Master Poets, Ritual Masters

The Art of Oral Composition
Among the Rotenese
of Eastern Indonesia

Master Poets, Ritual Masters

The Art of Oral Composition
Among the Rotenese
of Eastern Indonesia

JAMES J. FOX

PRESS

Published by ANU Press
The Australian National University
Acton ACT 2601, Australia
Email: anupress@anu.edu.au
This title is also available online at press.anu.edu.au

National Library of Australia Cataloguing-in-Publication entry

Creator: Fox, James J., 1940- author.

Title: Master poets, ritual masters : the art of oral composition among the Rotenese of eastern Indonesia / James J. Fox.

ISBN: 9781760460051 (paperback) 9781760460068 (ebook)

Subjects: Folk poetry, Indonesian--Indonesia--Rote Ndao.
Oral tradition--Indonesia--Rote Ndao.
Oral-formulaic analysis.
Folk literature, Indonesian--History and criticism.
Rote Ndao (Indonesia)--Poetry.

Dewey Number: 398.2095987

All rights reserved. No part of this publication may be reproduced, stored in a retrieval system or transmitted in any form or by any means, electronic, mechanical, photocopying or otherwise, without the prior permission of the publisher.

Cover design and layout by ANU Press. Cover photograph by James J. Fox.

This edition © 2016 ANU Press

Contents

List of Figures vii

List of Tables ix

Preface. xi

Acknowledgements xiii

Part I

1. Introduction: *Suti Solo do Bina Bane* 3
2. *Suti Solo do Bina Bane*:
   Version I from the Domain of Termanu 29
3. *Suti Solo do Bina Bane*:
   Version II from the Domain of Termanu 57
4. *Suti Solo do Bina Bane*:
   Version III from the Domain of Termanu. 77
5. *Suti Solo do Bina Bane*:
   Version IV from the Domain of Termanu 91
6. *Suti Solo do Bina Bane*:
   Version V from the Domain of Termanu. 111
7. *Suti Solo do Bina Bane*:
   Version VI from the Domain of Termanu 129
8. *Suti Solo do Bina Bane*:
   Version VII from the Domain of Termanu 145
9. *Suti Solo do Bina Bane*:
   Versions VIII and IX from the Domain of Termanu 163
10. *Suti Solo do Bina Bane* as a Personal Composition 183
11. Poetic Authority and Formulaic Composition 197

Part II

12. Historical Diversity and Dialect Differences on Rote. 229
13. *Suti Solo do Bina Bane*:
    A Version from the Domain of Landu 243
14. *Suti Solo do Bina Bane*:
    A Version from the Domain of Ringgou. 259
15. *Suti Solo do Bina Bane*:
    A Version from the Domain of Bilba 275
16. *Suti Solo do Bina Bane*:
    A Version from the Domain of Ba'a. 303
17. *Suti Solo do Bina Bane*:
    Version I from the Domain of Thie 313
18. *Suti Solo do Bina Bane*:
    Version II from the Domain of Thie 333
19. *Suti Saik ma Bina Liuk*:
    Two Versions from the Domain of Dengka 351
20. *Suti Saik ma Bina Liuk*:
    A Composition from the Domain of Dengka 365
21. *Suti Sai ma Bina Liu* from the Domain of Oenale. 377
22. Traditions of Oral Formulaic Composition
    across the Island of Rote 389

Postscript. 417

Appendix 419

Bibliography 435

Index 441

List of Figures

Figure 1: Rote Location Map. xv

Figure 2: Domain Map of Rote 19

Figure 3: Suti Solo and Bina Bane. 26

Figure 4: Stefanus Adulanu – 'Old Meno'. 31

Figure 5: Woman casting her scoop-net 39

Figure 6: Eli Pellondou – 'Seu Ba'i' 58

Figure 7: Petrus Malesi chanting at the Mortuary Ceremony for Old Meno. 79

Figure 8: Joel Pellondou. 146

Figure 9: Esau Markus Pono – 'Pak Pono'. 165

Figure 10: Zet Apulugi 185

Figure 11: Core Semantic Categories in Termanu Ritual Language 215

Figure 12: Group photo taken on 13 June 2009 after the fourth Bali recording session 228

Figure 13: Map of the Domains (*Nusak*) of Rote 230

Figure 14: A Tentative Map of the Dialects of Rote. 237

Figure 15: Alex Mada. 244

Figure 16: Ande Ruy 261

Figure 17: Ande Ruy reciting 262

Figure 18: Kornalius Medah 277

Figure 19: Woman with scoop-net 286

Figure 20: Samuel Ndun 315

Figure 21: N. D. Pah — 'Guru Pah' 316

Figure 22: Jonas Mooy 335

Figure 23: Simon Lesik 352

Figure 24: Frans Lau 367

Figure 25: Frans Lau conferring with Simon Lesik 368

Figure 26: Hendrik Foeh 378

Figure 27: Diagram of Key Signature Terms 412

List of Tables

Table 1: A Comparison of Dialogue Directives 86

Table 2: A Concordance of Corresponding Lines in the Two Versions of *Suti Solo do Bina Bane* by Mikael Pellondou 138

Table 3: Dialogue Directives in *Suti Solo do Bina Bane* Compositions in Termanu 209

Table 4: Dyadic Sets in All Versions of *Suti Solo do Bina Bane* from Termanu 218

Table 5: Principal Sound Variations in Rotenese Dialects 235

Table 6: Pronominal Systems of the Different Dialect Areas on Rote 236

Table 7: Dialect Terms in the Formation of Termanu's Dyadic Sets 238

Table 8: An Illustration of the Concatenation of Dyadic Sets Across Dialect Areas 240

Table 9: Termanu–Landu Dialect Comparisons I 254

Table 10: Termanu–Landu Dialect Comparisons II 254

Table 11: Termanu–Landu Dialect Comparisons III 254

Table 12: Termanu–Landu Dialect Comparisons IV 254

Table 13: Termanu–Landu Dialect Comparisons V 256

Table 14: Termanu–Ringgou Dialect Comparisons 270

Table 15: Termanu–Bilba–Ringgou Dialect Comparisons 298

Table 16: Ritual Sites in Thie's Two Versions of *Suti Solo do Bina Bane* 345

Table 17: Termanu–Thie Dialect Comparisons 347

Table 18: Termanu–Oenale Dialect Comparisons 385

Table 19: Encounters on the Journey of Suti and Bina
    in the Dialect Compositions of Rote 398

Table 20: Rotenese, Tetun and Atoni Canonical Pairs 414

Table 21: Dyadic Sets in Dialect Versions
    of *Suti Solo do Bina Bane* 419

Preface

This volume, *Master Poets, Ritual Masters*, is a study in oral formulaic composition. It takes its lead from one of the great classics in the study of oral composition, Albert Lord's *The Singer of Tales* (1960). From the outset, however, this study diverges from one of the premises of that study.

Drawing on the earlier researches of Milman Parry, Lord (1960) puts forward Parry's definition of an 'oral formula': 'a group of words which is regularly employed *under the same metrical conditions* to express a given essential idea' (1960: 4).

This definition assumes that all oral poetry is structured by metre, whereas much of the world's oral poetry does not rely on metre, but instead utilises other compositional devices. This is particularly the case with poetry composed according to rules of strict canonical parallelism.

Over many decades, I have endeavoured to document the extent and distribution of canonical parallelism in the world's oral literatures, from the earliest Sumerian poetry to contemporary practices in Asia and the Americas. These traditions are both diverse and persistent in South-East Asia, particularly in Indonesia and in the Maya world (see Fox 2014: 1–90).

Like Lord's study, this study is also a study of oral formulae, but it seeks to define the notion of the formula in other contexts. One could modify Parry's definition for this purpose by stating that an oral formula in this study consists of 'a group of words which is regularly employed *under the conditions of strict parallelism* to express a given essential idea'.

This study looks at simple formulae based on the strict pairing of words and also at more complex formulae that are composed of several recognisable formula pairs.

This study also differs from Lord's study in another fundamental way. Parry and Lord both carried out their research chiefly among a few remarkable oral poets. By contrast, in my research since 1965 on the island of Rote in eastern Indonesia, I have been able to work with and record many dozens of locally acknowledged and exceptionally able oral poets.

This book examines the oral compositions of some 17 different poets. The first half of this volume focuses on master poets from just one dialect or speech community on the island; the second half looks at the compositions of poets from six different dialect areas on the island.

This study is a strategic distillation of some of the finest examples of one of the most beautiful ritual compositions on the island. I was fortunate in being able to begin my recording of this particular composition in 1965, and have continued to record versions of it until 2014. This book thus covers a period of 50 years of research on Rotenese formulaic language.

Although it may differ from Lord's and Parry's work in particular respects, I hope this study may also be considered as a continuation of the research of the many scholars who have advanced research on oral poetic theory. This is a comparative study that ranges across time and place, but I would hope that each of the separate compositions recorded and translated here might also be appreciated individually as a distinctive expression of a striking mode of oral poetry.

Acknowledgements

A book like this, which is the work of some 50 years, would normally call for a great number of acknowledgements. This book is, however, focused specifically on the oral poetry of a group of remarkable and talented individuals and it is to these poets whom I feel I owe my greatest debt of gratitude. Many of them have long since died, but they are remembered by their families and ought to be remembered more widely. I must begin by thanking those poets whose recitations are included in this volume: Stefanus Adulanu, Eli Pellondou, Petrus Malesi, Mikael Pellondou, Joel Pellondou, Esau Pono, Zet Apulugi, Alex Mada, Anderias (Ande) Ruy, Kornalius Medah, Laazar Manoeain, Samuel Ndun, N. D. Pah, Jonas Mooy, Simon Lesik, Frans Lau and Hendrik Foeh. Of these master poets, I owe a special debt to Stefanus Adulanu ('Old Meno'), who taught me the beginnings of ritual language during my first period of fieldwork in 1965–66; Petrus Malesi, who was a frequent companion and my personal poet during my second period of fieldwork in 1972–73; and Esau Pono, who became, over many years, my closest Rotenese friend and confidant until his death in 2014. I was able to compose a short mortuary chant on his behalf and send it as an email to my former student and colleague Dr Lintje Pellu, in Kupang, who travelled to Termanu and saw that it was recited at his funeral.

These poets are only a small number of the poets whom I have recorded over the past 50 years. During my first fieldwork, Stefanus Adulanu and Stefanus Amalo—the two master poets in the domain of Termanu at that time—both competed and cooperated to provide me with a variety of recitations. I also recorded important recitations from A. Amalo and Lisbet Adulanu—a formidable figure and the only woman to offer to recite for me. N. D. Pah also supplied me with a wealth of materials from Thie. During my second period of fieldwork, I continued to record from Petrus Malesi and Eli Pellondou, who were rivals to one another.

I also recorded material from Hendrik Muskanan and obtained various recitations from Daniel Ndun from Talae, as I did from N. D. Pah and Samuel Ndun in Thie.

One special group of poets were those who took part in one or another of my nine recording sessions on Bali, which began in 2006. The list of these poets, besides those already named, is as follows: Yulius Iu and Jeskial Elimanafe from Landu; Mateos Poij from Oepao; Marthinus Teluain, Markus Bolla and Lefinus Penu from Bilba; Yunus Longo and Bernat S. Tasy, both Bilba-speakers from Semau; Efrain J. Ndeo and Jakobis Ndun from Korbaffo; Lief Keluanan and Yeri Fanggidae from Termanu; Chornelis Tuy from Keka; G. A. Foeh, Benjamin Sah and Alex Koan from Thie; and Gotlif Tungga and Lasarus Fanggi Idu from Dengka. My student and colleague Dr Tom Therik was an enthusiastic supporter of my Master Poets Project and he joined me on the first two recording sessions; when he died suddenly, another of my students, Dr Lintje Pellu, took over from him and helped organise each of the subsequent groups who travelled from Rote, via Kupang, to Bali. Apart from the occasional bout of malaria, which is endemic to the population of Rote, these gatherings on Bali were both fruitful and enjoyable.

The photographs in this volume cover the same period as my recordings. The black and white photographs were taken during my first two field trips: they date from the mid-1960s and the early 1970s. I wish to thank David Brazil for his help in digitising a large number of my early photographs. Colour photographs were taken on later visits to Rote and during various recording sessions on Bali. I would have liked to have photographs of all the poets whom I recorded but unfortunately I have no photographs of Mikael Pellondou and Laazar Manoeain.

It is essential that I acknowledge the support provided to me through an Australian Research Council (ARC) Discovery Grant (0663392) entitled 'The Semantics of Canonical Parallelism: Oral Composition among Rotenese Poets, Eastern Indonesia', which enabled me to carry out my initial recordings of Rotenese poets on Bali.

The maps and diagrams were made by Jennifer Sheehan of Coombs Cartography, and I thank her for her efforts. I also wish to thank Professor Frog of the University of Helsinki and Professor Elizabeth Traube of Wesleyan University for their comments on the manuscript. I would also like to thank Jan Borrie for her excellent copyediting of the manuscript and Elouise Ball and Emily Tinker for their proofreading. Finally, I wish to express my special thanks to my wife, Irmgard, who has read and reread drafts of the chapters in this book more often than I would wish to enumerate.

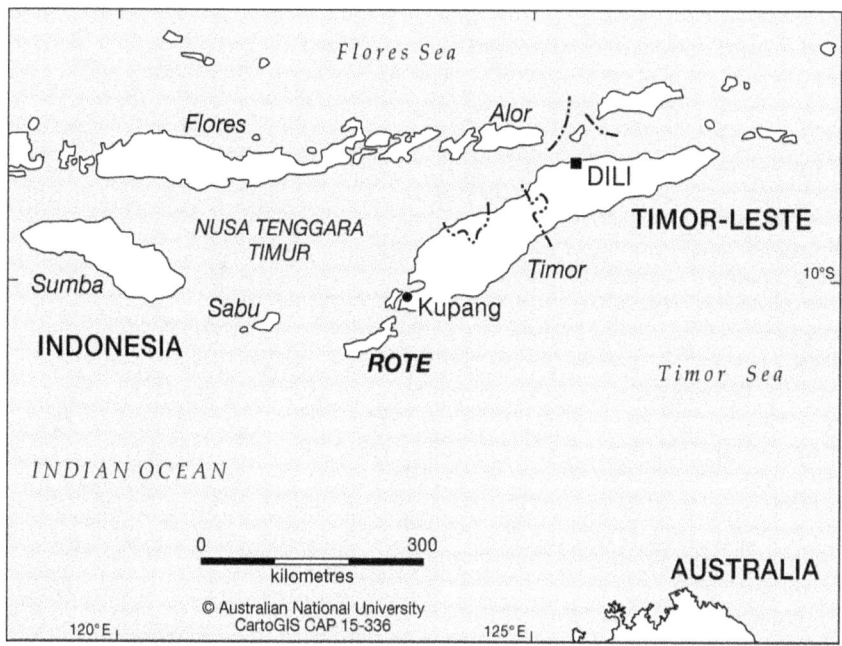

Figure 1: Rote Location Map
Source: © The Australian National University CartoGIS

PART I

1
Introduction: *Suti Solo do Bina Bane*

This is a study of oral composition. Specifically, it is a study of the way in which oral poets on the island of Rote in eastern Indonesia compose recitations within a tradition of strict canonical parallelism. It is thus a study of particular poets, their specific compositions and the tradition in which they operate. The materials for this study have been gathered from more than a dozen master poets over nearly 45 years. Before it is possible to begin an analysis of their compositions, it is essential to provide some background to this study and the tradition of analysis within which this study is situated.

A Personal Introduction

Soon after I arrived on the island of Rote in April 1965, I took a long walk with Jaap Amalo, the elder brother of the then Lord (*Manek*) of Termanu and District Head (*Camat*) of Rote, Ernst Amalo. Jaap Amalo had spent his career in the civil service, initially during the Dutch colonial period and thereafter in the period of Indonesian independence. Having left Rote as a young man, he had returned to the island on his retirement and reimmersed himself in Rotenese culture. He understood perhaps better than most others just what an anthropologist might wish to do on the island and he was anxious to give me thoughtful advice on Rote and its culture. He talked to me specifically about Rotenese ritual language, although at the time I hardly grasped what he was trying to tell me. I had brought with me a tape recorder and it was with this in mind that he advised me to begin my research by recording the chant *Suti Solo do Bina Bane*. He told me that he regarded *Suti Solo do Bina Bane* as the most beautiful and moving of Rotenese ritual compositions. Although I had, at the time, no idea what this composition might be like, I had a clear and specific directive to record the chant.

Some days later, Ernst Amalo took me to Feapopi where he had his official residence as *Manek* of Termanu and introduced me to an assembly of clan lords and elders. Since he had no idea of anthropology, he explained that I had come to be the historian of Termanu and had brought a 'voice-catcher' (*penangkap suara*) to record Termanu's oral traditions. At this gathering, I met, for the first time, Stefanus Adulanu, known as 'Old Meno' (*Meno Tua*), the senior most elder of clan Meno, who held the title of Head of the Earth (*Dae Langak*). Old Meno had served as the scribe to the court for at least four decades; he was one of the most respected elders of Termanu and was regarded as one of the most knowledgeable figures in the domain. Fortunately for me, he took on himself the task of teaching me the traditions of Termanu.

After this formal introduction, my wife and I were able to settle at Ufa Len in the house of a clan lord of Ingu-Beuk, Mias Kiuk, who was brother-in-law to the Acting *Manek* of Termanu (*Wakil Manek*), Frans Biredoko. From Ufa Len, I made regular visits to Ola Lain where Old Meno resided. Although he admitted to me some time later that he was first troubled and puzzled by my arrival, he explained that he saw in my voice-catcher the means for him to transmit to his grandson some of his most important traditional knowledge. In addition to reciting (or finding others to recite) key oral narratives and genealogies of the domain, Old Meno initiated me into an understanding of ritual language and slowly helped me to translate and comprehend ritual language compositions, many of which were gathered from an array of other local oral poets. At my request, Old Meno recited for me the composition *Suti Solo do Bina Bane* that Jaap Amalo had first urged me to record. The text of this composition is a superlative example of ritual language and is the first text examined in detail in this study.

This first text initiated a study that has continued for some 50 years—the entire time that I have spent studying ritual language. On subsequent visits over the years, primarily to Termanu, and more recently during recording sessions held on Bali with oral poets from different parts of Rote, I have repeatedly recorded versions of *Suti Solo do Bina Bane*.

I have asked some poets to recite this composition on different occasions at different intervals in their life, but I have also asked poets who are related to one another and are said to have learned their art from the same (or a closely related) source to provide me with their own version of this composition. Initially, I focused my efforts on Termanu, which constitutes a single speech community, but in time, I have recorded this chant from oral poets in other dialect areas.

I have purposely focused on *Suti Solo do Bina Bane* to understand, in specific detail, how individual poets compose their chants, how their compositions may differ from one recitation to another and how compositions vary from one speech community to another. This study is the result of these investigations. However, these focused, fine-grained investigations of a single named chant relate to wider issues in the study of oral traditions. Rotenese ritual compositions belong to a tradition of oral composition based on strict canonical parallelism. Composition in strict canonical parallelism is—and certainly once was—a widespread means of poetic creation. Thus, understanding a single tradition based on this form of composition—as in the case of the Rotenese—may contribute to a fuller understanding of other traditions of parallel composition.

Parallelism and Canonical Parallelism as Forms of Oral Composition

Rotenese ritual language is a special poetic register that relies on a strict—indeed obligatory—use of semantic parallelism. As such, it belongs to a tradition of composition that is common to much of the world's oral literatures. The term 'parallelism' dates to the eighteenth century and derives from the studies of Robert Lowth. In 1753, in a series of lectures delivered as Professor of Hebrew Poetry in the University of Oxford, Lowth noted that one of the major principles of composition in parts of the Old Testament was a carefully contrived pairing of line, phrase and verse. He described this form of composition as follows:

> The poetic conformation of the sentences, which has been so often alluded to as characteristic of the Hebrew poetry, consists chiefly in a certain equality, resemblance, or parallelism between the members of each period; so that in two lines (or members of the same period) things for the

most part shall answer to things, and words, to words, as if fitted to each other by a kind of rule or measure. This parallelism has much variety and graduations. (Lowth 1829: 157)

In a later lecture, in 1778, Lowth more explicitly defined his terminology for this form of composition, which he called *parallelismus membrorum:*

The correspondence of one verse or line with another, I call parallelism. When a proposition is delivered, and a second is subjoined to it, or drawn under it, equivalent, or contrasted with it in sense, or similar to it in the form of grammatical construction, these I call parallel lines; and the words or phrases, answering one to another in the corresponding lines, parallel terms. (Lowth 1834: ix)

Lowth's observations led to the recognition of similar forms of composition across a wide spectrum of the world's oral traditions as well as various written traditions based on oral models. Akkadian, Sumerian and early Egyptian texts were shown to be based on parallelism, and when Canaanite texts were discovered, it became evident that particular Biblical texts shared in a wider Semitic tradition of parallel composition. In Europe, the Finns were the first to take up Lowth's ideas, recognising in their own folk traditions a pervasive use of parallelism. Elias Lönnroth recorded, selected and compiled these compositions to create the *Kalevala*, perhaps the most frequently cited example of pervasive parallelism. Various other scholars noted and discussed similar forms of parallelism for Ostyak and Vogul folk poetry, for Hungarian, for Mongolian, and for Turkic. Still other researchers have established parallelism as the first principle of Náhuatl and of Mayan poetry, and others have taken up the study of parallelism in the poetry of contemporary Maya groups, in Cuna folk traditions and in Quechua poetry dating back to the time of the Incas.

Early in the nineteenth century, scholars pointed to parallelism in Chinese poetry. Since then, parallelism has been noted in a variety of linguistic forms: in early written documents, in the rhyme-prose of the Han Period, in 'parallel prose', in love songs, in proverbs and in popular poetry. Similar usages have been observed in the extensive ritual texts of Zhuang of south-west China, in Tibetan, as well as among the Thulung Rai of eastern Nepal, the Sadar of Jaspur and the Toda of South India. In mainland South-East Asia, the use of parallelism has been documented in compositions among the Kachin, Kmhmu and Khmer speakers, and in written and oral compositions in Vietnamese.

The largest textual literature on parallelism can be found in the Austronesian-speaking world, where extensive traditions of parallelism in poetry and ritual languages have been documented for the Rhade of Vietnam, the peoples of Nias, the Batak, a number of Dayak groups in Kalimantan, among Bugis and Toraja groups in Sulawesi and for numerous populations throughout eastern Indonesia where vibrant traditions of oral composition in parallelism persist, particularly on the islands of Sumba, Flores, Savu, Rote and Timor.[1]

While there can be no doubt about the prevalence of the use of parallelism in a great diversity of oral traditions, Lowth's qualification on his initial observations has still to be noted: 'parallelism has much variety and graduations.' Parallelism does not simply define a particular linguistic phenomenon, but rather points to a complex of intersecting phenomena. At times, parallelism may be considered to mask as much as it reveals.

The Jakobson Perspective on Canonical Parallelism

Throughout his career, the linguist Roman Jakobson returned repeatedly to parallelism as a special linguistic consideration, each time casting new reflections on the topic (see Fox 1977). It was Jakobson who coined the term 'canonical parallelism' to define parallel compositions 'where certain similarities between successive verbal sequences are compulsory or enjoy a high preference' (Jakobson 1966: 399). His purpose was to delimit traditions of oral composition in which specific pairings were culturally defined and specifically required for composition and, thus, to distinguish such traditions from others in which such pairings occur as poetic rhetoric that can be highly variable from composition to composition.

Distinguishing traditions of canonical parallelism and attempting to understand them shift the research agenda to a focus on the 'canonical coupling' of words—to what Jakobson described, in his own concise formulation, as the 'paradigmatic axis of selection' whose function in poetry is to create 'metaphor' by means of similarity (1956: 58 ff.). Canonical parallelism thus offers special insights by its explicit expression

---

1   See Fox (1977) for detailed documentation on the variety of the world's traditions of parallelism and Fox (1988, 2005) for detailed summaries of the Austronesian traditions of parallelism.

of this poetic function. Jakobson's frequently quoted statement that 'the poetic function projects the principle of equivalence from the axis of selection into the axis of combination' (1960: 358) has particular relevance in the study of traditions of canonical parallelism. Whereas in other forms of poetry, the 'poetic function' may be subtly concealed or entirely implicit, in canonical parallelism this function is given direct and explicit expression. Culturally defined linguistic equivalences, both semantic and syntactic, become manifest.

Many, perhaps most, of the major traditions of composition identified as based on parallelism may well be traditions of canonical parallelism, but the underlying canonical coupling on which they are based may not always be immediately manifest or consistently evident. Some of the oldest traditions of such canonical parallelism have been preserved in written form. This holds for magnificent early examples of parallelism from Akkadian and Sumerian cuneiform sources as well as from Egyptian hieroglyphic texts or from a rich array of early Chinese texts such as the Taoist *Yuandao* from the period of the Han Dynasty, but equally so for surviving Maya sources such as the *Popul Vuh*, the *Rabinal Achi* or the recently discovered Zhang corpus of ritual texts.

All of these materials reflect—some more directly than others—their basis in oral composition. The regular recurrence of specific paired terms can at times be strikingly apparent but often it requires a considerable effort, directed at a large corpus, to decipher the full range of these pairings and to discern their use in a tradition of oral composition. Much the same can be said for many excellent collections of oral compositions, compiled and published without adequate attention to their underlying principles of composition.

The Biblical Scholarly Focus on Canonical Pairs

Biblical scholarship, from the time of Lowth, has focused extraordinary attention on the use of parallelism, but this attention has more often been directed to what Lowth termed 'parallel lines' or 'parallel phrases' than to 'parallel terms'. Where the emphasis in this attention is to be placed remains a source of dispute. A considerable scholarship has been devoted to these issues, beginning with George B. Gray's *The Forms of Hebrew*

Poetry, which was first published in 1915 and then republished in 1972 with a substantial 'Prolegomenon' and extensive updated bibliography by David N. Freedman (Freedman 1972: vii–liii). Of equal relevance and comparative importance was Louis I. Newman and W. Popper's three-part *Studies in Biblical Parallelism* published between 1918 and 1923 (Newman and Popper 1918–23). Of these volumes, Newman's *Parallelism in Amos* (1918) was one of the first studies of its kind to point to comparative examples of parallelism in other Middle Eastern literary traditions.

A major impetus to the study of parallel terms came with the discovery in 1928 at Ras Shamra in the ruins of ancient Ugarit of a considerable corpus of Canaanite poetic texts dating from the fourteenth century BC. The eventual decipherment of these texts led to the recognition of a shared Hebrew–Canaanite tradition of composition based on recognisable paired terms, and this, in turn, opened a new wave of comparative scholarship that has continued to the present.[2]

Despite these new developments, differences in approach to the analysis of Hebrew parallelism persist. Thus, for example, James L. Kugel, in his book *The Idea of Biblical Poetry: Parallelism and its History* (1981: 1), asserts emphatically that the 'parallelistic line'—'a relatively short sentence-form that consists of two brief clauses'—is 'the basic feature of Biblical songs'. By contrast, Stanley Gevirtz is equally emphatic in his 'Prologue' to *Patterns in the Early Poetry of Israel*:

> More importantly, in the present context, it was found that the parallelistic structures evident in the Ugaritic poets were in all significant respects virtually identical with those known from Old Testament poetry. Still more central to the concerns of this present work was the recognition of a poetic diction common to the two literatures. Specific 'pairs' of words in fixed parallel relationship were found to occur in both Ugaritic and Hebrew literature with such frequency and regularity as to preclude the possibility of coincidence, while the differences in age and locale excluded the possibility of direct borrowing. (Gevirtz 1973: 3)

Gevirtz's analysis of specific pairs is particularly illuminating and has led to further deepening of scholarly research. Thus, following on earlier work by Cassuto, Held and Gevirtz, Mitchell Dahood embarked on an effort

---

2   Freedman, in the bibliography of his 'Prolegomenon' (1972), provides an excellent listing of useful publications on Ugaritic–Hebrew comparative scholarship to that date. In a valuable PhD thesis submitted to the University of Otago, Margaret R. Eaton (1994) examines the development of Biblical research on parallelism and word pairs and provides a further bibliography on this topic.

to compile a comprehensive 'thesaurus' of what he identified as 'Ugaritic–Hebrew parallel pairs'. His first compilation, prepared with assistance from Tadeusz Penar and included as an Appendix to his translation of *Psalms* (Dahood and Penar 1970: 445–56), consisted of 157 pairs of parallel words.[3] His next compilation (Dahood and Penar 1972: 71–382), again with Tadeusz Penar, added a further 609 parallel pairs. This was followed by the addition of another 66 pairs (Dahood 1975: 1–39) with supplementary information on 18 entries, and then a further 344 pairs and supplementary information on 105 entries (Dahood 1981: 1–219), bringing his total lexicon to some 1,176 parallel terms. In compiling this lexicon, Dahood's intention was to identify the semantic resources that poets of a common tradition relied on for their parallel compositions. He stated this clearly:

> The present work aims to recover from all of the published Ugaritic tablets and from the Hebrew Bible, including Ecclesiasticus or Ben Sira, the Canaanite thesaurus from whose resources Ugaritic and Hebrew poets alike drew. (Dahood and Penar 1972: 74)

The Focus on Word Pairs in Mayan Languages

The Náhuatl and Mayan language-speaking area of Mesoamerica is another region of the world that is notable for its traditions of canonical parallelism. In his *Pre-Columbian Literatures of Mexico*, Miguel León-Portilla (1969), the doyen of pre-Columbian language studies, noted the similarities to Biblical parallelism. In his words:

> [S]ome of the most frequent stylistic procedures ... were more or less alike in all the various early Mexican literatures and show a certain similarity to the forms of expression used in other ancient compositions also preserved by an unbroken tradition, as in the case of the Bible and other texts from the Eastern cultures. Anyone who reads indigenous poetry cannot fail to notice the repetition of ideas and the expression of sentiments in parallel form. (León-Portilla 1969: 76–77)

---

3   Dahood distinguishes between 'strict parallels', 'collocations' and 'juxtapositions', and includes all three of these categories in his Ugaritic–Hebrew parallel pair compilations. This is an important methodological distinction. By strict parallels, he refers to pairs found in both Ugaritic and Hebrew. Collocations and juxtapositions refer to terms that are found as pairs in one of the two languages but nevertheless occur in close association or juxtaposition in the other language. Most of his citations are strict parallels.

1. INTRODUCTION: *SUTI SOLO DO BINA BANE*

What makes this region different is a remarkable continuity of oral traditions. Local social and religious activities combine with a vibrant living tradition of composition in parallelism. This is particularly so among the Mayan-speaking populations of Mexico and Guatemala.[4] And nowhere is this continuity more significant than in the various studies of the *Popul Vuh*, or the *Book of Counsel*, of the Quiche Maya. With his collaborator, Earl Shorris, León-Portilla has described this extraordinary volume as one of the great treasures of literature:

> The *Popul Vuh* is the best connection we have to a Mesoamerican civilization that has lasted for more than a thousand years, and continues still; it is a compilation of a way of being in the world, a book of gods and humans, a work for all ages. (León-Portilla and Shorris 2001: 401)

Munro S. Edmonson has recounted the history of the survival of the manuscript of Quiche in the introduction to his translation of the *Popul Vuh*: its composition about 1550, the copying and translation of this manuscript by the Dominican parish priest Francisco Ximénez, between 1701 and 1703, and the succession of nearly a dozen translations of this work into a variety of different languages. In offering his translation, Edmonson was explicit in his conception of the underlying basis for the composition of the work:

> It is my conviction that the *Popul Vuh* is primarily a work of literature, and that it cannot be properly read apart from the literary form in which it is expressed. That this form is general to Middle America (and even beyond) and that it is common to Quiche discourse, ancient and modern, does not diminish its importance. The *Popul Vuh* is in poetry, and cannot be accurately understood in prose. It is entirely composed in parallelistic (i.e., semantic couplets). (Edmonson 1971: xi)[5]

---

4   For a classic study of these traditions, see Gossen (1974).
5   It is important to note that Edmonson (and various other authors writing on Mesoamerican parallelism) uses the term 'couplet' for what Dahood refers to as strict pairs or parallel pairs or what other Biblical scholars have called 'fixed pairs'. In his work on parallelism, Edmonson—as indeed León-Portilla—was inspired by K. Garibay (1971), who focused on the importance of parallelism in his *Historia de la Literatura Nahuatl*. Garibay coined the term '*difrasismo*' (diaphrasis) to describe the pairing of two metaphors to express a single thought.

MASTER POETS, RITUAL MASTERS

The opening lines of the Edmonson translation of the *Popul Vuh* illustrate this strict canonical/semantic parallelism:

This is the root of the former word
    Here is Quiche by name

Here we shall write then,
    We shall start out then, the former words,

The beginnings
    And the taproots

Of everything done in Quiche town,
    The tribe of the Quiche people.

So this is what we shall collect then,
    The decipherment,

The clarification,
    And the explanation

Of the mysteries
    And the illumination

By the Former
    And Shaper;

Bearer
    And Engenderer are their names,

Hunter Possum
    And Hunter Coyote

Great White Pig
    And Coati,

Majesty
    And Quetzal Serpent,

The Heart of the Lake
    And Heart of the Sea,

Green Plate Spirit
    And Blue Bowl Spirit, as it is said,

Who are likewise called,
    Who are likewise spoken of

As the Woman with Grandchildren
    And Man with Grandchildren

Xpiacoc
    And Xmucane by name,

Shelterer
>And Protector,

Great-Grandmother
>And Great-Grandfather

As it is said
>In Quiche words …

In a critically important paper, 'Semantic Universals and Particulars in Quiche' (Edmonson 1973), following the publication of his translation, Edmonson examined in detail the semantic parallelism in the first 94 lines of the *Popul Vuh*. Forty-nine pairs occur in these lines, of which there are five repeated pairs, thus reducing the number to 42 semantic pairs. These pairs—a small number in a work of more than 8,500 lines—are illustrative of the canonical pairs that form the basis of Quiche composition.

In his analysis, Edmonson grouped these pairs that he had identified into three classes: those that he considered 'universal' such as word//name or heaven//earth, root//tree or mother//father; those he considered 'widespread' such as bowl//plate, plant//root, lake//sea or tribe//town; and those that he considered 'particular' to Quiche culture such as possum//coyote, pig//coati, majesty//quetzal or heart//breath. He also noted that certain terms, as, for example, the term in Quiche translated as 'word', formed several different pairs: with the noun 'name', but also with the verbs 'to say', 'to do', 'to describe' and 'to be' as well as with the word for 'clear'.

Edmonson's short exploratory illustration of possible ways of analysing Quiche semantic couplets led to a much more thorough examination of these pairs in a Leiden PhD thesis, '*The Poetic Popul Vuh: An Anthropological Study*', by Robert de Ridder (1989). With close attention to Edmonson's translation, de Ridder provides an interpretation of the *Popul Vuh* based on a thoroughgoing analysis of specific word pairs, grouping them together and contrasting them with one another. Like Edmonson's paper, de Ridder's thesis is an exploration of the possibilities open to analysis by careful focus on culturally defined semantic equivalences.

Dennis Tedlock, a student of Edmonson, has produced his own translation of the *Popul Vuh* (Tedlock 1996) but he has done this in consultation with contemporary Quiche ritual officials whose interpretations allowed him to consider the *Popul Vuh* in terms of the possibilities of performance.[6] In a long paper, 'Hearing a Voice in an Ancient Text: Quiché Maya Poetics in Performance' (1987), Tedlock has described this cooperative 'ethnopaleographic project' in which he even attempts 'a reconstruction of the oral delivery' of particular passages from the *Popul Vuh*. His paper is a model of nuanced ethno-poetic analysis in which he is able to show similarities between passages in the *Popul Vuh* and the prayers recited by Quiche ritual specialists. For him, however, Edmonson 'let the search for parallel couplets dominate his entire reading of the text' (Tedlock 1987: 147). Tedlock is interested in Quiche triplets as well as couplets and in all sorts of syntactic shifts that occur between couplets. As he makes clear, recognition of canonical pairs is essential for an understanding of Quiche composition, but the use of the pairs and triplets can occur in varying syntactic contexts. As in the case of Biblical scholars in their examination of both Hebrew and Ugaritic texts, it is essential to provide a closely focused analysis of the various patterning within individual texts and variations in this patterning across texts.

Research on Mayan parallelism, which goes well beyond the research on the Quiche language, and similar research within Biblical scholarship represent two distinct fields of investigation—largely independent of one another—that are directed towards comparable ends and are suggestive of processes of oral composition. Both broad fields of research relate to and offer insights on similar processes that continue to be used by contemporary oral poets in eastern Indonesia.[7] This study of the oral composition among the oral poets of Rote is intended to carry forward this analysis.

A Focus on Semantic Parallelism on Rote

Since 1971, I have produced a succession of papers that examine the use of semantic parallelism in Rotenese oral compositions, and I have continued to rely on a number of conventions that I adopted in the first paper I published, 'Semantic Parallelism in Rotinese Ritual Language'

---

6   There are more than 750,000 'Quiche' living in Guatemala today, many of whom continue to maintain their traditional religious practices. Current classification divides 'Quiche' among at least six different but related languages, of which Central or South-Western Quiche has the largest number of speakers, with more than half a million.

7   For a compilation of papers on parallelism in different languages in eastern Indonesia, see Fox (1988).

(Fox 1971). Because all oral compositions based on canonical parallelism occur or are intended to occur in a ritual context and generally allude to matters of ritual significance, I have consistently referred to these oral compositions as a form of 'ritual language'. In Rotenese, the term *bini* is used to describe all poetic compositions in ritual language. These *bini* are then differentiated according to how they are performed—whether chanted, sung or recited with the accompaniment of a drum or according to their ritual context: an origin recitation, a funeral recitation, a lament and so forth.

From the outset, I have adopted, from Biblical scholarship, the use of the conventional '//' to identify canonical pairs and refer to all such pairs as 'dyadic sets'. A dyadic set consists of two semantic elements, x and y, but any element can occur in more than one dyadic set.[8] In semantic analysis of the lexicon of Rotenese ritual language, it is important to distinguish elements that form only a single dyadic set from those that form a 'range' of dyadic sets.

The following short poem from the dialect of the domain of Termanu provides an illustration of the use of pairs in this canonical parallelism. Analysis of this poem provides an opportunity to introduce the basic terminology and notation system that I use in this volume:

1.	*Lole faik ia dalen*	On this good day
2.	*Ma lada ledok ia tein na*	And at this fine time [sun]
3.	*Lae: tefu ma-nggona lilok*	They say: The sugar cane has sheaths of gold
4.	*Ma huni ma-lapa losik.*	And the banana has blossoms of copper.
5.	*Tefu olu heni nggonan*	The sugar cane sheds its sheath
6.	*Ma huni kono heni lapan,*	And the banana drops its blossom,
7.	*Tehu bei ela tefu okan*	Leaving but the sugar cane's root
8.	*Ma huni hun bai.*	And just the banana's trunk.
9.	*De dei tefu na nggona seluk*	But the sugar cane sheaths again
10.	*Fo na nggona lilo seluk*	The sheaths are gold again
11.	*Ma dei huni na lapa seluk*	And the banana blossoms again
12.	*Fo na lapa losi seluk.*	The blossoms are copper again.

---

8   By this convention, any so-called triplet that occurs in a composition can be represented simply as (a, b) + (a, c); such sets can be extended if particular elements form a variety of different pairs.

MASTER POETS, RITUAL MASTERS

This poem is composed of just eight semantic pairs or 'dyadic sets'. These dyadic sets are listed here together with a simple notation to distinguish them:

good//fine:	*lole//lada*	(a1//a2)
day//sun:	*fai(k)//ledo(k)*	(b1//b2)
inside//belly:	*dale(n)//tei(n)*	(c1//c2)
sugar cane//banana:	*tefu//huni*	(d1//d2)
sheath//blossom:	*-nggona//-lapa*	(e1//e2)
gold//copper:	*lilo//losi*	(f1//f2)
shed//drop:	*olu//kono*	(g1//g2)
root//trunk:	*oka//hu*	(h1//h2)

The poem also has various connectives, emphatics, time markers and verbal elements that are not subject to pairing: *ia* ('this'), *ma* ('and'), *tehu* ('but'), *de* ('but that'), *fo* ('that'), *heni* ('away', 'off'), *bei* ('still'), *bai* ('also'), *seluk* ('again'), *lae* ('they say').

Using the notation (a1//a2) to designate the various dyadic sets in this poem, it is possible to discern the poem's formulaic 'orderedness':

Lole faik ia dalen
  a1 b1   c1   a1, b1, c1

Ma lada ledok ia tein na
     a2   b2   c2   a2, b2, c2

Lae: tefu ma-nggona lilok
      d1   e1   f1   d1, e1, f1

Ma huni ma-lapa losik.
    d2   e2   f2   d2, e2, f2

Tefu olu heni nggonan
  d1 g1   h1   d1, g1, h1

Ma huni kono heni lapan
    d2 g2   h2   d2, g2, h2

Tehu bei ela tefu okan
             d1 h1   d1, h1

Ma huni hun bai.
    d2 h2   d2, h2

De dei tefu na-nggona seluk
        d1   e1   d1, e1

Fo na-nggona lilo seluk
    e1   f1   e1, f1
Ma dei huni na-lapa seluk
    d2   e2   d2, e2
Fo na-lapa losi seluk.
    e2   f2   e2, f2

A key to understanding these pairs and the way they function in composition is to recognise the varying range of the elements of which they are composed. For example, *lole* meaning 'good, beautiful' can also pair with *(ma-)na'a*, meaning 'striking, handsome, pretty'. Similarly, *fai(k)* ('day') also pairs with *leoda'e* ('night'); the verb *olu* ('to shed') forms a pair with *tui* ('to drop leaves'); while both *oka* and *hu* occur in multiple pairs: *oka* ('large root') with *samu* ('small root, tendril') and with *polo* ('shoot, growing tip of a plant'), and *hu* ('trunk, base') with *boa* ('fruit') and *do* ('leaf'). Only *tefu*//*huni* ('sugar cane'//'banana') forms a single, exclusive dyadic set. That sugar cane and banana are icons of male sexuality adds a further cultural dimension and sheds light on this short poetic passage, which is a metaphorical statement about male succession within a lineage.

The semantic pairs used in Rotenese compositions are not a collection of terms that are exclusive to a single pair. Underlying a large percentage of these pairs is a semantic network of connections. These connections are limited and culturally circumscribed. The knowledge of such pairs is a requirement of composition and learned within a particular speech community. Unacceptable pairing is quickly noted in a performance and usually leads to hissing a poet into silence. Previously, false pairings were considered to cause a poet sickness and even death for a ritual mistake. This poem is short and thus provides a simple illustration of the composition process. Most poetic compositions range from 100 lines to many hundreds of lines and correspondingly require the proper pairing of several hundred specific terms in all grammatical categories. The composition entitled *Dela Kolik ma Seko Bunak* that I analysed in detail in 'Semantic Parallelism in Rotinese Ritual Language' (Fox 1971) consisted of 224 lines that utilised 123 distinct dyadic sets plus seven dyadic chant character names and two dyadic place names.[9]

---

9   Each of these sets is identified and translated in the paper Fox (1971: 252–55).

The Speech Communities of Rote

The island of Rote—referred to in ritual language as *Lote do Kale*—is located off the western tip of the island of Timor. It extends roughly in an east–west direction so that what the Rotenese call the island's 'head' (*langa*) is 'east', and its 'tail' (*iko*) is west. These directional coordinates provide the basis for all ritual action in Rotenese poetic discourse. The island's population at present (2015) has grown to approximately 100,000.

The 'language' of the Rotenese constitutes a complex dialect chain stretching from one end of the island to the other. While neighbouring communities can understand each other, differences increase in terms of the distance of these communities from each other. At the two ends of this dialect chain intelligibility is a challenge.[10]

Rote's political history has contributed to this dialect diversity. In 1662, the Dutch East India Company began establishing contracts of trade with local rulers, thus recognising their authority in particular areas on the island. Initially, 12 domains were recognised. This process of Dutch recognition, however, continued through the eighteenth and into the nineteenth centuries, eventually dividing Rote into 17 separate domains plus a domain that embraced the offshore island of Ndao.[11] As a result, most Rotenese domains, referred to in Rotenese as *nusak*, have possessed a distinct social and political continuity since the seventeenth century.[12]

---

10   One of the first Rotenese to write about his own language, D. P. Manafe, a schoolteacher attached to a middle-level school in the town of Ba'a on Rote, prepared a document, '*Akan Bahasa Rotti*', in 1884. This was eventually published by the linguist H. Kern in the Dutch journal *Bijdragen tot de Taal-, Land- en Volkenkunde* in 1889 (see Kern 1889). In his paper, Manafe was at great pains to point out the considerable dialect variation on the island. He insisted, however, that Rotenese in the east of the island could, despite difficulties, still understand Rotenese in the west of the island. Some 120 years later, this proposition is questionable for the dialects at either end of the island and may have already been so at the time that Manafe wrote. Certainly some of the dialects within Manafe's east–west division of dialects are mutually intelligible but not necessarily all of them.

11   The population of the island of Ndao possesses a distinct language that has been heavily influenced by Rotenese but is more closely related to Savunese. Ndao figures prominently in the traditions of Rote; its ritual name is *Ndao Nusa do Folo Manu*. Most Ndaonese are bilingual and participate in Rotenese culture. A number of Ndaonese are master poets who recite in Rotenese ritual language.

12   For a discussion of the history of these political developments on Rote, see Fox (1971, 1977, 1979a, 1979b).

1. INTRODUCTION: *SUTI SOLO DO BINA BANE*

Each domain maintains its own traditions, claims its own special narratives and asserts the superiority of its rituals and its practices. Until the late 1960s, each domain had its own court to adjudicate on disputes based on its domain-specific customary law. It is a dogma among Rotenese on the island that all but one of these domains possess their own language. As a consequence, individuals often go to great lengths to elevate minor variations as evidence of major differences among domains. On an island with subtle dialect variation, the domains constitute distinct speech communities.

Each domain has its own ritual name—in fact, multiple ritual names—most of which are specific to a particular location within the domain. Among the poets, there is general, but by no means universal, consensus about the principal name of a domain. Although these names may vary slightly, as articulated by poets in their domain's dialect, they are broadly recognised throughout the island and are indispensable to ritual recitations.

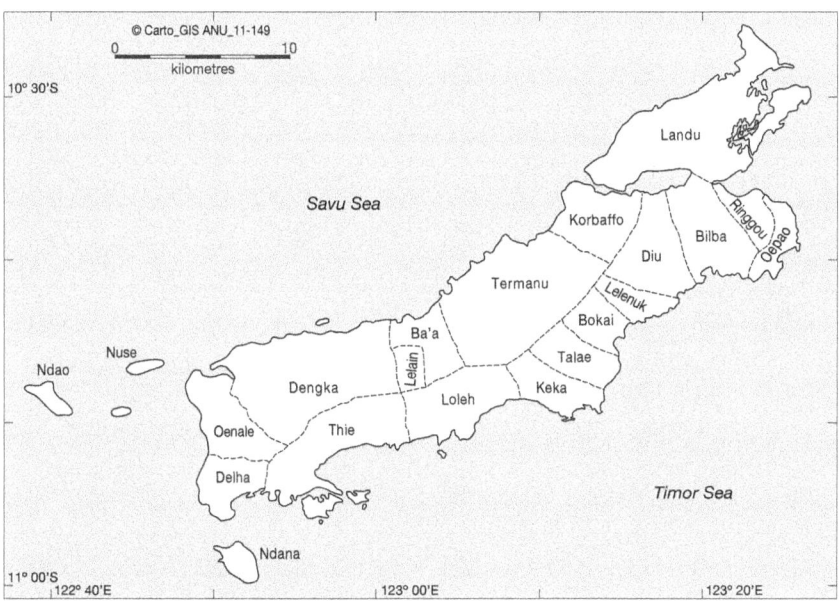

Figure 2: Domain Map of Rote
Source: © The Australian National University CartoGIS

This is the list of the principal names of the domains according to Termanu dialect.

The Principal Ritual Names of the Domains of Rote

Landu	Soti Mori ma Bola Tena
Oepao	Fai Fua ma Ledo Sou
Ringgou	Londa Lusi ma Batu Bela
Bilba	Pengo Dua ma Hilu Telu
Diu	Pele Pou ma Nggafu Lafa
Lelenuk	Lenu Petu ma Safe Solo
Bokai	Meda do Ndule
Korbaffo	Tunga Oli ma Namo Ina
Termanu	Koli do Buna
Keka	Tufa Laba ma Ne'e Fe'o
Talae	Pila Sue ma Nggeo Deta
Ba'a	Pena Pua ma Maka Lama
Dengka	Dae Mea ma Tete Lifu
Lelain	Nggede Ke ma Danda Mamen
Loleh	Ninga Ladi ma Hengu Hena
Thie	Tada Muli ma Lene Kona
Oenale	Tasi Puka ma Li Sonu
Delha	Dela Muli ma Ana Iko

All of this is highly significant for understanding traditions of composition and performance. All poets identify with their particular domains and regard themselves as responsible for conveying the 'true' ancestral traditions of their domain. Thus, each poet's composition is firmly situated in a particular speech community and is judged by members of that community. When poets from one domain encounter poets from other domains, they expect differences in the content of a composition (and would probably be upset were the composition from another domain to mirror too closely that of their own), but they are particularly attuned to the dyadic sets used in composition. Rotenese ritual language transcends the dialect differences among domains by utilising these differences as an essential component of its lexicon.

A considerable number of dyadic sets, particularly for synonyms, are composed of words taken from different dialects. Which word is the 'dialect' term and which word is 'local' depends on the particular speech community. A few examples may suffice. Adopting the perspective of the speech community of the domain of Termanu, in the dyadic set for 'human being' or 'person', *hataholi//daehena*, *hataholi* is the local term, whereas *daehena* comes from various dialects in the east of the island. In the dyadic set for 'cave' or 'grotto', *lea(k)//lua(k)*, *lea(k)* is the local term in Termanu, whereas *lua(k)* comes from the dialect of Korbaffo. Similarly, in the dyadic set for 'enough' or 'sufficient', *henu//sofe*, *henu* is the Termanu term, while *sofe* comes from the dialect of the south-western domain of Thie. It is possible that as much as 20 per cent of the lexicon of the ritual language used in any one speech community is made up of words from other dialects.[13]

In this study, an initial focus is on composition from the domain of Termanu. From Termanu, analysis shifts to similar compositions in other domains: Ba'a, Ringgou, Dengka and Thie.[14] This allows further insight into the variation in composition across dialects and speech communities.

The Poet as Custodian

This is a comparative study of the compositions of specific poets. The individuals to whom I refer as poets are, on Rote, known as *manahelo* ('chanters' or 'those who chant'). Whereas this general designation privileges one modality of performance, chanters can also sing (*soda*), speak (*kokola*) or tell (*tui*) their compositions. Sung recitations may be accompanied by the *sasandu*, a stringed bamboo instrument encased in a surrounding lontar leaf, or by the drum (*labu*). There is a variety of

---

13 It is essential at the outset of this study to emphasise the pervasive importance of dialect variation for the compositions of any particular speech community. However, from an island-wide perspective, the use of dialect variation is a more complex subject for analysis, involving a concatenation of dialect forms. Thus, to take a simple example, the word for 'person' in Termanu is *hataholi//daehena*; in the eastern dialect of Ringgou, it is *hataholi//laehenda*; whereas in the western dialect of Dengka, it is *hataholi//andiana*.

14 In this study, I rely on the historical (Dutch) spelling of the names for Rotenese domains—a convention I have followed in other publications. There is a variety of ritual names for each domain as well as other names. Use of the historical spelling for specific domains allows reference to a literature on the island that dates to the middle of the seventeenth century.

modes of performance, some specific and appropriate to the particular composition, and a general recognition that certain poets are more talented than others in singing or chanting.

Although the style of performance is important, the emphasis among all poets is on their substantive knowledge. Poets are primarily the custodians of a coded ancestral wisdom. They are all 'men of knowledge' (*hataholi malelak*) whose principal task is to communicate this ritual knowledge without alteration. As *manahelo*, they are judged by their fellow Rotenese on the depth of their ritual knowledge and this, in turn, is most evidently communicated by the quality and coherence of their compositions and their extensive citation of ritual names. As a consequence, with few exceptions, master poets are elders and the knowledge they convey in their compositions is a cultural accumulation acquired over decades. Relatively few individuals have the talent and inclination to accumulate the knowledge and fluency necessary to recite but there are individuals, usually prompted and facilitated by older relatives with whom they associate, who embark on this path and begin to emerge as promising poets when they are in their 40s or 50s. Gradually, by the time they are 60 or 70, they come to be regarded locally as capable *manahelo*. Recognition is locally conferred and invariably limited to a select number of individuals. At present, on Rote, there are only a few master poets in any of the island's speech communities.[15] This study will examine the compositions of some of these master poets and compare them with each other.

The Canon of Ritual Knowledge

Rotenese parallel poetry relates to the rituals of life on the island. All poetic compositions are referred to, in Rotenese, as *bini*. In turn, these *bini* are described according to a combination of subject matter, ritual context or performative mode, which usually identifies a specific ritual context. *Bini* can be used on all ceremonial occasions of the life cycle as well as on occasions of formal interaction, such as the greeting or farewelling of guests, making requests to superiors, installing officials or the negotiation of bride-wealth. Formerly, *bini* were also recited at the initiation of new

---

15 Nineteenth-century Dutch literature on the island suggests that there was much more mobility among chanters than at present. Large funeral ceremonies would attract poets from other domains who would compete with each other in mortuary chanting and would often be handsomely rewarded with pieces of gold placed on their tongues.

activities: the planting and harvesting of fields; the beginning of tying, dyeing and weaving of a new cloth; the start and ceremonial conclusion to the construction of a house; and, most importantly, at the annual 'origin' ceremonies (known as *hus* or *limbe*) in each domain. Most of these rituals have now ceased to be performed, but the knowledge of the composition associated with them continues to be maintained in poetry.

There are two major categories of *bini*: origin *bini* and mortuary *bini*. These categories are related to each other in terms of the rituals of life and death. Distinguishing them, however, provides the basis for an initial understanding.

Knowledge among the Rotenese is identified with the recognition of origins. To know and to be able to trace the origin of things constitute true cultural knowledge. All Rotenese activities as well as all of the key items of daily use, from rice and millet or water buffalo to the tools for building a house or weaving a cloth, possess distinctive 'origins' that are referred to and recounted in the poetry of the *bini*. The knowledge and recitation of this poetry upholds and ritually enlivens these Rotenese activities and links them properly to an ancestral past.

There is coherence to the recitation of these origins. Although never recited as a single successive recitation, most origin *bini* relate to what might be described as an epic account of relations between the Sun and Moon and their descendants and the Lords of the Sea with their adherents. These heavenly creatures and their counterparts in the ocean engage with each other, hunting together, exchanging goods, threatening war and intermarrying. This engagement occurs on the 'dry land' that divides them from each other and generates the cultural goods and practices that define Rotenese life. All of these goods, including fire for cooking, come from the sea. Hence most Rotenese rituals were concerned with the celebration of these oceanic origins.[16] After acknowledging these origins, a particular feature of many Rotenese poetic compositions involves the systematic recitation of the transmission and propagation of these goods throughout the island.[17]

---

16   I have discussed some of these origin *bini* in a number of publications: 1) the origin of fire (Fox 1975); 2) the origin of textile patterns (Fox 1980); 3) the origin of the house (Fox 1993); and I have tried to outline the structure of the Rotenese 'epic' narrative in Fox (1997a).

17   I use the term 'topogeny' to refer to the ordered recitation of a succession of place names. Such topogenies are common in chants that recount the origins of particular goods that come from the sea, such as rice and millet. See Fox (2007a).

In contrast with the various origin *bini*, there is less coherence and more diversity among the mortuary *bini*. All of these *bini*, however, follow similar ritual formats. In one such format, the spirit of the deceased is addressed directly, his or her life alluded to and the sorrow and distress of grieving relatives are emphasised; then the deceased is told to depart—to board the ship of the dead and sail westward—but at the same time reminded that it will return in spirit form to come among relatives. In another ritual format, the deceased is compared with a particular named chant character and the stereotyped life of this character is recounted. In some of the more elaborate of these compositions, the deceased is given voice to admonish his relatives before sailing to the west.[18] The use of these different formats varies from domain to domain and is now heavily influenced by Christian rituals and the use of Christian poetic parallelism. The domain of Termanu, in particular, has preserved a significant canon of mortuary *bini* identified with specific chant characters whose life course is the focus of the chant. The repertoire of these chants fits different social categories. There are set mortuary chants for nobles and for commoners; for young nobles or rich commoners; for girls who have died as 'unripe' virgins; and, above all, for 'widows and orphans'.[19] 'Widow and orphan' is a general category that invokes a particular view of life and can be used to fit virtually all human circumstances. There is thus a variety of 'widow and orphan' chants and, to make matters more complex, some origin *bini* can be recomposed and transformed into 'widow and orphan' mortuary chants. The chant *Suti Solo do Bina Bane* that is to be considered exhaustively in this study is a prime example of this potential for poetic transformation.

Suti Solo do Bina Bane as an Oral Composition

In an oral tradition, there is no one definitive composition. On Rote, each composition is judged by internal qualities and coherence supported by the authority of the particular poet who stands as custodian of an ancestral canon. There are many versions of *Suti Solo do Bina Bane* to be

---

18   I have discussed one such chant in Fox (2003).
19   The Rotenese concept of 'widow and orphan' carries with it a weight of understanding that will be discussed, at various points, throughout this study.

considered in this study. They are clearly related to one another but there is also variation not just in their narrative structure but also in the ritual focus of their composition.

Suti Solo do Bina Bane belongs to the class of Rotenese origin narratives and recounts the arrival of further beneficence from the sea. *Suti* in the name *Suti Solo* refers to a nautilus shell and *Bina* in the name *Bina Bane* refers to a bailer shell. In the poem, these two shells are personified as creatures from the sea who are washed up onto the tidal flats, gathered by two women while fishing and then carried from one location to another. In the origin versions of this composition, these creatures are eventually made into specific cultural objects. The nature of these cultural objects varies according to the speech community (*nusak*) in which this composition is told. In origin versions of the poem, there exists an esoteric dimension surrounding the reasons why the nautilus and bailer shells are 'expelled' from the depths of the sea. Poets who recite *Suti Solo do Bina Bane* as an origin narrative variously allude to this hidden aspect of the canon—some more fully than others—but in the end, this dimension remains shrouded in mystery.

Suti Solo do Bina Bane can also be recited as a 'widow and orphan' mortuary chant. In these versions, the displacement of the shells—generally as the result of a violent storm—and then their quest to find an appropriate social setting are taken to represent the human condition. Versions of this kind emphasise the search for companionship and generally end with the return of the shells to the sea. This kind of composition, when well composed, makes an ideal mortuary chant.

Figure 3: Suti Solo and Bina Bane

'Then I, Bina, with whom will I be
And I, Suti, with whom will I be
With whom will I talk
And with whom will I speak?'

It is in the nature of Rotenese oral composition for a poet's recitation to be ambiguous. The poet, as the custodian of a traditional knowledge, must allude to this ancestral knowledge but he does not expound at length nor make explicit all aspects of that knowledge. No composition is therefore entirely explicit. Indeed, the best poets are those who cleverly hint at what is to be known without openly revealing it.

In my experience, there is hardly a recitation that does not prompt discussion afterwards, with various interpretations and attempts at exegesis of its meaning. I was fortunate, when I first arrived on Rote and began trying to understand ritual language, to have the elderly poet Old Meno to guide me. I suspect that several of his recitations for me were possibly more elaborate than would have been the case if I had not been so naive and unknowing. For some of his compositions, even Old Meno would leave things unsaid, but he would hint at what he had omitted or left ambiguous and would then gently lead me towards some understanding of what this might be. Rotenese poetry is thus based on a different kind of pedagogy: one in which meaning is progressively encircled until, for some but not all, key ideas are grasped, although they may never be articulated.

By this same token, no recitation is a complete recitation.[20] Often among a group of poets, when one has finished his recitation, another will speak up and provide, from his perspective, other elements of the composition. Oral composition is thus a continuing process but can also be seen as part of a joint effort by different custodians of knowledge to contribute to the weaving of a larger whole.

---

20   It is possible that previously in the performance of critical rituals, there may have been stricter rules of exposition in communing with the ancestors. Now that the compositions are recited outside their ritual context, this is no longer the case. Disembodied from their ritual context, recitations take on new significance.

2
Suti Solo do Bina Bane: Version I from the Domain of Termanu

Introducing the First Text: *Suti Solo do Bina Bane* I

This chapter introduces *Suti Solo do Bina Bane* as a narrative text. It examines its internal structure and provides an exegesis on successive passages in it. The composition I have chosen for this purpose is the first version of this text that I recorded in 1965 from the poet 'Old Meno' (*Meno Tua*), Stefanus Adulanu. It is a composition of some 299 lines. Of all of the versions of *Suti Solo do Bina Bane* that I have recorded, this version remains the longest and, in my view, the most comprehensive version that I have gathered. In retrospect, I believe there were a number of reasons why Old Meno recited this composition for me as he did. I was newly arrived on Rote and had begun visiting him regularly—as a kind of apprentice—not just to learn ritual language, but also to gather the oral history of Termanu and to observe the court gatherings that were regularly held in his presence.[1] I was particularly insistent on recording *Suti Solo do Bina Bane* and had passed to Old Meno the instructions that had been

---

1   In the absence of the Lord (*Manek*) of Termanu, who was the *camat* of Rote at the time, the traditional court generally met in the village of Ola Lain because this was Old Meno's residential settlement; this made it easier for him, at his age, to preside at court with the Deputy *Manek*, Frans Biredoko. See Fox (2007b).

given to me by the elder brother of Termanu's ruler. Old Meno, in turn, saw my 'voice-catcher' as a means of some day passing on his words to his newly born grandson.

The result was a recitation that was more extensive than might otherwise have been the case. This, however, does not make analysis of the text easier. To the contrary, there are significant passages in the text that would—without appropriate exegesis—seem to be largely irrelevant to the core of the composition. These seemingly irrelevant passages are intended to identify the composition as an origin chant and allude to the role of the two creatures from the sea, Suti and Bina (nautilus and bailer shells), in relation to other origin chants concerned with the production of textiles. These internal references to the wider canon of origin chants were characteristic of Old Meno's style of composition and could be considered a hallmark of an elder poet with a mastery of the full poetic canon.

The Genealogical Introduction

This version of *Suti Solo do Bina Bane* begins with a genealogical introduction. This is a critical part of the chant because it recounts the origin of names of the principal chant character(s). For all poets, the knowledge of names—both of persons and of places—is considered paramount. A poet who is able to compose fluently but lacks the knowledge of names cannot be considered an authoritative custodian of tradition: a 'person of knowledge' (*hataholi malelak*). After any recitation, names are invariably the first topic of discussion—and of contention—because when poets dispute among themselves, such disputes are most often focused on differences in the citation of names.

In ritual languages, names are a complex subject. They always have significance, even though they can rarely be translated literally. Names hint at interpretable meaning: they can provide a context for a character or a place and thereby proclaim some intended sense.

2. VERSION I FROM THE DOMAIN OF TERMANU

Figure 4: Stefanus Adulanu – 'Old Meno'

This genealogy follows a common format. The poet announces the name of the focus of his recitation and then identifies the parents of this chant character. The lines describe the physical transfer of a woman from the woods and forests whose dual name, Hali Siku//Manu Koa, suggests a bird-like being. This woman marries a man from the sea whose dual name suggests a shell-like being. From this union of land and sea come the chant characters Suti Solo and Bina Bane, who are identified as nautilus (*suti*) and bailer (*bane*) shells. In Rotenese genealogical reckoning, children take the first name of their father: hence Bane Aka > Bina Bane and Solo Bane > Suti Solo.

1.	*La-fada Suti Solo*	They speak of Suti Solo
2.	*Ma la-nosi Bina Bane.*	And they talk of Bina Bane.
3.	*Ala soku Hali Siku nula*	They transfer Hali Siku of the woods
4.	*Ma ala ifa Manu Koa lasi.*	And they cradle Manu Koa of the forest.
5.	*Ala tu Bane Aka liun*	They wed Bane Aka in the sea
6.	*Ma sao Solo Bane sain.*	And marry Solo Bane in the ocean.
7.	*De besak a bongi-la Suti Solo*	And now they give birth to Suti Solo
8.	*Ma lae la Bina Bane.*	And they bring forth Bina Bane.

The Expulsion of the Two Shells from the Sea

With these introductory lines, the chant proceeds to recount the event that leads to the expulsion of Suti Solo do Bina Bane from the sea. Most other versions of this chant allude to the storm that casts the shells onto land. Old Meno's version describes the insult that provokes the storm.

Suti Solo do Bina Bane's father, Bane Aka//Solo Bina, hosts a lively origin feast. The woman Po'o Pau Ai//Latu Kai Do, who is, like Suti Solo do Bina Bane's mother, from the Forest and Wood, comes to dance at the feast and asks to dance with Suti Solo do Bina Bane. The shells refuse; the woman is shamed and expresses her outrage to the Heavens and Heights, who grow angry and create the storm that rages on the sea, forcing the shells to escape.

Here again the names provide some understanding. A possible translation of the names for the woman Po'o Pau Ai//Latu Kai Do, who is, in some way, a maternal relative, would be 'Mouldy Pau Trees//Withered Kai Leaves'. Although Suti Solo do Bina Bane's rejection might appear appropriate in regard to these less than attractive female relatives, the insult nonetheless constitutes a breach in relations between the sea and the upper world of the Heavens and Earth. Po'o Pau Ai//Latu Kai Do's complaint to the Heavens and Heights prompts the Heavens and Heights to create a cyclone that casts Suti Solo do Bina Bane from the sea.

9.	*Faik esa manunin*	On a certain day
10.	*Ma ledok esa mateben*	And at a particular time
11.	*Boe ma Bani Aka liun hun*	Bani Aka in the sea has his origin feast
12.	*Ma Solo Bina sain sion na*	Solo Bina in the ocean has his feast of nine
13.	*Sio lakadoto*	The feast of nine boils lively
14.	*Ma hus-sala lakase.*	The origin feast bubbles noisily.
15.	*Boe ma inak Po'o Pau Ai la*	The woman Po'o Pau Ai [Mouldy Pau Trees]
16.	*Po'o Pau Ai lasi*	Po'o Pau Ai of the Forest
17.	*Ma fetok Latu Kai Do la*	And the girl Latu Kai Do [Withered Kai Leaves]
18.	*Latu Kai Do nula*	Latu Kai Do of the Woods
19.	*Leu pela sio*	Comes to dance at the feast of nine
20.	*Ma leu leno hu.*	And comes to turn at the origin feast.
21.	*Boe ma ala pela sio kokolak*	While dancing at the feast of nine, they talk
22.	*Ma ala leno hu dede'ak ma lae:*	And while turning at the origin feast, they speak and say:
23.	*'Te Suti Solo nai be?*	'But where is Suti Solo?
24.	*Fo au pela akasusudik*	For I wish to dance next to him
25.	*Ma Bina Bane nai be?*	And where is Bina Bane?
26.	*Fo leno akaseselik.'*	For I wish to turn beside him.'
27.	*Boe ma Bina Bane na-fada ma nae*	Then Bina Bane speaks and says
28.	*Ma Suti Solo na-fada ma nae:*	And Suti Solo speaks and says:
29.	*'Oo ina Po'o Pau Ai la*	'Oh the woman, Po'o Pau Ai

30.	*Po'o Pau Ai lasi la*	Po'o Pau Ai of the Forest
31.	*Au senang ta no ndia*	I am no friend of hers
32.	*Ma feto Latu Kai Do la*	And the girl Latu Kai Do
33.	*Latu Kai Do Nula la*	Latu Kai Do of the Woods
34.	*Au tiang ta no ndia.'*	I am no companion of hers.'
35.	*Boe ma Ina Po'o Pau Ai la*	The woman Po'o Pau Ai
36.	*Ala mae leu dedein*	There is shame on her forehead
37.	*Ma Feto Latu Kai Do la*	And the girl Latu Kai Do
38.	*Ala bi neu mataboan.*	There is fear in her eyes.
39.	*Boe ma leu la-nosi Poin*	They go to talk to the Heights
40.	*Ma leu la-fada Lain*	And go to speak to the Heavens
41.	*Lain manakoasa*	The Heavens who have power
42.	*Ma Poin manakila.*	The Heights who see overall.
43.	*Boe ma Lain nggenggele*	The Heavens rage
44.	*Ma Poin namanasa.*	And Heights grow angry.
45.	*De sangu nala liun dale*	A storm strikes the ocean's depths
46.	*Ma luli nala sain dale.*	A cyclone strikes the sea's depths.
47.	*Hu ina Po'o Pau Ai la*	Because the woman Po'o Pau Ai
48.	*Po'o Pau Ai lasi*	Po'o Pau Ai of the Forest
49.	*Ma feto Latu Kai Do la*	The girl Latu Kai Do
50.	*Latu Kai Do nula nae-a:*	Latu Kai Do of the Wood says:
51.	*'Ala mamaek Po'o Pau Ai la*	'They shame Po'o Pau Ai
52.	*Ma ala lakabibik Latu Kai Do la.'*	And they frighten Latu Kai Do.'
53.	*Boe ma Poin namanasa*	The Heights grow angry
54.	*Ma Lain nggenggele.*	And the Heavens rage.
55.	*Neme ndia mai*	From this comes
56.	*Boe ma sangu nala liun dale*	A storm striking the ocean's depths
57.	*Ma luli nala sain dale.*	And a cyclone striking the sea's depths.
58.	*Boe ma besak ka Suti lama-edo nggi*	Now Suti exudes his pods
59.	*Ma Bina lamatoko-isi*	And Bina puts out his insides
60.	*De ana tolomu sasali*	He escapes quickly
61.	*Ma nalai lelena.*	And he flees hastily.

2. VERSION I FROM THE DOMAIN OF TERMANU

The Arrival of the Shells in the Tidal Flats of Tena Lai ma Mae Oe

The next lines tell of the arrival of Suti Solo do Bina Bane in the tidal shallows on the coast of Rote. The place of arrival, Tena Lai//Mae Oe, is a ritual site of great importance. Virtually all Rotenese chants identify this same site as the place where the various gifts from the sea reach Rote.[2]

62.	*De mai Tena Lai Loek lutun*	He comes to the fish wall in the shallows at Tena Lai
63.	*Ma Mae Oe Nggolok dean na.*	And the stone weir at the promontory at Mae Oe.
64.	*Bina mai ndia*	Bina comes there
65.	*De ana babi mafo neu ndia*	He conceals [himself] in the shade there
66.	*Ma Suti mai ndia*	And Suti comes there
67.	*De ana sulu sa'o neu ndia.*	He covers [himself] in the shadows there.

The Quest for the Ritual Fish

The following lines then set the scene for the 'gathering' of Suti Solo do Bina Bane and the transfer of these shells onto dry land. This passage introduces a number of new named characters without a full genealogical introduction. The characters in question are: 1) Manupui Peda//Kokolo Dulu, who, like Bane Aka//Solo Bina, wishes to hold an origin feast; 2) Bafa Ama Laik//Holu Ama Daek; and 3) his wife, Nggiti Seti//Pedu Hange. The character who is not yet mentioned is Lole Holu//Lua Bafa, the daughter who becomes the companion of Suti Solo do Bina Bane. She is introduced in a succeeding passage. Since Rotenese names follow a consistent pattern whereby the first name of the father becomes the last name of the child—Bafa Ama > Lua Bafa and Holu Ama > Lua Lole Holu—the relationship would be self-evident to a Rotenese listener.

---

2   These gifts include, among others, rice and millet, which are also gathered at Tena Lai ma Mae Oe and then transferred and propagated throughout Rote. For the chant that recounts these origins, see Fox (1997b).

MASTER POETS, RITUAL MASTERS

Although none of these names can be fully translated, they consist of words whose meaning is suggestive. Manupui//Kokolo, for example, connotes a bird-like being: *manupui* is the term for 'bird' and *kolo* (or *kokolo*) is a word used in the names for specific birds. Similarly, *nggiti* is the verb for 'working a loom' and *hange* is a variant of *henge*, the verb for 'tie-dyeing threads'. Thus the name Nggiti Seti//Pedu Hange indicates a character who is involved in weaving and dyeing, a connection that signals later developments in the composition and links this chant to another origin chant that recounts the origin of dyeing and weaving.

In this passage and throughout this composition, there is a clear opposition between the origin feast held on land and on sea. In this passage, Manupui Peda//Kokolo Dulu's feast is not lively. A divination is held and it is determined that a key ritual, *peda poi//fua bafa*, has not been carried out as part of the agricultural rituals for receiving harvested rice and millet into the house. Literally, these terms translate as 'placing at the tip'//'loading the mouth'; they require that an offering be made of two specific fish, referred to, in ritual language, as Tio Holu//Dusu La'e. As a consequence, Nggiti Seti//Pedu Hange has to prepare her scoop-net and go to the stone fish traps that are set out in the sea to catch fish as the tide recedes. These fish walls form a boundary between the land and the sea and therefore provide the point of contact between these worlds.

68.	*Faik esa manunin*	On a certain day
69.	*Ma ledok esa mateben*	And at a particular time
70.	*Boe ma Manupui Peda hun-na*	Manupui Peda holds his origin feast
71.	*Hus ta laka-doto*	The origin feast is not lively
72.	*Ma Kokolo Dulu sio-na*	Kokolo Dulu holds his feast of nine
73.	*Sio ta laka-se.*	The feast of nine is not noisy.
74.	*Boe ma ala kani batu dodo*	They divine by shaking the stone
75.	*Ma ala lea te ndanda.*	They consider by measuring the spear.
76.	*Boe ma lae:*	They [the diviners] say:
77.	*'O peda poin bei ta*	'You have not yet placed a fish on top of the rice
78.	*Ma fua bafa bei ta.'*	And you have not yet laid a fish on the basket's mouth.'
79.	*Boe ma ina Nggiti Seti*	The woman Nggiti Seti
80.	*Ma fetok ka Pedu Hange*	And the girl Pedu Hange

81.	*Bafa Ama Laik tun*	Bafa Ama Laik's wife
82.	*Ma Holu Ama Daek saon*	Holu Ama Daek's spouse
83.	*Ala kedi la mau don*	They cut a *mau* plant's leaves
84.	*De mau mana'a don*	A *mau* with a mouthful of leaves
85.	*Ma ala pena-la pole aban*	And they pluck a *pole* plant's cotton tufts
86.	*De pole masapena aban.*	A *pole* bursting with cotton tufts.
87.	*De ala teli kokolo ndai*	They string and wind a fishnet
88.	*De ndai mahamu lilok.*	A fishnet with a gold-weighted belly.
89.	*Ma ala ane seko bui seko*	They braid a scoop-net, twine a scoop-net
90.	*De seko matei besik.*	A scoop-net with iron-weighted insides.
91.	*De ana ndae ndai neu alun*	She hangs the fishnet over her shoulder
92.	*Ma ana su'u seko neu langan*	And she balances the scoop-net on her head
93.	*De leo Tena Lai neu*	And goes to Tena Lai
94.	*Ma leo Mae Oe neu,*	And goes to Mae Oe,
95.	*Neu nafa-nggao lutu limak*	Goes to grope in the 'arms' of the fish wall
96.	*Ma neu nafa-dama dea eik*	Goes to probe in the 'legs' of the stone weir
97.	*Dea ei manalek*	The 'legs' of the stone weir that hold good fortune
98.	*Ma lutu lima mauak.*	The 'arms' of the fish wall that bear good luck.
99.	*Nafanggao dea eik*	She gropes in the 'legs' of the stone weir
100.	*Ma nafadama lutu limak.*	And probes the 'arms' of the fish wall.

The Encounter with Suti Solo do Bina Bane

The next passage describes Nggiti Seti//Pedu Hange's encounter with Suti Solo and Bina Bane. Although Nggiti Seti//Pedu Hange is determined to catch only Tio Holu//Dusu La'e fish, all that she is able to scoop up is Suti

MASTER POETS, RITUAL MASTERS

Solo do Bina Bane, who declares himself 'an orphan wronged//a widow mistaken'. So, in the end, Nggiti Seti//Pedu Hange agrees to take the shells back to her daughter, Lole Holu//Lua Bafa.

101.	*Siluk bei ta dulu*	When morning is not yet in the east
102.	*Ma hu'ak bei ta langa dei*	And dawn is not yet at the head
103.	*Boe ma ana ndai ndano, ndai ndano*	She fish-catches, fish-catches
104.	*Ma ana seko toko, seko toko.*	And she scoop-throws, scoop-throws.
105.	*Boe ma ana seko nala Suti Solo*	She scoops up Suti Solo
106.	*Ma ana ndai nala Bina Bane*	And she fishes up Bina Bane
107.	*Boe ma lae:*	They say:
108.	*'Au seko Tio*	'I scoop for a Tio fish
109.	*Ma au ndai Dusu dei*	And I fished for a Dusu fish
110.	*Fo Dusu La'e dei*	A real Dusu La'e
111.	*Ma Tio Holu dei*	And a real Tio Holu
112.	*Tao neu peda-poik*	To place on top of the rice
113.	*Ma tao neu lua-bafak.'*	And to lay on the basket's mouth.'
114.	*Boe ma nae:*	Then he says:
115.	*'O ndai ndano meni au*	'Oh, fish me forth and take me
116.	*Ma seko toko meni au*	And scoop me up and take me
117.	*Fo ela tao neu namahenak*	To create expectation
118.	*Ma tao neu nakabanik.'*	And to create hope.'
119.	*Boe ma ana ndai ndano [heni] Suti*	But she fishes and throws Suti away
120.	*Ma ana seko toko heni Bina.*	And she scoops and throws Bina away.
121.	*Te hu inak Pedu Hange*	But when the woman Pedu Hange
122.	*Ma fetok ka Nggiti Seti*	And the girl Nggiti Seti
123.	*Seko nala lek dua*	Scoops in two waterholes
124.	*Na Bina nala lek dua*	Bina is there in the two waterholes
125.	*Ma ndai nala lifu telu*	And when she fishes in three pools
126.	*Na Suti nala lifu telu.*	Suti is there in the three pools.
127.	*Boe ma Suti, ana kokolak*	Then Suti, he talks
128.	*Ma Bina, ana dede'ak nae:*	And Bina, he speaks, saying:
129.	*'Ndai ndano muni au*	'Fish me forth and take me

130.	*Ma seko toko muni au dei.*	And scoop me up and take me then.
131.	*Au ana-ma ma-salak*	I am an orphan wronged
132.	*Ma au falu-ina ma-singok.'*	And I am a widow mistaken.'
133.	*Boe ma nae:*	The she says:
134.	*'Te au ndai ndano uni o*	'I will fish you forth and take you
135.	*Ma au seko toko uni o*	And I will scoop you up and take you
136.	*Fo mu mo Lole Holu*	That you may go with Lole Holu
137.	*Ma mu mo Lua Bafa.'*	And you may go with Lua Bafa.'

Figure 5: Woman casting her scoop-net

'She fish-catches, fish-catches
And she scoop-throws, scoop-throws.
She scoops up Suti Solo
And she fishes up Bina Bane.'

MASTER POETS, RITUAL MASTERS

The Dialogue Directives to the Shells

The next passage begins a remarkable dialogue between the two that is generally regarded as the defining component of *Suti Solo do Bina Bane* as a composition, whether it is recited as an origin narrative or as a mortuary chant. This dialogue extends for more than 80 lines and consists of a number of possibilities phrased in poetic formulae. For example, Suti//Bina agree to befriend Lole Holu//Lua Bafa but ask what would happen if the leaf container in which they were being carried broke. If this were to happen, Suti//Bina exclaim: 'Then, I, Suti, with whom would I be and I, Bina, with whom would I be? With whom will I talk and with whom will I speak?' This is the cry of the displaced orphan and widow.

138.	*Boe ma Suti, ana kokolak*	Then Suti, he talks
139.	*Ma Bina, ana dede'ak ma nae:*	And Bina, he speaks, and says:
140.	*'Te o ndai muni au*	'If you fish and take me
141.	*Fo au atia Lole Holu*	I will be a friend to Lole Holu
142.	*Ma seko muni au*	And if you scoop and take me
143.	*Fo au asena Lua Bafa.*	So that I will be a companion to Lua Bafa.
144.	*De malole-la so*	These things are good
145.	*Ma mandak-kala so.*	And these things are proper.
146.	*Te leo hai-paik la-tato*	But if the ends of the leaf bucket bump
147.	*Ma leo lepa-solak la-bebi*	And if the corners of the water carrier crash
148.	*Fo ala hika setele henin*	So they laugh with a shriek at losing me
149.	*Ma eki mata-dale henin,*	And they scream with a startle at losing me,
150.	*Na Bina, au o se*	Then I, Bina, with whom will I be
151.	*Ma Suti, au o se*	And I, Suti, with whom will I be
152.	*Fo au kokolak o se*	With whom will I talk
153.	*Ma au dede'ak o se?'*	And with whom will I speak?'

In response to Suti//Bina's query, Nggiti Seti//Pedu Hange proposes another possibility: an alternative resting place—to reside with the syrup vat and the rice basket. For Suti//Bina, however, this also offers only a transient possibility.

154.	*Boe ma inak-ka Nggiti Seti*	The woman Nggiti Seti
155.	*Ma fetok-ka Pedu Hange nae:*	And the girl Pedu Hange says:
156.	*'Te eki setele henin*	'If they scream with a shriek at losing you
157.	*Ma hika mata-dale henin na,*	And laugh with a startle at losing you,
158.	*Suti mo tua bou*	Then Suti, go with syrup vat
159.	*Ma Bina mo neka hade.'*	And Bina, go with the rice basket.'
160.	*Boe ma nae:*	Then he says:
161.	*'O malole-la so*	'Oh, these things are good
162.	*Ma mandak-kala so.*	And these things are proper.
163.	*Te leo bou lamakako fude*	But if the vat overflows with froth
164.	*Ma soka lamalua bafa*	And the sack runs over at the mouth
165.	*Fo bou lo totonon*	So that the vat must be overturned
166.	*Ma soka no lulunun*	And the sack must be rolled up
167.	*Na Suti au o se*	Then I, Suti, with whom will I be
168.	*Ma Bina au o se?'*	And I, Bina, with whom will I be?'

To each proposal that Nggiti Seti//Pedu Hange makes, Suti//Bina responds by emphasising its impermanence. This refrain accords with the Rotenese view of the human condition as transient and uncertain. In each response, Suti//Bina lays stress on the lack of someone with whom to speak. Thus, all of the various different settings that are proposed are botanic metaphors for community.

169.	*Boe ma nae:*	Then she says:
170.	*'Oo na mo bete pule kode ketuk*	'Oh, go with the millet grains that the monkey plucks
171.	*Ma pela po'o bafi ka'ak.'*	And with the ears of maize that the pig chews.'
172.	*Te hu Suti bei namatane*	But Suti continues to cry
173.	*Ma Bina bei nasakedu.*	And Bina continues to sob.
174.	*Boe ma nae:*	So he says:
175.	*'Te leo kode ketu neni betek*	'But if the monkey plucks the millet
176.	*Ma bafi ka'a neni pelak,*	And the pig chews the maize,
177.	*Na Suti au o se*	Then I, Suti, with whom will I be
178.	*Ma Bina au o se?'*	And I, Bina, with whom will I be?'

179.	*Boe ma Suti Solo na-fada*	Then Suti Solo speaks
180.	*Ma Bina Bane na-nosi ma nae:*	And Bina Bane answers and says:
181.	*'Oo ndia bei ta au alelak ndia.'*	'Oh, that I do not yet know at all.'

Once more, Nggiti Seti//Pedu Hange suggests a possible place to rest: in the trees' shade and the lontar palms' shadow, but such shade is fleeting.

182.	*Boe ma nae:*	Then she says:
183.	*'Na mo sa'o tua*	'Then go with lontar palms' shadow
184.	*Ma mo mafo ai.'*	And go with trees' shade.'
185.	*Boe ma nae:*	Then he says:
186.	*'Te leo mafo ai la hiluk*	'But if the trees' shade recedes
187.	*Ma sa'o tua la keko*	And the lontars' shadow shifts
188.	*Na Suti au o se*	Then I, Suti, with whom will I be
189.	*Ma Bina au o se*	And I, Bina, with whom will I be
190.	*Fo au kokolak o se*	With whom will I talk
191.	*Ma au dede'ak o se*	And with whom will I speak
192.	*Tao neu nakabanik*	To create hope
193.	*Ma tao neu namahenak?'*	And to create expectation?'

Finally, Nggiti Seti//Pedu Hange proposes yet another possibility, but this is also rejected specifically because it offers no community, no fellowship.

194.	*Boe ma nae:*	Then she says:
195.	*'Te na mu mo peu ai*	'Then go with boundary tree
196.	*Ma mu mo to batu.'*	And go with border stone.'
197.	*Boe ma Suti boe kokolak*	Still Suti talks
198.	*Ma Bina boe dede'ak ma nae:*	And still Bina speaks and says:
199.	*'Te hu ai dede'an ta*	'But a tree does not talk
200.	*Ma batu kokolan ta.'*	And a stone does not speak.'
201.	*Bina boe nasakedu*	Still Bina sobs
202.	*Ma Suti boe namatani.*	And still Suti cries.

Finally, Nggiti Seti//Pedu Hange proposes a return to the sea.

203.	*Besak-ka nae:*	Now she says:
204.	*'Mo doa lasi*	'Go with the forest cuckoo
205.	*Ma mo koloba'o le*	And go with the river watercock
206.	*[Fo] fa tunga-tunga le*	So that as current passes down the river
207.	*Ma fo ela udan tunga-tunga lasi*	And rain passes through the forest
208.	*Fo mu oli tatain*	You may go to the edge of the estuary
209.	*Ma mu le bibifan,*	And you may go to the lip of the river,
210.	*Fo ela fa oek ana mai*	So that when the current's water arrives
211.	*Ma ela epo oek ana mai*	And when the eddy's water arrives
212.	*Na bonu boa fo mu*	That bobbing like *boa* wood, you may go
213.	*Ma ele piko fo mu,*	And drifting like *piko* wood, you may go,
214.	*Leo sain dale mu*	To the sea, you may go
215.	*Ma leo liun dale mu.*	And to the ocean, you may go.
216.	*Te hu mu posi makamu mekon*	Thus go to the sea's edge, resounding like a gong
217.	*Fo nene fino tata*	To stop and listen there
218.	*Ma mu unu mali labun*	And go to the reef, rumbling like a drum
219.	*Fo dei dongo meme ndia*	To stand and wait there
220.	*Fo dei loe sain dale mu*	And then descend into the ocean
221.	*Ma dilu liun dale mu.'*	And turn downward into the sea.'

In many compositions in which *Suti Solo do Bina Bane* is told as a mortuary chant, the shells' return to the sea provides an appropriate ending. This version by Old Meno, however, is an origin chant and thus belongs to a larger set of interconnected chants. What follows is a long passage that makes specific connections to another chant about the origin of the particular tie-dye patterns that appear on traditional cloths. The actual subject of these lines is never stated but only alluded to: Suti, the nautilus shell, becomes the container for dye, particularly indigo dye; and Bina, the bailer shell, becomes the base on which the spindle for winding thread is turned. The two shells are ritual icons for the processes of preparing a cloth for weaving.

MASTER POETS, RITUAL MASTERS

The Return of the Shells to the Sea

The following passages first establish the close connection between Lua Bafa//Lole Holu and Suti Solo//Bina Bane and then emphasise her capacities as an extraordinary weaver of traditional cloth. The narrative proceeds in stages. Suti//Bina must return to the festivities in the sea and formally declare companionship with Lua Bafa//Lole Holu.

222.	*Boe ma besak ka*	Now it is that
223.	*Ina Po'o Ai la bei pela*	The woman Po'o Pau Ai is still dancing
224.	*Ma feto Latu Kai Do la bei longe.*	And the girl Latu Kai Do still does the *ronggeng*.
225.	*Ala teteni Suti Solo*	They request Suti Solo
226.	*Ma ala tata Bina Bane.*	And they ask for Bina Bane.
227.	*'Boe ma oo te nakas sa ia*	'Oh, just a while ago
228.	*Fo Suti namaedo nggi*	Suti exuded his pods
229.	*Hu inak nde*	Because of this woman
230.	*Oo bei huas a ia*	Oh, just yesterday
231.	*Fo Bina lamatoko isi*	Bina put forth his insides
232.	*Hu inak ka nde.*	Because of this woman.
233.	*O de au senang ta no o*	Oh I am no companion of yours
234.	*Ma au tiang ta no o.*	And I am no friend of yours.
235.	*Au atia Lua Bafa Au a*	I am a friend of Lua Bafa
236.	*Ma asena Lole Holu dei.'*	And I am a companion of Lole Holu.'

As in the beginning of this chant, here there is an occurrence of origin feasts both on land and in the sea. Instead of Nggiti Seti//Pedu Hange going in search of the ritual fish needed for the feast on land, Lua Bafa//Lole Holu goes to the sea in search of these creatures. What is indicated here is that Suti Solo//Bina Bane's relationship with Lua Bafa//Lole Holu has re-established a harmonious relationship between the land and the sea. This is signalled by the fact that when the Ruler of the Sea holds his celebration of origin, Lua Bafa//Lole Holu is able to gather the ritual fish that allow Kokolo Dulu//Manupui Peda to hold his origin feast.

237.	*Faik esa manunin*	On a certain day
238.	*Ma ledok esa mateben,*	And at a particular time,
239.	*Boe ma la-fada,*	So they say,

240.	*Danga Lena liun hun-na*	The Ruler of the Ocean holds his origin feast
241.	*Hus sala lakadoto.*	The origin feast boils.
242.	*Ma Mane Tua sain sion-na*	And the Lord of the Sea holds his feast of nine
243.	*Sio la laka-se.*	The feast of nine bubbles.
244.	*Boe ma besak-ka inak-ka Lole Holu*	Now the woman Lole Holu
245.	*Ma fetok-ka Lua Bafa*	And the girl Lua Bafa
246.	*Neu sanga Dusu peda-poik*	Goes to seek a Dusu to place on top
247.	*Ma neu sanga Tio fua-bafak*	And goes to seek a Tio to lay on the mouth
248.	*Fo ana tao neu peda-poik*	That she might do the 'top-placing rite'
249.	*Ma tao neu fua-bafak*	And she might do the 'mouth-laying ritual'
250.	*Neu Kokolo Dulu hun*	For Kokolo Dulu's origin feast
251.	*Ma Manupui Peda sion na.*	And Manupui Peda's feast of nine.

The next passage identifies Lua Bafa//Lole Holu as a weaver: a woman who knows how to spin, dye and weave bright-coloured cloths.

252.	*Boe ma besak-ka inak-ka Lua Bafa*	Now the woman Lua Bafa
253.	*Ma fetok-ka Lole Holu*	And the girl Lole Holu
254.	*Lima ku'u dao kin*	The left fingers of her hand
255.	*Na leleak ifa lolek*	Know how to cradle the winding rack
256.	*Ma pu lete lai konan-na*	And the right side of her thigh
257.	*Na-lelak dipo ine.*	Knows how to turn the spindle on its base.
258.	*Boe ina besak ka ana tenu dedele pou*	Now she weaves a woman's sarong tightly
259.	*Fo dula kakaik lo pana-dai esa,*	A patterned sarong with multi-coloured design,
260.	*Boe ma ana henge dedele lafa*	She ties a man's cloth tightly
261.	*Fo sidi soti busa-eik,*	A supplemented cloth with dog-leg stitch,
262.	*Ma pou leu pana-dai*	A woman's sarong with multicoloured design
263.	*Ma sidi soti busa-eik.*	And a supplemented cloth with dog-leg stitch.

Lua Bafa//Lole Holu appears at the great feast in the sea and is proclaimed the good friend and proper companion of Suti//Bina. This is essentially a restatement of restoration of the continuing good relationship between the land and the sea.

264.	*Besak-ka leu pela sio nai liun*	Now they go to dance at the feast of nine in the sea
265.	*Ma leu leno hun nai sain.*	And they go to spin at the origin feast in the ocean.
266.	*Boe ma besak-ka lae:*	So now they say:
267.	*'Oo Suti tian nde ia*	'Oh, that is Suti's friend
268.	*Ma Bina senan nde ia*	And that is Bina's companion
269.	*Ma inak-ka Lua Bafa*	The woman Lua Bafa
270.	*Fo Bafo Ama Laik anan*	Bafa Ama Laik's child
271.	*Ma fetok-ka Lole Holu*	And the girl Lole Holu
272.	*Fo Holu Aina Daek anan.'*	Holu Ama Daek's child.'
273.	*Ma nae:*	And it is said:
274.	*'Sena mandak kia*	'This is a proper companion
275.	*Ma tia malole ia.'*	And this is a good friend.'

Origin References and Ritual Outcomes

The final passage in this chant is not so much a continuation of the previous passage as a statement of a ritual outcome. Because of the relation of Lua Bafa//Lole Holu with Suti Solo//Bina Bane, relations between the land and the sea are restored and the origin feasts on land can be celebrated properly. However, with the further knowledge of dyeing and weaving, these feasts can be performed with dancers arrayed in multi-coloured cloths. The chant concludes with a direct reference to the chant *Pata Iuk ma Dula Foek*, which recounts the origin of weaving.

276.	*Besak-ka ala kokolak sio bafi la*	Now they talk of the pigs of the feast of nine
277.	*Ma ala dede'ak hu kapa.*	And they speak of the buffalo of the origin feast.
278.	*Hu kapa la tola*	The buffalo of the origin appear
279.	*Ma sio bafi la dadi,*	And the pigs of nine come forth,
280.	*Hu Holu Ama Daek hu-na*	There at Holu Ama Daek's origin feast

281.	*Ma hu Bafa Ama Laik sion-na.*	And Bafa Ama Laik's feast of nine.
282.	*Ma besak ka neu pela sio*	Now they go to dance at the feast of nine
283.	*Ma leno hu.*	And spin at the origin feast.
284.	*Besak-ka neni pou la mai*	Now they bring women's sarongs
285.	*Ma neni sidik la mai,*	And bring supplemented cloths,
286.	*Sidi soti busa eik*	Supplemented cloth with dog-leg stitch
287.	*Ma pou le'u pana dai.*	And women's sarongs in multicoloured strips.
288.	*Pela ngganggape liman-na*	They dance with outstretched arms
289.	*Pana-dai la tuda*	The multicoloured cloth falls
290.	*Ma leno sosodo ein-nala*	And they turn with shuffling feet
291.	*Ma tola-te-la monu.*	And the spear-patterned cloth drops.
292.	*Besak-ka lae:*	Now they say:
293.	*'Ninga do Hena bei nde ia*	'This is still Ninga do Hena
294.	*Fo lae Dula Foek*	So they say: Dula Foek [Pattern Crocodile]
295.	*Fo lae Pata Iuk*	Thus they say: Pata Iuk [Figure Shark]
296.	*Pata Iuk tete'ek*	Truly, Pata Iuk
297.	*Ma Dula Foe tete'ek.*	And truly, Dula Foek.
298.	*De pana-dai la tuda*	The multicoloured cloth falls
299.	*Ma tola-te la monu.'*	And the spear-patterned cloth drops.'

Old Meno's chant is a complex but subtly structured composition: a narrative that both reveals and hides its meaning. It provides an appropriate starting point for the analysis of ritual language composition.

Initial Composition Analysis

Old Meno's *Suti Solo do Bina Bane* comes to 299 lines and is composed on the basis of a full 103 dyadic sets, including a number of compound dyadic sets. In it is a great variety of oral formulae and a number of these formulae recur, at intervals, in the composition. It is useful therefore to begin the analysis of this composition by focusing on some of these recurrent formulae.

Formulae for Speaking: -fada//-nosi; kokola(k)// dede'a(k)

Speaking is at the core of Rotenese culture. Speeches, sermons and ceremonial presentations—tale-telling, debate, repartee, argument—are all essential elements of sociality. Among Rotenese, talk never ceases. In a class society, however, with hierarchies of order, there are some constraints on speech. In gatherings, nobles speak more than commoners, men more than women, elders more than juniors; yet commoners, women and youth, when given the opportunity, invariably display the same prodigious fondness for speaking.

Only in certain rituals is silence required. Yet Rotenese find even these occasional ritual injunctions hard to observe. In ordinary situations, a lack of talk is an indication of distress. Rotenese repeatedly explain that if their 'hearts' are confused or dejected, they keep silent. Thus, the act of speaking is critical to all human engagement, and from an early age, every Rotenese engages in the rhetorical presentation of self.

The composition *Suti Solo do Bina Bane* emphasises this central feature of Rotenese life. The shells repeatedly ask:

> Then I, Bina, with whom will I be
> And I, Suti, with whom will I be
> With whom will I talk
> And with whom will I speak?

From this perspective, 'being' is equated with 'talking'.

The vocabulary of speaking in ritual language is both extensive and elaborate. In the lexicon of ritual language, there are no less than 25 different verbs for speaking, cajoling, requesting, stating, asserting and conversing.[3] It is therefore perhaps significant but in no way surprising that this first version of *Suti Solo do Bina Bane* begins with an assertion based on a key dyadic set for speaking, *-fada//-nosi*:

1.	*La-fada Suti Solo*	They speak of Suti Solo
2.	*Ma la-nosi Bina Bane.*	And they talk of Bina Bane.

---

3   I examine the semantic network of these verbs of speaking in Fox (1974: 77–79).

Here Old Meno is following a convention used by most poets to assert that they are simply recounting the words of the elders and ancestors. Although they are the ones who 'speak', what they say has come down from past generations. Meno uses a succinct formula to make this assertion, whereas some poets offer substantial perorations to their compositions to make this same point. The dyadic set that he uses combines the verb *-fada*, which is the most general term 'to speak', with the verb *-nosi*, which is a term that, in ordinary speech of Termanu, means 'to drip'. Thus, in ritual language, *-nosi* takes its meaning from its pair, *-fada*. Both verbs are the third-person plural without a preceding pronoun.[4] This is intended to convey a sense of general agency.

The same set occurs elsewhere in the composition. The first of these occurrences is when the women dancers who are insulted by the shells raise their complaint to the Heavens:

39.	*Boe ma leu la-nosi Poin*	They go to talk to the Heights
40.	*Ma leu la-fada Lain*	And go to speak to the Heavens

A further occurrence is when the two shells make a direct statement. In this case, another verb for 'speaking', *nae* (third-person singular: 'to say'), is added.

179.	*Boe ma Suti Solo na-fada*	Then Suti Solo speaks
180.	*Ma Bina Bane na-nosi ma nae:*	And Bina Bane answers and says:

---

4   Rotenese has three kinds of verbs: 1) those with formative prefixes, all of which indicate person, number and form of action; 2) those without formative prefixes; and 3) a small number of irregular verbs whose formative elements, indicating person and number, are part of the verb itself. Rotenese has the following verbal formative prefixes (third-person singular): *na-, nama-, nafa-, nasa-, naka-*. The paradigm for the verb 'to speak' (*-fada* in Termanu dialect, *-fade* in Dengak dialect), with appropriate pronouns, offers an illustration:

	Termanu		Dengka	
I speak	*au*	*a-fada*	*au*	*u-fade*
You (sg.) speak	*o*	*ma-fada*	*ho*	*mu-fade*
(S)he/it speaks	*ana/ndia*	*na-fada*	*eni*	*na-fade*
We (incl.) speak	*ita*	*ta-fada*	*hita*	*ta-fade*
We (excl.) speak	*ami*	*ma-fada*	*hai*	*mi-fade*
You (pl.) speak	*emi*	*ma-fada*	*hei*	*mi-fade*
They speak	*ala/sila*	*la-fada*	*sila*	*la-fade*

The textual presentation utilises hyphenation to highlight the root terms that constitute canonical sets.

Generally, in ritual language compositions, *nae* is used to indicate that what follows is a direct statement.⁵ As such, *nae* (singular) and *lae* (plural) occur frequently throughout the *Suti Solo do Bina Bane* compositions because of their emphasis on dialogue. *Nae/lae* occur in 'orphan' lines that lack a corresponding line. All these orphan lines introduce the next statement in a dialogue.

The same phrase, *Boe ma nae* ('Then he or she says'), occurs eight times in Meno's composition (lines 114, 133, 160, 169, 174, 182, 185 and 194) with two other occurrences in variant form, *Besak-ka nae* ('Now he says') (line 203), or simply as *Ma nae* ('And it is said') (line 273). It also occurs in plural form, *Boe ma lae* ('Then they say'), in two lines (76 and 107) and once in the variant form *Boe ma besak-ka lae* ('So now they say') (line 266) and again as *Besak-ka lae* ('Now they say') (line 292).

There are also two occurrences of *nae* on its own where it functions to introduce statements by specific chant characters:

50.	*Latu Kai Do nula nae-a:*	Latu Kai Do of the Wood says:
155.	*Ma fetok-ka Pedu Hange nae:*	And the girl Pedu Hange says:

Some poets combine *nae/lae* with *-fada* to form a dyadic set. Although acceptable, this is generally judged as unsuitable among some poets. Meno appears to do this in his recitation, but it is also possible that he has simply repeated *-fada* where he should have used *-nosi*:

27.	*Boe ma Bina Bane na-fada ma nae*	Then Bina Bane speaks and says
28.	*Ma Suti Solo na-fada ma nae:*	And Suti Solo speaks and says:

Another dyadic set that denotes 'speaking' also occurs strategically throughout this composition. This set combines the term *kokola(k)* with *dede'a(k)*. Both verbs in this set are in reduplicated form. Their root form is *kola/de'a*. Neither verb takes a formative prefix. Both of these verbs are commonly used in ordinary language, more often in their reduplicated

---

5 The paradigm for this verb is:

I speak	au	ae
You speak	o	mae
(S)he/it speaks	ndia/ana	nae
We (incl.) speak	ita	tae
We (excl.) speak	ami	mae
You (pl.) speak	emi	mae
They speak	sila/ala	lae

form. *Kokolak* describes conversational speech whereas *dede'ak* refers to a more directed form of speech, involving turn-taking, argument and debate. As a noun, *dede'ak* is the term for a court case or ongoing litigation.

The same set occurs twice (lines 127–28 and 138–39) to describe the speech of the two shells:

| *Boe ma Suti, ana kokolak* | Then Suti, he talks |
| *Ma Bina, ana dede'ak nae:* | And Bina, he speaks, saying: |

The set also occurs twice (lines 152–53 and 190–91) as part of the plaintive refrain of the shells in response to the possibility of a lack or loss of fellowship:

| *'Fo au kokolak o se* | 'With whom will I talk |
| *Ma au dede'ak o se?'* | And with whom will I speak?' |

And it occurs again towards the end of the composition:

| 276. | *Besak-ka ala kokolak sio bafi la* | Now they talk of the pigs of the feast of nine |
| 277. | *Ma ala dede'ak hu kapa.* | And they speak of the buffalo of the origin feast. |

Formulae for Marking Time: *fai(k)//ledo*

The first of these is a set marker of time that is regularly used by poets throughout Rote to define the occurrence of a particular event. In Old Meno's chant, this formula occurs in lines 9–10, 68–69 and 237–38:

| *Faik esa manunin* | On a certain day |
| *Ma ledok esa mateben* | And at a particular time |

Meno's use of this formula, however, is interesting in that it does not follow strict canonical rules. Were these lines to follow canonical rules, they would be composed as follows:[6]

| *Faik esa manunin* | On a certain day |
| *Ma ledok dua mateben* | And at a particular time |

---

6   This is the formula used, for example, by the poet Petrus Malesi, whose composition will be considered in Chapter 4.

Thus, in formal terms, the formula should be made up of three dyadic sets:

1) *fai(k)//ledo(k)*: 'day'//'sun'
2) *esa//dua*: 'one'//'two'
3) *ma-nunin//ma-teben* 'certain, exact'//'particular, true'

Old Meno's usage, which in this case is a minor deviation from the rules of composition, is in fact one of the 'key signatures' that distinguishes his compositions from others.

Formulae for Scoop-Net Fishing: *seko//ndai*

Another set of formulae of significance in all *Suti Solo do Bina Bane* compositions is formed by those based on the dyadic set *seko//ndai*, which occurs both in noun and verb forms.[7] The terms *seko//ndai* refer to a simple fishing apparatus: a stretch of net set between two poles. This is the principal device that women use for fish gathering in tidal flats along the shore. Women use the poles of the net to plunge the net into the water, then lift it out. If nothing of value has been caught or the net contains only useless detritus from the sea, women simply lift the poles further, turn the net with a flip of the wrist to clear it, and then once more plunge it into the water.

On Rote, stone weirs are built out into the sea. As the tide goes out, these weirs trap small fish, which women can gather up in their nets as they walk through the receding waters. The monthly cycle of tides is named and determines the time of day or night when fishing occurs.[8]

In the chant, this simple Rotenese fishing net is described in poetic terms:

88.	*De ndai mahamu lilok.*	A fishnet with a gold-weighted belly.
90.	*De seko matei besik.*	A scoop-net with iron-weighted insides.

The formula, which occurs in other versions of the chant, is made of three dyadic sets:

1) *ndai//seko* 'fishnet'//'scoop-net'
2) *ma-hamu//ma-tei* 'belly'//'inside, stomach'

---

7   In strict terms, *ndai* refers to the net itself while *seko* is the verb for fishing with this net. Linking these terms in a single dyadic set allows them to be used as both noun and verb.
8   See Fox (2008: 145–54, particularly p. 148).

2. VERSION I FROM THE DOMAIN OF TERMANU

3) *lilo(k)//besi(k)* 'gold'//'iron'

The dyadic set *seko//ndai* occurs more frequently in verbal form—for example, this set can be found in lines 103–4 and again in lines 105–6:

103.	*Boe ma ana ndai ndano, ndai ndano*	She fish-catches, fish-catches
104.	*Ma ana seko toko, seko toko.*	And she scoop-throws, scoop-throws.
105.	*Boe ma ana seko nala Suti Solo*	She scoops up Suti Solo
106.	*Ma ana ndai nala Bina Bane*	And she fishes up Bina Bane

The combination set *ndai ndano//seko toko* beautifully describes the fishing process of plunging, lifting and then casting out debris from the net.

Twice Suti Solo do Bina Bane ask the woman Pedu Hange//Nggiti Seti to scoop them up from the sea. The phrasing of their request is nearly identical:

115.	*'O ndai ndano meni au*	'Oh, fish me forth and take me
116.	*Ma seko toko meni au'*	And scoop me up and take me'
129.	*'Ndai ndano muni au*	'Fish me forth and take me
130.	*Ma seko toko muni au dei.'*	And scoop me up and take me then.'

Finally Pedu Hange//Nggiti Seti relents and scoops them up.

| 134. | *'Te au ndai ndano uni o* | 'I will fish you forth and take you |
| 135. | *Ma au seko toko uni o'* | And I will scoop you up and take you' |

Perhaps the most notable feature of *Suti Solo do Bina Bane* as a composition is the extended dialogue that occurs between the shells and the woman who has scooped them from the sea. She proposes different possible symbolic sites to which she directs the shells but each of these possibilities is rejected as transient or ephemeral. Every *Suti Solo do Bina Bane* composition contains a number of these 'dialogue directives', each of which is largely formulaic.

Old Meno's chant contains the following six such dialogue directives, which are identifiable by their opening lines:

1) Lole Holu//Lua Bafa

| 134. | *'Te au ndai ndano uni o* | 'I will fish you forth and take you |

135.	*Ma au seko toko uni o*	And I will scoop you up and take you
136.	*Fo mu mo Lole Holu*	That you may go with Lole Holu
137.	*Ma mu mo Lua Bafa.'*	And you may go with Lua Bafa.'

2) Syrup vat//rice basket

158.	*'Suti mo tua bou*	'Then Suti, go with syrup vat
159.	*Ma Bina mo neka hade.'*	And Bina, go with the rice basket.'

3) Millet grains//ears of maize

170.	*'Oo na mo bete pule kode ketuk*	'Oh, go with the millet grains that the monkey plucks
171.	*Ma pela po'o bafi ka'ak.'*	And with the ears of maize that the pig chews.'

4) Palm shadow//tree shade

183.	*'Na mo sa'o tua*	'Then go with lontar palms' shadow
184.	*Ma mo mafo ai.'*	And go with trees' shade.'

5) Boundary tree//border stone

195.	*'Te na mu mo peu ai*	'Then go with boundary tree
196.	*Ma mu mo to batu.'*	And go with border stone.'

6) Forest cuckoo//river watercock

204.	*'Mo doa lasi*	'Go with the forest cuckoo
205.	*Ma mo koloba'o le'*	And go with the river watercock'

Four of these dialogue passages end with the similar formulaic refrain, in either shorter or longer format.

The shorter format is the same.

167.	*'Na Suti au o se*	'Then I, Suti, with whom will I be
168.	*Ma Bina au o se?'*	And I, Bina, with whom will I be?'
177.	*'Na Suti au o se*	'Then I, Suti, with whom will I be
178.	*Ma Bina au o se?'*	And I, Bina, with whom will I be?'

The longer format expands on this.

150.	*'Na Bina, au o se*	'Then I, Bina, with whom will I be
151.	*Ma Suti, au o se*	And I, Suti, with whom will I be
152.	*Fo au kokolak o se*	With whom will I talk
153.	*Ma au dede'ak o se?'*	And with whom will I speak?'
188.	*'Na Suti au o se*	'Then I, Suti, with whom will I be
189.	*Ma Bina au o se*	And I, Bina, with whom will I be
190.	*Fo au kokolak o se*	With whom will I talk
191.	*Ma au dede'ak o se*	And with whom will I speak
192.	*Tao neu nakabanik*	To create hope
193.	*Ma tao neu namahenak?'*	And create expectation?'

Once, however, when told to go with 'boundary tree//border stone', another formulaic reply is offered.[9]

199.	*'Te hu ai dede'an ta*	'But a tree does not talk
200.	*Ma batu kokolan ta.'*	And a stone does not speak.'

---

9   This couplet uses noun forms of the set *kokolak//dede'ak*, so it might be more appropriate to translate these lines as:

199.	*'Te hu ai dede'an ta*	'But a tree has no talk
200.	*Ma batu kokolan ta.'*	And a stone has no speech.'

3
Suti Solo do Bina Bane: Version II from the Domain of Termanu

Introducing the Second Text: *Suti Solo do Bina Bane II*

The second version in this successive investigation of the chant *Suti Solo do Bina Bane* was recited by the poet Eli Pellondou of clan Dou Danga, who was more commonly known by the name Seu Ba'i. In 1966, when I recorded this composition, Seu Ba'i was in his late 40s. He lived in the settlement of Namo Dale, not far from Old Meno's residence in Ola Lain, and I would often meet him at Old Meno's house, where he, too, was learning from the old man. Seu Ba'i belonged to a cluster of individuals in Namo Dale—including two of his younger cousins—who had obtained their earliest knowledge from senior clan relatives, but during the time of my first fieldwork, Seu Ba'i was involved in extending his knowledge by associating with Old Meno.

Figure 6: Eli Pellondou – 'Seu Ba'i'

3. VERSION II FROM THE DOMAIN OF TERMANU

Not surprisingly, Seu Ba'i's version of *Suti Solo do Bina Bane* shows a clear relationship to Old Meno's version. Its narrative, however, is not as well structured as Old Meno's and it is shorter by one-third. Similarly, the names of the chant characters in Seu Ba'i's version are virtually the names in Old Meno's version, with only minor differences. Where Old Meno speaks of Kokolo Dulu//Manupui Peda, Seu Ba'i refers to this character as Boko Dulu//Manupui Peda. But the chant assumes knowledge of the relationships among these characters rather than making them explicit. Unlike Old Meno, who begins with a genealogical introduction, Seu Ba'i begins with the attempt to celebrate the origin feast that requires the woman Nggiti Seti//Peda Hange to prepare her scoop-net and go to fish in the receding tide.

The Origin Feast and the Preparation of the Fishing Net

1.	*Boko Dulu hun-na*	Boko Dulu's origin feast
2.	*Ma Manupui Peda sio-na.*	And Manupui Peda's feast of nine.
3.	*Hus-sa ta laka-se*	The origin feast is not lively
4.	*Ma lutu ta laka-doto.*	And the ringed stones do not resound.
5.	*Boe te ala kedi-la mau-don-na*	So they cut a *mau* plant's leaves
6.	*Ma ala pena-la pole-aban-na*	And they pluck a *pole* plant's cotton tufts
7.	*Pole masa-fali pena*	A *pole* with repeated cotton bolls
8.	*Mau ma-na'a do-na.*	A *mau* with a mouthful of leaves.
9.	*Ala teli kokolo ndai*	They string and wind a fishnet
10.	*Ma ala ane balu-bui seko la*	And they braid and twine scoop-nets
11.	*Seko ma-tei besik*	A scoop-net with iron-weighted insides
12.	*Ma ndai ma-hamu lilok.*	And a fishnet with a gold-weighted belly.
13.	*Boe te ala fe inak-ka Pedu Hange*	They give it to the woman Pedu Hange
14.	*Ma fetok-ka Nggiti Seti.*	And the girl Nggiti Seti.
15.	*Ana tenga-nala ndai tasi*	She takes up the fishnet for the sea
16.	*Ma ana nggama-nala seko meti.*	And she picks up the scoop-net for the tide.

The next passage describes Pedu Hange//Nggiti Seti's encounter with Suti Solo do Bina Bane as she searches for the ritual fish Tio Holu//Dusu La'e. The chant makes clear that this occurs at the ritually important site Tena Lai//Mae Oe.

The Quest for the Ritual Fish at Tena Lai ma Mae Oe

17.	*De siluk bei ta dulu*	Morning is not yet in the east
18.	*Ma hu'ak bei ta langa.*	And dawn is not yet at the head.
19.	*Te ana tenga-nala ndai tasi*	But she takes up the fishnet for the sea
20.	*Ma ana nggama-nala seko meti.*	And she picks up the scoop-net for the tide.
21.	*De neu nafa-loe dea eik*	She goes to probe in the 'legs' of the stone weir
22.	*Ma neu nafa-nggao lutu limak*	And goes to grope in the 'arms' of the fish catch
23.	*Fo Tena Lai Laok dean*	Tena Lai Laok's stone weir
24.	*Ma Mae Oe Loek lutun,*	And Mae Oe Loek's fish wall,
25.	*Neu seko sanga Tio peda-poik*	Goes to scoop for a Tio to place on top
26.	*Ma neu ndai sanga Dusu fua-bafak.*	And goes to fish for a Dusu for the basket's mouth.
27.	*Fo Dusu La'e ma Tio Holu*	A Dusu La'e and a Tio Holu
28.	*Tao neu peda-poik*	To place on top of the rice
29.	*Ma tao neu fua-bafak.*	And to lay on the basket's mouth.
30.	*Fo hus-sala laka-se*	So that the origin feast can be made lively
31.	*Ma sio-la laka-doto.*	And the feast of nine can be made noisy.
32.	*Seko basa-lek-kala*	She scoops in all the waterholes
33.	*Ma ndai basa lifu-la*	And she fishes in all the pools
34.	*Te ta ndai nita Tio*	But she does not fish or see a Tio
35.	*Ma ta seko nita Dusu fa.*	And does not scoop or see a Dusu.
36.	*Ndai nita kada Suti Solo*	She fishes but sees only Suti Solo
37.	*Ma seko nita kada Bina Bane.*	And she scoops but sees only Bina Bane.

A Genealogy of Suti Solo do Bina Bane

It is at this point that Seu Ba'i provides a short genealogical introduction to identify Suti//Bina.

38.	*Solo Bane sain anan*	The child of Solo Bane of the sea
39.	*Ma Bane Aka liun anan.*	And the child of Bane Aka of the ocean.
40.	*Inak-ka Manu Koa Lasi*	The woman Manu Koa of the forest
41.	*Fetok-ka Hali Siko Nula*	And the girl Hali Siko of the wood
42.	*Ana tu Solo Bane sain*	She marries Solo Bane of the sea
43.	*Ma sao Bane Aka liun.*	And she weds Bane Aka of the ocean.
44.	*De lae Bina Bane*	She brings forth Bina Bane
45.	*Ma bongi Suti Solo.*	And she gives birth to Suti Solo.

Seu Ba'i reverts to recounting Nggiti Seti//Pedu Hange's fishing efforts.

46.	*Seko basa lek-kala*	She scoops in all the waterholes
47.	*Ma ndai basa lifu-la*	And she fishes in all the pools
48.	*Te seko toko heni Bina*	But she fishes and throws Bina away
49.	*Ma ndai ndano heni Suti.*	And she scoops and tosses Suti away.

The Dialogue with the Shells

Suti Solo do Bina Bane addresses Nggiti Seti//Pedu Hange and asks to be taken home and to be used as the ritual substitute for the Tio Holu//Dusu La'e fish.

50.	*Boe te Suti neu dede'ak*	So Suti begins to speak
51.	*Ma Bina neu kokolak, nae:*	And Bina begins to talk, saying:
52.	*'Ndai ndano mala au*	'Fish catch and take me
53.	*Ma seko toko mala au*	Scoop throw and take me
54.	*Tao neu peda-poik*	To place on top of the rice
55.	*Ma tao neu fua-bafak*	And to lay on the basket's mouth
56.	*Fo hus-sala laka-se*	So that the origin feast can be made lively
57.	*Ma sio-la laka doto.'*	And the feast of nine can be made noisy.'

The Shells Call for Lole Holu//Lua Bafa

As soon as Suti//Bina are taken up into the house, the shells begin to cry and ask for Lole Holu//Lua Bafa. In this version of the chant, however, Lole Holu//Lua Bafa is not given any formal genealogical introduction.

58.	*Boe-ma lo Suti mai uma*	So they bring Suti home
59.	*Fo mai lao dale*	To the inner cooking fire
60.	*Ma lo Bina mai uma lai.*	And they bring Bina to the upper house.
61.	*Boe te Suti neu nama-tani*	But Suti begins to cry
62.	*Ma Bina neu nasa-kedu*	And Bina begins to sob
63.	*Nasa-kedu Lole Holu*	Sobs for Lole Holu
64.	*Ma nama-tani Lua Bafa.*	And cries for Lua Bafa.

It is at this point that the dialogue begins between Nggiti Seti//Pedu Hange and Suti//Bina as to where the shells should best be located in their quest for companionship. Lole Holu//Lua Bafa is invoked as the ideal companion. The first dialogue stanza is similar to that of Old Meno's version, although it lacks one parallel line.

65.	*Boe te ana dede'ak no Suti*	So she speaks with Suti
66.	*Ma ana kokolak no Bina, lae:*	And she talks with Bina, saying:
67.	*'Mo tua bou*	'Go with the syrup vat
68.	*Ma mo neka hade*	And go with the rice basket
69.	*Fo masa-lai tua bou.'*	That you may lean on the syrup vat.'
70.	[Line missing]	[And that you may sit with rice basket].
71.	*Boe te Bina neu kokolak*	But Bina begins to talk
72.	*Ma Suti neu dede'ak, nae:*	And Suti begins to speak, saying:
73.	*'Au u o tua bou*	'I will go with the syrup vat
74.	*Ma au o neka hade.*	And I go with the rice basket.
75.	*De malole ndia so*	This is good
76.	*Do mandak ndia so.*	Or this is proper.
77.	*Te neka lama-kako bafa*	But if the baskets overflow at the mouth
78.	*Fo soka lo lulunun*	So that the sacks must be rolled up
79.	*Ma tua lama-lua fude*	And the syrup runs over with froth
80.	*Fo bou lo totonon,*	So that the vats must be overturned,
81.	*Au dede'ak o se*	With whom will I speak

82.	*Ma au kokolak o se*	And with whom will I talk
83.	*Sama leo Lua Bafa*	[With someone] just like Lua Bafa
84.	*Ma deta leo Lole Holu?'*	And exactly like Lole Holu?'

For the study of oral composition, the next passage, which conflates two consecutive dialogue stanzas, is particularly revealing. The stanza that refers to 'boundary tree and border stone' and that which refers to 'pig chews and monkey plucks' are combined in a way that does not make much sense. However, the knowledge that Seu Ba'i was trying to model this version on Old Meno's version allows one to recognise the conflation that has occurred. These flaws provide insight into a poet's approach to composition.

85.	*Boe te dede'ak no Suti bai*	But she speaks with Suti again
86.	*Ma kokolak no Bina bai, lae:*	And she talks with Bina again, saying:
87.	*'Mu mo peu ai lasi*	'Go with boundary tree of the forest
88.	*Ma mu mo to batu nula.'*	And go with border stone of the wood.'
89.	*Boe te Bina, ana kokolak*	But Bina, he talks
90.	*Ma Suti, ana dede'ak, nae:*	And Suti, he speaks, saying:
91.	*'Malole ndia so*	'This is good
92.	*Ma mandak ndia so.*	And this is proper.
93.	*Au o peu ai lasi*	I will be with boundary tree of the forest
94.	*Ma au o to batu nula*	And I will be with border stone of the wood
95.	*Te bafi ka'a neni pelak*	But if the pig chews the maize
96.	*Au dede'ak o se*	With whom will I speak
97.	*Ma kode ketu neni betek*	And if monkey plucks the millet
98.	*Au kokolak o se*	With whom will I talk
99.	*Do se'ek o se*	Or be noisy with whom
100.	*Ma oku-boluk o se*	And shout with whom
101.	*Sama leo Lua Bafa*	[With someone] just like Lua Bafa
102.	*Ma deta leo Lole Holu?'*	And exactly like Lole Holu?'

Seu Ba'i follows this passage with another that introduces a set stanza of dialogue that does not occur in Old Meno's chant but does often occur in other versions. Thus Seu Ba'i's recitation is not simply an attempt at replication but rather one that combines Seu Ba'i's previous knowledge with what he has derived from Old Meno.

103.	*Boe te ala dede'ak lo Suti*	So they speak with Suti
104.	*Ma ala kokolak lo Bina, lae:*	And they talk with Bina, saying:
105.	*'Mu mo pila kumea letek*	'Go with the red *kumea* grass on the hill
106.	*Ma mu mo nggeo kuku telas.'*	And go with the black *kuku* shrub in the underbrush.'
107.	*Boe te Suti lole halan-na neu*	But Suti lifts his voice
108.	*Ma Bina ae dasin-na neu ma nae:*	And Bina raises his speech and says:
109.	*'Au o pila kumea letek*	'I will go with the red *kumea* grass on the hill
110.	*Ma au o nggeo kuku telas.*	And I go with the black *kuku* shrub in the underbrush.
111.	*Malole ndia so*	This is good
112.	*Ma mandak ndia so.'*	And this is proper.'
113.	*Boe te ala dede'ak lo Suti ma lae:*	But they speak with Suti and say:
114.	*'Mu mo pila kumea letek*	'Go with red *kumea* grass on the hill
115.	*Ma mu mo nggeo kuku telas.'*	And go with black *kuku* shrub in the underbrush.'
116.	*Boe te Suti lole halan-na neu*	But Suti lifts his voice
117.	*Ma Bina ae dasin-na neu:*	And Bina raises his speech:
118.	*'Au o pila kumea letek*	'I will be with red *kumea* grass on the hill
119.	*Ma au o nggeo kuku telas.*	And I will be with black *kuku* grass in the underbrush
120.	*De malole a so*	It is good
121.	*Ma mandak a so.*	And it is proper.
122.	*Te timu lama-tua dulu*	But when the east monsoon grows great in the east
123.	*Ma fak lama-nalu langa*	And the west monsoon lengthens at the head
124.	*Fo pila kumea letek-kala*	The red *kumea* grass on the hill

3. VERSION II FROM THE DOMAIN OF TERMANU

125.	*Lama-dilu leu kalen*	Bends down its heavy top
126.	*Ma nggeo kuku telas*	And the black *kuku* shrub in the underbrush
127.	*Lama-sesu leu bu'un-na*	Breaks its heavy joints
128.	*Au dede'ak o se*	Then with whom will I speak
129.	*Ma au kokolak o se*	And with whom will I talk
130.	*Sama leo Lua Bafa*	[With someone] just like Lua Bafa
131.	*Ma deta leo Lole Holu?'*	And exactly like Lole Holu?'

The final segment of dialogue is again similar to that in Old Meno's version. In this stanza, Nggiti Seti//Pedu Hange advises the shells to follow 'the current through the river' and 'the rain through the forest' to return to the sea.

132.	*Boe te ala dede'ak seluk lo Suti*	So they speak once more with Suti
133.	*Ma kokolak seluk lo Bina, lae:*	And they talk once more with Bina, saying:
134.	*'Mu mo doa lasi*	'Go with the forest cuckoo
135.	*Ma mu mo koloba'o le*	And go with the river watercock
136.	*Fo ba'o-ba'o tunga le*	To [cry] *ba'o-ba'o* along the river
137.	*Ma do-do tunga tunga lasi*	And *do-do* through the forest
138.	*Fo udan tunga-tunga lasi*	So when the rain passes through the forest
139.	*Ma fa tunga-tunga le*	And the current passes down the river
140.	*Bonu boa fo mu*	Then bobbing like *boa* wood, you may go
141.	*Ma ele piko fo mu.*	And drifting like *piko* wood, you may go.
142.	*Leo sain mu*	To the sea you may go
143.	*Ma leo liun mu.'*	And to the ocean you may go.'
144.	*Boe te Suti neu dedeak*	But Suti begins to speak
145.	*Ma Bina neu kokolak, nae:*	And Bina begins to talk, saying:
146.	*'Malole ndia so*	'This is good
147.	*Ma mandak ndia so.*	And this is proper.
148.	*Au bonu boa fo au u*	I will bob like *boa* wood and go
149.	*Ma au ele piko fo u.'*	And I will drift like *piko* wood and go.'
150.	*Boe te nae:*	But she says:
151.	*'Mu le bibifan*	'Go to the lip of the river

152.	*Ma mu oli tatain*	And go to the edge of the estuary
153.	*Nene-fino mu ndia*	Go to stop and listen there
154.	*Ma dei-dongo mu ndia.*	And go to stand and wait there.
155.	*Udan tunga-tunga lasi*	The rain passes through the forest
156.	*Ma fa tunga-tunga le*	And the current passes down the river
157.	*Fo bonu boa fo mu*	Then bobbing like *boa* wood, you may go
158.	*Ele piko fo mu.'*	And drifting like *piko* wood, you may go.'

The Shells' Return to the Sea

Suti Solo do Bina Bane follows this advice and returns to the sea. It is only at this point in this recitation that Seu Ba'i proceeds to tell of the origin feast in the sea's depths and the shaming of the two shells that occurs when Mouldy Pau Trees//Withered Kai Leaves attempts to dance beside Suti Solo do Bina Bane as 'wife and spouse'. The Heavens grow angry and, as a result, the shells exude their insides, thus becoming the empty creatures that are found on the beaches and tidal flats of Rote. Seu Ba'i ends his recitation with a common formula that emphasises that what he has recounted has consequences 'to this day and until this time'.

159.	*Boe te sama leo halak*	So precisely according to the voice
160.	*Boe ma deta leo dasik*	And exactly according to the speech
161.	*Boe nene-fino neu ndia*	He stops and listens there
162.	*Ma dei-dongo mu ndia*	And he stands and waits there
163.	*Neu oli tatain*	Goes to the estuary's edge
164.	*Ma neu le bibifan.*	And goes to the river's lip.
165.	*Fa oek lali namo*	The current's water moves harbour
166.	*Ma uda hedu(?) tunga le*	And rain's flow(?) follows the river
167.	*Ma bonu boa de neu*	And bobbing like *boa* wood, he goes
168.	*Ma ele piko de neu*	And drifting like *piko* wood, he goes
169.	*Neu Liun dale na-taladan*	Goes to the bounded ocean [depths]
170.	*Neu Sain dale naka-ton.*	And goes to the bordered sea [depths].
171.	*Boe neu tongo lololo*	Then he encounters with arms
172.	*Ma neu nda lilima*	And he meets with hands
173.	*Mila-Ana Daik labun*	Mila Ana Daik's drum
174.	*Ma O-Ana Selan mekon-na.*	And O Ana Selan's gong.

175.	*Ala delu laka-ndu'un hu na*	They strike a steady beat at the origin feast
176.	*Ala sali laka-sasaän [sio-na].*	And they beat a continuing flurry [at the feast of nine].
177.	*Boe te ala fe Bina neu pela*	Then they make Bina dance
178.	*Ma ala fe Suti neu sodok.*	And they make Suti sing.
179.	*De Suti ta sodok nalelak*	But Suti knows not how to sing
180.	*Ma Bina ta longe nalelak.*	And Bina knows not how to dance the *ronggeng*.
181.	*Boe te Ina Po'o Pau Ai lasi*	Then the woman Mouldy Pau Trees of the Forest
182.	*Feto Latu Kai Do nulan*	And the girl Withered Kai Leaves of the Woods
183.	*Neu sodo do neu pela.*	Goes to sing or goes to dance.
184.	*De ana pela seli Suti Solo*	She dances beside Suti Solo
185.	*Ma ana leno seli Bina Bane.*	And she turns beside Bina Bane.
186.	*Boe te Suti bi neu dedein*	But for Suti there is fear on his forehead
187.	*Ma Bane mae neu mata-boan.*	And for Bane there is shame in his eyes.
188.	*Boe te halak esa nae neme dea neu ma nae:*	But a voice speaks from outside and says:
189.	*'Ina Po'o Pau Ai lasi-la*	'The woman Mouldy Pau Trees of the Forest
190.	*Do fetok Latu Kai Do nula-la*	And the girl Withered Kai Leaves of the Woods
191.	*De ala pela seli Suti Solo na ndia*	She dances beside Suti Solo there
192.	*Sanga na-seti [setu?] tu*	Trying to appear intimate like a wife
193.	*Ma ala leno seli Bina Bane na ndia*	And she turns beside Bina Bane there
194.	*Sanga na-hope sao.'*	Trying to be close like a spouse.'
195.	*Boe te halak-a leo Lain neu*	But a voice goes to Heaven
196.	*Ma dasik-kala leo Poi leu lae:*	And speeches go to the Heights and it is said:
197.	*Te Poin nggenggele*	The Heights rage
198.	*Ma Lain nama-nasa.*	And the Heavens grow angry.
199.	*Ala fe ni ledok kala mai [?]*	[Unintelligible line]

200.	*Poin neu nama-nasa*	The Heights grow angry
201.	*Ma Lain nggenggele.*	And the Heavens rage.
202.	*De luli nala liun dale*	A storm strikes the ocean depths
203.	*Ma sangu nala sain dale*	And a cyclone strikes the sea depths
204.	*Liun dale na-hopo*	The ocean depths are upset
205.	*Ma sain dale na-foki.*	The sea depths are shaken.
206.	*Boe te Suti nama-toko isi*	So Suti expels his insides
207.	*Ma Bina [nama-]edo nggi*	And Bina exudes his pods
208.	*Losa faik-ka*	To this day
209.	*Ma nduku ledok-ka.*	And until this time.

Composition Analysis: Old Meno–Seu Ba'i comparisons

Seu Ba'i's version of *Suti Solo do Bina Bane* consists of 209 lines and is composed of 85 dyadic sets, 49 of which are identical to those in Old Meno's version of this composition. It is appropriate to begin by noting some of the common formulae used in both these compositions. These formulae are not specific to these two compositions but are among the most common formulae that occur in ritual language.

Similar Formulae

The first of these formulae is used to indicate the day's dawn. In Seu Ba'i's composition, this formula occurs early.

Seu Ba'i

17.	*De siluk bei ta dulu*	Morning is not yet in the east
18.	*Ma hu'ak bei ta langa.*	And dawn is not yet at the head.

Old Meno's use of this formula occurs further on in his composition.

Old Meno

101.	*Siluk bei ta dulu*	When morning is not yet in the east
102.	*Ma hu'ak bei ta langa dei*	And dawn is not yet at the head

The formula is based on two dyadic sets: 1) *siluk//hu'ak* ('morning'//'dawn'); and 2) *dulu//langa* ('east'//'head'). The combination of 'east' and 'head' reflects the Rotenese directional system. Rote is a long, relatively narrow island. The eastern end of the island is conceived of as the island's head (*langa*) and its western end its tail (*iko*). Although Rote is mostly flat, these directional coordinates imply that one goes 'up' to the east and 'down' to the west. In mortuary chants, the west is the direction of death: the ship of the dead sails westward to the afterworld.

Another formula used frequently in both compositions is perhaps the single most common formula used in virtually all compositions. Seu Ba'i uses this formula five times at different points in his composition. Three of these uses are identical: lines 91–92, 111–12 and 146–47; the two other uses are phrased with a slight change.

Seu Ba'i

91/111/146.	*'Malole ndia so*	'This is good
92/112/147.	*Ma mandak ndia so.'*	And this is proper.'
75.	*'De malole ndia so*	'This is good
76.	*Do mandak ndia so.'*	Or this is proper.'

Old Meno relies on this same formula, but in his composition, he uses the formula in its plural form.

Old Meno

144.	*'De malole-la so*	'These things are good
145.	*Ma mandak-kala so.'*	And these things are proper.'
161.	*'O malole-la so*	'Oh, these things are good
162.	*Ma mandak-kala so.'*	And these things are proper.'

Meno, however, also uses the *malole//mandak* set in another context:

| 274. | *'Sena mandak kia* | 'This is a proper companion |
| 275. | *Ma tia malole ia.'* | And this is a good friend.' |

In addition to these common formulae, both poets use the same formula for speaking and make use of the same refrain that is a distinctive feature of *Suti Solo do Bina Bane*.

Old Meno

127.	*Boe ma Suti, ana kokolak*	Then Suti, he talks
128.	*Ma Bina, ana dede'ak nae:*	And Bina, he speaks, saying:

Seu Ba'i

89.	*Boe te Bina, ana kokolak*	But Bina, he talks
90.	*Ma Suti, ana dede'ak, nae:*	And Suti, he speaks, saying:

Where Meno phrases his refrain one way:

150.	*'Na Bina, au o se*	'Then I, Bina, with whom will I be
151.	*Ma Suti, au o se*	And I, Suti, with whom will I be
152.	*Fo au kokolak o se*	With whom will I talk
153.	*Ma au dede'ak o se?'*	And with whom will I speak?'

Seu Ba'i extends this refrain in another way:

96.	*'Au dede'ak o se …*	'With whom will I speak …
98.	*Au kokolak o se*	With whom will I talk
99.	*De se'ek o se*	Or be noisy with whom
100.	*Ma oku-boluk o se'*	And shout with whom'

Similarities in Differently Phrased Passages

There are various passages in Seu Ba'i's composition that closely resemble those in Meno's composition and yet follow a slightly different arrangement and use somewhat different dyadic sets. Several of these passages are worth careful examination for what they reveal about the processes of composition.

Preparing the Scoop-Net

Old Meno

83.	*Ala kedi-la mau don*	They cut a *mau* plant's leaves
84.	*De mau mana'a don*	A *mau* with a mouthful of leaves
85.	*Ma ala pena-la pole aban*	And they pluck a *pole* plant's cotton tufts
86.	*De pole masapena aban.*	A *pole* bursting with cotton tufts.

87.	*De ala teli kokolo ndai*	They string and wind a fishnet
88.	*De ndai ma hamu lilok*	A fishnet with a gold-weighted belly.
89.	*Ma ala ane seko, bui seko*	They braid a scoop-net, twine a scoop-net
90.	*De seko ma tei besik.*	A scoop-net with iron-weighted insides.

Seu Ba'i

5.	*Boe te ala kedi-la mau-don-na*	So they cut a *mau* plant's leaves
6.	*Ma ala pena-la pole-aban-na*	And they pluck a *pole* plant's cotton tufts
7.	*Pole masa-fali pena*	A *pole* with repeated cotton bolls
8.	*Mau ma-na'a do-na.*	A *mau* with a mouthful of leaves.
9.	*Ala teli kokolo ndai*	They string and wind a fishnet
10.	*Ma ala ane balu-bui seko la*	And they brand and twine scoop-nets
11.	*Seko ma-tei besik*	A scoop-net with iron-weighted insides
12.	*Ma ndai ma-hamu lilok.*	And a fishnet with a gold-weighted belly.

In these two passages, there is a host of similarities, although the arrangement of lines is different. For comparison, Seu Ba'i's composition is in bold.

83.	*Ala kedi-la mau don*	They cut a *mau* plant's leaves
5.	***Boe te ala kedi-la mau-don-na***	**So they cut a *mau* plant's leaves**
85.	*Ma ala pena-la pole aban*	And they pluck a *pole* plant's cotton tufts
6.	***Ma ala pena-la pole-aban-na***	**And they pluck a *pole* plant's cotton tufts**
84.	*De mau mana'a don*	A *mau* with a mouthful of leaves
8.	***Mau ma-na'a do-na.***	**A *mau* with a mouthful of leaves.**
86.	*De pole masa pena aban.*	A *pole* bursting with cotton tufts.
7.	***Pole masa-fali pena***	**A *pole* with repeated cotton bolls**

Seu Ba'i's line seven differs from that of Meno in a way that seems to violate the expected pairing of *don//aban* ('leaves'//'cotton tufts'). Moreover, *masa-fali* is not a term that normally pairs with *mana'a*; it implies a notion of 'return', which I have had to translate awkwardly as 'repeated'. Comparison of the lines therefore suggests that this is probably a simple mistake in composition.

| 87. | *De ala teli kokolo ndai* | They string and wind a fishnet |

9.	*Ala teli kokolo ndai*	They string and wind a fishnet
89.	*Ma ala ane seko, bui seko*	They braid a scoop-net, twine a scoop-net
10.	*Ma ala ane balu-bui seko la*	**And they braid and twine scoop-nets**
88.	*De ndai ma-hamu lilok.*	A fishnet with a gold-weighted belly.
12.	*Ma ndai ma-hamu lilok.*	**And a fishnet with a gold-weighted belly.**
90.	*De seko ma-tei besik.*	A scoop-net with iron-weighted insides.
11.	*Seko ma-tei besik*	**A scoop-net with iron-weighted insides**

The Sequence of Dialogue Directives

In both versions of *Suti Solo do Bina Bane,* Pedu Hange//Nggiti Seti offers the shells six distinct directives. These directives, however, differ. Four of these dialogue directives are similar but two are different and they are proposed in a different sequence.

In Meno's version, the shells are directed first to: 1) Lole Holu//Lua Bafa as companion; and then in sequence to 2) syrup vat//rice basket, 3) millet grains//ears of maize, 4) palm shadow//tree shade, 5) boundary tree//border stone, and 6) forest cuckoo//river watercock, before following the passage of the rains and flow of the river to the sea.

In Seu Ba'i's version, the shells are first taken home to: 1) cooking fire//upper house, which is, in some ways, the equivalent to being taken to Lole Holu//Lua Bafa, though in this version, the shells continue to cry for these two as companions. Thereafter they are directed to 2) syrup vat//rice basket, and 3) boundary tree//border stone. They are then directed to 4) *kumea* grass//*kuku* shrub, and finally to 5) forest cuckoo//river watercock, before drifting to the sea. Thus, in Seu Ba'i's composition, the *kumea* grass//*kuku* shrub passage replaces palm shadow//tree shade.[1]

Of the four directives shared by these two compositions, it is most useful to compare similar passages in Pedu Hange//Nggiti Seti's proposal to the shells to join the forest cuckoo and river watercock. It is the longest and, in terms of composition, the most complex of any of the directives.

---

1   Since these dialogue directives are one of the distinctive aspects of this composition, the way different poets phrase these passages will be a continuing focus of subsequent chapters. Here only one passage has been selected for this comparison between Seu Ba'i and Old Meno.

3. VERSION II FROM THE DOMAIN OF TERMANU

In Meno's composition, this passage comprises 18 lines. In Seu Ba'i's composition, this passage occurs in two parts, the first of which comprises 10 lines, the second eight lines.

Old Meno

204.	*'Mo doa lasi*	'Go with the forest cuckoo
205.	*Ma mo koloba'o le*	And go with the river watercock
206.	*[Fo] fa tunga-tunga le*	So that as current passes down the river
207.	*Ma fo ela udan tunga-tunga lasi*	And rain passes through the forest
208.	*Fo mu oli tatain*	You may go to the edge of the estuary
209.	*Ma mu le bibifan,*	And you may go to the lip of the river,
210.	*Fo ela fa oek ana mai*	So that when the current's water arrives
211.	*Ma ela epo oek ana mai*	And when the eddy's water arrives
212.	*Na bonu boa fo mu*	That bobbing like *boa* wood, you may go
213.	*Ma ele piko fo mu,*	And drifting like *piko* wood, you may go,
214.	*Leo sain dale mu*	To the sea, you may go
215.	*Ma leo liun dale mu.*	And to the ocean, you may go.
216.	*Te hu mu posi makamu mekon*	Thus go to the sea's edge, resounding like a gong
217.	*Fo nene fino tata*	To stop and listen there
218.	*Ma mu unu mali labun*	And go to the reef, rumbling like a drum
219.	*Fo dei dongo meme ndia*	To stand and wait there
220.	*Fo dei loe sain dale mu*	And then descend into the ocean
221.	*Ma dilu liun dale mu.'*	And turn downward into the sea.'

Seu Ba'i

134.	*'Mu mo doa lasi*	'Go with the forest cuckoo
135.	*Ma mu mo koloba'o le*	And go with the river watercock
136.	*Fo ba'o-ba'o tunga le*	To [cry] *ba'o-ba'o* along the river
137.	*Ma do-do tunga-tunga lasi*	And *do-do* through the forest
138.	*Fo udan tunga-tunga lasi*	So when the rain passes through the forest
139.	*Ma fa tunga-tunga le*	And the current passes down the river

140.	*Bonu boa fo mu*	Then bobbing like *boa* wood, you may go
141.	*Ma ele piko fo mu.*	And drifting like *piko* wood, you may go.
142.	*Leo sain mu*	To the sea you may go
143.	*Ma leo liun mu.'*	And to the ocean you may go.'

...

151.	*'Mu le bibifan*	'Go to the lip of the river
152.	*Ma mu oli tatain*	And go to the edge of the estuary
153.	*Nene-fino mu ndia*	Go to stop and listen there
154.	*Ma dei-dongo mu ndia.*	And go to stand and wait there.
155.	*Udan tunga-tunga lasi*	The rain passes through the forest
156.	*Ma fa tunga-tunga le*	And the current passes down the river
157.	*Fo bonu boa fo mu*	Then bobbing like *boa* wood, you may go
158.	*Ele piko fo mu.'*	And drifting like *piko* wood, you may go.'

The first two lines in both compositions are similar. While Old Meno relies only on a verbal phrase, Seu Ba'i uses both verb and verbal phrase, which mean 'to go' and 'to go with'.

204.	*Mo doa lasi*	Go with the forest cuckoo
134.	***Mu mo doa lasi***	**Go with the forest cuckoo**
205.	*Ma mo koloba'o le*	And go with the river watercock
135.	***Ma mu mo koloba'o le***	**And go with the river watercock**

Seu Ba'i then adds two lines that take their meaning from the sounds made by these birds.

| 136. | *Fo ba'o-ba'o tunga le* | To [cry] *ba'o-ba'o* along the river |
| 137. | *Ma do-do tunga tunga lasi* | And *do-do* through the forest |

The next lines are again virtually identical, though they occur in different order.

206.	*[Fo] fa tunga-tunga le*	So that as the current passes down the river
207.	*Ma fo ela udan tunga-tunga lasi*	And rain passes through the forest
138.	***Fo udan tunga-tunga lasi***	**So when the rain passes through the forest**
139.	***Ma fa tunga-tunga le***	**And the current passes down the river**

3. VERSION II FROM THE DOMAIN OF TERMANU

Meno then uses two lines as an embedded clause where Seu Ba'i renders these lines as a direct injunction in the second part of his dialogue with the shells.

208.	*Fo mu oli tatain*	You may go to the edge of the estuary
209.	*Ma mu le bibifan.*	And you may go to the lip of the river.
151.	***Mu le bibifan***	**Go to the lip of the river**
152.	***Ma mu oli tatain***	**And go to the edge of the estuary**

Meno then follows with two lines that Seu Ba'i does not use.

| 210. | *Fo ela fa oek ana mai* | So that when the current's water arrives |
| 211. | *Ma ela epo oek ana mai* | And when the eddy's water arrives |

Then both poets use the metaphor of two pieces of wood that float to the sea.[2]

212.	*Na bonu boa fo mu*	That bobbing like *boa* wood, you may go
213.	*Ma ele piko fo mu*	And drifting like *piko* wood, you may go,
214.	*Leo sain dale mu*	To the sea, you may go
215.	*Ma leo liun dale mu.*	And to the ocean, you may go.
140.	***Bonu boa fo mu***	**Then bobbing like *boa* wood, you may go**
141.	***Ma ele piko fo mu.***	**And drifting like *piko* wood, you may go.**
142.	***Leo sain mu***	**To the sea you may go**
143.	***Ma leo liun mu.***	**And to the ocean you may go.**

Meno then concludes this passage with six lines that invoke a common poetic formula that describes the sea's edge pounding like a gong and the reef rumbling like a drum.[3]

| 216. | *Te hu mu posi makamu mekon* | Thus go to the sea's edge, resounding like a gong |
| 217. | *Fo nene-fino tata* | To stop and listen there |

---

2 Although I have not yet been able to identify these species of trees, poets have told me that both are light and buoyant and can often be seen as driftwood on the waters.
3 Although Seu Ba'i does not use this formula in his composition, it is a common formula that regularly occurs in other ritual compositions.

218.	*Ma mu unu mali labun*	And go to the reef, rumbling like a drum
219.	*Fo dei-dongo meme ndia*	To stand and wait there
220.	*Fo dei loe sain dale mu*	And then descend into the ocean
221.	*Ma dilu liun dale mu.*	And turn downward into the sea.

Among these six lines are two lines that Seu Ba'i uses in his composition.

153.	***Nene-fino mu ndia***	**To stop and listen there**
154.	***Ma-dei dongo mu ndia.***	**And to stand and wait there.**

Seu Ba'i then concludes his second passage of dialogue by repeating lines that he previously used in his first passage.

155.	*Udan tunga-tunga lasi*	**The rain passes through the forest**
156.	*Ma fa tunga-tunga le*	**And the current passes down the river**
157.	*Fo bonu boa fo mu*	**Then bobbing like *boa* wood, you may go**
158.	*Ele piko fo mu.'*	**And drifting like *piko* wood, you may go.'**

Although composed and arranged somewhat differently, in Seu Ba'i's composition, 12 of 18 lines are nearly identical to those of his mentor, Old Meno.

4

Suti Solo do Bina Bane: Version III from the Domain of Termanu

In 1972, after an absence of more than six years, I returned to Rote to continue my research. As soon as I arrived back on the island, I began to record new ritual language recitations. During the period of my first fieldwork, I had gathered three versions of the chant *Suti Solo do Bina Bane*.[1] On my return, I decided that I would try to gather additional recitations for comparative purposes.

By 1972, Old Meno had died. Another of the great master poets of Termanu, Stefanus Amalo, had also died. Although I had recorded other chants from him, I had never recorded a version of *Suti Solo do Bina Bane* and this has always been a considerable regret. On the other hand, Seu Ba'i was still alive, but during my second fieldwork, I saw him only on a few occasions. He was particularly concerned to provide me with material that he felt was connected with my previous work with Old Meno. For example, Old Meno had recited a beautiful chant, *Dela Koli do Seko Buna*, which I published as my first example of a long ritual language recitation (Fox 1971). Old Meno had structured his recitation as a mortuary chant and Seu Ba'i was aware of this fact. He wanted me, however, to recognise

---

1   I gathered my third version of *Suti Solo do Bina Bane* from the blind master poet of the domain of Ba'a, L. Manoeain. His version of this recitation will be discussed with versions of this text from other non-Termanu dialect areas.

that *Dela Koli do Seko Buna* was in fact an origin chant connected with the two prominent rock formations known as Sua Lai and Batu Hun that dominated the entrance to the harbour of Namodale, near where he lived. He therefore recited a version of this chant to make explicit its origin foundations.

In 1965–66, I had begun to record recitations by the relatively young poet Petrus Malesi or Pe'u Malesi, who was usually referred to simply as Malesi.[2] During that first fieldwork, I recorded three chants from Malesi. One of these was a chant that recounted the origin of fire, a version of which I had also recorded from Old Meno; the second was a mortuary chant of less than 100 lines; the third was a version of the origin of rice and millet, whose transcription I showed to Old Meno. He regarded Malesi's recitation as inadequate and, as a consequence, extended it to make it acceptable. Thus, in 1965–66, Pe'u Malesi was only beginning to demonstrate his skills as a poet; he was not yet regarded as a mature *manahelo*. But by 1972–73, with only Seu Ba'i as his rival, Malesi was coming into his prime. During my second period on Rote, Malesi, who lived nearby, became a regular visitor at Ufa Len ma Batu Bongo, where I lived, and for a time, he provided me with more material than any other poet in Termanu. He was available for all rituals we carried out, including the mortuary performance, the *Lutu Tutus*, that Meno's son and I sponsored in honour of Old Meno.[3]

Thus in 1973, I recorded a version of *Suti Solo do Bina Bane* from Pe'u Malesi. This recitation is constructed to portray a cycle that carries Suti Solo do Bina Bane from the sea through the land and back to the sea. No genealogy is provided for any of the chant characters and no explanation is given for the expulsion of the shells from the sea. Nor is there any attempt to link these shells to a transformation into implements for dyeing and spinning. This version is not an origin recitation but rather is presented as a mortuary recitation: a widow and orphan chant.

---

2   Malesi was sometimes also called Suara Malesi ('Voice of Malesi') in mock recognition of Suara Malaysia ('Voice of Malaysia') whose broadcasts could occasionally be heard by those who had a radio. My first fieldtrip coincided with the period of 'Confrontation' with Malaysia and listening to 'Voice of Malaysia' was supposedly forbidden. Since no one in Termanu (that I know of) had a radio, listening to 'Voice of Malaysia' was hardly an issue but one could joke that no one needed to listen to 'Suara Malaysia' because we had 'Suara Malesi', which was much better and certainly clearer.
3   I have described this performance and the chanting associated with it in Fox (1989).

4. VERSION III FROM THE DOMAIN OF TERMANU

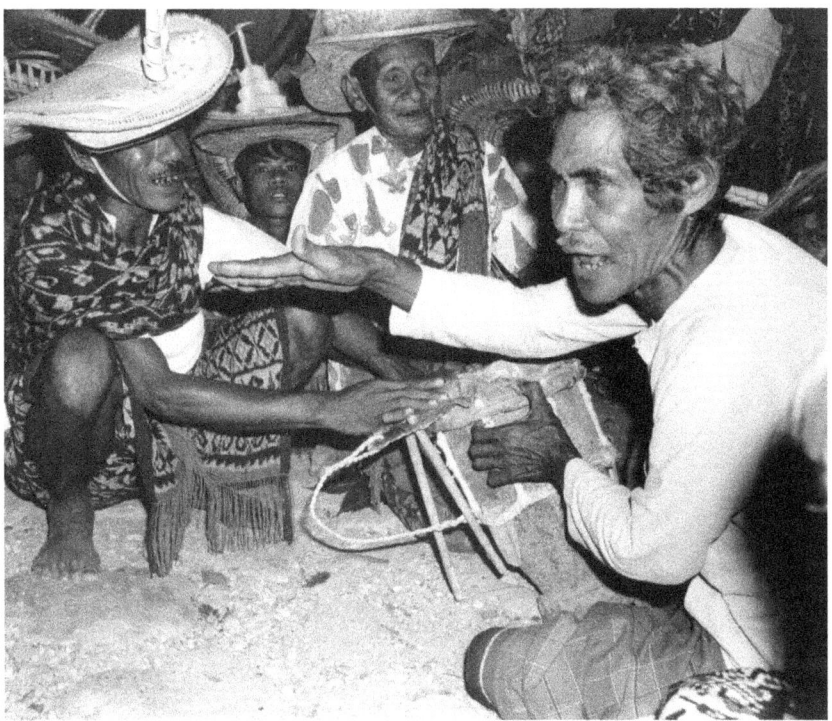

Figure 7: Petrus Malesi chanting at the mortuary ceremony for Old Meno

The Ocean Storm that Carries the Shells to Tena Lai ma Mae Oe

The recitation begins with the storm that drives the two shells from the ocean and then describes the search for the ritually required fish that results only in the scooping forth of the shells, Suti Solo do Bina Bane.

1.	*Luli nala liun dale*	A storm arises in the ocean's depths
2.	*Ma sangu nala sain dale*	And a cyclone arises in the sea's depths
3.	*Bina nama-toko isi*	Bina puts out its insides
4.	*Suti nama-edo nggi*	Suti exudes its pods
5.	*Suti Solo namatani*	Suti Solo cries
6.	*Ma Bina Bane nasakedu*	Bina Bane sobs
7.	*De ele piko basa meti*	Floating forth through all the tides

79

8.	*Ma bonu boa basa namo*	And bobbing along in all harbours
9.	*Neu Teni Lai Laok meti na [dean na]*	Goes to Tena Lai Laok's tide [wall]
10.	*Ma Mae Oe Loek lutun na*	And Mae Oe Loek's fish catch
11.	*Ana lili dela nai ndia*	He likes it there
12.	*Ma neka nita nai ndia.*	And enjoys it there.

The Preparation of the Scoop-Net and the Search for the Ritual Fish

13.	*Faik esa manunin*	On a certain day
14.	*Ma ledok dua matebe*	And at a particular time
15.	*Teke Hulu Hutu tina na*	Teke Hulu Hutu's garden
16.	*Ma Sio Pale Enge osi na*	And Sio Pale Enge's field
17.	*Pelak ka nggona-hano*	The corn cobs have ripened
18.	*Ma betek kala dio-hu.*	And the millet stalks have matured.
19.	*Ana doko-doe peda-poi na*	He seeks to perform the *peda-poi* ritual
20.	*Ma ana tai-boni fua-bafa na*	And he requests to do the *fua-bafa* ritual
21.	*Ana lulua Lole Holu*	He selects Lole Holu
22.	*Ma ana heheli Lua Bafa.*	And he chooses Lua Bafa.
23.	*Boe ma inak kia Sama Dai*	So the woman Sama Dai
24.	*Ma fetok kia Kuku Nou*	And the girl Kuku Nou
25.	*Ana pena na pole aba*	She picks bolls of cotton
26.	*De pole dai lena aban*	Bolls enough for thread
27.	*Ma kedi na lata do*	And cuts strips of lontar leaf
28.	*De lata tolesi don*	Leaf enough for strips
29.	*Ana neni neu seko*	She makes them into a scoop-net
30.	*Fo seko matei besi*	A scoop-net with iron-weighted insides
31.	*Ma tale na neu ndai*	And fashions them into a fishnet
32.	*Fo ndai mahamu lilok*	A fishnet with a gold-weighted belly
33.	*Neu seko sanga Dusu La'e*	She goes to scoop for a Dusu La'e
34.	*Ma ndai sanga Tio Holu*	And goes to fish for a Tio Holu
35.	*Mai Tena Lai Laok lutun*	In Tena Lai Laok's fish catch

4. VERSION III FROM THE DOMAIN OF TERMANU

36.	*Do Mae Oe Loek lutun*	Or Mae Oe Loek's fish catch.
37.	*Seko nala meti dua*	She scoops in two tides
38.	*Na Suti nala meti dua*	Suti is in those two tides
39.	*Ma ndai nala namo telu*	And she fishes in three harbours
40.	*Na Bina nala namo telu.*	Bina is in those three harbours.
41.	*Seko na Suti Solo*	She scoops up Suti Solo
42.	*Na seko fo ndaso heni*	She scoops and throws him away
43.	*Ma ndai na Bina Bane*	She fishes up Bina Bane
44.	*Na ndai fo toko henin.*	She fishes and throws him away.

The Dialogue with the Shells

It is at this point that the dialogue with Suti Solo and Bina Bane begins.

45.	*Suti Solo dede'ak*	Suti Solo speaks
46.	*Ma Bina Bane kokolak ma nae:*	And Bina Bane talks and says:
47.	*'Seko heni Suti Solo*	'If you scoop but throw away Suti Solo
48.	*Ma ndai heni Bina Bane*	And fish but throw away Bina Bane
49.	*Na Suti, au o se*	I, Suti, with whom will I be
50.	*Ma Bina, au o se?*	And I, Bina, with whom will I be?'
51.	*Inak kia Sama Dai*	The woman Sama Dai
52.	*Lole halan na neu*	Lifts her words
53.	*Ma fetok kia Kuku Nou*	And the girl Kuku Nou
54.	*Selu dasin na neu:*	Raises her voice:
55.	*'Mu mo timi di'i*	'Go with the *timi* post
56.	*Ma mu mo lungu tua.'*	And go with the *lungu* beam.'
57.	*Bina Bane kokolak*	Bina Bane speaks
58.	*Ma Suti Solo dede'ak ma nae:*	And Suti Solo replies and says:
59.	*'Malole la so*	'That would be good
60.	*Ma mandak kala so*	And that would be proper.
61.	*Au o timi di'i*	I will go with the *timi* post
62.	*Ma au o lungu tua,*	And I will go with the *lungu* beam,
63.	*Te hu lungu tua natahi*	But if the *lungu* beam sags
64.	*Ma timi di'i na so'o*	And the *timi* post tilts

65.	*Au asalai o se*	On whom will I recline
66.	*Ma au angatu o se*	And on whom will I sit
67.	*Fo se-tele o se*	With whom will I laugh
68.	*Ma ata-dale o se?'*	And with whom will I take heart?'
69.	*Inak kia Sama Dai*	The woman Sama Dai
70.	*Ma fetok kia Kuku Nou*	And the girl Kuku Nou
71.	*Ana lole lele halan*	She lifts her words encouragingly
72.	*Ma selu doko-doe dasin, nae:*	And raises her voice coaxingly, saying:
73.	*'Mu no bou tua*	'Go with the lontar syrup vat
74.	*Ma mu mo neka hade.'*	And go with the rice basket.'
75.	*Bina Bane kokolak*	Bina Bane speaks
76.	*Ma Suti Solo dede'ak ma nae:*	And Suti Solo replies and says:
77.	*'Malole la so*	'That would be good
78.	*Ma mandak kala so*	And that would be proper
79.	*Bou tua na tono*	[But if] the syrup vat is overturned
80.	*Ma neka hade lulunu*	And the rice basket is rolled up
81.	*Na au asalai o se*	Then with whom will I recline
82.	*Ma au angatu o se?'*	And with whom will I sit?'
83.	*Inak kia Sama Dai*	The woman Sama Dai
84.	*Ana lole lekek halan*	She lifts her words sweetly
85.	*Ma fetok kia Kuku Nou*	And the girl Kuku Nou
86	*Selu doko-doe dasin, nae:*	Raises her voice coaxingly, saying:
87.	*'Mu mo peu ai*	'Go with the boundary tree
88.	*Ma mu mo to batu.'*	And go with the border stone.'
89.	*Bina Bane kokolak*	Bina Bane talks
90.	*Ma Suti Solo dede'ak ma nae:*	And Suti Solo speaks and says:
91.	*'Malole la so*	'That would be good
92.	*Ma mandak kala so.*	And that would be proper.
93.	*Au u o to batu*	I will go with the border stone
94.	*Ma ami meu mo peu ai*	And we will go with the boundary tree
95.	*Te hu ala ketu heni ndoto osin*	But if they snap off spreading beans
96.	*Ma se heni tuli hena*	And they clear away the pigeon peas
97.	*Na to ai la hiluk*	Then the border tree will go down

98.	*Ma lane batu la keko*	And the marker stone will shift
99.	*Na ami masalai mo se*	Then with whom will we recline
100.	*Ma ami magatu mo se?'*	And with whom will we sit?'
101.	*De Bina bei nasakedu*	So Bina continues to sob
102.	*Ma Suti bei namatani.*	And Suti continues to cry.
103.	*Boe ma Sama Dai kokolak*	Then Sama Dai speaks
104.	*Ma Kuku Nou nafada na nae:*	And Kuku Nou replies, saying:
105.	*'Meu mo kumea letek*	'Go with the *kumea* grass on the hill
106.	*Ma meu mo kuku telas.'*	And go with the *kuku* shrub in the underbrush.'
107.	*Boe ma nae:*	Then he says:
108.	*'Malole la so*	'That would be good
109.	*Ma mandak kala so*	And that would be proper.
110.	*Te hu pila kumea letek*	But if the red *kumea* on the hills
111.	*Lamadilu neu kalen*	Bends at its top
112.	*Ma nggeo kuku telas*	And the black *kuku* of the underbrush
113.	*Lamasesu leu bu'un*	Breaks at its joints
114.	*Bina Bane neu se*	To whom will Bina Bane go
115.	*Fo setele no se*	With whom to laugh
116.	*Ma Suti Solo no se*	And with whom will Suti Solo go
117.	*Fo nata-dale no se?'*	With whom to take heart?'
118.	*Fo Suti bei namatani*	So Suti continues to cry
119.	*Ma Bina bei nasakedu.*	And Bina continues to sob.
120.	*Boe ma inak ka Sama Dai*	The woman Sama Dai
121.	*Ma fetok ka Kuku Nou*	And the girl Kuku Nou
122.	*Ana lole halan na neu*	She lifts her words
123.	*Ma selu dasin na neu ma nae:*	And raises her voice and says:
124.	*'Mu mo doa lasi*	'Go with the forest cuckoo
125.	*Ma mu mo koloba'o le.'*	And go with the river woodcock.'
126.	*Boe ma Bina Bane nahala*	Then Bina Bane gives voice
127.	*Ma Suti Solo nafada ma nae:*	And Suti Solo speaks and says:
128.	*'Au o kolobao le*	'I will go with the river woodcock
129.	*Na malole la so*	Such would be good

130.	*Ma mandak kala so.*	And such would be proper.
131.	*Te timu lamatua dulu*	But if the wind increases in the east
132.	*Ma hu'ak [fak] lamanalu langa*	And the monsoon extends at the headlands
133.	*Na kulu kolobao le*	Then the river woodcock
134.	*Ba'o-ba'o tunga le*	[Cries] *ba'o-ba'o* along the river
135.	*Ma betu doa lasi la*	And the forest woodcock
136.	*Do'o-do'o tunga lasi*	[Cries] *do'o-do'o* through the forest
137.	*Na Bina Bane no se*	Then with whom will Bina Bane be
138.	*[Fo] setele no se*	With whom to laugh
139.	*Ma Suti Solo no se*	And with whom will Suti Solo be
140.	*Fo nata-dale no se?'*	With whom to take heart?'
141.	*Boe Bina bei pinu idu*	So Bina still drips snot from the nose
142.	*Ma Suti bei lu mata.*	And Suti still drops tears from the eyes.

The Final Directive to Return to the Sea

143.	*Boe ma inak ka Sama Dai*	So the woman Sama Dai
144.	*Do fetok ka Kuku Nou*	Or the girl Kuku Nou
145.	*Lole hala na neu*	Lifts her words
146.	*Lole hala di'u dua*	Lifts words to repeat
147.	*Ma selu dasi nasafali ma nae:*	And raises her voice to say again:
148.	*'Mu le titian*	'Go along the river's bank
149.	*Ma mu oli tatain.'*	And go along the estuary's edge.'
150.	*Besaka ifa-la Suti Solo*	So she lifts Suti Solo
151.	*Ma ko'o-la Bina Bane*	And she cradles Bina Bane
152.	*De leu le titian*	Then they go to the river bank
153.	*Ma leu oli tatain*	And they go to the estuary's edge.
154.	*Boe ma besak ka timu lamatua dulu*	Now the wind increases in the east
155.	*Ma hu'ak [fak] lamanalu langa*	And the monsoon extends at the headlands
156.	*Boe ma timu nggefu neu Suti Solo*	The monsoon blows Suti Solo

157.	*Ma ani fupu neu Bina Bane*	And the wind strikes Bina Bane
158.	*De ele piko neu liun*	Floating forth like *piko* wood to the sea
159.	*Ma ana bonu boa neu sain*	And bobbing forth like *boa* wood to the ocean
160.	*Nde lili dela neu sain*	He likes going to the ocean
161.	*Ma neka nita neu liun*	And enjoys going to the sea
162.	*De leo faik ia dalen*	As on this day
163.	*De neka nita nai liun*	He likes it in the sea
164.	*Ma leo ledok ia tein.*	And as at this time.

Composition Analysis: Old Meno–Seu Ba'i–Malesi Comparisons

Malesi's composition is shorter than either Meno's or Seu Ba'i's compositions. It consists of 164 lines based on 73 dyadic sets. Of these 73 sets, 31 are shared in common with Meno's composition, which comprises 103 sets. Some 31 sets, although not all the same, are shared with Seu Ba'i's composition, which comprises 85 sets. Only 27 of the same sets are used in all three compositions. Based on shared dyadic sets, Malesi's composition is more closely related to that of Seu Ba'i than to that of Meno.

Ritual Names: People and Places

Malesi introduces new chant characters in his composition. In both Meno's and Seu Ba'i's compositions, the woman who scoops up the shells is Pedu Hange//Nggiti Seti. In Malesi's composition, this woman is named Sama Dai//Kuku Nou. All three compositions indicate the need to search for ritual fish in order to carry out the ceremony of the *peda-poi// fua-bafa* harvest ritual. But each chant differs as to whose ritual this is. For Meno, this is Manupui Peda//Kokolo Dulu's origin feast//feast of nine; for Seu Ba'i, it is Manupui Peda//Boko Dulu's ceremony. For Malesi, it is Teke Hulu Hutu//Sio Pale Enge's ritual. All three compositions agree, however, on the importance of Lole Holu//Lua Bafa. Meno's composition provides her genealogy, but only Malesi makes clear her significance. She is the woman designated to perform the critical harvest ritual. All three compositions also agree on the sacred site of Tena Lai//Mae Oe as the place where the encounter with the shells occurs and where they are scooped from the sea. In his composition, Malesi identifies this site by making it into the personal name of the 'owner' of the fish weir, Tena Lai Laok//Mae Oe Loek, where the shells are found.

Directives in the Dialogue with the Shells

Most of Malesi's composition consists of the dialogue with the shells. This dialogue contains five separate directives, whereas both Meno's and Seu Ba'i's compositions have six distinctive directives. Of Malesi's five directives, three are shared with Meno and four with Seu Ba'i. It could also be argued that Malesi's first directive to the house shares a similarity to the other compositions. Meno's first directive is for the shells to make their home with Lole Holu//Lua Bafa, whereas Seu Ba'i designates a part of the house, the cooking fire//upper house, which is a different part of the house to that designated by Malesi. Malesi's five directives are the following:

Table 1: A Comparison of Dialogue Directives

	Meno	Seu Ba'i
1) house post//floor beam		
2) syrup vat//rice basket	X	X
3) boundary tree//border stone	X	X
4) *kumea* grass//*kuku* shrub		X
5) forest cuckoo//river watercock	X	X

Of these various passages, it is worth comparing the three compositions in relation to boundary tree//border stone. Whereas for Meno this passage is only eight lines, for Seu Ba'i and for Malesi, their equivalent passages comprise 15 to 16 lines.

Old Meno

195.	*Te na mu mo peu ai*	'Then go with boundary tree
196.	*Ma mu mo to batu.'*	And go with border stone.'
197.	*Boe ma Suti boe kokolak*	Still Suti talks
198.	*Ma Bina boe dede'ak ma nae:*	And still Bina speaks and says:
199.	*'Te hu ai dedean ta*	'But a tree does not talk
200.	*Ma batu kokolan ta.'*	And a stone does not speak.'
201.	*Bina boe nasakedu*	Still Bina sobs
202.	*Ma Suti boe namatani.*	And still Suti cries.

4. VERSION III FROM THE DOMAIN OF TERMANU

Seu Ba'i

87.	*'Mu mo peu ai lasi*	'Go with boundary tree of the forest
88.	*Ma mu mo to batu nula.'*	And go with border stone of the wood.'
89.	*Boe te Bina, ana kokolak*	But Bina, he talks
90.	*Ma Suti, ana dede'ak, nae:*	And Suti, he speaks, saying:
91.	*'Malole ndia so*	'This is good
92.	*Ma mandak ndia so.*	And this is proper.
93.	*Au o peu ai lasi*	I will be with boundary tree of the forest
94.	*Ma au o to batu nula*	And I will be with border stone of the wood
95.	*Te bafi ka'a neni pelak*	But if pig chews the maize
96.	*Au dede'ak o se*	With whom will I speak
97.	*Ma kode ketu neni betek*	And if monkey plucks the millet
98.	*Au kokolak o se*	With whom will I talk
99.	*Do se'ek o se*	Or be noisy with whom
100.	*Ma oku-boluk o se*	And shout with whom
101.	*Sama leo Lua Bafa*	[With someone] just like Lua Bafa
102.	*Ma deta leo Lole Holu?'*	And [someone] exactly like Lole Holu?'

Malesi

87.	*'Mu mo peu ai*	'Go with the boundary tree
88.	*Ma mu mo to batu.'*	And go with the border stone.'
89.	*Bina Bane kokolak*	Bina Bane talks
90.	*Ma Suti Solo dede'ak ma nae:*	And Suti Solo speaks and says:
91.	*'Malole la so*	'That would be good
92.	*Ma mandak kala so.*	And that would be proper.
93.	*Au u o to batu*	I will go with the border stone
94.	*Ma ami meu mo peu ai*	And we will go with the boundary tree
95.	*Te hu ala ketu heni ndoto osin*	But if they snap off spreading beans
96.	*Ma se heni tuli hena*	And they clear away the pigeon peas
97.	*Na to ai la hiluk*	Then the border tree will go down
98.	*Ma lane batu la keko*	And the marker stone will shift
99.	*Na ami masalai mo se*	Then with whom will we recline

100.	*Ma ami magatu mo se?'*	And with whom will we sit?'
101.	*De Bina bei nasakedu*	So Bina continues to sob
102.	*Ma Suti bei namatani.*	And Suti continues to cry.

Old Meno
195.	*'Te na mu mo peu ai*	'Then go with boundary tree
196.	*Ma mu mo to batu.'*	And go with border stone.'

Seu Ba'i
87.	*'Mu mo peu ai lasi*	'Go with boundary tree of the forest
88.	*Ma mu mo to batu nula.'*	And go with border stone of the wood.'

Malesi
87.	*'Mu mo peu ai*	'Go with the boundary tree
88.	*Ma mu mo to batu.'*	And go with the border stone.'

In a comparison of the three compositions, Malesi's lines directing the shells on where to go are virtually the same as those of Old Meno. Seu Ba'i's lines require some consideration because he attaches a place marker to 'boundary tree//border stone' as if to imply that this is a personal name. His personification of each entity to which the shells are directed is more explicit than either Meno's or Malesi's. Each entity is, in effect, given a name.

Following this directive, the response in Meno's composition is blunt and to the point:

199.	*'Te hu ai dedean ta*	'But a tree does not talk
200.	*Ma batu kokolan ta.'*	And a stone does not speak.'

In Seu Ba'i's and Malesi's compositions, by contrast, the following six lines are more similarly extended:

Seu Ba'i
89.	*Boe te Bina, ana kokolak*	But Bina, he talks
90.	*Ma Suti, ana dede'ak, nae:*	And Suti, he speaks, saying:
91.	*'Malole ndia so*	'This is good

92.	*Ma mandak ndia so.*	And this is proper.
93.	*Au o peu ai lasi*	I will be with boundary tree of the forest
94.	*Ma au o to batu nula*	And I will be with border stone of the wood

Malesi

89.	*Bina Bane kokolak*	Bina Bane talks
90.	*Ma Suti Solo dede'ak ma nae:*	And Suti Solo speaks and says:
91.	*'Malole la so*	'That would be good
92.	*Ma mandak kala so.*	And that would be proper.
93.	*Au u o to batu*	I will go with the border stone
94.	*Ma ami meu mo peu ai*	And we will go with the boundary tree

Although these particular lines resemble each other closely, Malesi adds a flourish that some poets utilise to enhance the parallelism of their composition. Thus, in Malesi's composition (lines 93–94), the shells reply by combining a singular 'I' with a plural 'we'.

After these similar lines, their compositions diverge. Seu Ba'i invokes the image of a bounded corn and millet field that is pillaged by pig and monkey, whereas Malesi invokes the image of a temporary bean and pea garden that is harvested. In the end, in Malesi's composition, the shells are left on their own to sob and to cry. And eventually they return to the sea.

5
Suti Solo do Bina Bane: Version IV from the Domain of Termanu

Some years later, in 1977, when I visited Rote with the filmmaker Tim Asch, I asked Pe'u Malesi to recite a number of *bini* including that of *Suti Solo do Bina Bane*. To my surprise, his recitation took a different turn. This time, instead of a mortuary rendition of the chant, Malesi set out to recite *Suti Solo do Bina Bane* as an origin chant. This version was intended as a revelation.

Malesi's performance was not, however, straightforward. He initially hesitated on how to present the chant. He began with a comment: '*Suti Solo do Bina Bane*: our recitation comes from the west house—indeed from the deeds of the Almighty that extend to this day.'[1] Mention of the 'west house' is, I assume, a reference to the house of the dead, which is located in the west. In numerous mortuary chants, the deceased is described as setting sail to the west from whence there is, on specific occasions, the possibility of a return of the spirit on a visitation to the living. Malesi's comment thus indicates that his intention is to recite *Suti Solo do Bina Bane* as a mortuary chant.

---

1   *Suti Solo do Bina Bane: Ita kokolakana neme uma muli—hu meme Manakuasa tata nonoin fo nakatok losa faik-ia.*

He then began by describing the storm that carried the shells to land, but after only 10 lines, he interrupted his recitation, apologised for beginning in the middle of the narrative, and began his recitation again, asserting that he would begin at the beginning. His first 10 lines were as follows:

1.	*Luli nala liun dalek*	A storm arises in the ocean's depths
2.	*Ma sangu nala sain dalek.*	And a cyclone arises in the sea's depths.
3.	*Liun neu na-edo*	The ocean exudes
4.	*Ma sain neu na-pode.*	The sea puts forth.
5.	*De pode heni Suti aten*	It puts forth Suti's liver
6.	*Ma edo heni Bina nggin.*	And it exudes Bina's pods.
7	*De ana ele piko*	He floats forth
8	*Ma ana bonu boa*	And he bobs along
9.	*Ana ele piko*	He floats
10.	*Ma ana bonu boa …*	And he bobs along …

When he stopped his recitation, his comment was emphatic: 'Ah, this is the middle of the recitation. Sorry. I will trace things from the beginning … Suti Solo do Bina Bane's origins from the very beginning.'[2]

He then continued for some 110 lines but at the point when the shells return to the sea, he interrupted himself again and began to recount how the shells were made into objects for dyeing and spinning. Thus, his telling of *Suti Solo do Bina Bane* is essentially a combination of two versions. The first half of the recitation is a mortuary chant; the second half is an origin chant rendition.

For this first rendition, Malesi began his recitation not unlike his other version, with the origin feast and the need to search for the required ritual fish at Tena Lai//Mae Oe.

The Origin Feast and the Search for Tio Holu do Dusu La'e

1.	*Touk-a Kafi Dulu tina-na*	The man Kafi Dulu's garden
2.	*Ma ta'ek-a Kule Langa osi-na*	And the boy Kule Langa's field

---

2 'Ah! Kokolakana nai talada ia. Maaf dei. Tao neme hu-na mai dei, te au lilin … Suti Solo no Bina Bane dadina makasososana.'

3.	*Bete-kala dio hu'u*	The millet has ripened grains
4.	*Fo ala sanga ketu*	So they are ready to pick
5.	*Ma pela-kala lona nggona*	And the maize is full of cobs
6.	*Fo sanga sei.*	So they are ready to pluck.
7.	*Boe-ma sanga peda poina*	They want to celebrate 'placing on top'
8.	*Ma sanga fua bafana.*	And want to perform 'setting on the mouth'.
9.	*Boe ma ala lali lala Sama Dai*	So they bring forth Sama Dai
10.	*Do soko lala Kuku Nou*	And they carry forth Kuku Nou
11.	*Tenga na ndai tasina*	She takes a fishnet for the sea
12.	*Ndai mahamu lilok*	A fishnet with a gold-weighted belly
13.	*Ma nggao na seko metina*	And she picks up a scoop-net for the tide
14.	*Seko matei besik*	A scoop net with iron-weighted insides
15.	*Neu seko sisi'u enggak*	She goes to scoop, lifting seaweed
16.	*Nai Mae Oe loek lutun na*	In Mae Oe's fish catch
17.	*Ma ndai huhuka batu*	And goes to net fish, turning rocks
18.	*Nai Tena Lai la'ok de'an na.*	At Tena Lai's stone weir.

The Encounter and Dialogue with the Shells

19.	*Ana seko sanga Dusu La'e*	She goes scoop fishing seeking Dusu La'e
20.	*Fo seko nala meti dua*	Scoop fishing in two tides
21.	*Na Suti nala meti dua*	But Suti is there in the two tides
22.	*Ndai sanga Tio Holu*	She goes net fishing, seeking Tio Holu
23.	*Fo ndai nala namo telu*	Net fishing in three bays
24.	*Na Bina nala namo telu.*	But Bina is there in the three bays.
25.	*Na ana ta hapu Dusu La'e*	She does not get Dusu La'e
26.	*Ma ana ta hapu Tio Holu*	And she does not get Tio Holu
27.	*Te ana seko nala Suti Solo*	But she does scoop up Suti Solo
28.	*Ma ana ndai nala Bina Bane.*	And she does fish forth Bina Bane.
29.	*Boe ma ana ndai neni Bina Bane*	So she fishes forth Bina Bane

30.	*Ma seko neni Suti Solo*	And she scoops up Suti Solo
31.	*De mai enok telu tai-lolona*	But coming to the three winding paths
32.	*Ma dalak dua bobongona*	And the two rounding roads
33.	*Boe ma ana tu'u heni Suti Solo*	She throws Suti Solo away
34.	*Ma ana tapa heni Bina Bane.*	And she casts Bina Bane away.
35.	*Boe ma Bina Bane kokolak*	So Bina Bane speaks
36.	*Ma Suti Solo dedeak ma nae:*	And Suti Solo talks and says:
37.	*'Ah! Tu'u au neu eno teluna*	'Ah! Throw me to the three paths
38.	*Ma tapa au neu dala duana*	And cast me at the two roads
39.	*De au Suti, au o se*	Then I, Suti, with whom will I be
40.	*Fo asalai o se*	On whom will I recline
41.	*Ma au Bina, au o se*	And I, Bina, with whom will I be
42.	*Fo au angatu'u o se?'*	With whom will I sit?'
43.	*De Bina bei pinu idu*	Bina has snot coming from his nose
44.	*Ma Suti bei lu mata.*	And Suti has tears in his eyes.
45.	*Boe ma inaka Kuku Nou*	So the woman Kuku Nou
46.	*Ma fetoka Sama Dai*	And the girl Sama Dai
47.	*Lole halana neu*	Raises her voice
48.	*Ma selu dasi na neu ma nae:*	And lifts her speech and says:
49.	*'Meu mo neka hade*	'Go with the rice basket
50.	*Ma meu mo bou tuana.'*	And go with the lontar syrup vat.'
51.	*Boe ma Suti Solo nafada*	Then Suti Solo talks
52.	*Ma Bina Bane kokolak ma nae:*	And Bina Bane speaks and says:
53.	*'Ah, malole la so*	'Ah, that would be good
54.	*Ma mandak kala so*	And that would be proper
55.	*[Te] bou tua la heok*	But if the lontar syrup vats turn
56.	*Ma neka hade la keko*	And if the rice baskets shift
57.	*Na au asalai o se*	Then with whom shall I recline
58.	*Ma au angatu o se?'*	And with whom shall I sit?'
59.	*Suti bei namatani*	Suti continues to cry
60.	*Ma Bina bei nasakedu.*	Bina continues to sob.
61.	*Boe ma inak leo Kuku Nou*	So the woman like Kuku Nou
62.	*Do fetok leo Sama Dai nae:*	Or the girl like Sama Dai says:

63.	*'Mu mo doa-lasi*	'Go with the forest cuckoo
64.	*Ma mo koloba'o le.'*	And with the river woodcock.'
65.	*Boe ma Bina Bane kokolak*	So Bina Bane speaks
66.	*Ma Suti Solo dedeak ma nae:*	And Suti Solo answers and says:
67.	*'Ah, malole la so*	'Ah, such would be good
68.	*Ma mandakala so.*	And such would be proper.
69.	*Hu koloba'o le la ba'o-ba'o tunga le*	But if the woodcocks *ba'o-ba'o* down the river
70.	*Ma betu doa lasi la do'o-do'o tunga lasi,*	And the cuckoos *do'o-do'o* through the forest,
71.	*Na Suti au o se*	Then for me, Suti, with whom will I be
72.	*Fo au asalai o se*	With whom will I recline
73.	*Ma Bina au o se*	And with me, Bina, with whom will I be
74.	*Fo au angatu o se?'*	And with whom will I sit?'
75.	*De Bina bei nasakedu*	Thus Bina continues to sob
76.	*Ma Suti bei namatani.*	And Suti continues to cry.
77.	*Boe ma inaka Sama Dai*	So the woman Sama Dai
78.	*Do fetoka Kuku Nou nae:*	And the girl Kuku Nou says:
79.	*'Mu mo mafo ai*	'Go with the trees' shade
80.	*Ma mu mo sa'o tua.'*	And go with the lontar palms' shadow.'
81.	*Boe ma Bina Bane kokolak*	So Bina Bane speaks
82.	*Ma Suti Solo dede'ak ma nae:*	And Suti Solo answers and says:
83.	*'Ah, malole la so*	'Ah, such would be good
84.	*Ma mandakala so*	And such would be proper
85.	*Mafo ai la heok*	[If] the trees' shade turns aside
86.	*Ma sa'o ai la hiluk*	And the lontar palms' shadow recedes
87.	*Na au asalai o se*	Then with whom will I recline
88.	*Na au angatu'u o se*	Then with whom will I sit
89.	*Fo Suti Solo no se*	With whom will Suti Solo be
90.	*Ma Bina Bane no se?'*	And with whom will Bina Bane be?'
91.	*De Bina bei nasakedu*	Thus Bina continues to sob
92.	*Ma Suti bei namatani.*	And Suti continues to cry.
93.	*Boe ma inaka Kuku Nou*	Then the woman Kuku Nou
94.	*Do fetoka Sama Dai*	Or the girl Sama Dai

95.	*Lole di'u doe halana*	Raises her voice softly
96.	*Ma hele tai boni dasina ma nae:*	And lifts her voice gently and says:
97.	*'Ah, mu oli titian*	'Ah, go along the estuary's edge
98.	*Ma mu le tatain*	And go along the river's bank
99.	*Fo timu lamatua dulu*	So when the wind increases in the east
100.	*Do fak lamanalu langana*	And the monsoon arises in the headlands
101.	*Na timu nggefu Suti Solo*	The east wind sweeps Suti Solo away
102.	*Do fak foki Bina Bane.'*	Or the west wind carries Bina Bane away.'

The Return of the Shells to the Sea

103.	*De fak fupu Bina Bane*	The west wind blows Bina Bane
104.	*De dilu neu [mu] liun dalek*	Descending into the sea's depths
105.	*Timu nggefu Suti Solo*	The east wind sweeps Suti Solo
106.	*De loe neu [mu] sain dalek.*	Turning down into the ocean's depths.
107.	*Tama ota neu liun*	Crowded together in the sea
108.	*Ma tesa bela [isi] neu sain.*	And packed tightly in the ocean.
109.	*Boe ma luli nala sain dalek*	Then a cyclone arises in the ocean's depths
110.	*Ma sangu nala sain dalek.*	A storm strikes the ocean's depths.

Malesi's Further Interruption and the Redirection of the Chant

Having carried his recitation to this point, Malesi interrupted his performance with the following interjection: 'Our Lord wishes to do this tale to the present.'[3] The term 'Our Lord' has to be taken as a Christian reference and his remark can be interpreted to mean that Malesi sees himself as the vehicle of revelation on God's behalf. What follows is sacred revelation.

---

3   *'Ita Lamatua sanga tao dede'a nakatok losa faikia.'*

5. VERSION IV FROM THE DOMAIN OF TERMANU

The resumed recitation gives the genealogy of the woman who scoops up the shells and is the first to use them for spinning cotton and preparing indigo dye as 'whorl shell' (*ifa bina*) and 'indigo pot' (*tena tau*). This is not, however, the woman who then does the tying and dyeing of the cloth. Another woman is named who performs this task and, when it is completed, a search is begun to find yet another woman who can weave. This search leads to the far eastern end of Rote where there is a woman who can weave particular named textile patterns. The chant concludes by naming a succession of places—all in eastern Rote.

In the general context of Rotenese culture, this revelation of the origin of weaving is notable because other origin chants that recount the origin of weaving, including one from Old Meno, give another account of the origin of weaving and specifically name a woman associated with the west of the island. Across the island, the assertion of different origins is common. Specifically, for Malesi as a chanter, this revelation confirms what many in Termanu said to me about him: that his knowledge came from eastern Rote where he was said to have spent some time before he was married and settled down in Termanu.

Not all of the lines in what follows are in strict canonical parallelism: Malesi seems more intent on conveying the narrative of his revelation than in maintaining its proper form. As he proceeds to his conclusion, the composition becomes a recitation of the ritual names of the various domains of the eastern side of the island.

This version of *Suti Solo do Bina Bane* proceeds as follows (continuing with the numbering from before the interruption):

111.	*Ana fe luli a mai*	He causes a cyclone to come
112.	*De luli neu liun dalek*	The cyclone moves on the sea's depths
113.	*Ma ana fe sangu mai*	And he causes a storm to come
114.	*De sangu neu sain dalek.*	The storm moves on the ocean's depths.
115.	*De sain neu napode*	The ocean moves, extending forth
116.	*Ma liun neu naedo*	The sea moves, exuding forth
117.	*De edo heni Suti nggina*	Exuding forth Suti's pod
118.	*Ma pode heni Bina atena.*	Extending forth Bina's liver.
119.	*Nate inaka Pasa Paku*	The woman Pasa Paku
120.	*Ma fetoka Finga Fiti*	And the girl Finga Fiti

121.	*[Ana] tu Kokolo Dulu*	She marries Kokolo Dulu
122.	*Ma ana sao Manupui Peda.*	And she weds Manupui Peda.
123.	*De Manupui Peda osina*	Manupui Peda's garden
124.	*Ma Kokolo Dulu tinana.*	Kokolo Dulu's field.
125.	*Tauk-ala mofa ndana*	The indigo grows grey branches
126.	*Ma abas-ala sai oka.*	The cotton lets out its tendrils.
127.	*Boe ma inaka Pasa Paku*	The woman Pasa Paku
128.	*Ma fetok Finga Fiti*	And the girl Finga Fiti
129.	*Ana pena na abasa*	She picks the cotton
130.	*De naleo nan.*	And draws it out.
131.	*Tehu ifa binan bei ta*	But there is no winding stick shell
132.	*Ma tena taun bei ta.*	And there is no indigo pot.
133.	*Boe ma neu seko pepei oli*	So she goes to scoop deliberately in the estuary
134.	*Ma ndai ndondolo le*	And she goes to fish steadily in the river
135.	*De neu hapu Suti louna*	She finds Suti's shell
136.	*Ma neu tongo Bina louna.*	And she encounters Bina's shell.
137.	*Boe ma ana hai neni Suti louna*	She picks up Suti's shell
138.	*Ma ana tenga neni Bina louna, fe mai*	And she takes up Bina's shell, bringing it back
139.	*De besaka ana dipo ine*	Then she turns the spindle on its base
140.	*Ma ana lole aba.*	And she winds the cotton.
141.	*Boe ma kolu tauk*	So she picks the indigo
142.	*De ana dopo lifu,*	She stirs the liquid,
143.	*De tao neu Suti dea-na*	She puts it into Suti's outside
144.	*Le'a na abasa.*	Draws the cotton forth.
145.	*De ana dadi aba do.*	It becomes cotton thread.
146.	*Boe ma ana lolo nan,*	So she stretches it out,
147.	*De ana dadi futus.*	It becomes a bundle of thread.
148.	*Boe ma ana du'a sanga manahenge.*	So she thinks and plans to be the one who ties.
149.	*Inaka Kuku Dula*	The woman Kuku Dula
150.	*Boe ma pila nggeon,*	She wishes to use red and black dyes,

5. VERSION IV FROM THE DOMAIN OF TERMANU

151.	*Fetoka Lima Le'u.*	The girl Lima Le'u.
152.	*Kuku Dula ana henge nan ndia dale dulak,*	Kuku Dula ties a pattern in it,
153.	*De ana tao nan,*	So she works it through,
154.	*De ana dadi futus.*	It becomes a bundle of thread.
155.	*Tehu pila-nggeon bei ta.*	But it is not yet red and black.
156.	*Boe ma inaka Lima Le'u,*	So the woman Lima Le'u,
157.	*Ana tao pilana*	She makes it red
158.	*Fo pila manukudu-na*	Making it *morinda*-red
159.	*Ma ana tao nggeona*	And she makes it black
160.	*Fo tao nggeo tau isi-na.*	Making it indigo-black.
161.	*Tata nan boe ma.*	When this is done.
162.	*Boe ma ala sanga ina manando selu*	Then they seek a woman who can work the shuttle
163.	*Ma feto mananggiti atis.*	And a girl who can weave on a loom.
164.	*De ala losa Dulu Balaha oli-na*	They go to the estuary of Dulu Balaha
165.	*Fo losa Diu Dulu*	All the way to Diu Dulu
166.	*Ma Langa Mangaledo le-na*	And to the river of Langa Mangaledo
167.	*Fo losa Kana Langa.*	All the way to Kana Langa.
168.	*Ina bei Lata Nae la*	The woman still at Lata Nae
169.	*Inaka Adu Pinga*	The woman Adu Pinga
170.	*Ma [feto] bei Pinga Dai la*	And the girl still at Pinga Dai
171.	*Fetoka Leo Lapa*	The girl Leo Lapa
172.	*Lole halana neu*	Raises her voice
173.	*Ma selu dasi na neu, nae:*	And lifts her words, saying:
174.	*'Ah, au ta alelak tetenuka.*	'I do not know how to weave.
175.	*De nggele boo nggenggele*	Rage, do not rage
176.	*Ma nasa boo mamanasa.'*	Angry, do not be angry.'
177.	*Boe ma besak fetoka Kuku Dula*	So then the girl Kuku Dula
178.	*Ma inaka Lima Le'u*	And the woman Lima Le'u
179.	*Latane seluk bai*	They ask once again
180.	*Fo latane manatenu*	Asking for someone who can weave

181.	*Ma ala teteni seluk bai*	And request once again
182.	*Fo teteni managgiti atis.*	Requesting someone who can weave on a loom.
183.	*Boe ma leo Dulu Balaha olina*	So at the estuary of Dulu Balaha
184.	*Fo Pota Popo delan*	Is Pota Popo's *delas* tree
185.	*Ma Langa Mangaledo le-na*	And at Langa Mangaledo's river
186.	*Fo Solu Oebau nitan*	Is Solu Oebau's *nitas* tree
187.	*Leu te inaka Menge Solu*	There the woman Menge Solu
188.	*Ana ndo selu nai ndia*	She works the shuttle there
189.	*Fetoka Li Pota*	The girl Li Pota
190.	*Ana nggiti ati nai ndia.*	She weaves on the loom there.
191.	*Besaka inaka Kuku Dula*	Now the woman Kuku Dula
192.	*De fetoka Lima Le'u fe futusa neu.*	And the girl Lima Le'u gives her the thread bundle.
193.	*De inaka Menge Solu*	The woman Menge Solu
194.	*Ma fetoka Li Pota, ana tenun.*	And the girl Li Pota, she weaves.
195.	*De ana tenu nan dadi pou*	She weaves it to become a woman's cloth
196.	*Fo lae pou dula selu-kolo*	They call this woman's cloth the *selu-kolo* pattern
197.	*Ma ana tenu nan dadi lafa*	And she weaves it to become a man's cloth
198.	*Fo lae lafa dula tema-nggik*	They call this man's cloth the *tema-nggik* pattern
199.	*Losa faik ia.*	To this day.
200.	*Pou dula selu-kolo la*	Women's cloths with the *selu-kolo* pattern
201.	*Bei lai Dulu Balaha olin*	Are still [found] at the Dulu Balaha's estuary
202.	*Fo bei lai Diu Dulu*	Still at Diu Dulu
203.	*Ma lafa langa tema-nggika la*	And men's cloths with the *tema-nggik* pattern
204.	*[Bei] lai Langa Mangaledo le-na*	Are still [found] at Langa Mangaledo's river
205.	*Fo bei Kana Langa*	Still at Kana Langa
206.	*Fo bei lai Bolo Tena*	Still at Bolo Tena

207.	*Ma bei lai Soti Mori*	And still at Soti Mori
208.	*Bei lai Londa Lusi*	Still at Londa Lusi
209.	*Ma bei lai Batu Bela*	And still at Batu Bela
210.	*Bei lai Tua Nae*	Still at Tua Nae
211.	*Ma bei lai Selu Beba*	And still at Selu Beba
212.	*Bei lai Fai Fua*	Still at Fai Fua
213.	*Ma bei lai Ledo Sou*	And still at Ledo Sou
214.	*Bei lai Oe Manu*	Still at Oe Manu
215.	*Ma bei lai Kunu Iko*	And still at Kunu Iko
216.	*Leo faik ia*	To this day
217.	*Ma leo ledok ia.*	And to this time.
218.	*Pou dula selu-kolo*	The woman's cloths with *selu-kolo* pattern
219.	*Do lafa langa tema-nggikala*	Or the men's cloths with *tema-nggik* pattern
220.	*Bei lai Diu Dulu*	Are still [found] in Diu Dulu
221.	*Ma bei lai Kana Langa*	And are still [found] in Kana Langa
222.	*Fo bei lai Lamak-anan fo losa faika.*	Still [found] in Lamak-anan to this day.

Composition Analysis: Malesi Versions I and II–Old Meno–Seu Ba'i Comparisons

Malesi's second version of *Suti Solo do Bina Bane* consists of 222 lines. If one adds the additional 10 lines with which he began his recitation, the entire chant extends for 232 lines. It is shorter than Meno's composition (299 lines) but longer than either Seu Ba'i's composition (209 lines) or his own first version (164 lines) of this chant. It is composed on the basis of 75 dyadic sets and shares 23 sets with Meno's version, 19 sets with Seu Ba'i's version and 28 sets with the first version of his composition.[4] Although there are a few passages that closely resemble his first version,

---

4 In counting the number of dyadic sets for each composition, ritual names are not included. In Meno's composition with its dyadic genealogies and in Malesi's second recitation with its interwoven succession of ritually named people and places, there are a considerable number of additional dyadic sets.

the composition as a whole is a distinctive chant. As an origin chant, it is in accord with Meno's composition in linking the use of the shells to spinning and dyeing. In this, it is more explicit than Meno's composition, but in the naming of places and of textile patterns, it points to eastern Rote, whereas Meno's composition, though not explicit, suggests an association with western Rote.[5]

Despite the evident difference among these four chants, it is useful to focus, at least initially, on compositional similarities. Perhaps most notable are the opening lines of both of Malesi's versions, which are similar and, in certain formulaic phrases, virtually identical to the passages in Meno's and Seu Ba'i's compositions.

The opening lines of both of Malesi's versions describe the storm that expels the shells—or, more specifically, expels the 'insides' of these shells. The first version consists of four lines; the second has six lines. The first two lines in each passage are identical.

Malesi I

1. *Luli nala liun dale*   A storm arises in the ocean's depths
2. *Ma sangu nala sain dale*   And a cyclone arises in the sea's depths
3. *Bina nama-toko isi*   Bina puts out its insides
4. *Suti nama-edo nggi*   Suti exudes its pods

Malesi II

1. *Luli nala liun dalek*   A storm arises in the ocean's depths
2. *Ma sangu nala sain dalek.*   And a cyclone arises in the sea's depths.
3. *Liun neu na-edo*   The ocean exudes
4. *Ma sain neu na-pode.*   The sea puts forth.
5. *De pode heni Suti aten*   It puts forth Suti's liver
6. *Ma edo heni Bina nggin.*   And it exudes Bina's pods.

Meno and Seu Ba'i rely on a similar phrasing.

---

5   This is a judgement that cannot be made on the basis of Meno's version of *Suti Solo do Bina Bane* alone, but rather in the context of his recitation of the origin of weaving, which constitutes a separate composition.

Meno

56.	*Boe ma sangu nala liun dale*	A storm striking the ocean's depths
57.	*Ma luli nala sain dale.*	And a cyclone striking the sea's depths.
58.	*Boe ma besak ka Suti lama-edo nggi*	Now Suti exudes his pods
59.	*Ma Bina lamatoko-isi*	And Bina puts out his insides

Seu Ba'i

202.	*De luli nala liun dale*	A storm strikes the ocean depths
203.	*Ma sangu nala sain dale*	And a cyclone strikes the sea depths
204.	*Liun dale na-hopo*	The ocean depths are upset
205.	*Ma sain dale na-foki.*	The sea depths are shaken.
206.	*Boe te Suti nama-toko isi*	So Suti expels his insides
207.	*Ma Bina [nama-]edo nggi*	And Bina exudes his pods

In their first lines, all three poets combine the set *luli//sangu* with the set *liun//sain*. Malesi and Seu Ba'i combine *luli* with *liun* and *sangu* with *sain* to create an alliterative formula, whereas Meno does not. The rules of composition allow either possibility.

Interestingly, in his first version, Malesi combines the set *-toko//-edo* with the set *isi//nggi*. This is the same formulaic combination as Meno and Seu Ba'i use. In his second version, however, Malesi uses a different combination of sets: *-edo//-pode* with *ate//nggi*. This combination allows him to use the same verbal set, *-edo//-pode*, to describe the eruption of the sea and expulsion of the shells' insides.

Another similarity in composition across all versions is one that describes the scoop-net used to fish forth Suti Solo do Bina Bane. All compositions refer to this simple apparatus, with the same recognisable formula, as 'a scoop-net with iron-weighted insides'//'a fishnet with gold-weighted belly' (*seko matei besi//ndai mahamu lilok*).

Malesi I

29.	*Ana neni neu seko*	She makes them into a scoop-net
30.	*Fo seko matei besi*	A scoop-net with iron-weighted insides
31.	*Ma tale na neu ndai*	And fashions them into a fishnet
32.	*Fo ndai mahamu lilok*	A fishnet with a gold-weighted belly

Malesi II

11.	*Tenga na ndai tasina*	She takes a fishnet for the sea
12.	*Ndai mahamu lilok*	A fishnet with a gold-weighted belly
13.	*Ma nggao na seko metina*	And she picks up a scoop-net for the tide
14.	*Seko matei besik*	A scoop-net with iron-weighted insides

Meno

87.	*De ala teli kokolo ndai*	They string and wind a fishnet
88.	*De ndai mahamu lilok.*	A fishnet with a gold-weighted belly.
89.	*Ma ala ane seko, bui seko*	They braid a scoop-net, twine a scoop-net
90.	*De seko matei besik.*	A scoop-net with iron-weighted insides.

Seu Ba'i

9.	*Ala teli kokolo ndai*	They string and wind a fishnet
10.	*Ma ala ane balu-bui seko la*	And they braid and twine scoop-nets
11.	*Seko ma-tei besik*	A scoop-net with iron-weighted insides
12.	*Ma ndai ma-hamu lilok.*	And a fishnet with a gold-weighted belly.

Compositional Comparison: Malesi I – Malesi II

The most noticeable differences between Malesi's two versions are in the way in which the dialogue directives to the shells are reworked. Malesi's first version contains five distinct proposals directing the shells to: 1) house post//cross beam, 2) syrup vat//rice basket, 3) boundary tree//border stone, 4) *kumea* grass//*kuku* shrub, and 5) forest cuckoo//river watercock. The fifth proposal directs the shells to follow the cuckoo and watercock through the forest and along the river to 'the estuary's edge and river's bank' and then out to sea.

Malesi's second version retains the rice basket//syrup vat directive but not the boundary tree//border stone or the *kumea* grass//*kuku* shrub directives. Instead, in his second version, Malesi introduces a new directive to go with the trees' shade//lontar palms' shadow—a directive also used by Meno in his chant. Malesi also recomposes the long directive in his first version to follow the forest cuckoo and river watercock into two separate directives: first to the cuckoo//watercock and then to the river bank//estuary's edge. In his second version, Malesi's four directives are the following:

49.	*'Meu mo neka hade*	'Go with the rice basket
50.	*Ma meu mo bou tuana.'*	And go with the lontar syrup vat.'
63.	*'Mu mo doa-lasi*	'Go with the forest cuckoo
64.	*Ma mo koloba'o le.'*	And with the river woodcock.'
79.	*'Mu mo mafo ai'*	'Go with the trees' shade
80.	*Ma mu mo sa'o tua.'*	And go with the lontar palms' shadow.'
97.	*'Ah, mu oli titian*	'Ah, go along the estuary's edge
98.	*Ma mu le tatain*	And go along the river's bank

Comparison of Malesi's composition of the directives to rice basket// syrup vat in the two versions is particularly instructive. The eight lines of these two compositions are virtually identical except for the use of two particular dyadic sets. The two compositions are as follows:

Malesi I

73.	*'Mu no bou tua*	'Go with the lontar syrup vat
74.	*Ma mu mo neka hade.'*	And go with the rice basket.'
75.	*Bina Bane kokolak*	Bina Bane speaks
76.	*Ma Suti Solo dede'ak ma nae:*	And Suti Solo replies and says:
77.	*'Malole la so*	'That would be good
78.	*Ma mandak kala so.*	And that would be proper.
79.	*Bou tua na tono*[6]	[But if] the syrup vat is overturned
80.	*Ma neka hade lulunu*	And the rice basket is rolled up
81.	*Na au asalai o se*	Then with whom will I recline
82.	*Ma au angatu o se?'*	And with whom will I sit?'

Malesi II

| 49. | *'Meu mo neka hade* | 'Go with the rice basket |
| 50. | *Ma meu mo bou tuana.'* | And go with the lontar syrup vat.' |

---

6   It is worth noting that here one would expect the semi-reduplicated form *totono* in order to conform with the semi-reduplicated *lulunu*. Whether this is simply a minor mistake in performance or, possibly, a mistake in the transcription of Malesi's words cannot be determined.

51.	*Boe ma Suti Solo nafada*	Then Suti Solo talks
52.	*Ma Bina Bane kokolak ma nae:*	And Bina Bane speaks and says:
53.	*'Ah, malole la so*	'Ah, that would be good
54.	*Ma mandak kala so*	And that would be proper
55.	*[Te] bou tua la heok*	But if the lontar syrup vats turn
56.	*Ma neka hade la keko*	And if the rice baskets shift
57.	*Na au asalai o se*	Then with whom shall I recline
58.	*Ma au angatu o se?'*	And with whom shall I sit?'

Where in lines 75–76, Malesi uses the set *kokolak//dede'ak* ('to speak'//'to reply'), in lines 51–52 of his second version, he uses an alternative set, *kokolak//na-fada* ('to speak'//'to talk').

Similarly, but more unusually, where in lines 79–80, Malesi uses the common set *tono//lunu* ('to overturn'//'to roll up'), whereas in lines 55–56 he uses the set *heok//keko* ('to turn aside'//'to shift').

Both Meno and Seu Ba'i use the formulaic set *tono//lunu* in their compositions, as does Malesi in his first version.

Meno

| 165. | *Fo bou lo totonon* | So that the vat must be overturned |
| 166. | *Ma soka no lulunun* | And the sack must be rolled up |

Seu Ba'i

| 78. | *Fo soka lo lulunun* | So that the sacks must be rolled up |
| 80. | *Fo bou lo totonon* | So that the vats must be overturned |

Malesi's use of *heok//keko* is highly idiosyncratic. The verb *keko* generally occurs in two sets, either with *lali* (*keko//lali*), when describing the transfer of a bride after marriage, or with *hiluk*, in reference to the shifting of shadows, as in the directive regarding the lontar palms' shadow//trees' shade.

Meno, for example, uses the set *keko//hiluk*:

| 186. | *Te leo mafo ai la hiluk* | But if the trees' shade recedes |
| 187. | *Ma sa'o tua la keko* | And the lontars' shadow shifts |

5. VERSION IV FROM THE DOMAIN OF TERMANU

By contrast, Malesi Version II uses the set *heok//hiluk*:

| 85. | *Mafo ai la heok* | [If] the trees' shade turns aside |
| 86. | *Ma sa'o ai la hiluk* | And the lontar palms' shadow recedes |

In all of the chants I have gathered from Termanu, this is the only occurrence of *keko//heok* as a set. The use of this set has to be considered idiosyncratic and not part of recognisable formulaic convention.

Malesi's use in both versions of the set *nasa-lai//na-ngatu* ('to recline'//'to sit') in the shells' plaintive refrain 'with whom shall I recline//with whom shall I sit' is distinctive of his composition but the use of this set is not uncommon.

Both Meno and Seu Ba'i use the plaintive query about speaking in their compositions. Thus in Meno, the shells utter this refrain:

150.	*'Na Bina, au o se*	'Then I, Bina, with whom will I be
151.	*Ma Suti, au o se*	And I, Suti, with whom will I be
152.	*Fo au kokolak o se*	With whom will I talk
153.	*Ma au dede'ak o se?'*	And with whom will I speak?'

By contrast, Malesi Version II uses a refrain that evokes a sense of resting in a secure location:

39.	*'De au Suti, au o se*	'Then I, Suti, with whom will I be
40.	*Fo asalai o se*	On whom will I recline
41.	*Ma au Bina, au o se*	And I, Bina, with whom will I be
42.	*Fo au angatu'u o se?'*	With whom will I sit?'

In cultural terms, reclining and sitting are closely linked; reclining, however, is superior to sitting. In a traditional house, the head of the household is entitled to recline on a resting platform located at the eastern end of the house. This honour may also be accorded to an esteemed guest, whereas most guests will sit on other raised platforms arrayed under the extended roof of the house. Standing is reserved for those outside or for those who serve within the house.

MASTER POETS, RITUAL MASTERS

The Second Half of Malesi's Composition: An Origin Chant

Malesi's second version of *Suti Solo do Bina Bane* is, in effect, two chants. The first 110 lines are a mortuary chant conceived as a metaphoric journey of two shells through a variety of symbolic locations from the sea and back to the sea; the second 115 lines are an origin chant that recounts the transformation of these same two shells—the nautilus shell, Suti, into a container for dyes and the bailer shell, Bina, into a base on which to spin cotton. Although more explicit on the transformation of the shells than Meno's origin chant, much of the second half of Malesi's composition is elusive. It is a text that requires some exegesis to be deciphered.

The second half begins with the storm at sea and the expulsion of the shells, as do the first eight lines with which Malesi began his composition before starting over again. Malesi then introduces new chant characters. Instead of Kafi Dulu//Kule Langa, with his field of corn and millet, and the woman (presumably his wife) Sama Dai//Kuku Nou, in the first half, Malesi invokes Manupui Peda//Kokolo Dulu with his field of indigo and cotton and his wife, Pasa Paku//Finga Fiti. Manupui Peda//Kokolo Dulu is the same chant character identified in Meno's chant, but where Meno speaks of Nggiti Seti//Pedu Hange, Malesi has Pasa Paku//Finga Fiti. It is Pasa Paku//Finga Fiti who scoops Suti Solo//Bina Bane from the sea.

What follows is a narrative of the transformation of the two shells that runs from line 147 to line 163. These lines are, however, for the most part not in strict parallelism. They have the appearance of parallelism by the use of a number of canonical dyadic sets—*feto//ina* ('girl'//'woman'), *nggeo//pila* ('black'//'red') and the chant character Kuku Dula//Lima Le'u—but many seeming pairs in these lines do not follow the canon. Thus, for example, in line 139, *dipo ine* ('to turn the spinning stick on its base') should pair with *ifa lolek* ('to cradle the winding rack') (see Meno: lines 255–57); *kolu* ('to pick or pluck') should pair with *ketu* ('to break, pluck or snap').

5. VERSION IV FROM THE DOMAIN OF TERMANU

The canonical format resumes with line 163 and continues, with a few orphan lines, to the end of the composition.[7] These lines describe a search for a woman who can weave the cloth that has been dyed by Kuku Dula// Lima Le'u. At first sight, they offer a confusing succession of both personal chant character names and specific place names. The place names, all in eastern Rote, form an ordered succession of identifiable locations—an interpretable topogeny of particular places.[8]

The whole of Rote is blanketed in ritual names. Some of these names are specific and only locally known; others are more generally known and are taken to represent the various domains and prominent landmarks on the island. Knowledge of these names is essential for all poets, but some poets, like Malesi, are noted for the extensive knowledge of these names and the frequent insertion of topogenies in their recitations.

In this recitation, Malesi identifies the initial area in which the search for a woman to weave begins:

164.	*De ala losa Dulu Balaha oli-na*	They go to the estuary of Dulu Balaha
165.	*Fo losa Diu Dulu*	All the way to Diu Dulu
166.	*Ma Langa Mangaledo le-na*	And to the river of Langa Mangaledo
167.	*Fo losa Kana Langa.*	All the way to Kana Langa.

Dulu Balaha//Langa Mangaledo refers to eastern Rote.[9] Diu Dulu// Kana Langa refers to the domain of Diu located to the east of Termanu. Both names are formed around the same set, *dulu//langa*, which links the idea of 'east' (*dulu*) with the 'head' (*langa*) of the island. The island extends physically in an east–west direction, so that by a similar directional

---

7   Even though line 156 is an 'orphan' line ('So the woman Lima Le'u'), its pair ('And the girl Kuku Dula') is implied by the use of these same lines just a few lines earlier. (Another 'orphan' line occurs at line 174.)
8   I have coined the word 'topogeny' to refer to the recitation of an ordered succession of place names, the equivalent to a genealogy, which consists of the recitation of an ordered succession of personal names. See Fox (1997b). In this article, as an example of a topogeny, I examine an origin chant by Malesi that recounts the origin of rice and millet and includes a topogeny of 32 distinct places that moves in a cycle around the island of Rote from the ritual site Tena Lai//Mae Oe, in eastern Rote, which is mentioned in virtually all versions of *Suti Solo do Bina Bane*, back to this same ritual site.
9   Translated literally, *Dulu Balaha//Langa Mangaledo* means 'East Tomorrow//Head Dawning'. Another name for eastern Rote is Timu Dulu ma Sepe Langa, which, translated, literally would be 'Eastern East//Brightening Head'. See Fox (1973: 356–64) for a further discussion of the Rotenese orientation system and its ritual significance.

logic the 'west' (*muli*) is linked with the 'tail' (*iko*) of the island. Rote is often spoken of as if it were a living creature—generally associated with the body of a crocodile floating in the sea. Thus, Rote's southern coast (*kona*) is synonymous with 'right' (*kona*) and its northern coast (*ki*) is synonymous with 'left' (*ki*). Ritual names often reflect this quadripartite orientation/directional system.

The first woman to be contacted, Adu Pinga//Leo Lapa, at the site Lata Nae//Pinga Dai, apparently within the domain of Diu, states that she cannot weave, so Kuku Dulu//Lima Le'u go to find the woman Menge Solu//Li Pota, the daughter of Solu Oebau//Pota Popo. This woman is able to weave and she creates a special design pattern, *selu-kolo*, on the woman's cloth that she weaves and another design pattern, *tema-nggi*, on the man's cloth she weaves.[10] This pattern, Malesi asserts, is still found in the domain of Diu and in other domains in eastern Rote. This assertion is then reiterated in a short topogeny that recalls the names of the different domains of eastern Rote:

1.	*Bolo Tena//Soti Mori*	Landu
2.	*Londa Lusi//Batu Bela*	Ringgou
3.	*Tua Nae//Selu Beba*	Ringgou
4.	*Fai Fua//Ledo Sou*	Oepao
5.	*Oe Manu//Kunu Iko?*	Bilba?
6.	*Diu Dulu//Kana Langa*	Diu

As a poet, Pe'u Malesi demonstrates his standing as a 'man of knowledge' through recitations that explicitly embrace the island of Rote as a whole rather than simply the domain of Termanu.

---

10 Neither *tema-nggi* nor *selu-kolo* is a textile pattern in Termanu, but since both *tema* and *kolo* occur in the names of various birds, there would appear to be some association of these patterns with bird-like motifs.

6
Suti Solo do Bina Bane: Version V from the Domain of Termanu

Introduction

In 1988 I made a brief visit to Rote. I had been given a cabin on board the *Asmara Lomba-Lomba*, an Indonesian-owned tourist vessel that visited the islands between Bali and Kupang, in exchange for providing lectures on the culture of eastern Indonesia. The *Asmara Lomba-Lomba* included Rote on its tour and put into the port town of Ba'a for a short stay. As it happened, at the time, there were several men from Termanu in Ba'a who had come to buy supplies. Among them was the former *Wakil Manek* of Termanu, Frans Biredoko, whom I had known since 1965.

The moment we were together, the *Wakil* began to recount for me the latest news from Termanu. One of the first things he had to tell me was that Eli Pellondou, whom we all knew as Seu Ba'i, had died. Termanu, we agreed, had lost one of its great poets but we had hardly begun to speak about Seu Ba'i when the *Wakil* introduced me to someone whom I did not know among the group, a cousin of Seu Ba'i, Mikael Pellondou. The *Wakil* assured me that Mikael was also a fine poet and would continue the traditions of his cousin.

The Rotenese place great stress on continuity. They express this in various ways, often in short poems that emphasise a continuation from generation to generation. A short poem, given to me by Old Meno, describes this continuity from father to son by describing the way a father's mortuary monument—a tree ringed by stones—becomes a son's place to rest.

1.	*Nggongo Ingu Lai lalo*	Nggongo of the Highland dies
2.	*Ma Lima Le Dale sapu*	And Lima of the Riverbed perishes
3.	*De lalo ela Latu Nggongo*	He dies leaving Latu Nggongo
4.	*Ma sapu ela Engga Lima.*	And perishes leaving Engga Lima.
5.	*Boe te ela batu nangatun*	But he leaves a stone to sit on
6.	*Ma ela ai nasalain.*	And leaves a tree to recline upon.
7.	*De koluk Nggongo Ingu Lai*	Plucked is Nggongo from the Highland
8.	*Te Latu Nggongo nangatu*	But now Latu Nggongo sits
9.	*Ma haik Lima Le Dale*	And grasped is Lima from the Riverbed
10.	*Te Engga Lima nasalai.*	But now Engga Lima reclines.
11.	*Fo lae Nggongo tutuu batun*	They say: Nggongo's sitting stone
12.	*Na tao ela Latu Nggongo*	Was made for Latu Nggongo
13.	*Ma Lima lalai ain*	And Lima's resting tree
14.	*Na peda ela Engga Lima.*	Was placed for Engga Lima.

Another short poem, also from Meno, describes this continuity figuratively in a botanic idiom:

1.	*Tefu ma-nggona lilok*	The sugar cane has sheaths of gold
2.	*Ma huni ma-lapa losik.*	And the banana has blossoms of copper.
3.	*Tefu olu heni nggonan*	The sugar cane sheds its sheath
4.	*Ma huni kono heni lapan.*	And the banana drops its blossoms.
5.	*Te hu bei ela tefu okan*	Still leaving but the sugar cane's root
6.	*Ma huni hun bai.*	And the banana's trunk too.
7.	*De dei tefu na nggona seluk*	So that the sugar cane sheathes again
8.	*Fo na nggona lilo seluk*	The sheaths are gold again
9.	*Ma dei huni na lapa seluk*	And the banana blossoms again
10.	*Fo na lapa losi seluk.*	The blossoms are copper again.

In response to the *Wakil*'s praise of his abilities, Mikael agreed to recite something for me. I happened to have a small cassette recorder with me and I asked Mikael to recite *Suti Solo do Bina Bane*—a chant that I told him I had already recorded from Seu Ba'i. An opportunity had presented itself unexpectedly and Mikael was keen to demonstrate his poetic skills. The following is Mikael Pellondou's version of *Suti Solo do Bina Bane*.

Prefatory Lines

Mikael's recitation follows the format of a mortuary chant and its composition is similar to other such versions. Many of the features of his narrative are, however, distinctive, indeed idiosyncratic. Whereas most poets when they recite tend to press forward with their narrative as a revelation, in this recitation (and in others I have recorded) Mikael has a more repetitive style, often repeating lines in similar, sometimes almost identical, form.

The recitation begins with a few prefatory lines that situate Suti Solo and Bina Bane as creatures from sea:

1.	*Sona leo iak lae:*	Like this they say:
2.	*Bina nai liun*	Bina in the ocean
3.	*Ma Suti nai sain dei*	And Suti in the sea
4.	*O tao Bina Bane le'e*	What do you do with Bina Bane
5.	*Ma o tao Suti Solo le'e*	And what do you do with Suti Solo
6.	*Fo o masena Suti Solo*	That you may be a companion to Suti Solo
7.	*Ma o matiak Bina Bane?*	And that you may be a friend to Bina Bane?
8.	*Te Bina nai liun*	For Bina is in the ocean
9.	*Ma Suti nai sain.*	And Suti is in the sea.

The Introduction of the Chief Chant Character

The chief chant character in this version—the woman who eventually gathers the shells and engages in dialogue with them—is identified as Lole Holu//Fua Bafo (or Fua Bafa). This is a slightly different chant name from that used by Meno and Seu Ba'i in their recitations: Lole Holu//Lua Bafa. The recitation begins with Lole Holu//Fua Bafo tending her fields, which are ready for harvest. There is no explicit mention of an origin or harvest ceremony, but this is implied in the need to search for the appropriate ritual fish.

10.	*Boe te inaka Fua Bafo*	So the woman Fua Bafo
11.	*Ma fetoka Lole Holu*	And the girl Lole Holu
12.	*Na-nea pelak*	Cares for maize
13.	*Ma na-nea betek*	And cares for millet
14.	*De ana oko boluk tunga seli*	She shouts on one side
15.	*Ma ana do-se'ek tunga seli*	And she screams at one side
16.	*Ma bafi na'a tunga seli*	And the pig eats on one side
17.	*Ma kode ketu tunga seli.*	And the monkey plucks at one side.
18.	*Boe ma ana dodo neu dalen*	So she thinks within herself
19.	*Ma ana dudu'a neu teina,*	And she ponders within her insides,
20.	*Nai du'a taon leo be*	Thinking what to do
21.	*Fo kode boso na'a pelak*	So the monkey does not eat the maize
22.	*Ma bafi boso na'a pelak [betek].*	And the pig does not eat the maize [millet].
23.	*Ah, ledo lama-tetetun*	The sun is at its height
24.	*Ma fai lama-hahanan*	And the day is at its hottest
25.	*Boe ma ana nggao na ndai tasin na*	She takes up her sea fishnet
26.	*Ma tenga na seko metin*	And picks up her tidal scoop-net
27.	*Fo seko matei besik*	The scoop-net with iron-weighted insides
28.	*Fo ndai mahamu lilok*	The fishnet with gold-weighted belly
29.	*Ndae ndai neu alun*	Hangs the fishnet over her shoulder
30.	*[Ma seko matei besi-na]*	[And the scoop-net with iron-weighted insides]
31.	*Su'u seko neu langan.*	Balances the scoop-net on her head.

6. VERSION V FROM THE DOMAIN OF TERMANU

The Search for the Ritual Fish

In other recitations of *Suti Solo do Bina Bane*, the search for the ritual fish is said to occur at a sacred site known as Mae Oe//Tena Lai at the eastern end of Rote. By contrast, Mikael explicitly locates the search for these fish along the coast of Termanu at Fopo Sandika//Tefi Noe Mina, not far, in fact, from where both he and his cousin Seu Ba'i lived at Namodale.

32.	*De ana lipa naka nanae*	She looks around carefully
33.	*Ma ana lelu nala mumula.*	And she glances intently.
34.	*De tasi Fopo Sandika*	The sea at Fopo Sandika
35.	*Ma meti Tefi Noe Mina*	And the tide at Tefi Noe Mina
36.	*Tasi la huka papa*	The sea shows its shallows
37.	*Ma meti la si'unu.*	And the tide begins to ebb.
38.	*Boe ma neu seko sisi'u engga*	She goes to scoop, lifting *engga* seaweed
39.	*Ma neu ndai huhuka batu,*	And goes to fish, overturning rocks,
40.	*Neu seko sanga Dusu La'e*	Goes to scoop in search of a Dusu La'e[1]
41.	*Ma neu ndai sanga Tio Holu*	And goes to fish in search of a Tio Holu
42.	*Fo Dusu la la'e ao*	For Dusu fish that support one another
43.	*Ma Tio la holu ao.*	The Tio fish that embrace one another.
44.	*Fo ana seko nala lifu esa*	So she scoops in one pool
45.	*Ma ndai nala lek dua na*	And fishes in two waterholes
46.	*Ta ndai nala Tio*	But does not fish up a Tio fish
47.	*Ma ta seko nala Dusu.*	And does not scoop up a Dusu fish.
48.	*De ana ndai ndano heni Dusu*	She fishes and throws for a Dusu
49.	*Ma seko toko heni Tio.*	And she scoops and casts for a Tio.
50.	*De ana ndai nala lifu dua*	She fishes in two pools
51.	*Ma seko nala lek telu na*	And she scoops in three waterholes
52.	*Bina nala lek dua*	Bina is in the two waterholes
53.	*Ma Suti nala lek telu.*	And Suti is in the three waterholes.
54.	*De ana ndai ndano heni Bina*	She fishes and throws away Bina

---

1 Implied in the following lines 41–42 and again in lines 57–58 is an interpretative play on words. The term *la'e* in the ritual name Dusu La'e is here interpreted as the verb *la'e* ('to support, to care for'), and the term *holu* in the ritual name Tio Holu is interpreted as the verb 'to embrace'—hence the lines about the Dusu and the Tio loving and embracing one another.

55.	*Seko toko heni Suti,*	Scoops and casts away Suti,
56.	*Ana seko sanga Dusu La'e*	She scoops, seeking a Dusu La'e
57.	*Ma ana seko sanga Tio Holu dei*	And she scoops, seeking only a Tio Holu
58.	*Fo ela Tio la holu ao*	So that the Tio may embrace one another
59.	*Ma Dusu la la'e ao.*	And the Dusu may support one another.

The Initial Dialogue with the Shells

In this version, the initial response by Suti Solo//Bina Bane to Fua Bafo//Lole Holu is of interest, particularly because the opening lines of this chant begin with the problem of pigs and monkeys stealing grain from the ripening fields. The shells propose that they be attached to a rock and tree and be used as clappers whose sound will drive away the pigs and monkeys. This is significant in terms of the wider traditions of Rote. Thus, according to origin versions of this chant from other domains, such as the domain of Ringgou, the shells are not made into objects for dyeing and spinning, but instead are used as clappers to drive away animals that disturb the fields.

60.	*Boe ma besaka ana a'e dasi na*	Now he [Suti] lifts her words
61.	*Ma ana lole hala na neu ma nae:*	And he [Bina] raises her voice and says:
62.	*'Bo senango nei*	'Oh, dear companion
63.	*Do bo tiango nou*	Or oh, dear friend
64.	*O ma hala*	You may say
65.	*Do o ma dasi mae:*	Or you give voice, saying:
66.	*"Kode ketu betek*	"The monkey plucks the millet
67.	*Ma bafi na'a pelak.*	And the pig eats the maize.
68.	*De ketu bei tolesi*	Plucking yet still some remains
69.	*Ma na'a bei ela."*	And eating yet still something is left."
70.	*Tehu mafa ndendelek*	So remember, do remember
71.	*Ma masa nenedak*	And recall, do recall
72.	*Teu te isa au [nai] ai*	Go tie me to the wood
73.	*Ma pa'a au nai batu*	And fasten me to the stone

74.	*Fo au bengo bengo u ai*	That I may shake and shake with the wood
75.	*Ma toto toto o batu*	And knock and knock on the rock
76.	*Fo daenga kode ana tolo mu*	So that the monkey will run
77.	*Ma bafi ana nalai*	And the pig will flee
78.	*Lo nula dale neu*	Deep into the woods
79.	*Ma lo ai lai neu*	And high into the trees
80.	*Fo kode boso ketu betek*	So that the monkey does not pluck the millet
81.	*Ma bafi bo'o na'a pelak.'*	And the pig does not eat the maize.'
82.	*De dasi leo la hala*	The words just like the voice
83.	*Ma deta leo dasi ma*	And just like the words
84.	*De ana oku-boluk*	She shouts
85.	*Ma ana do-se'ek dei*	And she screams
86.	*Bafi ta na'a pelak*	The pig does not eat the maize
87.	*Ma kode ta ketu betek.*	And the monkey does not pluck the millet.
88.	*De sama leo hala*	Just like the voice
89.	*Ma deta dasi*	And like the words
90.	*Ma ana oku-boluk*	And she shouts
91.	*Ma ana do-se'ek.*	And she screams.
92.	*De kode ta ketu betek*	The monkey does not pluck the millet
93.	*Ma bafi ta na'a pelak.*	And the pig does not eat the maize.
94.	*De pela lai la lama-tasa*	The corn is ripe in the field
95.	*Ma betekala dio hu'u*	And the millet has ripened grains
96.	*Ma hade la modo peda*	And the rice is green-tipped
97.	*De ala dio hu'u kokolun*	They are ripe with grain to be harvested
98.	*Ma ala modo peda keketun.*	And they are green-tipped to be plucked.
99.	*De Bina Bane o fali uma*	Bina Bane, return to your home
100.	*Ma Suti Solo tulek lon.*	And Suti Solo, turn back to your house.

MASTER POETS, RITUAL MASTERS

The Directives to the Shells

The number of directives that Mikael includes in this composition is limited compared with that in other versions. Some are similar to those of other versions but at least one is specific to his recitation.

101.	*Boe ma kokolak no inaka Lole Holu*	So he speaks to the woman Lole Holu
102.	*Ma dede'ak no fetoka Fua Bafo, nae:*	And he talks to the girl Fua Bafo, saying:
103.	*'Au u'u o se sama leo o bai?'*	'With whom—with the likes of you—can I go?'
104.	*Boe ma nae:*	So she says:
105.	*'Mu mo pila kumea letek*	'Go with the red *kumea* grass on the hill
106.	*Ma mu mo nggeo kuku telas.'*	And go with the black *kuku* shrub in the underbrush.'
107.	*'Boe ma malole lai ndia*	'Such things would be good
108.	*Ma mandak lai ndia,*	And such things would be proper,
109.	*Te pila kumea letek*	But the red *kumea* grass on the hill
110.	*Ma nggeo kuku telas-a,*	And the black *kuku* shrub in the underbrush,
111.	*Timu lama tua dulu*	[When] the east monsoon grows great in the east
112.	*Do fak lama nalu langa,*	And the west monsoon lengthens at the head,
113.	*De lama dilu neu kalen*	Bends down its heavy top
114.	*Ma lama sesu neu bu'un*	And breaks its heavy joints
115.	*De au kokolak o se*	Then with whom will I speak
116.	*Ma au dede'ak o se*	And with whom will I talk
117.	*Fo sama leo Lole Holu*	[With someone] just like Lole Holu
118.	*Ma sama leo Fua Bafo?'*	And exactly like Fua Bafo?'
119.	*Boe ma nae:*	So she says:
120.	*'Mu mo titi'i letek*	'Go with the *titi'i* shrub on the hill
121.	*Ma mu mo kai-hule mok.'*	And go with *kai-hule* bush of the field.'
122.	*Boe ma nae:*	So he says:
123.	*'Malole lai ndia*	'Such would be good

6. VERSION V FROM THE DOMAIN OF TERMANU

124.	*Ma mandak lai ndia*	And such would be proper
125.	*Lafada lae:*	But they say:
126.	*"Titi'i letek*	"The *titi'i* shrub on the hill
127.	*Ma kai-hule mok*	And the *kai-hule* bush of the field
128.	*Ndia mesakana nai mok esa*	It is all alone in the field
129.	*Ma ndia mesakana nai letek esa,"*	And it is all alone on the hill,"
130.	*De au dede'ak o se*	So with whom will I speak
131.	*Ma au kokolak o se*	And with whom will I talk
132.	*Fo sama leo Lole Holu*	[Someone] like Lole Holu
133.	*Deta leo Fua Bafo?'*	And just like Fua Bafo?'
134.	*Boe ma nae:*	So she says:
135.	*'Te o mu mo se bai*	'But with whom will you go
136.	*Ma sama leo au bai?'*	And who is like me?'
137.	*Boe ma nae:*	But she says:
138.	*'Nah, mu mo a dini ana nau.'*	'Nah, go with the fine *dini* grass.'
139.	*Boe ma nae:*	So he says:
140.	*'Au u o dini ana nau*	'If I go with the fine *dini* grass
141.	*O sama leo kumea letek*	It is just like going with the *kumea* grass on the hill
142.	*Ma kuku telas,*	And with the *kuku* shrub in the underbrush,
143.	*De fak lama nalu langa*	[When] the west monsoon lengthens at the head
144.	*Ma timu lama tua dulu na*	And the east monsoon grows great in the east
145.	*De lama dilu neu bu'un*	It bends at its heavy joints
146.	*Ma lama sesu neu kalen,*	And it breaks at its heavy head,
147.	*Nah, au kokolak o se*	Then with whom will I speak
148.	*Ma au dede'ak o se*	And with whom will I talk
149.	*Fo sama leo o boe*	[With someone] just like you, too
150.	*Ma deta leo o boe.'*	And exactly like you, too.'

MASTER POETS, RITUAL MASTERS

The Directive to Return to the Sea

The final directive to the shells is simply to return to the sea, specifically to the women Po'o Pau Ai//Latu Kai Do. There is no mention of following the birds through the forest and along the river to the resounding sea.

151.	*Boe ma inaka Fua Bafo*	So the woman Fua Bafo
152.	*Ma fetoka Lole Holu nae:*	And the girl Lole Holu says:
153.	*'Bo senango nou*	'Oh dear friend
154.	*Ma bo tiango nou*	And oh dear companion
155.	*Te o mu mo se bai?*	But with whom will you go?
156.	*Au du'a dodo doak*	I ponder on it with difficulty
157.	*Ma afi ndanda doak,*	And I think on it with difficulty,
158.	*Mo se fo o dede'ak mon*	With whom for you to talk
159.	*Sama leo au bai.'*	With someone like myself.'
160.	*Boe ma nae:*	So she says:
161.	*'Mu mo inak Po'o Pau Ai*	'Go with the woman Po'o Pau Ai
162.	*Ma mu mo fetok Latu Kai Do.*	And go with the girl Latu Kai Do.
163.	*Inak Po'o Pau Ai*	The woman Po'o Pau Ai
164.	*Ma fetok Latu Kai Do*	And the girl Latu Kai Do
165.	*Nai le bibifa*	At the river's lip
166.	*Ma nai oli tatain.'*	And at the estuary's edge.'
167.	*Boe ma ana lole halan*	So he lifts his words
168.	*Ma ana a'e dasi na ma nae:*	And he raises his voice and says:
169.	*'Bo Fua Bafo o*	'Oh, dear Fua Bafo
170.	*Do bo Lole Holu o*	Or oh dear Lole Holu
171.	*Malole ndia*	This is good
172.	*Ma mandak ndia*	And this is proper
173.	*De fo au bonu boa*	For me to bob like *boa* wood
174.	*Ma au ele piko*	And me to float like *piko* wood
175.	*Fo fali u'ung lo liun*	For me to return to the sea
176.	*Ma tulek u'ung leo sain.'*	And to turn back to the ocean.'
177.	*De leo halan ma leo dasin*	According to his word and voice
178.	*Tasi mai de nala oli dale*	The sea comes into the estuary
179.	*Boe ma ana bonu boa*	Then he floats like *boa* wood
180.	*Ma ana ele piko.*	And he bobs like *piko* wood.

6. VERSION V FROM THE DOMAIN OF TERMANU

The Brief Return to the Sea

In this version, the return to the sea leads to the humiliation of the shells as they try to dance at a celebration of origin. This leads to their return to Rote.

181.	*De fali neu leo sain*	He returns to the sea
182.	*Ma fali neu leo liun.*	And returns to the ocean.
183.	*Neu de ana tongo lolo*	He goes and he meets
184.	*De neu nda lilima,*	He goes and he encounters,
185.	*Neu, te ala foti hus-ala*	He goes, but they are celebrating their origin feast
186.	*Ma be'e Lipa*	And they are performing their *Lipa* celebration
187.	*Leme liun ma leme sain*	In the oceans and in the sea
188.	*Fo neme Nggusi Buin do Pinga Dale.*	From Nggusi Bui or Pinga Dale.
189.	*Neu te inak liu-kala*	He goes but the women of the ocean
190.	*Ma feto sai-kala*	And the girls of the sea
191.	*Ala pela ma ala longe*	They dance and they turn
192.	*Ala pela ngganggafu aon*	They dance, swaying their bodies
193.	*Ma ala leno sosodo aon*	And they spin, shuffling their bodies [feet]
194.	*De dae sopukala ta lapu*	Fine dust does not fly
195.	*[Ma batu lutu la ta pela]*	[And tiny stones do not dance]
196.	*Boe ma Bina Bane do Suti Solo*	Bina Bane and Suti Solo
197.	*Ala pela ngganggafu aon*	They dance, swaying their bodies
198.	*Ma leno sosodo aon.*	And they spin, shuffling their feet.
199.	*Besaka dae sopu-kala lapu*	Now the dust flies
200.	*Ma batu lutu la pela.*	And the small stones spin.
201.	*Boe ma ina liu-kala*	So the women of the ocean
202.	*Ma feto sai-kala*	And the girls of the sea
203.	*Ala kokola ma ala dede'ak*	They speak and they converse
204.	*'Wah, te beuk Bina Bane bai*	'Wah, something new for Bina Bane
205.	*Ma fe'ek Suti Solo boe dei.'*	And something strange for Suti Solo.'

The Return to Rote

The final trajectory of the shells is to the domain of Delha, at the southwestern corner of Rote, identified by its ritual name, Dela Muli//Ana Iko ('Dela in the West'//'Ana at the Tail'). It is at the far western end of the island that they obtain the companions they seek.

Mikael gives no explanation for the shells' return nor does he provide any indication of the relationship of Suti Solo do Bina Bane to the chant character Ka Lau Ao//Tena Hu Dulu, who becomes companion to the shells.

206.	*Bina lama toko isi*	Bina throws forth his insides
207.	*Ma Suti lama edo nggi.*	And Suti puts forth his pods.
208.	*Boe ma ala bi do mae*	They feel fear or shame
209.	*Boe ma ala tolu mu leo sain*	They flee into the sea
210.	*Ma lalai leo liun*	And they rush into the ocean
211.	*De ana leo Dela Muli neu*	He goes to Dela Muli [Dela in the West]
212.	*De ana leo Ana Iko neu.*	He goes to Ana Iko [Ana at the Tail].
213.	*Boe ma ana hapu senan*	He has a friend
214.	*Ma hapu tian*	And has a companion
215.	*Nade Ka Lau Ao ma Tena Hu Dulu*	Named Ka Lau Ao and Tena Hu Dulu
216.	*Boe ma nae:*	So he says:
217.	*'Bo senango nou*	'Oh dear friend
218.	*Ma bo tiango nou*	And oh dear companion
219.	*Ita dua tia mai ia*	Let us two come here as friends
220.	*Do sena mai ia.'*	And come here as companions.'
221.	*Boe ma nae:*	So she says:
222.	*'Leo meme ia leon*	'Stay here then
223.	*Do tapa-lasa teme ia leon.'*	Or let us stay here then.'
224.	*De ana leo neme Dela Muli*	He goes to stay at Dela Muli
225.	*Ma napalasa neme Ana Iko.*	And remains at Ana Iko.

Composition Analysis: Meno and Seu Ba'i Comparisons

Mikael Pellondou's *Suti Solo do Bina Bane* is based on a repertoire of 75 dyadic sets. Twenty-eight of these 75 sets are shared with Meno's composition and 26 sets are shared with Malesi's first version of *Suti Solo do Bina Bane*. By contrast, 38 of these sets (51 per cent) are shared with his cousin Seu Ba'i's composition. Because Mikael tends to repeat passages in his composition, it is actually longer—225 lines compared with 209 lines—than Seu Ba'i's composition but it has fewer dyadic sets (75 compared with 85 sets).

Of the various repeated or partially repeated passages in Mikael's composition, the one that is most immediately apparent is what might be called the 'monkey plucks' (*kode ketu*) formula. This formula is used four separate times in the composition. At the very beginning of his recitation, rather than announce the need for special ritual fish for the harvest ceremony, Mikael describes the ripening field that signals the coming of the harvest ceremony. He then proceeds to describe the hunt for the ritual fish, as if to imply that the search for the fish is the means to protecting the field. The first use of the 'monkey plucks' formula describes the way Fua Bafo//Lole Holu shouts to drive away monkeys//pigs from the field.

First Passage of 'Monkey Plucks'

14.	*De ana oko boluk tunga seli*	She shouts on one side
15.	*Ma ana do-se'ek tunga seli*	And she screams at the other side
16.	*Ma bafi na'a tunga seli*	And the pig eats on one side
17.	*Ma kode ketu tunga seli.*	And the monkey plucks at one side.
18.	*Boe ma ana dodo neu dalen*	So she thinks within herself
19.	*Ma ana dudu'a neu teina,*	And she ponders within her insides,
20.	*Nai du'a taon leo be*	Thinking what to do
21.	*Fo kode boso na'a pelak*	So the monkey does not eat the maize
22.	*Ma bafi boso na'a pelak.*	And the pig does not eat the maize.

The second use of this formula occurs in the initial dialogue between Fua Bafo//Lole Holu. The shells describe the situation that Fua Bafo//Lole Holu faces and instruct her to make them into sounding clappers that will drive away the monkeys//pigs. As in the first passage, the formula is used twice, but in this second passage, line 80 is composed correctly, whereas in the first passage, line 21 is composed incorrectly.

Second Passage of 'Monkey Plucks'

66.	*"Kode ketu betek*	"The monkey plucks the millet
67.	*Ma bafi na'a pelak.*	And the pig eats the maize.
68.	*De ketu bei tolesi*	Plucking yet still some remains
69.	*Ma na'a bei ela."*	And eating yet still something is left."
70.	*Tehu mafa ndendelek*	So remember, do remember
71.	*Ma masa nenedak*	And recall, do recall
72.	*Teu te isa au [nai] ai*	Go tie me to the wood
73.	*Ma pa'a au nai batu*	And fasten me to the stone
74.	*Fo au bengo bengo u ai*	That I may shake and shake with the wood
75.	*Ma toto toto o batu*	And knock and knock on the rock
76.	*Fo daenga kode ana tolo mu*	So that the monkey will run
77.	*Ma bafi ana nalai*	And the pig will flee
78.	*Lo nula dale neu*	Deep into the woods
79.	*Ma lo ai lai neu*	And high into the trees
80.	*Fo kode boso ketu betek*	So that the monkey does not pluck the millet
81.	*Ma bafi bo'o na'a pelak.'*	And the pig does not eat the maize.'

Immediately after this passage, Mikael repeats virtually the same six lines twice. These repeated lines include the 'monkey plucks' formula and another formula, which could be called the 'shout//scream' (*do-se'ek//oku-boluk*) formula, which occurs in the first passage.

Third Passage of 'Monkey Plucks'

84.	*De ana oku-boluk*	She shouts
85.	*Ma ana do-se'ek dei*	And she screams
86.	*Bafi ta na'a pelak*	The pig does not eat the maize
87.	*Ma kode ta ketu betek.*	And the monkey does not pluck the millet.

Fourth Passage of 'Monkey Plucks'

90.	*Ma ana oku-boluk*	And she shouts
91.	*Ma ana do-se'ek.*	And she screams.
92.	*De kode ta ketu betek*	The monkey does not pluck the millet
93.	*Ma bafi ta na'a pelak.*	And the pig does not eat the maize.

Malesi does not use the 'monkey plucks' formula in his version of *Suti Solo do Bina Bane*, but both Meno and Seu Ba'i do. Their use of this formula, however, differs from that of Mikael's. Whereas Mikael's formula is *kode ketu//bafi na'a*, Meno and Seu Ba'i's formula is *kode ketu// bafi ka'a*. The difference is in the use of two verbs. Mikael's /*na'a*/ (third-person singular) is the verb 'to eat', whereas Meno and Seu Ba'i's /*ka'a*/ (third-person singular) is the verb 'to bite or to chew'.

Both Meno and Seu Ba'i use the 'monkey plucks' formula in one of the directives to the shells. Meno's usage is as follows:

Old Meno

170.	*'Oo na mo bete pule kode ketuk*	'Oh, go with the millet grains that the monkey plucks
171.	*Ma pela po'o bafi ka'ak.'*	And with the ears of maize that the pig chews.'
172.	*Te hu Suti bei namatane*	But Suti continues to cry
173.	*Ma Bina bei nasakedu.*	And Bina continues to sob.
174.	*Boe ma nae:*	So he says:
175.	*'Te leo kode ketu neni betek*	'But if the monkey plucks the millet
176.	*Ma bafi ka'a neni pelak,*	And the pig chews the maize,
177.	*Na Suti au o se*	Then I, Suti, with whom will I be
178.	*Ma Bina au o se?.'*	And I, Bina, with whom will I be?'

Seu Ba'i's usage is similar to Meno's but includes the 'shout//scream' formula that Mikael uses in several of his similar passages.

Seu Ba'i

93.	*Au o peu ai lasi*	I will be with boundary tree of the forest
94.	*Ma au o to batu nula*	And I will be with border stone of the wood

95.	*Te bafi ka'a neni pelak*	But if the pig chews the maize
96.	*Au dede'ak o se*	With whom will I speak
97.	*Ma kode ketu neni betek*	And if monkey plucks the millet
98.	*Au kokolak o se*	With whom will I talk
99.	*Do se'ek o se*	Or be noisy [scream] with whom
100.	*Ma oku-boluk o se*	And shout with whom
101.	*Sama leo Lua Bafa*	[With someone] just like Lua Bafa
102.	*Ma deta leo Lole Holu?'*	And exactly like Lole Holu?'

There is, however, another remarkable similarity in composition between Seu Ba'i's version and Mikael's. In both compositions, this passage consists of 14 lines that make up one of the directives to the shells. The composition of this same passage is so similar that it could be considered as a distinctive 'Pellondou' family resemblance. A line-by-line comparison shows the use of exactly the same dyadic sets and formulae based on these sets throughout the two passages. Seu Ba'i's version of this passage is as follows:

Seu Ba'i

109.	*'Au o pila kumea letek*	'I will go with the red *kumea* grass on the hill
110.	*Ma au o nggeo kuku telas.*	And I go with the black *kuku* shrub in the underbrush.
111.	*Malole ndia so*	This is good
112.	*Ma mandak ndia so.*	And this is proper.
...		
122.	*Te timu lama-tua dulu*	But when the east monsoon grows great in the east
123.	*Ma fak lama-nalu langa*	And the west monsoon lengthens at the head
124.	*Fo pila kumea letek-kala*	The red *kumea* grass on the hill
125.	*Lama-dilu leu kalen*	Bends down its heavy top
126.	*Ma nggeo kuku telas*	And the black *kuku* shrub in the underbrush
127.	*Lama-sesu leu bu'un-na*	Breaks its heavy joints
128.	*Au dede'ak o se*	Then with whom will I speak
129.	*Ma au kokolak o se*	And with whom will I talk
130.	*Sama leo Lua Bafa*	[With someone] just like Lua Bafa

6. VERSION V FROM THE DOMAIN OF TERMANU

131.	*Ma deta leo Lole Holu?'*	And exactly like Lole Holu?'

In Mikael's version, this same passage is as follows.

Mikael Pellondou

105.	*'Mu mo pila kumea letek*	'Go with the red *kumea* grass on the hill
106.	*Ma mu mo nggeo kuku telas.'*	And go with the black *kuku* shrub in the underbrush.'
107.	*'Boe ma malole lai ndia*	'Such things would be good
108.	*Ma mandak lai ndia,*	And such things would be proper,
109.	*Te pila kumea letek*	But the red *kumea* grass on the hill
110.	*Ma nggeo kuku telas-a,*	And the black *kuku* shrub in the underbrush,
111.	*Timu lama tua dulu*	[When] the east monsoon grows great in the east
112.	*Do fak lama nalu langa,*	And the west monsoon lengthens at the head,
113.	*De lama dilu neu kalen*	Bends down its heavy top
114.	*Ma lama sesu neu bu'un*	And breaks its heavy joints
115.	*De au kokolak o se*	Then with whom will I speak
116.	*Ma au dede'ak o se*	And with whom will I talk
117.	*Fo sama leo Lole Holu*	[With someone] just like Lole Holu
118.	*Ma sama leo Fua Bafo?'*	And exactly like Fua Bafo?'

Mikael is consistent in his reliance on this arrangement of formulae. He repeats a variant of this passage some 22 lines further on in his composition.

140.	*'Au u o dini ana nau*	'If I go with the fine *dini* grass
141.	*O sama leo kumea letek*	It is just like going with the *kumea* grass on the hill
142.	*Ma kuku telas,*	And the *kuku* shrub in the underbrush,
143.	*De fak lama nalu langa*	[When] the west monsoon lengthens at the head
144.	*Ma timu lama tua dulu na*	And the east monsoon grows great in the east
145.	*De lama dilu neu bu'un*	It bends at its heavy joints

146.	*Ma lama sesu neu kalen,*	And it breaks at its heavy head,
147.	*Nah, au kokolak o se*	Then with whom will I speak
148.	*Ma au dede'ak o se*	And with whom will I talk
149.	*Fo sama leo o boe*	[With someone] just like you, too
150.	*Ma deta leo o boe.'*	And exactly like you, too.'

7
Suti Solo do Bina Bane: Version VI from the Domain of Termanu

Introduction

My first meeting with Mikael Pellondou in 1988 was brief and quite unexpected. My request for a recitation of *Suti Solo do Bina Bane* may have taken him by surprise but he hardly hesitated. His response was immediate. He took little time to reflect or prepare himself before beginning his recitation.

Five years later, on another visit to Rote, I was able to meet Mikael again and once more ask him to recite *Suti Solo do Bina Bane* for me. My second request prompted a similar, immediate response. Unlike Malesi, whose second recitation is significantly different from his first, Mikael's second recitation, some five years after his first composition for me, produced a version of *Suti Solo do Bina Bane* that was remarkably similar to his first version. The similarity between these two versions provides further understanding of poetic memory and composition.

In presenting this composition, I have divided it at the same junctures as the first composition.

Prefatory Lines

1.	*Ita kokolak Bina Bane*	We speak of Bina Bane
2.	*Ma ita dede'ak Suti Solo*	And we talk of Suti Solo
3.	*Te hu Bina nai liun*	But Bina is in the ocean
4.	*Ma Suti nai sain.*	And Suti is in the sea.
5.	*Hu lae:*	Hence they say:

Introduction of the Chief Chant Character

6.	*Inaka Fua Bafa*	The woman Fua Bafa
7.	*Ma fetoka Lole Holu*	And the girl Lole Holu
8.	*Na-nea pelak*	Cares for the maize
9.	*Ma na-nea betek.*	And cares for the millet.
10.	*De ana oku boluk tunga seli*	She shouts at one side
11.	*Ma do se'ek tunga seli*	And she screams at one side
12.	*Ma bafi na'a tunga seli*	And the pig eats at one side
13.	*Ma kode ketu tunga seli.*	And the monkey plucks at one side.
14.	*De faik esa manunin*	At a certain day
15.	*Do ledok esa mate'ena*	Or at a particular time
16.	*Boe ma ana teli kokolo ndai*	She strings, winding a fishnet
17.	*Fo ndai mahamu lilok*	A fishnet with a gold-weighted belly
18.	*Ma ana ane seseko meti*	And she braids, twining a scoop-net
19.	*Fo seko matei besik.*	A scoop-net with iron-weighted insides.
20.	*De neu seko sisi'u enggak*	Then she goes to scoop, lifting *enggak* seaweed
21.	*Ma neu ndai huhuka batu.*	And goes to net fish, overturning rocks.
22.	*Ana lipa neu nakanae*	She looks around carefully
23.	*Ma lelu nala mumula*	And glances intently
24.	*Neu meti Tefi Noe Mina la*	Goes to the tide at Tefi Noe Mina
25.	*Tasi Fopo Sandi-kala*	The sea at Fopo Sandi-kala
26.	*Ma meti Tefi Noe Mina la*	And the tide at Tefi Noe Mina
27.	*Leu huka papa*	[The sea] shows its shallows

28.	*Ma meti la si'unu.*	And the tide begins to ebb.
29.	*Ma ana ane seko la*	And she braids the scoop-net
30.	*Fo seko matei besik*	The scoop-net with iron-weighted insides
31.	*Ma ana teli kokolo ndai*	And she strings, winding the fishnet
32.	*Fo ndai mahamu lilok.*	The fishnet with a gold-weighted belly.
33.	*Tasi la huka papa*	The sea shows its shallows
34.	*Ma meti la si'unu.*	And the tide begins to ebb.
35.	*Boe ma ndae ndai neu alun*	So she hangs the fishnet over her shoulder
36.	*Su seko neu langa.*	Balances the scoop-net on her head.

The Search for the Ritual Fish

37.	*De neu seko sisi'u enggak*	Then she goes to scoop, lifting *enggak* seaweed
38.	*Ma neu ndai huhuka batu*	And goes to net fish, overturning rocks.
39.	*Fo ana ndai sanga Tio Holu*	She fishes, seeking a Tio Holu fish
40.	*Ma seko sanga Dusu La'e*	And scoops, seeking a Dusu La'e fish
41.	*Fo ela Tio la holu ao*	Tio that embrace one another
42.	*Ma Dusu la'e ao.*	And Dusu that support one another.
43.	*Te hu ana seko nala lifu esa*	But she scoops in one pond
44.	*Ma ndai nala lek esa,*	And fishes in one pool,
45.	*Na, te ta ndai nala Tio*	Nah, but she does not fish a Tio
46.	*Ma ana ta seko nala Dusu*	And she does not scoop a Dusu
47.	*Te seko nala lifu esa*	But she scoops in one pond
48.	*Na Bina nala lifu esa*	Nah, Bina is in that pond
49.	*Ma ana ndai nala lek dua*	And she fishes in two pools
50.	*Na Suti nala lek dua.*	Nah, Suti is in the two pools.

The Initial Dialogue with the Shells

51.	*De ana kokolak*	Then she speaks
52.	*Ma ana dede'ak:*	And she talks:

53.	*'O, au mai seko sanga Dusu La'e dei*	'Oh, I only come to scoop for a Dusu La'e
54.	*Ma ndai sanga Tio Holu dei*	And only fish for a Tio Holu
55.	*Te seko uni o*	But I scoop you up
56.	*Ma ndai uni o*	And I fish you up
57.	*Fo soa be ma o nda be?'*	For what purpose and what gain?'
58.	*Boe ma Bina lole halan*	Then Bina raises his voice
59.	*Ma Suti a'e dasi na, nae:*	And Suti lifts his words, saying:
60.	*'Seko muni Bina*	'Scoop up Bina
61.	*Ndai muni Suti*	Fish up Suti
62.	*Te Suti ta, dae hena*	Not Suti, but a human being
63.	*Ma Bina ta, hataholi.'*	And not Bina, but a living being.'
64.	*Boe ma ana ndai ndano neni Bina*	So she fishes forth, taking Bina
65.	*Ma seko solu neni Suti.*	And she scoops up, taking Suti.
66.	*'Na kode a ketu betek*	'The monkey plucks the millet
67.	*Ma bafi bei na'a pelak*	And the pig still eats the maize
68.	*De na'a bei tolesi*	He eats, but still some remains
69.	*Ma ketu bei ela.*	And plucks, but there is still some left.
70.	*Mafa ndendelek*	So remember, do remember
71.	*Ma masa nenedak*	And recall, do recall
72.	*Mu sona*	Go, then
73.	*Pa'a au u ai*	Tie me to the tree
74.	*Isa au neu batu*	Fasten me to the rock
75.	*Fo toto-toto no batu*	To knock and knock against the rock
76.	*Ma bengo-bengo no ai.*	And shake and shake against the tree.
77.	*Kode tolo mu*	The monkey will run
78.	*Fo lo ai lai neu*	High into the trees
79.	*Ma bafi nalai*	And the pig will flee
80.	*Fo lo nula dale neu.*	Deep into the woods.
81.	*Sama leo hala ma*	Just as my voice
82.	*Deta leo dasi ma*	Just like my words
83.	*Kode ana tolo mu*	The monkey, he will run
84.	*Ma bafi ana nalai*	And the pig, he will flee

85.	*De leo nula dale neu*	Deep into the woods
86.	*Ma leo ai lai neu.*	And high into the trees.
87.	*Boe te pela-lai la fali uma*	The corn harvest is returned to the house
88.	*Ma bete-lai la tuke lo.*	And the millet harvest is brought to the home.
89.	*Boe ma Bina o fali uma*	So Bina, you return to the house
90.	*Ma Suti o tulek lo.'*	And Suti, you go back to the home.'

The Directives to the Shells

The only significant difference in this section from the similar section of the first composition is in the addition of the directive to go with the forest cuckoo bird and the river watercock.[1]

91.	*Boe ma ana kokolak*	So he speaks
92.	*No ina Po'o Pau Ai [Lole Holu]*	With the woman Po'o Pau Ai [Lole Holu][1]
93.	*Ma feto Latu Kai Do [Fua Bafa], nae:*	And with the girl Latu Kai Do [Fua Bafa], saying:
94.	*'Bo tiango nou*	'Dear, dear friend
95.	*Au sanga tulek ma falik.'*	I seek to go back and to return.'
96.	*Boe ma nae:*	Then she says:
97.	*'Mu mo se?'*	'With whom will you go?'
98.	*Inak a Fua Bafa*	The woman Fua Bafa
99.	*Ma fetok a Lole Holu nae:*	And the girl Lole Holu says:
100.	*'Na, mu mo titi'i letek*	'Go with the *titi'i* bush on the hill
101.	*Ma mu mo kai-hule mok.'*	And go with the *kai-hule* shrub in the field.'
102.	*'Malole lai ndia*	'Such things are good there
103.	*Ma mandak lai ndia.*	And such things are proper right there.
104.	*Te kai-hule mok*	But the *kai-hule* shrub in the field
105.	*Ndia mesakana nai mok esa*	It is all alone in the field

---

1   In lines 92–93, Mikael refers to Po'o Pau Ai//Latu Kai Do where he should have referred to Fua Bafa//Lole Holu. This was a mistake that was immediately recognised. I have not altered the text, if only to emphasise that poets can make 'mistakes' in their compositions.

106.	*Ma ndia mesakana nai letek esa*	And it is all alone on the hill
107.	*De au kokolak o se*	So with whom will I speak
108.	*Ma au dede'ak o se*	And with whom will I talk
109.	*Sama leo Lole Holu*	[Someone] just like Lole Holu
110.	*Ma sama leo Fua Bafa?'*	And just like Fua Bafa?'
111.	*Boe ma nae:*	So she says:
112.	*'Na, mu mo dini ana na'u.'*	'Nah, go with the *dini* grass.'
113.	*'Te dini ana na'u*	'But the *dini* grass
114.	*Leo timu lama tua dulu*	When the east monsoon grows great in the east
115.	*Ma se lama dilu do lama sesu*	It will bend or break
116.	*Neu kalena ma neu bu'una,*	At this head and at its joint,
117.	*Na, au kokolak o se*	Then with whom will I speak
118.	*Ma au dede'ak o se?'*	And with whom will I talk?'
119.	*Boe ma nae:*	So she says:
120.	*'Mu mo pila kumea letek*	'Go with the red *kumea* grass on the hill
121.	*Ma mu mo nggeo kuku telas.'*	And go with the black *kuku* shrub in the forest.'
122.	*'Te timu lama tua dulu na*	'But when the east monsoon grows great in the east
123.	*Ma fak lama nalu langa na*	And the west monsoon lengthens at the head
124.	*Se pila kumea letek*	The red *kumea* grass on the hill
125.	*Do nggeo kuku telas*	Or the black *kuku* shrub in the forest
126.	*Se lama dilu neu bu'un*	Will bend at its heavy joints
127.	*Ma lama sesu neu kalen,*	And will break at its heavy head,
128.	*Na, au kokolak o se*	Nah, then with whom will I speak
129.	*Ma au dede'ak o se*	And with whom will I talk
130.	*Sama leo Lole Holu*	[Someone] just like Lole Holu
131.	*Ma deta leo Fua Bafa?'*	And exactly like Fua Bafa?'
132.	*Boe ma ana lole hala na neu*	So she raises her voice
133.	*Ma ana a'e dasi no neu, nae:*	And lifts her words, saying:
134.	*'Na, o mu mo se*	'Nah, with whom will you go

135.	*Fo sama leo au bai*	[Someone] just like me
136.	*Do deta leo au bai?'*	Or exactly like me?'
137.	*Boe ma nae:*	Then she says:
138.	*'Na, mu mo doa lasi anakala*	'Nah, go with the tiny forest cuckoos
139.	*Ma mu mo koloba'o le anakala.'*	And go with the little river watercocks.'
140.	*'Malole lai na*	'Such things are good there
141.	*Ma mandak lai ndia.'*	And such things are proper there.'
142.	*Lafada ma ladasi, lae:*	They speak and they talk, saying:
143.	*'Doa lasi ana-kala*	'[When] the tiny forest cuckoos
144.	*Bedoa tunga lasi*	Sing *doa-doa* through the forest
145.	*Na udan tunga tunga lasi*	As the rain follows through the forest
146.	*Ma kolo ba'o le ana-kala*	And the little river watercocks
147.	*Beba'o tunga le*	Sing *ba'o-ba'o* along the river
148.	*Na fa tunga tunga le,*	As the current follows along the river,
149.	*Au dede'ak o se*	With whom will I speak
150.	*Ma dede'ak o se?'*	And with whom will I speak?'

The Directive to Return to the Sea

151.	*Boe ma nae:*	So she says:
152.	*'Mu mo ina Po'o Pau Ai la*	'Go with the woman Po'o Pau Ai
153.	*Ma feto Latu Kai Do la*	And with the girl Latu Kai Do
154.	*Nai le [bi]bifan*	At the river's lip
155.	*Ma nai oli tatain.'*	And the estuary's edge.'
156.	*Boe ma Bina a'e dasi na neu*	So Bina lifts his words
157.	*Ma Suti lole hala a neu ma nae:*	And Suti raises his voice and says:
158.	*'Bo senango nou*	'Oh dear friend
159.	*Ma bo tiango nou*	And oh dear companion
160.	*Malole lai ndia*	Such things are good there
161.	*Ma mandak lai na,*	And such things are proper right there.
162.	*De au kokolak o ina Po'o Pau Ai la*	I will speak with the woman Po'o Pau Ai

163.	*Ma au dede'ak o feto Latu Kai Do*	And I will talk with the girl Latu Kai Do
164.	*Nai le bifan ma oli tatain*	At the river's lip and estuary's edge
165.	*Sama deta leo dasima:*	Just as you say:
166.	*"Mu mo ina Po'o Pau Ai la*	"Go with the woman Po'o Pau Ai
167.	*Do feto Latu Kai Do."'*	Or the girl Latu Kai Do."'

The Brief Return to the Sea

168.	*Boe ma besak tasi mai*	Now the sea comes in
169.	*De nala oli dale.*	And enters the estuary.
170.	*Boe ma Bina ana bonu boa*	Bina, he floats like *boa* wood
171.	*Ma Suti ana ele piko*	And Suti, he bobs like *piko* wood
172.	*De ana ele piko leo liun*	He bobs into the ocean
173.	*Ma ana bonu boa leo sain neu.*	And he floats off into the sea.
174.	*Te seko-ma nai liun do sain*	As it happens in the ocean or sea
175.	*Laka-doto kokolo*	It is as lively as a *kokolo* bird
176.	*Ma laka-se bebengu,*	And as noisy as horses' bells,
177.	*Te hu ana ta bubuluk*	But he is not aware
178.	*Do ana ta nalelak.*	Or he does not know.
179.	*Seko-ma ala be'e Lipe la*	As it happens, they perform at the *Lipe* feast
180.	*Ma ala doi dosa*	And they are suffering
181.	*Leme liun do sain.*	In the ocean and the sea.
182.	*De ina liu-kala*	The women of the ocean
183.	*Ma feto sai-kala*	And the girls of the sea
184.	*Ala foti ma leno lai sain.*	They dance and turn in the sea.
185.	*De dae sopuka ta lapu*	Fine dust does not fly
186.	*Ma batu lutu la ta pela.*	And small stones do not rise/dance.
187.	*Besak ka Bina Bane no Suti Solo*	Now Bina Bane or Suti Solo
188.	*Ala pela nggangafu aon*	They dance, swaying their bodies
189.	*Ma leno sosodo aon.*	And they turn, shuffling their feet.
190.	*Boe ma dae sopuka lapu*	Fine dust flies

191.	*Ma batu lutu la pela.*	And small stones rise.
192.	*Boe ma ina liu-kala*	The women of the ocean
193.	*Do feto sai-kala*	Or girls of the sea
194.	*Lahala ma lae.*	'Wah.'
195.	*De lae: 'Beuk Suti Solo boe*	They say: 'Something new for Suti Solo
196.	*Do fe'ek Bina Bane boe.'*	Or something strange for Bina Bane.'

The Return to Rote

197.	*De Bina nama toko isi*	So Bina throws forth his insides
198.	*Ma Suti nama edo nggi.*	And Suti puts forth his pods.
199.	*Boe ma ana bi'i*	He is fearful
200.	*Do ana mae.*	Or he is ashamed.
201.	*Boe ma ana tolu mu sasali*	He flees forth quickly
202.	*Ma nalai lelena.*	And he rushes forth hastily.
203.	*De ana tolo mu*	He flees
204.	*De leo Dela Muli neu*	To Dela Muli [Dela in the West]
205.	*Ma nalai*	And rushes
206.	*De leo Ana Iko neu.*	To Ana Iko [Ana at the Tail].
207.	*De ana nduku Ana Iko*	He arrives at Ana Iko
208.	*Ana losa Dela Muli.*	He reaches Dela Muli.
209.	*Boe ma neu tongo senan*	He goes to meet a friend
210.	*Ma neu nda tian*	And goes to encounter a companion
211.	*Fo neu nda tia na nai Dela Muli.*	Goes to meet a companion at Dela Muli.
212.	*Boe ma nae:*	He says:
213.	*'Bo tiango nou*	'Oh dear companion
214.	*Seko-ma nggolok nai ia.*	As it happens the village is here.
215.	*Boe ma taduk nai ia boe.'*	The settlement is here too.'
216.	*Boe ma nae:*	So she says:
217.	*'Leo do mapa lasa meme ia*	'Stay and remain here
218.	*Te o mai nda au.*	You have come to meet me.
219.	*De ita dua senak*	Let the two of us be friends
220.	*Ma ita dua tiak.*	And let the two of us be companions.

221. *De neme Dela Muli*   Here in Dela Muli
222. *Do neme Ana Iko.'*   Or here in Ana Iko.'

Composition Analysis: Mikael's Versions I and II and Seu Ba'i's Recitation

The immediate point of comparison for this version of *Suti Solo do Bina Bane* is Mikael's first version. The two compositions are nearly the same length. Version I has 224 lines; version II 222 lines. Both versions include the repetition and rephrasing of particular passages. Version I is based on a repertoire of 75 dyadic sets; version II has 79 sets. The two versions have 59 sets in common—in both cases, 75 per cent or more of their dyadic repertoire. Version I shares 38 sets with Seu Ba'i's composition while version II—largely because of the inclusion of the directive that refers to the 'forest cuckoo and river watercock'—shares 42 sets with Seu Ba'i. The compositional links among these various recitations are considerable.

Although both of Mikael's recitations are similar and share a majority of sets in common, the composition arrangement of these two versions—the sequence of lines one to another—is more complex. The general succession of the narrative is much the same but particular lines, couplet lines and sometimes longer passages follow different sequences. Seeming similarity masks a good deal of compositional difference. Table 2 provides a concordance of corresponding lines in the two versions and allows for closer scrutiny of the specifics of composition.

Table 2: A Concordance of Corresponding Lines in the Two Versions of *Suti Solo do Bina Bane* by Mikael Pellondou

Mikael Pellondou II		Mikael Pellondou I
3	<>	2 + 8
4	<>	3 + 9
6 – 13	<>	10 – 17
17	<>	28
19	<>	27 + 30
22 – 23	<>	32 – 33
25 – 28	<>	34 – 37
30	<>	27 + 30

7. VERSION VI FROM THE DOMAIN OF TERMANU

Mikael Pellondou II		Mikael Pellondou I
32	<>	28
37 – 42	<>	38 – 43
43 – 46	<>	44 – 47
47 + 49	<>	50 – 51
48 + 50	<>	52 – 53
58 – 59	<>	60 – 61
66 – 71	<>	66 – 71
73 – 80	<>	72 – 79
81 – 82	<>	82 – 83
83 – 86	<>	76 – 79
89 – 90	<>	99 – 100
100 – 101	<>	120 – 121
102 – 103	<>	123 – 124
104 – 110	<>	126 – 133
111 – 112	<>	137 – 138
114 – 115	<>	144 – 146
117 – 118	<>	147 – 148
120 – 121	<>	105 – 106
122 – 123	<>	111 – 112
124 – 125	<>	109 – 110
126 – 127	<>	113 – 114
128 – 131	<>	115 – 116
132 – 133	<>	60 – 61
134 – 135	<>	135 – 136
151 – 155	<>	161 – 162 + 165 – 166
160 – 161	<>	171 – 172
166 – 167	<>	161 – 162
170 – 171	<>	179 – 180
179	<>	186
181	<>	187
182 – 183	<>	189 – 190
185 – 186	<>	194 – [195]
188 – 189	<>	197 – 198
190 – 191	<>	199 – 200
195 – 200	<>	204 – 208

Mikael Pellondou II		Mikael Pellondou I
197 – 198	<>	206 – 207
199 – 200	<>	208
201 – 202	<>	209 – 210
204 + 206	<>	211 – 212
213	<>	218
216 – 217	<>	221 – 223

It is probably best to compare some of the longer passages in the two versions before focusing on particular lines and couplets. Thus, near the beginning of both compositions, there is a sequence of eight lines that are virtually identical.

Passage 1

Version I

10.	*Boe te inaka Fua Bafo*	So the woman Fua Bafa
11.	*Ma fetoka Lole Holu*	And the girl Lole Holu
12.	*Na-nea pelak*	Cares for maize
13.	*Ma na-nea betek*	And cares for millet
14.	*De ana oko boluk tunga seli*	She shouts on one side
15.	*Ma ana do-se'ek tunga seli*	And she screams at one side
16.	*Ma bafi na'a tunga seli*	And the pig eats on one side
17.	*Ma kode ketu tunga seli.*	And the monkey plucks at one side.

Version II

6.	*Inaka Fua Bafa*	The woman Fua Bafa
7.	*Ma fetoka Lole Holu*	And the girl Lole Holu
8.	*Na-nea pelak*	Cares for the maize
9.	*Ma na-nea betek.*	And cares for the millet.
10.	*De ana oku boluk tunga seli*	She shouts at one side
11.	*Ma do se'ek tunga seli*	And she screams at one side
12.	*Ma bafi na'a tunga seli*	And the pig eats at one side
13.	*Ma kode ketu tunga seli.*	And the monkey plucks at one side.

7. VERSION VI FROM THE DOMAIN OF TERMANU

Except for the use of different connectives—*boe te* at the beginning of Version I and the optional use of the pronoun *ana* in line 14 of Version I—these two passages are identical both in their use of dyadic sets and in the order or sequence of lines. One could speculate that these lines constitute a personal routine or extended formula that allows Mikael to begin his recitation on a secure basis.

After this passage, the compositions diverge. In Version I, Mikael has Fua Bafa//Lole Holu ponder how she can prevent the monkey and pig from eating her crops. It is only after this that she takes up her fishing net and goes to the sea. In Version II, Mikael launches immediately into the fishing sequence.

Another early passage of some 12 lines in Version I can be compared with similar lines in Version II. However, the corresponding lines in Version II do not form a single sequence nor do they appear in the same order as in Version I.

Passage 2

Version I

A

32.	*De ana lipa naka nanae*	She looks around carefully
33.	*Ma ana lelu nala mumula.*	And she glances intently.
34.	*De tasi Fopo Sandika*	The sea at Fopo Sandika
35.	*Ma meti Tefi Noe Mina*	And the tide at Tefi Noe Mina
36.	*Tasi la huka papa*	The sea shows its shallows
37.	*Ma meti la si'unu.*	And the tide begins to ebb.

B

38.	*Boe ma neu seko sisi'u engga*	She goes to scoop, lifting *enggak* seaweed
39.	*Ma neu ndai huhuka batu,*	And goes to fish, overturning rocks,
40.	*Neu seko sanga Dusu La'e*	Goes to scoop in search of a Dusu La'e
41.	*Ma neu ndai sanga Tio Holu*	And goes to fish in search of a Tio Holu
42.	*Fo Dusu la la'e ao*	For Dusu fish that support one another
43.	*Ma Tio la holu ao.*	The Tio fish that embrace one another.

Version II

A

20.	*De neu seko sisi'u enggak*	Then she goes to scoop, lifting *enggak* seaweed
21.	*Ma neu ndai huhuka batu.*	And goes to fish, overturning rocks.
22.	*Ana lipa neu nakanae*	She looks around carefully
23.	*Ma lelu nala mumula*	And glances intently
24.	*Neu meti Tefi Noe Mina la*	Goes to the tide at Tefi Noe Mina
25.	*Tasi Fopo Sandi-Kala*	The sea at Fopo Sandi-Kala
26.	*Ma meti Tefi Noe Mina la*	And the tide at Tefi Noe Mina
27.	*Leu huka papa*	[The sea] shows its shallows
28.	*Ma meti la si'unu.*	And the tide begins to ebb.
...		
33.	*Tasi la huka papa*	The sea shows its shallows
34.	*Ma meti la si'unu.*	And the tide begins to ebb.

B

37.	*De neu seko sisi'u enggak*	Then she goes to scoop, lifting *enggak* seaweed
38.	*Ma neu ndai huhuka batu.*	And goes to fish, overturning rocks.
39.	*Fo ana ndai sanga Tio Holu*	She fishes, seeking a Tio Holu fish
40.	*Ma seko sanga Dusu La'e*	And scoops, seeking a Dusu La'e fish
41.	*Fo ela Tio la holu ao*	Tio that embrace each other
42.	*Ma Dusu la'e ao.*	And Dusu that support each other.

If one takes the sequence of lines in Version I as a starting point, the first six lines (32–37) correspond to six of the last seven lines (22–28) in the sequence in Version II. Both sequences use exactly the same dyadic sets in the same order as follows:

32/22	*lipa – nae*
33/23	*lelu – mula*
34/25	*tasi –* [name: Fopo Sandika]
35/26	*meti –* [name: Tefi Noe Mina]
36/27	*tasi – huka-papa*
37/28	*meti – si'unu*

There are, however, a number of compositional differences, six of which are notable. 1) There is a difference in line 22 (Version II) where a verbal, non-reduplicated *neu nakanae* is used instead of the reduplicated *naka nanae* in line 32, as in Version I. 2) Line 24 is an (unnecessary) insertion, which is made redundant by the repetition in line 26. 3) The place names in lines 24–26 are given in plural form (*la* or *kala*) in Version II, but singular form in Version I. This is a permissible feature of Rotenese parallel poetry where dyadic characters are cited as often in singular as in plural form, with some poets using a singular form as a contrastive pair with a plural form. 4) The noun *tasi* ('sea') is omitted but clearly implied in line 27 of Version II. 5) In Version II, lines 27 and 28 are repeated as lines 33 and 34. 6) Also in Version II, lines 20 and 21 are repeated as lines 37 and 38.

As a result, lines 38–43 in Version I correspond to lines 37–42 in Version II. Although the lines regarding the Tio and Dusu are in reverse order, in terms of the use of dyadic sets, these lines are the same. The varied evidence of these two versions of *Suti Solo do Bina Bane* shows the formulaic continuity in the compositional capabilities of the poet Mikael Pellondou.

8

Suti Solo do Bina Bane: Version VII from the Domain of Termanu

Introduction

In 2006, I began a renewed effort to study ritual language by setting out to record the finest chanters—the master poets—from all the dialect areas of Rote. For more than 40 years, I had recorded chanters, mainly from the domains of Termanu and Thie. Most of these recordings were made when the occasion arose. Although I sought out particular chanters and often made requests of them, most chanters preferred to choose the occasion and the setting for their recitation and most recitations were those of their own choosing. On numerous occasions, I would ask about a specific chant only to be told that its recitation was too dangerous to be spoken of without the proper offerings and would be told of someone who had recited without proper heed and had suffered the consequences.

Often these recitations would occur during a ritual gathering, where there were large numbers gathered and various animals slaughtered, thus creating a favourable setting for a recitation as public revelation. On a number of occasions, a particular chanter would simply appear—once near midnight—and announce that he had come to recite a specific chant. This would be an entirely private recording and, having heard the replay of his recitation, the chanter would leave.

Figure 8: Joel Pellondou

As a result, I gathered what I could when I could—occasionally and opportunistically. In retrospect, it now seems to me that only Old Meno had the idea in mind to provide me with a broad comprehension of the most important ritual knowledge that he possessed, but unfortunately I was only at the beginning of my study of Rotenese life and did not have the proper basis to understand everything he was trying to communicate.

The other limitation of my study was its restricted basis. I did most of my fieldwork in Termanu and concentrated on learning the dialect of Termanu. I had a place in Termanu, was comfortable there and, on return visits, was eager to catch up with what had happened in a community I knew well. I had briefly gathered material from one of the great poets of Ba'a and had recorded excellent ritual language materials from two of the finest chanters in Thie, but this was the limit of my recording of other dialects.

So in 2006, with a research grant from the Australian Research Council, I set out to bring Rotenese chanters for a week at a time to Bali where I rented the top floor of a small family hotel at Sanur. Here in a setting entirely removed from restrictions that would apply on Rote, I was able to record more freely and could carry on, without interruptions, the discussions and close exegesis needed to understand particular recitations.

The project took on a momentum of its own. After the first recording session I was helped by each group of chanters, who spread the word of their time on Bali. Two elderly chanters who came to Bali at different times described Bali as like being in paradise. Neither had ever left Rote, so that having flown above the clouds to reach Bali, they felt themselves in a wondrous place.

For the first session, which was organised as a trial effort, I invited three notable chanters from Termanu and a master poet and performer from the domain of Ringgou, whom I had met just the year before on a visit to Rote and from whom I had failed to record a single chant.

Among the three chanters from Termanu was Mikael Pellondou's cousin Joel Pellondou. By this time, Mikael had died and it was Joel who was carrying on the Pellondou traditions. As Joel explained to me, he and his cousin Mikael (his father's brother's son) learned from the same source: their grandfather, Dou Ba'i Adu. When I told Joel that I had already recorded *Suti Solo do Bina Bane* from Mikael and from Eli Pellondou (that is, Seu Ba'i) and that I needed to record his version, he had no reservations. His recitation was much shorter than Mikael's recitations and that of Seu Ba'i, but it nonetheless bears comparison with these compositions.

Joel Pellondou's version of *Suti Solo do Bina Bane* is as follows:

1.	*Meti la si'unu*	The tide begins to ebb
2.	*Ma tasi la huka papa*	The sea shows its shallows
3.	*Boe ma inak Ole Masi*	The woman Ole Masi
4.	*Ma fetok ka Bisa Oli*	And the girl Bisa Oli

5.	*Ana nggao na ndai tasi na*	She takes up her sea fishnet
6.	*[Fo] ndai ma hamu lilok*	The fishnet with a gold-weighted belly
7.	*Ma tenga na seko meti*	And picks up her tidal scoop-net
8.	*Fo seko ma tei besik.*	The scoop-net with iron-weighted insides.
9.	*Neu seko sisi'u enggak*	Goes to scoop and gather *engga* seaweed
10.	*Ma ndai huhuka batu*	And to fish and turn the rocks
11.	*Fo neu seko sanga Dusu La'e*	Goes scooping in search of Dusu La'e
12.	*Ma neu ndai sanga Tio Holu.*	And goes fishing in search of Tio Holu.
13.	*Boe te ana seko nala lifu esa*	But she scoops in one pool of water
14.	*Na, Bina nala lifu esa*	Nah, Bina is in that pool of water
15.	*Ma ana ndai nala lek esa,*	And she fishes in one waterhole,
16.	*Na Suti nala lek esa.*	Nah, Suti is in that waterhole.
17.	*Seko toko heni Bina*	She scoops but throws Bina away
18.	*Ma ndai ndano heni Suti.*	And fishes but casts Suti away.
19.	*Boe ma Bina ana a'e dasi*	So Bina, he raises his voice
20.	*Ma Suti ana lole halana, nae:*	And Suti, he lifts his words, saying:
21.	*'Seko toko muni au*	'Scoop and take me up
22.	*Te Bina ta, te dae hena*	For I am not Bina, but a human being
23.	*Ma ndai ndano muni au,*	And fish and take me up,
24.	*Te Suti ta, te hataholi.'*	For I am not Suti, but a human person.'
25.	*Boe ma inaka nahala ma nae:*	So the woman speaks and says:
26.	*'Au o o fo o mo se?'*	'If I take you, with whom will you go?'
27.	*Boe ma nae:*	Then she says:
28.	*'Mu mo feto Titi Letek*	'Go with the girl Titi of the Hill
29.	*Ma inak Ai Huule Mok.'*	And with the woman Huule of the Field.'
30.	*Boe ma nae:*	Then he says:
31.	*'Malole la so*	'That is good
32.	*Te mesa ma letek esa*	But alone with a hill
33.	*Ma mesa ma mok esa*	And alone with a field
34.	*Na, se kokolak no se?'*	Nah, with whom will I speak?'
35.	*Boe ma nae:*	Then she says:
36.	*'Mu mo pila kumea letek*	'Go with the red *kumea* grass on the hill
37.	*Ma mu mo nggeo koko [kuku] telas.'*	And go with the black *kuku* shrub in the forest.'

8. VERSION VII FROM THE DOMAIN OF TERMANU

38.	*Boe ma nae:*	Then he says:
39.	*'Malole so*	'That is good
40.	*Tehu timu lama tua dulu*	But when the east monsoon builds in the east
41.	*Na pila kumea letekala*	Nah, the red *kumea* grass on the hill
42.	*Lama dilu neu kalen*	Bends at the heads of its stalks
43.	*Ma fak nama nalu langa na*	And when the west monsoon grows at the head
44.	*Nggeo koko [kuku] telasala*	The black *kuku* shrub in the underbrush
45.	*Lama sesu neu bu'un,*	Breaks at the weight of its joints,
46.	*Fo au kokolak o se*	With whom will I talk
47.	*Ma au dedea'k o se?'*	And with whom will I speak?'
48.	*Boe ma nae:*	Then she says:
49.	*'Mu mo fetok Po'o Pau Ai la*	'Go with the girl Mouldy Pau Tree
50.	*Ma mu mo inak Latu Kai Do la*	And go with the woman Withered Kai Leaves
51.	*Nai le bibifa-na*	At the mouth of the river
52.	*Ma nai oli tatain*	And at the edge of the estuary
53.	*Fo kolo ba'o le anakala*	There the river watercock birds
54.	*Beba'o tunga le*	Cry *ba'o-ba'o* along the river
55.	*Na fa tunga-tunga le*	As the monsoon follows the river
56.	*Ma do[a] lasi anakala*	And the forest cuckoo birds
57.	*Bedo'o tunga lasi,*	Cry *do-do* through the forest,
58.	*Na udan tunga-tunga lasi*	As rain follows through the forest
59.	*Fo daenga fa tunga-tunga le*	So as the monsoon follows the river
60.	*Fo o bonu boa fo liun*	Go bobbing like *boa* wood to the ocean
61.	*Fo o ele piko fo sain.'*	Go drifting like *piko* wood to the sea.'
62.	*Boe ma be'uk Suti Solo bai*	So the new-one Suti Solo
63.	*Ma fe'ek Bina Bane bai*	And the stranger-one Bina Bane
64.	*De [Bina] lama edo nggi*	So Bina exudes its pods
65.	*Ma Suti lama toko isi.*	And Suti issues forth its insides.
66.	*De ala bonu boa fo liun*	They bob like *boa* wood to the ocean
67.	*Ma ele piko fo sain.*	And they drift like *piko* wood to the sea.

This is the shortest version of *Suti Solo do Bina Bane* that I recorded from Termanu. It assumes some considerable background knowledge and some acquaintance with other versions of this chant. In itself, it is a mere outline of other longer chants.

Composed of 67 lines, this version comprises just 37 different dyadic sets. Comparing it with Meno's version, which is composed of 299 lines and comprises 103 dyadic sets, this version is particularly succinct. It has a higher percentage of different dyadic sets per line of composition. As a poetic composition, it has the bare minimum of necessary elements to qualify as an 'orphan and widow' mortuary chant. It recounts the gathering of the shells and their return to the sea. It mentions the search for the Tio Holu//Dusu La'e fish but makes no attempt to explain the reason for this search; nor does it explain the cause of the appearance of Suti Solo and Bina Bane in the waterhole where they are gathered up. It does, however, contain three dialogue directives: 1) to go with the girl Titik Letek and the woman Huule Mok ('Titik of the Hill' and 'Huule of the Field'); 2) to go with the red *kumea* grass and the black *kuku* shrub; and then finally 3) to go with the girl Mouldy Pau Tree and the woman Withered Kai Leaves. The invocation of these names in this third directive alludes to the origin incident that drove Suti Solo and Bina Bane from the depths of the sea and is linked with the directive to follow the *koloba'o* river birds and the *doa* forest birds back to the sea.

This directive (in lines 49 to 61) is similar to other directives that refer to the *koloba'o* and *doa* birds. The directive to go with the *koloba'o* and *doa* birds is a key admonition in virtually all versions of *Suti Solo do Bina Bane* because it leads to the return of the shells to the sea. Joel Pellondou's version thus calls for closer comparison with these other directives and for closer examination of just how these passages are constructed in terms of a variety and combination of formulae.

Comparison of Formulae in the *Koloba'o* and *Doa* Bird Directives

With the exception of Mikael Pellondou's first version of *Suti Solo do Bina Bane*, all of the versions so far considered have included the directive to go with the *koloba'o* and *doa* birds. Some involve a single long statement; others involve an exchange of dialogue. Each is made of several formulae in different variations.

8. VERSION VII FROM THE DOMAIN OF TERMANU

The *koloba'o* and *doa* bird directive can be analysed in terms of its constituent formulae and these formulae can, in turn, be analysed in terms of their variations.

Formula I

To begin with, *doa lasi* and *koloba'o le* ('forest cuckoo' and 'river watercock') is itself a formula. *Doa*//*koloba'o* form a dyadic set, as do *lasi*//*le* ('forest'//'river'), but the combination of *doa* with *lasi* and *koloba'o* with *le* constitutes an invariant relation and this invariance is evidence of a formulaic (synthetic or syntagmatic) relationship. (It is, for example, unacceptable to combine *doa* with *le* or *koloba'o* with *lasi*: *doa le*//*koloba'o lasi** does not occur.)

Seu Ba'i and Malesi rely on exactly the same formula.

Seu Ba'i

134.	*'Mu mo doa lasi*	'Go with the forest cuckoo
135.	*Ma mu mo koloba'o le'*	And go with the river watercock'

Malesi I

124.	*'Mu mo doa lasi*	'Go with the forest cuckoo
125.	*Ma mu mo koloba'o le.'*	And go with the river woodcock.'

Malesi II

63.	*'Mu mo doa-lasi*	'Go with the forest cuckoo
64.	*Ma mo koloba'o le.'*	And with the river woodcock.'

Mu is the second-person singular of the verb 'to go', while *mo* is the second-person singular verbal term meaning 'with'. Old Meno uses the same formula, but without the verb *mu*.

Old Meno

204.	*'Mo doa lasi*	'Go with the forest cuckoo
205.	*Ma mo koloba'o le'*	And go with the river watercock'

Mikael Pellondou uses this same formula but adds a diminutive plural form to indicate many small birds.

Mikael Pellondou II

138.	*'Na, mu mo doa lasi anakala*	'Nah, go with the tiny forest cuckoos
139.	*Ma mu mo koloba'o le anakala.'*	And go with the little river watercocks.'

He reiterates this formula again a few lines further in his directive.

143.	*'Doa lasi ana-kala*	'[When] the tiny forest cuckoos
146.	*Ma kolo ba'o le ana-kala'*	And the little river watercocks'

He then follows this with the directive to go with the woman Po'o Pau Ai and the girl Latu Kai Do.

152.	*'Mu mo ina Po'o Pau Ai la*	'Go with the woman Po'o Pau Ai
153.	*Ma feto Latu Kai Do la'*	And with the girl Latu Kai Do'

Thus, the '*Mu mo*' command can itself be considered a formula whose framework can take various sets.

Joel Pellondou's use of this formula is similar to Mikael's. In his version, the command to go with the woman Po'o Pau Ai and the girl Latu Kai Do precedes his invocation of cuckoo and river watercock.

49.	*'Mu mo fetok Po'o Pau Ai la*	'Go with the girl Mouldy Pau Tree
50.	*Ma mu mo inak Latu Kai Do la'*	And go with the woman Withered Kai Leaves'

Formula II

Another formula associated with *doa lasi*//*koloba'o le* is a 'formulaic frame' that has various possibilities and is used in two variant forms in the same directive. It consists of the frame *x ... tunga-tunga le*//*y ... tunga-tunga lasi*. This formulaic frame is made up of the reduplicated verbal/preposition *tunga-tunga* ('follow through/down/along') and the dyadic set *lasi*//*le* ('forest'//'river'). Various dyadic sets can be inserted in the x/y slot. The most frequent is the set *fa*//*uda(n)* ('current/monsoon flood'//'rain').

Old Meno uses this formula with the simple connectives *fo* or *fo ela*, whose meaning can be translated as 'so' or 'so that'.

Old Meno

206.	*[Fo] fa tunga-tunga le*	So that as current passes down the river
207.	*Ma fo ela udan tunga-tunga lasi*	And rain passes through the forest

Seu Ba'i uses the same formula as Meno but he also uses it to describe the sound of the birds as they pass through the forest and down the river.

Seu Ba'i

Variant I

138.	*Fo udan tunga-tunga lasi*	So when the rain passes through the forest
139.	*Ma fa tunga-tunga le*	And the current passes down the river

Variant II

136.	*Fo ba'o-ba'o tunga le*	To [cry] *ba'o-ba'o* along the river
137.	*Ma do-do tunga tunga lasi*	And *do-do* through the forest

Malesi uses only variant II of this formula.

Malesi I

134.	*Ba'o-ba'o tunga le*	[Cries] *ba'o-ba'o* along the river
136.	*Do'o-do'o tunga lasi*	[Cries] *do'o-do'o* through the forest

Malesi II

69.	*Hu koloba'o le la ba'o-ba'o tunga le*	But if the woodcocks *ba'o-ba'o* down the river
70.	*Ma betu doa lasi la do'o-do'o tunga lasi,*	And the cuckoos *do'o-do'o* through the forest,

Mikael Pellondou interweaves the two variants.

Mikael Pellondou II

143.	*'Doa lasi ana-kala*	'[When] the tiny forest cuckoos
144.	*Bedoa tunga lasi*	Sing *doa-doa* through the forest
145.	*Na udan tunga tunga lasi*	As the rain follows through the forest
146.	*Ma kolo ba'o le ana-kala*	And the little river watercocks

| 147. | *Beba'o tunga le* | Sing *ba'o-ba'o* along the river |
| 148. | *Na fa tunga tunga le,* | As the current follows along the river, |

In this sequence of lines, Mikael skilfully uses *tunga* on its own in one formula variation and a reduplicated *tunga* in his second variant.

Joel Pellondou's version follows closely that of Mikael. His interweaving of the two formulae is less well constructed and, as a consequence, he repeats the formula *fa tunga-tunga le* (lines 55 and 59).

Joel Pellondou

53.	*Fo kolo ba'o le anakala*	There river watercock birds
54.	*Beba'o tunga le*	Cry *ba'o-ba'o* along the river
55.	*Na fa tunga-tunga le*	As the monsoon follows the river
56.	*Ma do[a] lasi anakala*	And the forest cuckoo birds
57.	*Bedo'o tunga lasi,*	Cry *do-do* through the forest,
58.	*Na udan tunga-tunga lasi*	As rain follows through the forest
59.	*Fo daenga fa tunga-tunga le*	So as the monsoon follows the river

Formula III

Another formula that recurs in these passages is the locative reference to the *oli tatain*//*le bibifan* ('edge of the estuary'//'lip of the river') to which the shells are directed. Here *tatain* is the semi-reduplicated form of the noun *tai(n)*, meaning 'edge, side', and *bibifan* is the semi-reduplicated form of the noun for 'lip'.

Old Meno

| 208. | *Fo mu oli tatain* | You may go to the edge of the estuary |
| 209. | *Ma mu le bibifan,* | And you may go to the lip of the river, |

Seu Ba'i

| 151. | *'Mu le bibifan* | 'Go to the lip of the river |
| 152. | *Ma mu oli tatain* | And go to the edge of the estuary |

The poet Malesi does not use this formula but both Mikael and Joel Pellondou use it in a similar way.

Mikael Pellondou II

154.	*Nai le [bi]bifan*	At the river's lip
155.	*Ma nai oli tatain.*	And the estuary's edge.

Joel Pellondou

51.	*Nai le bibifa-na*	At the mouth of the river
52.	*Ma nai oli tatain*	And at edge of the estuary

Formula IV

Yet another formula often associated with this passage but one that recurs more generally in most versions of *Suti Solo do Bina Bane* is *bonu boa*//*ele piko* ('to bob like *boa* wood'//'to drift like *piko* wood'). (It is a formulaic combination in that syntactic connection between verb and comparator cannot be altered. Thus, *bonu piko*//*ele boa** is not acceptable.)

Among the various poets, only Meno, Seu Ba'i and Joel Pellondou use this formula in their *doa lasi*//*koloba'o le* directive. Meno and Joel Pellondou each use this formula once, while Seu Ba'i uses it three times in his passage. In all these instances, this formula is associated with a return to the sea, whereas earlier in *Suti Solo do Bina Bane*, it is associated with the arrival of the shells from the sea.

Old Meno

212.	*Na bonu boa fo mu*	That bobbing like *boa* wood, you may go
213.	*Ma ele piko fo mu,*	And drifting like *piko* wood, you may go,

Joel Pellondou

60.	*Fo o bonu boa fo liun*	Go bobbing like *boa* wood to the ocean
61.	*Fo o ele piko fo sain.*	Go drifting like *piko* wood to the sea.

Seu Ba'i

140.	*Bonu boa fo mu*	Then bobbing like *boa* wood, you may go
141.	*Ma ele piko fo mu.*	And drifting like *piko* wood, you may go.
148.	*Au bonu boa fo au u*	I will bob like *boa* wood and go
149.	*Ma au ele piko fo u.*	And I will drift like *piko* wood and go.

157.	*Fo bonu boa fo mu*	Then bobbing like *boa* wood, you may go
158.	*Ele piko fo mu.*	And drifting like *piko* wood, you may go.

Other Formulae

Three of the poets—Seu Ba'i, Malesi and Mikael Pellondou—make use of one of the most common of all formulae, one that occurs repeatedly as a refrain in most ritual compositions. Seu Ba'i uses the singular variant of this formula while both Malesi and Mikael use plural forms.

Seu Ba'i
146.	*Malole ndia so*	This is good
147.	*Ma mandak ndia so.*	And this is proper.

Malesi I
129.	*Na malole la so*	Such would be good
130.	*Ma mandak kala so.*	And such would be proper.

Malesi II
67	*Ah, malole la so*	Ah, such would be good
68.	*Ma mandakala so.*	And such would be proper.

Mikael Pellondou II
140.	*'Malole lai na*	'Such things are good there
141.	*Ma mandak lai ndia.'*	And such things are proper there.'

Meno and Seu Ba'i both make use of another common formula: *nene fino*//*dei dongo* ('stop and listen'//'stand and wait').

Old Meno
217.	*Fo nene fino tata*	To stop and listen there
219.	*Fo dei dongo meme ndia*	To stand and wait there

Seu Ba'i
153.	*Nene-fino mu ndia*	Go to stop and listen there
154.	*Ma dei-dongo mu ndia.*	And go to stand and wait there

Finally, Old Meno uses a formula that none of the other poets uses in this same passage: *posi maka-mu mekon//unu ma-li labun* ('the sea's edge resounding like a gong'//'the reef rumbling like a drum'). This is a complex formulaic construction since it is based on the combination of three dyadic sets: 1) *posi//unu* ('sea's edge'//'reef'); 2) *maka-mu//ma-li* ('resounding'//'rumbling'); and 3) *meko(n)//labu(n)* ('gong'//'drum').

216.	*Te hu mu posi makamu mekon*	Thus go to the sea's edge, resounding like a gong
218.	*Ma mu unu mali labun*	And go to the reef, rumbling like a drum

This formula is one that Meno used in other of his compositions, such as the chant *Dela Koli ma Seko Buna*, which tells of an eagle and hawk that steal a child in revenge for the theft of their eggs.[1]

The formula in two lines in that chant is identical to that in *Suti Solo do Bina Bane*.

172.	*De neu posi maka-mu mekon*	She goes toward the edge, resounding like a gong
173.	*Ma unu ma-li labun-na*	And the reef, rumbling like a drum

Koloba'o and *Doa* Bird Reference Passages

To understand the processes of oral composition, it is essential to analyse specific passages in terms of their constituent formulae, but it is also necessary to consider how these various formulae are deftly combined to produce poetic compositions. The following poetic segments contain all of the reference passages that have been analysed in terms of specific formulae. It is useful to go further and consider these various segments in their wider compositional contexts.

Old Meno

Lines 204–21: 18 lines in a single statement.

204.	*'Mo doa lasi*	'Go with the forest cuckoo
205.	*Ma mo koloba'o le*	And go with the river watercock

---

[1] I have published this chant, *Dela Koli do Seko Buna*, in Fox (1971). It is a magnificent specimen of Old Meno's art.

206.	*[Fo] fa tunga-tunga le*	So that as current passes down the river
207.	*Ma fo ela udan tunga-tunga lasi*	And rain passes through the forest
208.	*Fo mu oli tatain*	You may go to the edge of the estuary
209.	*Ma mu le bibifan,*	And you may go to the lip of the river,
210.	*Fo ela fa oek ana mai*	So that when the current's water arrives
211.	*Ma ela epo oek ana mai*	And when the eddy's water arrives
212.	*Na bonu boa fo mu*	That bobbing like *boa* wood, you may go
213.	*Ma ele piko fo mu,*	And drifting like *piko* wood, you may go,
214.	*Leo sain dale mu*	To the sea, you may go
215.	*Ma leo liun dale mu.*	And to the ocean, you may go.
216.	*Te hu mu posi makamu mekon*	Thus go to the sea's edge, resounding like a gong
217.	*Fo nene fino tata*	To stop and listen there
218.	*Ma mu unu mali labun*	And go to the reef, rumbling like a drum
219.	*Fo dei dongo meme ndia*	To stand and wait there
220.	*Fo dei loe sain dale mu*	And then descend into the ocean
221.	*Ma dilu liun dale mu.'*	And turn downward into the sea.'

Seu Ba'i

Lines 134–58: 25 lines of a dialogue exchange.

134.	*'Mu mo doa lasi*	'Go with the forest cuckoo
135.	*Ma mu mo koloba'o le*	And go with the river watercock
136.	*Fo ba'o-ba'o tunga le*	To [cry] *ba'o-ba'o* along the river
137.	*Ma do-do tunga tunga lasi*	And *do-do* through the forest
138.	*Fo udan tunga-tunga lasi*	So when the rain passes through the forest
139.	*Ma fa tunga-tunga le*	And the current passes down the river
140.	*Bonu boa fo mu*	Then bobbing like *boa* wood, you may go
141.	*Ma ele piko fo mu.*	And drifting like *piko* wood, you may go.
142.	*Leo sain mu*	To the sea you may go
143.	*Ma leo liun mu.'*	And to the ocean you may go.'
144.	*Boe te Suti neu dedeak*	But Suti begins to speak
145.	*Ma Bina neu kokolak, nae:*	And Bina begins to talk, saying:
146.	*'Malole ndia so*	'This is good

		8. VERSION VII FROM THE DOMAIN OF TERMANU
147.	*Ma mandak ndia so.*	And this is proper.
148.	*Au bonu boa fo au u*	I will bob like *boa* wood and go
149.	*Ma au ele piko fo u.'*	And I will drift like *piko* wood and go.'
150.	*Boe te nae:*	But she says:
151.	*'Mu le bibifan*	'Go to the lip of the river
152.	*Ma mu oli tatain*	And go to the edge of the estuary
153.	*Nene-fino mu ndia*	Go to stop and listen there
154.	*Ma dei-dongo mu ndia.*	And go to stand and wait there.
155.	*Udan tunga-tunga lasi*	The rain passes through the forest
156.	*Ma fa tunga-tunga le*	And the current passes down the river
157.	*Fo bonu boa fo mu*	Then bobbing like *boa* wood, you may go
158.	*Ele piko fo mu.'*	And drifting like *piko* wood, you may go.'

Malesi I

Lines 124–40: 17 lines in a single dialogue exchange.

124.	*'Mu mo doa lasi*	'Go with the forest cuckoo
125.	*Ma mu mo koloba'o le.'*	And go with the river woodcock.'
126.	*Boe ma Bina Bane nahala*	Then Bina Bane gives voice
127.	*Ma Suti Solo nafada ma nae:*	And Suti Solo speaks and says:
128.	*'Au o kolobao le*	'I will go with the river woodcock
129.	*Na malole la so*	Such would be good
130.	*Ma mandak kala so.*	And such would be proper.
131.	*Te timu lamatua dulu*	But if the wind increases in the east
132.	*Ma hu'ak [fak] lamanalu langa*	And the monsoon extends at the headlands
133.	*Na kulu kolobao le*	Then the river woodcock
134.	*Ba'o-ba'o tunga le*	[Cries] *ba'o-ba'o* along the river
135.	*Ma betu doa lasi la*	And the forest woodcock
136.	*Do'o-do'o tunga lasi*	[Cries] *do'o-do'o* through the forest
137.	*Na Bina Bane no se*	Then with whom will Bina Bane be
138.	*[Fo] setele no se*	With whom to laugh
139.	*Ma Suti Solo no se*	And with whom will Suti Solo be
140.	*Fo nata-dale no se?'*	With whom to take heart?'

Malesi II

Lines 63–74: 12 lines in a single dialogue exchange.

63.	*'Mu mo doa lasi*	'Go with the forest cuckoo
64.	*Ma mo koloba'o le.'*	And with the river woodcock.'
65.	*Boe ma Bina Bane kokolak*	So Bina Bane speaks
66.	*Ma Suti Solo dedeak ma nae:*	And Suti Solo answers and says:
67.	*'Ah, malole la so*	'Ah, such would be good
68.	*Ma mandakala so.*	And such would be proper.
69.	*Hu koloba'o le la ba'o-ba'o tunga le*	But if the woodcocks *ba'o-ba'o* down the river
70.	*Ma betu doa lasi la do'o-do'o tunga lasi,*	And the cuckoos *do'o-do'o* through the forest,
71.	*Na Suti au o se*	Then for me, Suti, with whom will I be
72.	*Fo au asalai o se*	With whom will I recline
73.	*Ma Bina au o se*	And with me, Bina, with whom will I be
74.	*Fo au angatu o se?'*	And with whom will I sit?'

Mikael Pellondou II

Lines 138–55: 18 lines in a single dialogue exchange.

138.	*'Na, mu mo doa lasi anakala*	'Nah, go with the tiny forest cuckoos
139.	*Ma mu mo koloba'o le anakala.'*	And go with the little river watercocks.'
140.	*'Malole lai na*	'Such things are good there
141.	*Ma mandak lai ndia.'*	And such things are proper there.'
142.	*Lafada ma ladasi, lae:*	They speak and they talk, saying:
143.	*'Doa lasi ana-kala*	'[When] the tiny forest cuckoos
144.	*Bedoa tunga lasi*	Sing *doa-doa* through the forest
145.	*Na udan tunga tunga lasi*	As the rain follows through the forest
146.	*Ma kolo ba'o le ana-kala*	And the little river watercocks
147.	*Beba'o tunga le*	Sing *ba'o-ba'o* along the river
148.	*Na fa tunga tunga le,*	As the current follows along the river,
149.	*Au dede'ak o se*	With whom will I speak
150.	*Ma dede'ak o se?'*	And with whom will I speak?'

8. VERSION VII FROM THE DOMAIN OF TERMANU

151.	*Boe ma nae:*	So she says:
152.	*'Mu mo ina Po'o Pau Ai la*	'Go with the woman Po'o Pau Ai
153.	*Ma feto Latu Kai Do la*	And with the girl Latu Kai Do
154.	*Nai le [bi]bifan*	At the river's lip
155.	*Ma nai oli tatain.'*	And the estuary's edge.'

Joel Pellondou:

Lines 49–61: 13 lines in a single statement.

49.	*'Mu mo fetok Po'o Pau Ai la*	'Go with the girl Mouldy Pau Tree
50.	*Ma mu mo inak Latu Kai Do la*	And go with the woman Withered Kai Leaves
51.	*Nai le bibifa-na*	At the mouth of the river
52.	*Ma nai oli tatain*	And at the edge of the estuary
53.	*Fo kolo ba'o le anakala*	There the river watcock birds
54.	*Beba'o tunga le*	Cry *ba'o-ba'o* along the river
55.	*Na fa tunga-tunga le*	As the monsoon follows the river
56.	*Ma do[a] lasi anakala*	And the forest cuckoo birds
57.	*Bedo'o tunga lasi,*	Cry *do-do* through the forest,
58.	*Na udan tunga-tunga lasi*	As rain follows through the forest
59.	*Fo daenga fa tunga-tunga le*	So as the monsoon follows the river
60.	*Fo o bonu boa fo liun*	Go bobbing like *boa* wood to the ocean
61.	*Fo o ele piko fo sain.'*	Go drifting like *piko* wood to the sea.'

The shortest of these poetic segments weaves together just 12 lines; the longest segment some 25 lines. Each is, however, a distinctive compositional creation.

9

Suti Solo do Bina Bane: Versions VIII and IX from the Domain of Termanu

In 2010, some 45 years after I began my research on Rote, much had changed in Termanu. Most of the poets whose compositions I recorded had died and what remained of their poetry were memories and my recordings. One poet, Esau Markus Pono, whom I first met in 1965, spanned this period of change and was, at the time, regarded as Termanu's leading chanter. In 1965, 'Pak Pono' lived in the coastal settlement of Hala, a walk of some 40 minutes from the cluster of settlements, Sosa-Dale, Ufa-Len and Kola, where my wife and I were located. As a young man at that time, Pak Pono was involved in a protracted and eventually unsuccessful attempt to marry a woman from the clan Nggofa-Laik. We met and knew of each other but had no close association. By 1973, on my next long stay on Rote, Pak Pono had married and had begun to establish his reputation as a preacher and a poet. At that time, I was involved in sponsoring the final mortuary ceremony—erecting a ring of stones around a large living tree to create a *tutus*—in honour of Old Meno and needed someone to act as primary speaker at this ritual.[1]

Pak Pono was the ideal person for this task because of his evident speaking skills and because, as a preacher, his presence would allay any Christian objections to my reviving so significant a traditional ritual. I was also

---

1 I have described this ceremony and set out, in detail, the background to it in Fox (1989).

interested in acquiring animals for the accompanying feast and was able to barter my watch for Pak Pono's largest pig. His performance at the *tutus* ceremony established what was to become our continuing relationship.

Some years later, in 1977 and again in 1978, I visited Rote with the filmmaker Tim Asch. By this time, Pak Pono was widely recognised for his use of ritual language in his preaching, and we were able to film him conducting a church service.[2] He was also a member of the groom's party in a bridewealth payment ceremony that we filmed. As a result of his close involvement in our filming efforts, we invited him for a visit to Canberra to help in the preparation of the film.[3] One of his tasks was to transcribe a great deal of Rotenese that we recorded during filming.

By the 1980s, Pak Pono and I had become close friends and on all subsequent visits to Rote, he was my first point of contact in Termanu. For the past 30 years, as his own skills as an accomplished poet increased, he became my most dedicated advisor on all matters relating to ritual language. On all occasions when I gathered poets for recording sessions on Bali, he joined the group. In short, we two grew old together in a continual effort to document the beauty and intricacies of Rotenese ritual language.

Although I had heard Pak Pono recite *Suti Solo do Bina Bane* to other poets, I did not record him directly until 2008, and having recorded him in 2008, I asked to record him again (and video him at the same time) in 2009. With an interval of only a year, his two versions are similar to one another. Neither version is long. The 2008 version runs to 126 lines; the 2009 version is somewhat longer and comes to 150 lines. The 2008 version comprises 50 dyadic sets; the 2009 version shares 48 sets with the 2008 version but utilises a dozen additional dyadic sets including several additional longer formulae.

---

2   I have written on Pak Pono's use of ritual language in his preaching in Fox (1982).
3   A film was made of the bridewealth payment ceremony, *Spear and Sword: A Payment of Bridewealth* (Fox with Asch and Asch 1988), but no film was ever made from the footage of the church service. All of the footage is stored in the archives of the Smithsonian Institution.

9. VERSIONS VIII AND IX FROM THE DOMAIN OF TERMANU

Figure 9: Esau Markus Pono – 'Pak Pono'

As compositions, the two versions are worth comparing one with the other: their use of constituent dyadic sets, their order of composition and their reliance on recognisable formulae can provide further insights into the art of composition.

I will therefore compare the two compositions in sequence with one another.

MASTER POETS, RITUAL MASTERS

Introduction and Search for the Ritual Fish

2008 Version

1.	*Faik esa manunin*	On one particular day
2.	*Do ledok esa mate'e-na*	Or one certain time
3.	*Inaka Mo Bisa*	The woman Mo Bisa
4.	*Ma fetoka Ole Masi*	And the girl Ole Masi
5.	*Ana nggao na seko meti-na*	She takes up her tidal scoop-net
6.	*Fo seko matei besin*	The scoop-net with iron-weighted insides
7.	*Ma tenga na ndai tasi-na*	And picks up her sea fishing net
8.	*Fo ndai mahamu lilo-na.*	The fishing net with gold-weighted belly.
9.	*De leu seko sisi'u enggak*	They go to scoop lift the *enggak* seaweed
10.	*Ma leu ndai huhuka batu.*	And they go to uncover the rocks.
11.	*De seko sanga Dusu La'e*	They scoop in search of Dusu La'e fish
12.	*Ma leu ndai sanga Tio Holu.*	And they go to fish in search of Tio Holu fish.
13.	*De ala ndai basa namo-la*	They fish in all the harbours
14.	*Ma seko basa lek-ala.*	And they scoop in all the waterholes.
15.	*Te ta hapu Tio Holu*	But do not find Tio Holu
16.	*Ma ta hapu Dusu La'e.*	And do not find Dusu La'e.

2009 Version

1.	*Au kokolak Suti Solo*	I speak of Suti Solo
2.	*Ma au dede'ak Bina Bane.*	And I tell of Bina Bane.
3.	*Neu faik esa manunina*	On one particular day
4.	*Ma ledok esa mate'ena,*	And at a certain time,
5.	*Boe ma inaka Mo Bisa*	The woman Mo Bisa
6.	*Ma fetoka Masi Tasi*	And the girl Masi Tasi
7.	*Tenga la ndai tasi-na*	Pick up their sea fishing net
8.	*Ma nggao la seko meti-na*	And take up their tidal scoop-net
9.	*Fo seko matei besik*	The scoop-net with iron-weighted insides

10.	*Ma ndai mahamu lilok.*	And the fishing net with gold-weighted belly.
11.	*Neu lelek fo meti la si unu*	At a time when the tide begins to ebb
12.	*Ma tasi la huka papa*	And the sea shows its shallows
13.	*Boe duas leu seko meti*	The two go to scoop in the tide
14.	*Ma duas leu ndai tasi.*	And the two go to fish in the sea.
15.	*Leu seko sisi'u enggak*	Go to scoop and lift the *enggak* seaweed
16.	*Ma leu ndai huhuka batu,*	And go to fish and uncover the rocks,
17.	*Seko sanga Dusu La'e*	Scoop in search of Dusu La'e fish
18.	*Ma ndai sanga Tio Holu.*	And fish in search of Tio Holu fish.
19.	*Tehu ala seko basa lifu la*	But they scoop in all the pools
20.	*Ma ala ndai basa lek ala,*	And they fish in all the waterholes,
21.	*Te ta hapu Tio Holu*	But they do not find Tio Holu
22.	*Ma ta hapu Dusu La'e.*	And do not find Dusu La'e.

The Gathering of Suti Solo do Bina Bane

2008 Version

17.	*Te lala lifu dua na*	But when they look in two pools
18.	*Suti nala lifu dua*	Suti is in the two pools
19.	*Ma lala lek telu*	And when they look in three waterholes
20.	*Na Bina nala lek telu.*	Bina is in the three waterholes.
21.	*Boe ma ala seko ndano leni Suti*	So they scoop up and take Suti
22.	*Ma ala ndai ndano leni Bina.*	And they fish forth and take Bina.

2009 Version

23.	*Te ala seko lala lifu dua*	But when they scoop in two pools
24.	*Na Bina nala lifu dua*	Bina is in the two pools
25.	*Ma ndai lala lek telu*	And when they fish in three waterholes
26.	*Na Suti nala lek telu.*	Suti is in the three waterholes.
27.	*Boe ma ala dudu'a*	So they ponder

28.	*Ma ala a'afi*	And they think
29.	*De lae le baik*	It would be better if
30.	*Seko teni Suti Solo*	We scoop and take Suti Solo
31.	*Ma ndai teni Bina Bane.*	And we fish and take Bina Bane.
32.	*Boe ma ala ndai ndano*	So they fish forth
33.	*Leni Bina Bane*	Taking Bina Bane
34.	*Ma ala seko toko*	And they scoop up
35.	*Leni Suti Solo.*	Taking Suti Solo.

Initial Dialogue and First Directive

2008 Version

23.	*De ala mai dalak dua bobongo*	They come to where two roads circle
24.	*Ma mai enok telu tai lolona.*	And come to where three paths cross.
25.	*Boe ma Suti neu kokolak*	Suti begins to speak
26.	*Ma Bina neu dede'ak, nae:*	And Bina begins to talk, saying:
27.	*'Ndele mafa ndendelek*	'Remember, do remember
28.	*Ma nesa masa nanedak*	And keep in mind, do keep in mind
29.	*Bo inango nou*	My dear mother
30.	*Ma bo te'ongo nei*	And my dear aunt
31.	*O mu losa lo*	[When] you go to your home
32.	*Ma o mu nduku uma*	And you go to your house
33.	*Na boso masu ndalu au*	Do not smoke me
34.	*Ma boso pila nuli au,*	And do not burn me,
35.	*Te au daehena*	For I am a human being
36.	*Ma au ia hataholi.*	And I am indeed a person.
37.	*Au ia ana-mak*	I am indeed an orphan
38.	*Ma au ia falu-inak.'*	And I am indeed a widow.'
39.	*Boe ma ala kokolak*	So they speak
40.	*Ma ala dede'ak ma lae:*	And they talk, saying:
41.	*'Sona mu dalak dua bobongon*	'Then go to where two roads circle
42.	*Ma mu enok telu tai lolon.'*	And go to where the three paths cross.'

43.	*Boe ma Suti Solo do Bina Bane*	So Suti Solo or Bina Bane
44.	*Ala kokolak*	They speak
45.	*Ma ala dede'ak ma lae:*	And they talk and say:
46.	*'Malole basa sila*	'All this is good
47.	*Ma mandak basa sila.*	And all this is proper.
48.	*Tehu hataholi mai*	But if people come
49.	*Ma daehena mai*	And humans come
50.	*Na ala momolo tatabu ami*	They will step and tread upon us
51.	*Na ami kokolak mo se*	Then with whom will we speak
52.	*Ma ami dede'ak mo se?'*	And with whom will we talk?'

2009 Version

36.	*De ala mulai*	They then begin
37.	*Ala tulek do ala falik,*	They go back or they return,
38.	*Falik mai leo uma*	Return to the home
39.	*Ma tulek mai leo lon.*	And go back to the house.
40.	*De ala bela'o*	As they go
41.	*Boe ma Suti ana dede'ak*	Suti, he talks
42.	*Ma Bina ana kokolak, nae:*	And Bina, he speaks, saying:
43.	*'Bo inango nou*	'My dear mother
44.	*Do bo te'ongo nou*	Or my dear aunt
45.	*Neda masa-nenedak*	Keep in mind, do keep in mind
46.	*Ma ndele mafa ndendelek*	And remember, do remember
47.	*Fo teu losa uma sona,*	When we reach the house,
48.	*Boso pila nuli ami*	Do not burn us
49.	*Do boso masu ndalu ami,*	Or do not smoke us,
50.	*Te ami ia dae-hena*	For we indeed are human beings
51.	*Ma ami ia hataholi,*	And we indeed are people,
52.	*Ami falu-ina Bina Bane la*	We are the widows, Bina Bane
53.	*Ma ami ana-ma Suti Solo la.'*	And we are the orphans, Suti Solo.'
54.	*Boe ma ala dede'ak*	So they talk
55.	*Ma ala kokolak lo duas lae:*	And they speak with the two, saying:
56.	*'Ita nai enok dua bobongon*	'We are where two paths circle

57.	*Ma nai dalak telu tai lolona*	And where three roads cross
58.	*Ela emi dua meme ia.'*	Let us leave you here.'
59.	*Boe ma nae:*	So he says:
60.	*'Malole ndia so*	'That would be good
61.	*Ma manda ndia so,*	That would be proper,
62.	*Tehu daehena mai*	But if humans come
63.	*Ma hataholi mai*	And people come
64.	*Na ala momolo ami*	They will step on us
65.	*Ma ala tatabu ami,*	And they will tread on us,
66.	*Na ami maka bani neu se*	Then on whom will we rely
67.	*Ma ami mama hena neu se?'*	And on whom will we depend?'

Second Dialogue Directive

2008 Version

53.	*Boe ma lae:*	So they say:
54.	*'Sona mu mo sa'o tua*	'Then go be with the lontar shadow
55.	*Ma mu mo mafo ai.'*	And go be with the tree shade.'
56.	*Boe ma Suti Solo nahala*	So Suti Solo gives voice
57.	*Ma Bina Bane nadasi ma nae:*	And Bina Bane lifts words and says:
58.	*'Ami [mo] mafo ai*	'We [can] go with the tree shade
59.	*Te mafo ai la heok*	But if the tree shade shifts
60.	*Ma ami mo sa'o tua*	And we can go with the lontar shadow
61.	*Fo sa'o tua lahiluk.*	But if the lontar shadow moves
62.	*Na ami kokolak mo se*	Then with whom will we speak
63.	*Ma ami dede'ak mo se?'*	And with whom will we talk?'

2009 Version

68.	*Boe ma lae:*	So they say:
69.	*'Sona dua ma*	'So the two of you
70.	*Meu mo mafo tua*	Go with lontar shade
71.	*Ma meu mo sa'o ai.'*	And go with the tree shadow.'

72.	*Boe ma lae:*	Then they say:
73.	*'Ndia boe o malole ndia*	'That indeed would be good
74.	*Tehu neu faik*	But during the day
75.	*Mafo ai la heok*	If the tree shade shifts
76.	*Ma sa'o tua hiluk,*	And the lontar shadow moves,
77.	*Na ami kokolak mo se*	Then with whom will we speak
78.	*Ma ami dede'ak mo se?'*	And with whom will we talk?'

Third Dialogue Directive

2008 Version

64.	*'Na sona mu mo neka hade*	'Then go with the rice basket
65.	*Ma mu mo bou tua.'*	And go with the lontar syrup vat.'
66.	*Boe ma lae ndia:*	So they say this:
67.	*'Boe o malole ndia so*	'Oh, that would be good
68.	*Ma mandak ndia so,*	And that would be proper,
69.	*Tehu fui-ana la kae*	But if strangers climb up [into the house]
70.	*Ma ae-ana la hene na*	And if neighbours ascend [into the house]
71.	*Basa bou tua la*	The syrup vat will be finished
72.	*Ma basa neka hade la.*	And the rice basket emptied,
73.	*Na ami kokolak mo se*	Then with whom will we speak
74.	*Ma ami dede'ak mo se?'*	And with whom will we talk?'

2009 Version

79.	*Boe lahala ma lae: 'A sona*	So they give voice and say: 'If so,
80.	*Dua ma meu mo neka hade*	Then you two go with the rice basket
81.	*Ma dua ma meu mo bou tua.'*	And you two go with the lontar syrup vat.'
82.	*Boe ma lae:*	So they say:
83.	*'Tete'ek ndia nde malole*	'Truly, that would be good
84.	*Ma na nde mandaka*	And that would be proper
85.	*Tehu neu fai-na ma ledo-na*	But on a certain day and time
86.	*Fo fui ana la kae*	If strangers climb [into the house]

87.	*Ma ae ana la hena*	And neighbours ascend [into the house]
88.	*Na basa neka hade*	Then the rice basket will be emptied
89.	*Ma basa bou tua,*	And the syrup vat finished
90.	*Na ami mama hena neu se*	Then on whom will we depend
91.	*Ma ami maka bani neu se?'*	And on whom will we rely?'

Fourth Dialogue Directive

2008 Version

75.	*Boe ma nae:*	So she says:
76.	*'Mu mo lete nalu kala*	'Go be with the high hills
77.	*Mu mo mo loa kala.'*	And go be with the wide fields.'
78.	*Boe ma nae:*	So he says:
79.	*'Ndia boe malole*	'That would be good
80.	*Ma ndia boe o manda-kala*	And that would be proper
81.	*Tehu neu fai-na fo bote-la mai*	But some day a flock of goats will come
82.	*Ma neu ledo na tena-la mai*	And at a certain time a herd of buffalo will come
83.	*Fo ala heheta [ami]*	They will trample us into the mud
84.	*Ma hahapa ami*	And they will tread us into the dirt
85.	*Na ami dede'ak mo se*	Then with whom will we speak
86.	*Ma ami kokolak mo se?'*	And with whom will we talk?'

2009 Version

92.	*Boe ma nae: 'Sona,*	So she says: 'If so,
93.	*Dua ma meu mo mo naluk*	You two should go with the long field
94.	*Ma meu mo lete lepak.'*	And go with the mountain ridge.'
95.	*Boe ma nae:*	Then he says:
96.	*'Auwe, sona ndia faik*	'Oh dear, if that day
97.	*Fo bote la lama da'a mai*	Goats come and scatter about
98.	*Ma tena la lama nggela main a*	And buffalo come and spread out
99.	*Nau ta nau fa o*	Wish it or not
100.	*Ala heheta do hahapa ami so,*	They will tramp or tread upon us,

9. VERSIONS VIII AND IX FROM THE DOMAIN OF TERMANU

| 101. | *Sona ami nama henak ta* | For us, there is nothing to depend on |
| 102. | *Ma ami naka banik ta.'* | And for us, there is nothing to rely upon.' |

Fifth and Final Dialogue Directive

2008 Version

87.	*'Sona mu le tatai-na*	'Then go to the edge of the river
88.	*Ma mu oli titiana*	And go to the side of the estuary
89.	*Fo ela leo bena*	So that it may be so
90.	*Faik fo betu doa lasi*	Each day the forest cuckoos
91.	*Ala bedoa tunga lasi*	They cry *doa-doa* through the forest
92.	*Na udan tunga lasi*	As the rain comes through the forest
93.	*Ma koloba'o le la taona*	And the river woodcocks do the same
94.	*Bebao tunga le*	[They] cry *bao-bao* along the river
95.	*Na fa tunga-tunga le.*	As the monsoon flood moves down the river.
96.	*Sona dilu mu sain dale*	So that descending, you go into the sea
97.	*Ma loe mu liun dale.'*	And lowering, you go into the ocean.'
98.	*Boe ma nae:*	So he says:
99.	*'Malole ndia so*	'That would be good
100.	*Ma mandak ndia.*	And that would be proper.
101.	*Fak ala foki le na*	When the monsoon rains beat the river
102.	*Foki leni ami*	They will beat and carry us
103.	*Meu leo sain dale*	That we may go into the sea
104.	*Ma ami meu liun dale.*	And we may go into the ocean.
105.	*De ami bonu boa fo liun*	We will bob like *boa* wood to the ocean
106.	*Ma ami ele piko fo sain.'*	And we will drift like *piko* wood to the sea.'

2009 Version

| 103. | *Boe ma nae: 'Sona mai,* | So she says: 'If that happens, |
| 104. | *Fo meu le titiana* | Then go to the side of the river |

105.	*Ma meu oli tatai-na*	And go to the edge of the estuary
106.	*Fo meu faik fo de'eka [?]*	So that you go each day
107.	*Doa lasi la bedoa*	The forest cuckoos cry *doa-doa*
108.	*Fo lae betu doa lasi la*	Thus the forest cuckoos
109.	*Bedoa tunga lasi na*	They cry *doa-doa* through the forest
110.	*Udan tunga tunga lasi,*	As the rain comes through the forest,
111.	*Boe ma kolo ba'o le la*	So the river woodcocks along the river
112.	*Ala beba'o tunga tunga le*	They cry *bao-bao* along the river
113.	*Na fa tunga tunga le.*	And the monsoon flood moves down the river.
114.	*De neu faik fo betu doa lasi la,*	So each day the forest cuckoos,
115.	*Ala bedoa tunga lasi*	They cry *doa-doa* through the forest
116.	*Boe ma udana boe*	Just as the rain comes
117.	*Tunga tunga lasi*	Following through the forest
118.	*De fa boe ana mai*	Just as the monsoon flood comes
119.	*Menik koloba'o a*	To carry away the woodcock
120.	*Ana ba'o-ba'o tunga le.'*	Who crys *bao-bao* along the river.'
121.	*Lae: 'Malole ndia.'*	They say: 'That is good.'
122.	*De duas lae:*	The two say:
123.	*'Ia sona nda dalek ma tesa teik.'*	'This is pleasing and satisfying.'

The Return to the Sea and Concluding Lines

2008 Version

107.	*Boe ma neu nduku sain*	So he goes to the sea
108.	*Ma leu nduku liun.*	And they go to the ocean.
109.	*Boe ma liun na e'edo*	The sea continually casts out
110.	*De ana edo heni Suti nggi*	It casts forth Suti's pod
111.	*Ma ana toko heni Bina isin.*	And it throws out Bina's contents.
112.	*Ana edo heni Suti nggi*	It casts out Suti's pod

113.	*Ma ana toko heni Bina isin.*	And throws out Bina's contents.
114.	*Boe ma ana bonu boa*	He bobs like *boa* wood
115.	*Ma ana ele piko*	And he drifts like *piko* wood
116.	*Basa namo la*	[Through] all the harbours
117.	*Ma basa tasi la.*	And all the seas.
118.	*De losa faika*	So to this day
119.	*Ma nduku ledo ka*	And until this time
120.	*Mita kada Bina loun*	We see only Bina's shell
121.	*Ma hapu kada Suti loun.*	And find only Suti's shell.
122.	*Te isin ta.*	But no contents.
123.	*Bina bei ma-isik*	Bina still has contents
124.	*Tehu Suti isin ta.*	But Suti has no contents.
125.	*Losa faik ia*	To this day
126.	*Ma nduku ledok ia.*	And until this time.

2009 Version

124.	*De dua leu*	So the two go
125.	*Le tatai-na ma oli titiana.*	To river's edge and estuary's side.
126.	*De faika fo fa ana mai*	Then one day the monsoon comes
127.	*Nafa foki neni Bina*	The waves beat and carry Bina
128.	*Ma nafa foki neni Suti.*	And the waves beat and carry Suti.
129.	*De ala bonu boa de [neu] liu*	They bob like *boa* wood and go to the ocean
130.	*Ma ala ele piko de [neu] sain.*	And they drift like *piko* wood and go to the sea.
131.	*Tehu leu sain boe ma*	But when they are in the sea
132.	*Liun neu na-pode*	The ocean throws them back
133.	*Ma sain boe o na-edo*	And the sea casts them out
134.	*Nai fak lama nalu langa*	When the monsoon lengthens its head
135.	*De liun pode heni Bina isin*	The ocean throws away Bina's contents
136.	*Ma sain edo heni Suti nggin.*	And the sea casts away Suti's pods.
137.	*Nalak duas bonu boa selu*	Then the two bob back like *boa* wood
138.	*De ala dae mai*	They come to land
139.	*De ala madak mai.*	They come to dry land.

140.	*Tehu Bina bei ma isik*	But Bina still has some contents
141.	*Ma Suti isi ta.*	And Suti has no contents.
142.	*De losa besaka.*	So it is to the present.
143.	*Ala tao Bina neu dipo ina*	They make Bina into a spinning base
144.	*Ma tao Suti neu tena tauk*	And make Suti into an indigo container
145.	*Fo ina mana pa'a abasala*	So the woman who winds cotton
146.	*Ma feto ma feo futusala*	And the girl who dyes the threads
147.	*Tao neu dipo inak*	They make a spinning base
148.	*Ala tao neu tena tauk.*	And they make an indigo container.
149.	*De losa besaka Bina bei ma isik*	Until now, Bina still has content
150.	*Te Suti isin ta kada louna.*	But Suti has only its shell.

Compositional Analysis

As is evident from the very beginning, there are various subtle differences between Pak Pono's 2008 and 2009 recitations. Most notably, in terms of the ritual knowledge of names, Pak Pono gives slightly different names to the women who scoop up Suti Solo do Bina Bane. In the 2008 version, they are named Mo Bisa//Ole Masi, while in the 2009 version, they are named Mo Bisa//Masi Tasi. Significantly as well, the 2009 version is longer, and to reach each equivalent point in the chant narrative, this version utilises more lines. Thus illustratively, in its initial sequence, the 2009 version has six more lines than the 2008 version, beginning with the opening lines: 'I speak of Suti Solo and I tell of Bina Bane.' For each of the 16 lines in the 2008 version, however, there is a similar equivalent line. Although the ordering of these lines varies, they are all—with one exception—composed of the same dyadic sets.

There is yet another significant difference between these two versions. Given the dyadic nature of compositions, poets have the option of presenting their recitation in single or plural format—or, as commonly occurs, in a mix of singular and plural formats. Thus, for example, in its early lines and throughout the narrative, the 2008 version mixes singular and plural. Thus, on line five, *ana* is the singular, third-person pronoun 'she', while in line 13, *ala* is the plural, third-person pronoun 'they'. (As a consequence, verbal agreements, where necessary, are either singular or plural.) By contrast, the 2009 version is consistently presented in the plural. In lines seven and eight, for example, both verbs *tenga-la* and *nggao-la* are plural forms; in lines 13, 14, 15 and 16, the plural form *leu* of the verb 'to go' is used, and the third-person plural pronoun is used throughout the composition.

As a consequence of these differences and the order of composition, the various lines in the two recitations differ slightly, even though they are, for the most part, based on the same dyadic sets. In the initial sequence, only lines 13 and 14 of the 2008 version use a different dyadic set from lines 19 and 20 in the 2009 version. The 2008 version uses the dyadic set *namo//lek* ('harbour'//'waterhole'), whereas the 2009 version uses the set *lifu//lek* ('pool'//'waterhole'). Notably, however, several lines further on in the 2008 version (lines 17–20), Pak Pono uses the set *lifu//lek,* as he does consistently in his 2009 version.

As a simple illustration, it is useful to compare the first 16 lines of the 2008 version with their equivalent lines in the 2009 version.

The First 16 Lines of the 2008 Version Compared

1.	*Faik esa manunin*	On one particular day
(3)	***Neu faik esa manunina***	**On one particular day**
2.	*Do ledok esa mate'e-na*	Or one certain time
(4)	***Ma ledok esa mate'ena,***	**And at a certain time,**
3.	*Inaka Mo Bisa*	The woman Mo Bisa
(5)	***Boe ma inaka Mo Bisa***	**The woman Mo Bisa**
4.	*Ma fetoka Ole Masi*	And the girl Ole Masi
(6)	***Ma fetoka Masi Tasi***	**And the girl Masi Tasi**
5.	*Ana nggao na seko meti-na*	She takes up her tidal scoop-net
(8)	***Ma nggao la seko meti-na***	**And take up their tidal scoop-net**
6.	*Fo seko matei besin*	The scoop-net with iron-weighted insides
(9)	***Fo seko matei besik***	**The scoop-net with iron-weighted insides**
7.	*Ma tenga na ndai tasi-na*	And picks up her sea fishing net
(7)	***Tenga la ndai tasi-na***	**Pick up their sea fishing net**

8.	*Fo ndai mahamu lilo-na.*	The fishing net with gold-weighted belly.
(10)	**Ma ndai mahamu lilok.**	**And the fishing net with gold-weighted belly.**
9.	*De leu seko sisi'u enggak*	They go to scoop lift the *enggak* seaweed
(15)	**Leu seko sisi'u enggak**	**Go to scoop and lift the *enggak* seaweed**
10.	*Ma leu ndai huhuka batu.*	And they go to uncover the rocks.
(16)	**Ma leu ndai huhuka batu,**	**And go to fish and uncover the rocks,**
11.	*De seko sanga Dusu La'e*	They scoop in search of Dusu La'e fish
(17)	**Seko sanga Dusu La'e**	**Scoop in search of Dusu La'e fish**
12.	*Ma leu ndai sanga Tio Holu.*	And they go to fish in search of Tio Holu fish.
(18)	**Ma ndai sanga Tio Holu.**	**And fish in search of Tio Holu fish.**
13.	*De ala ndai basa namo-la*	They fish in all the harbours
(19)	**Tehu ala seko basa lifu la**	**But they scoop in all the pools**
14.	*Ma seko basa lek-ala.*	And they scoop in all the waterholes.
(20)	**Ma ala ndai basa lek ala,**	**And they fish in all the waterholes,**
15.	*Te ta hapu Tio Holu*	But do not find Tio Holu fish
(21)	**Te ta hapu Tio Holu**	**But they do not find Tio Holu fish**
16.	*Ma ta hapu Dusu La'e.*	And do not find Dusu La'e fish.
(22)	**Ma ta hapu Dusu La'e.**	**And do not find Dusu La'e fish.**

As these recitations proceed, the play on singular and plural continues. Thus, in Suti Solo do Bina Bane's first dialogue, the 2008 version uses the singular 'I' (*au*) while the 2009 version begins with the use of the third-person singular pronoun (*ana*) and a first-person singular possessive pronoun (*-ngo*) but then uses the plural 'we' (*ami*) throughout the actual dialogue.

It is useful to compare the slightly different ways in which these passages are composed. The only compositional flaw that is apparent in comparing the passages is in the 2009 version, which lacks a corresponding line for line 47. Lines 31 and 32 in the 2008 version reveal the expected and appropriate pairing of the sets *losa*//*nduku* ('up to'//'towards, until, at') and *uma*//*lo* ('house'//'home'). The arrangement of the lines is similar but not entirely identical. The lines with 'My dear mother and my dear aunt' either precede or follow the lines with 'Remember, do remember and keep in mind, do keep in mind'.

2008 Version: Initial Dialogue

25.	*Boe ma Suti neu kokolak*	Suti begins to speak
26.	*Ma Bina neu dede'ak, nae:*	And Bina begins to talk, saying:
27.	*'Ndele mafa ndendelek*	'Remember, do remember
28.	*Ma nesa masa nenedak*	And keep in mind, do keep in mind
29.	*Bo inango nou*	My dear mother
30.	*Ma bo te'ongo nei*	And my dear aunt
31.	*O mu losa lo*	[When] you go to your home
32.	*Ma o mu nduku uma*	And you go to your house
33.	*Na boso masu ndalu au*	Do not smoke me
34.	*Ma boso pila nuli au,*	And do not burn me,
35.	*Te au dae-hena*	For I am a human being
36.	*Ma au ia hataholi.*	And I am indeed a person.
37.	*Au ia ana-mak*	I am indeed an orphan
38.	*Ma au ia falu-inak.'*	And I am indeed a widow.'

2009 Version: Initial Dialogue

41.	*Boe ma Suti ana dede'ak*	Suti, he talks
42.	*Ma Bina ana kokolak, nae:*	And Bina, he speaks, saying:
43.	*'Bo inango nou*	'My dear mother
44.	*Do bo te'ongo nou*	Or my dear aunt
45.	*Neda masa-nenedak*	Keep in mind, do keep in mind
46.	*Ma ndele mafa ndendelek*	And remember, do remember
47.	*Fo teu losa uma sona,*	When we reach the house,
48.	*Boso pila nuli ami*	Do not burn us
49.	*Do boso masu ndalu ami,*	Or do not smoke us,
50.	*Te ami ia dae-hena*	For we indeed are human beings
51.	*Ma ami ia hataholi,*	And we indeed are people,
52.	*Ami falu-ina Bina Bane la*	We are the widows, Bina Bane
53.	*Ma ami ana-ma Suti Solo la.'*	And we are the orphans, Suti Solo.'

Although with their various uses of singular and plural and the missing line in the 2009 version these two passages are indeed different, their composition is in fact based on the same eight dyadic sets: 1) *kokolak// dede'ak*; 2) *ina//te'o*; 3) *nedak//ndelek*; 4) *losa//nduku*; 5) *uma//lo*; 6) *pila nuli//masu ndalu*; 7) *daehena//hataholi*; 8) *falu-ina//ana-mak*.

In both versions, this passage asserts the dominant theme of the composition: that the shells Suti Solo do Bina Bane are orphans in search of a permanent place of refuge and genuine fellowship. In the 2008 version, immediately after this passage, Pak Pono begins the familiar refrain that marks most versions of *Suti Solo do Bina Bane*:

Na ami kokolak mo se	Then with whom will we speak
Ma ami dede'ak mo se?	And with whom will we talk?

In the 2008 version, this refrain, which is first enunciated in lines 51/52, is repeated in lines 62/63, 73/74 and 85/86—each time in reply to one of the directives on where to seek refuge.

The 2009 version also uses this formulaic refrain but alternates with another formulaic refrain:

Na ami maka bani neu se	Then on whom will we rely
Ma ami mama hena neu se?	And on whom will we depend?

This refrain occurs first in lines 66/67 and is followed in lines 77/78 by the same refrain that is used throughout the 2008 version:

Na ami kokolak mo se	Then with whom will we speak
Ma ami dede'ak mo se?	And with whom will we talk?

This refrain is then followed by a return to the first refrain in lines 90/91 but with the order of the two lines reversed:

Na ami mama hena neu se	Then on whom will we depend
Ma ami maka bani neu se?	And on whom will we rely?

Finally, where one expects a return to the alternative refrain in lines 101/102, Pak Pono offers another, more emphatic variant of his initial refrain:

Sona ami nama henak ta	For us, there is nothing to depend on
Ma ami naka banik ta.	And for us, there is nothing to rely upon.

Coming as the last in a succession of these refrains, this is a powerful poetic assertion.

Like other versions of *Suti Solo do Bina Bane*, the concluding passages of both of Pak Pono's recitations recount the return of the shells to the sea.

The 2008 version presents this return to the sea with what is a commonplace observation that is frequently heard on Rote. Whereas a bailer shell (*bina*) is occasionally found with some remnant fleshy content, a nautilus shell is always found without its content. This observation is the basis for the concluding lines of the 2008 version:

120.	*Mita kada Bina loun*	We see only Bina's shell
121.	*Ma hapu kada Suti loun.*	And find only Suti's shell.
122.	*Te isin ta.*	But no contents.
123.	*Bina bei ma-isik*	Bina still has contents
124.	*Tehu Suti isin ta.*	But Suti has no contents.
125.	*Losa faik ia*	To this day
126.	*Ma nduku ledok ia.*	And until this time.

Technically, the composition of lines 120–24 is not based on pairs and should probably be considered as a commentary on the recitation rather than as an integral part of it. Lines 125/126 simply repeat lines 118/119 as an appropriate conclusion.

The 2009 version has a more complex conclusion. It recounts the passage of the shells to the sea, but then recounts their return to the land and their transformation into specific cultural objects: the first spinning base and first indigo container. As, for example, in Old Meno's composition, this statement—just six lines out of a total of 150 lines—links this recitation to a special corpus of sacred origin chants, even though the precise connections to this corpus are not articulated. Were these connections not articulated in other versions, the concluding lines in this version would make little sense, especially when they are inserted with observations about the content or lack of content in the two types of shell.

135.	*De liun pode heni Bina isin*	The ocean throws away Bina's contents
136.	*Ma sain edo heni Suti nggin.*	And the sea casts away Suti's pods.
137.	*Nalak duas bonu boa selu*	Then the two bob back like *boa* wood
138.	*De ala dae mai*	They come to land

139.	*De ala madak mai.*	They come to dry land.
140.	*Tehu Bina bei ma isik*	But Bina still has some contents
141.	*Ma Suti isi ta.*	And Suti has no contents.
142.	*De losa besaka.*	So it is to the present.
143.	*Ala tao Bina neu dipo ina*	They make Bina into a spinning base
144.	*Ma tao Suti neu tena tauk*	And make Suti into an indigo container
145.	*Fo ina mana pa'a abasala*	So the woman who winds cotton
146.	*Ma feto ma feo futusala*	And the girl who dyes the threads
147.	*Tao neu dipo inak*	They make a spinning base
148.	*Ala tao neu tena tauk.*	And they make an indigo container.
149.	*De losa besaka Bina bei ma isik*	Until now, Bina still has content
150.	*Te Suti isin ta kada louna.*	But Suti has only its shell.

In ritual terms, if a version of *Suti Solo do Bina Bane* recounts the passage of the nautilus and bailer shells from the sea through a series of impermanent stations and then finally back to the sea, it can be used as a mortuary chant symbolic of the passage of a human being, as an orphan and widow, through the course of a lifetime. If, however, a recitation alludes to the creation and use of the nautilus and bailer shells as key ritual objects in the processes of weaving and dyeing, it constitutes an origin chant and forms part of a larger corpus of sacred knowledge. Pak Pono's 2008 version can appropriately be considered a mortuary chant whereas his 2009 version—because of the brief ritual allusions at its conclusion—can more appropriately be considered as an origin chant.

These versions of *Suti Solo do Bina Bane* were among the last recitations of Esau Pono. Although he continued to preside at our recording sessions in Bali, he grew ever weaker at each gathering and eventually he was too weak to join our ninth session in 2014. Sometime after midnight on the 16th of December 2014, he died. At his funeral his fellow poets gathered to chant his farewell and with the help of Dr Lintje Pellu, who travelled from Kupang to Rote, I was able to send a chant that I composed to give voice to our long friendship.

10
Suti Solo do Bina Bane as a Personal Composition

This is a version of *Suti Solo do Bina Bane* that belongs within the speech community of Termanu. It is entirely in the dialect of Termanu, but as a composition, it is not grounded in Termanu's traditional ritual knowledge. It is a beautiful, personal composition by an unusual poet, Zet Apulugi.

Zet Apulugi, as his name indicates, is a Ndaonese, the descendant of settlers from the tiny island at the western end of Rote.[1] I first encountered Zet in 1973 as a young man who was then living in the Mok Dae, a settlement in the village of Ono Tali. At the time, with Old Meno's son, I sponsored a final mortuary ceremony for Old Meno. The ceremony, known as *Lutu Tutus,* involved the creation of a raised stone platform surrounding a living tree as a monument in Meno's honour.[2]

The night before the main ceremony and feast was dedicated to chanting in remembrance of Old Meno. A number of leading chanters came from Termanu and from the neighbouring domain of Korbaffo and engaged, as was expected, in competition with one another. Pe'u Malesi was a prominent figure among these chanters because he was considered the representative

---

1   Ndaonese are settled in virtually every domain on the island of Rote. In some domains, Ndaonese are assimilated to a specific clan; in other domains, as in Termanu, individual Ndaonese settlers are incorporated in various clans. In Zet Apulugi's case, he retains his Ndaonese name: Apulugi. This suggests that his family is in an early stage of the process of assimilation to being considered fully 'Rotenese'.
2   I have described this ceremony and the preparations leading to its performance in Fox (1989).

of the village where I was living, Nggodi Meda. A particularly focused competition developed between Pe'u Malesi on behalf of Nggodi Meda and Zet Apulugi on behalf of Ono Tali. To me, Zet was clearly the more fluent speaker but in the judgement of all the elders who listened intently, Malesi's chanting was far superior. Repeatedly I was told that Zet's words were empty. He did not have ritual knowledge for proper chanting. At the time, I attributed these opinions to the fact that Zet was a young man in his early 20s and hardly of the age to be allowed to speak at a ceremony.

Although I had no chance to meet him after the ceremony in 1973, I remained interested in recording him at greater length. Fortunately, more than 30 years later, in 2006, I was able to invite him to join the first group of poets whom I recorded on Bali. On Bali, he related to me his background and the origins of his ritual language fluency. Unlike other Rotenese poets, for whom the transmission of ritual knowledge is crucial and who therefore invariably related their family situation and from which specific relative they learned their knowledge, Zet explained that his knowledge and fluency had come in a dream when he was still in school. An old man appeared to him holding a staff; slowly he prepared betel and areca nut and began to chew. After chewing for a while, he took a portion of the betel and areca nut from his mouth and put it into Zet's mouth. This was the spiritual transmission that transformed him. After the dream, Zet became fluent in ritual language. He told me that he would regularly join the older men of Termanu when they would gather and speak in ritual language. He would insist on speaking in their company, even though they objected to his impertinence. Thus, from an early age, Zet defined himself as an insistent ritual speaker but one who had little ritual knowledge to support his ritual speech.

Zet, it would seem, has little or no concern with the ritual underpinnings of the compositions that he produces. His compositions can be beautifully clear and uncomplicated. He knows enough to be able to fabricate ritual names to enhance his compositions. This is particularly maddening for those Rotenese who regard ritual knowledge as both the reason and the basis for composition. For this reason, Zet is more often shunned than he is appreciated.

10. *SUTI SOLO DO BINA BANE* AS A PERSONAL COMPOSITION

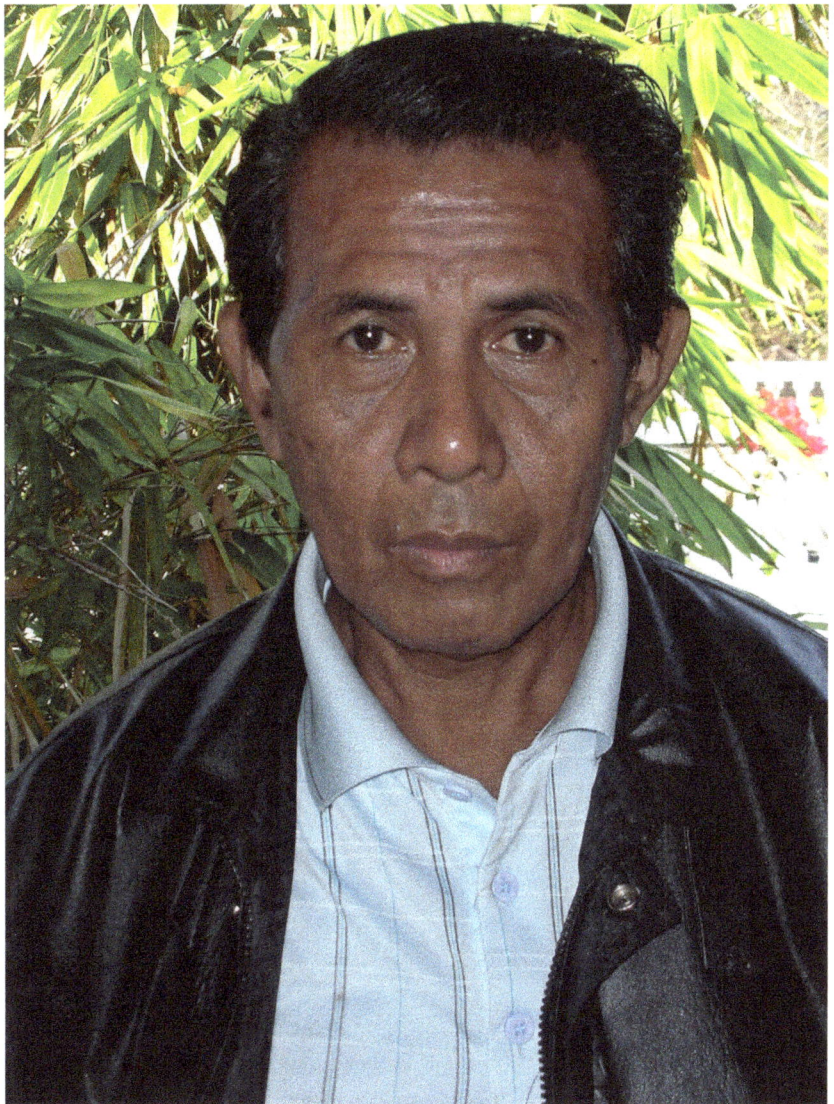

Figure 10: Zet Apulugi

This recitation, recorded on 4 July 2006, is a good example of Zet Apulugi's oral artistry.

Zet's *Suti Solo do Bina Bane* narrative is straightforward compared, for example, with Old Meno's recitation, with its complex interweaving of sites and relations linking the Heavens, the Earth and the Sea. A woman with the ritual name Masi Bisa//Bisa Oli is credited with scooping the shells from the sea. (These names resemble the names used by Joel Pellondou, Ole Masi//Bisa Oli, in his recitation during the same recording session in 2006.) Suti Solo//Bina Bane speak up and declare that they are widow and orphan, having lost their mother, Solo Saik//Suti Liun ('Solo of the Sea'//'Suti of the Ocean'), who has died in the depths of the sea. Zet emphasises the weeping and sadness of being orphaned and being left to float on one's own in the sea. In response, Masi Bisa//Bisa Oli offers to scoop up the shells and to place them on the earth but as Suti Solo//Bina Bane insist, in their reply, being on earth is insufficient without companionship. Suti Solo//Bina Bane ask for this companionship but also ask that eventually they be returned to the sea. Masi Bisa//Bisa Oli agrees to be a companion but, after a certain time, she returns the shells to the sea.

Zet's version is a unique telling of *Suti Solo do Bina Bane*. It is well composed with the full dyadic conventions of ritual language. Although it does not have the set of successive directives that are prominent in other versions of this composition from Termanu, it nevertheless constructs its own dialogue and beautifully conveys the theme of the orphan and widow.

Introduction: The Search for the Ritual Fish

1.	*Inaka Masi Bisa*	The woman Masi Bisa
2.	*Ma fetoka Bisa Oli*	And the girl Bisa Oli
3.	*Ana lu'a na ndai tasin*	She lifts the fishnet for the sea
4.	*Ma ana lo'a na seko metin*	And she takes the scoop-net for the tide
5.	*Neu ndai sanga Dusu La'e*	Goes to fish in search of Dusu La'e
6.	*Ma neu sanga Tio Holu*	And goes to seek for Tio Holu
7.	*Fo Dusu la la'e ao*	For the Dusu that support themselves
8.	*Fo Tio la holu ao.*	For the Tio that embrace themselves.

Suti Solo do Bina Bane's Lament

9.	*Te ana seko nai lifu be,*	But in whatever pool she scoops,
10.	*Na Suti bonu nai lifu ndia*	Suti bobs in that pool

10. *SUTI SOLO DO BINA BANE* AS A PERSONAL COMPOSITION

11.	*Ma ana ndai neu lek be,*	And in whatever waterhole she fishes,
12.	*Na Bina ele nai lek ndia.*	Bina floats in that waterhole.
13.	*Te kada ana bonu nai lek ndia*	But he just bobs in that waterhole
14.	*Te ana bonu no nama-tani bobolu*	But he bobs, crying tearfully
15.	*Ma nasakedu dodopo.*	And sobbing weepingly.
16.	*Boe ma Suti Solo mulai dede'ak*	Then Suti Solo begins to speak
17.	*Ma Bina Bane mulai kokolak, nae:*	And Bina Bane begins to talk, saying:
18.	*'[Au] asa-kedu ma ama-tani nana,*	'I am sobbing and crying,
19.	*Au momoli ana-mak*	I have turned into an orphan
20.	*Ma au dadadi falu-ina.*	And I have become a widow.
21.	*Au ina tebengo ta*	I have no true mother
22.	*Ma au te'ong hungo ta.*	And no origin aunt.
23.	*Au inang Solo Saik*	My mother, Solo Saik
24.	*De ana sapu nai sain dalek*	She has perished in the depths of the sea
25.	*Ma au te'ong Suti Liun*	And my aunt, Suti Liun
26.	*De ana lalo nai liun dalek.*	She has died in the depths of the ocean.
27.	*Besak ia au bonu boa nai li poik*	Now I bob like *boa* wood on top of the waves
28.	*Ma au ele piko nai tasi bafak,*	And I drift like *piko* wood on the sea's surface,
29.	*Au ele piko o nasakeduk*	I drift like *piko* wood, sobbing
30.	*Ma au bonu boa o namatanik,*	And I bob like *boa* wood, crying,
31.	*Lu ko-boa nau-na*	Tears like *bidara* fruit in the grass
32.	*Nama titi ate-lasi*	Drip like sap as from an old *ate* tree
33.	*Ma pinu kaitio telana*	Snot like *kaitio* [leaves] in the underbrush
34.	*Nama nosi oba-tula.*	Pour forth like juice from a tapped *gewang*.
35.	*Au mole duanga*	My welfare is in twos
36.	*Ta tona kale hade*	Does not sprout like proper rice
37.	*Ma au soda telunga*	And my well-being is in threes
38.	*Ta le'a bu'u bete.*	Does not grow like good millet.

39.	*Au doi doso an'seli*	I am suffering terribly
40.	*De au ele piko mai meti-ia*	I have drifted like *piko* wood to this tidal site
41.	*Ma au bonu boa mai namo ia.*	And I have bobbed like *boa* wood to this harbour.
42.	*Sueka mateik lai se*	Who will have pity on me
43.	*Madalek lai se,*	And who will have sympathy with me,
44.	*Na ana lipa nita au sodang*	To look and see to my well-being
45.	*Ma ana mete nita au moleng*	And focus and see my welfare
46.	*Nai lu mata pinu iduka,*	With tears from my eyes, snot from my nose,
47.	*Nai nasakeduk dodopok dale.'*	Sobbing, inwardly weeping.'

The Reply to Suti Solo do Bina Bane's Lament

48.	*Boe ma inaka Masi Bisa*	So the woman Masi Bisa
49.	*Ma fetoka Bisa Oli*	And the girl Bisa Oli
50.	*Ana ndai toko nan*	She fishes him up
51.	*Ma ana seko toko nan.*	And she takes him up.
52.	*Boe ma nae:*	Then she says:
53.	*'Au o o leo batu poi*	'I will take you to dwell on the top of the rocks
54.	*Ma au o o leo dae bafaka*	And I will take you to dwell on the earth's surface
55.	*Te o soda ma nai li poik*	Instead of your being on top of the waves
56.	*O soda ma nai tasi bafak.*	Instead of your being on the sea's surface.
57.	*De o mu dae bafak*	So you will go to the earth's surface
58.	*Ma o mu batu poi o*	And you will go to the top of the rocks
59.	*O se masa kedu dodopo ia*	You will continue to sob weepingly
60.	*Fo lu ta mada matam*	For your tears will not dry from your eyes
61.	*Ma pinu ta meti idum.*	And your snot will not ebb from your nose.
62.	*De o dudu'a fe au dudu'ak esa*	Your pondering gives me to ponder

63.	*Ma o kokolak fe au kokolak esa,*	And your talk gives me to talk,
64.	*Fo au bei dudu'a dalanga*	For I am still pondering a way
65.	*Ma au bei a'afi enong*	And I am still thinking of a path
66.	*Fo au amopo o lu matam*	That I may dispel the tears from your eyes
67.	*Ma au amopo o pinu idum.'*	And I may dispel the snot from your nose.'

Suti Solo do Bina Bane's Reply

68.	*Boe ma Suti Solo nahala ma nae:*	So Suti Solo gives voice and says:
69.	*'Faik ia o ndai ndano ma au*	'This day you fish me forth
70.	*Ma o seko toko ma au.*	And scoop me up.
71.	*Nde ndia tehu hataholi mai seko metina*	When someone comes to scoop in the tide
72.	*Ana sanga du'u lalu-na*	That person seeks morsels for their beer
73.	*Ma ana sanga eke nggeto na*	And that person seeks snacks for their drink
74.	*Tehu losa na sona*	But for that reason
75.	*Boso nasu hihilu au,*	Do not put me aside,
76.	*Te au ia momoli ane-ana [?]*	For I am here to grow into a person
77.	*Ma au dadi hataholi.*	And to become a human.
78.	*De au leo dae bafok*	So that I may dwell on the earth's surface
79.	*Ma au leo batu poi.*	And I may dwell on the top of the rocks.
80.	*Te neuko-se au ta lili do neka*	But if I am not attached or cared for
81.	*Au sodanga nai liun mananggenggeon*	Then my well-being will be in the dark ocean
82.	*Ma [au] molanga nai sain manatatana.*	And my welfare will be in the pounding sea.
83.	*De o ndai muni au nde ia*	So when you fish and carry me here
84.	*Tehu [au moli] neu tiak esa*	I [will grow] to be a companion
85.	*Ma au dadi neu senak esa.*	And I will become a friend.
86.	*De faik esa mate'ena*	But on one particular day
87.	*Ma ledo dua ma nuni*	And at a certain time

88.	*Na sona mo fali au leo liun dale*	You will return me to the ocean's depths
89.	*Do mo fali au leo sain dalek.*	Or will return me to the sea's depths.
90.	*Fo o po'i fali au*	You will throw me back
91.	*Leo liun do sain dalek.'*	To dwell in the ocean and sea's depths.'

The Return to the Sea

92.	*Boe ma ledo la soko muli*	The sun inclines to the west
93.	*Ma fai la loe iko*	And the day descends at the tail
94.	*Ledo soko leo muli*	As the sun inclines toward the west
95.	*Fo leo iko beku-ten*	So that its tail hangs down
96.	*Ma fai loe leo iko*	And the day descends toward the tail
97.	*Fo leo langa loloen.*	So that its head is lowered.
98.	*Boe ma inaka Masi Bisa*	Then the woman Masi Bisa
99.	*Ma fetoka Bisa Oli*	And the girl Bisa Oli
100.	*Ana dudu'a neu dalen*	She ponders in her heart
101.	*Ma ana a'afi neu tein.*	And she thinks within herself.
102.	*Ia momoli na momoli ana-mak*	He grows, indeed grows as an orphan
103.	*Ma ia dadadi na dadadi falu-ina.*	And he becomes, indeed becomes a widow.
104.	*Tehu esako mamana leleo napa lasan*	But now in these surroundings
105.	*Ndia neu oe manaleleuk*	He goes to the winding waters
108.	*Ma au nai dae bafak.*	While I am on the earth's surface.
109.	*Ami dua de'a-de'a*	We two converse together
110.	*Ma ami dua kola-kola.*	And we two speak together.
111.	*Nafada nae:*	She speaks and says:
112.	*'Ami dadi neu tiak*	'We have become companions
113.	*Ma ami dadi neu senak.*	And we have become friends.
114.	*Te hu ana ta lili-neka nai dae bafak*	But he has no attachment to the earth's surface
115.	*Ma ana [ta] ingu-leo nai batu poi.*	And he has no clanship on top of the rocks.

116.	*De malole lenak,*	It would be far better if,
117.	*Au uni falik la loe iko*	I bring him back to the lowered tail
118.	*Meti sai-kala nggonga*	The tidal seas sounding
119.	*Ma unu pedakala mada.*	And the edge of the dry reef
120.	*Neni falik ana neu tasi tatain*	Taking him back to sea's edge
121.	*Ma neni falik ana neu oli bibifan.*	And taking him back to estuary's lip.
122.	*Ana ele piko de neni leo liun*	That he may drift like *piko* wood to the ocean
123.	*Ma ana bonu boa de neni leo sain.*	And bob like *boa* wood to the sea.
124.	*De ana fali leo liun*	So that he may return to the ocean
125.	*Ma ana fali leo sain.'*	And that he may return to the sea.'
126.	*Boe ma besaka ana le'a bu'u bete*	Now he sprouts like good millet
127.	*Ma ana tona kale hade.*	And grows like proper rice.
128.	*Nama tua kada nai liun dalek*	Grows large only in the ocean's depths
129.	*Ma nama nalu kada nai sain dalek.*	And grows long only in the sea's depths.
130.	*Te ta nama-nalu nai batu poi*	He does not grow long on the top of the rocks
131.	*Ma ta nama-tua nai dae bafak.*	And does not grow large on the earth's surface.
132.	*De ana losa kada ndia*	He has only gone there
133.	*Fo besaka ita tuti popo selukana.'*	So that now we may be connected again.

Compositional Analysis and Comparison

Zet's recitation of *Suti Solo do Bina Bane* is composed of 52 dyadic sets expressed in 133 lines. As a formal composition, Zet's version is well constructed: lines pair beautifully and successively. Nonetheless, compared with the versions of the other poets of Termanu, it is notably different. The differences are not so much in what the composition does but what it does not do. There is, for example, very little ritual grounding to the composition. Apart from Suti Solo//Bina Bane, the only ritual name evoked is that of the woman who scoops up the orphaned shells, Masi Bisa//Bisa Oli. More significantly, there is relatively little of the recurrent formulaic phrasing that characterises most compositions. Suti Solo//Bina Bane's plaintive refrain is a pertinent example because it is considered one of the distinguishing features of the chant.

Old Meno uses the refrain:

'Na Bina, au o se	'Then I, Bina, with whom will I be
Ma Suti, au o se	And I, Suti, with whom will I be
Fo au kokolak o se	With whom will I talk
Ma au dede'ak o se?'	And with whom will I speak?'

Seu Ba'i follows Meno closely:

'Au dede'ak o se	'With whom will I speak
Ma au kokolak o se?'	And with whom will I talk?'

Pe'u Malesi uses a variation on this refrain:

'Na au asalai o se	'Then with whom will I recline
Ma au angatu o se?'	And with whom will I sit?'

Mikael Pellondou's refrain is like that of his cousin Seu Ba'i:

'Nah, au kokolak o se	'Then with whom will I speak
Ma au dede'ak o se?'	And with whom will I talk?'

Even in Joel Pellondou's short version of this chant, this refrain is used:

'Fo au kokolak o se	'With whom will I talk
Ma au dedea'k o se?'	And with whom will I speak?'

Pak Pono alternates between two refrains. One is the familiar refrain:

'Na ami dede'ak mo se	'Then with whom will we speak
Ma ami kokolak mo se?'	And with whom will we talk?'

The other, like that of Malesi, is a variant on this refrain:

Na ami mama hena neu se	'Then on whom will we depend
Ma ami maka bani neu se?'	And on whom will we rely?'

Where one might expect this refrain to occur, Zet provides a multiline peroration, rather than the simple, expected formulaic phrase. Thus, for example, Zet's phrasing is:

16.	*Boe ma Suti Solo mulai dede'ak*	Then Suti Solo begins to speak
17.	*Ma Bina Bane mulai kokolak, nae:*	And Bina Bane begins to talk, saying:
18.	*'[Au] asa-kedu ma ama-tani nana,*	'I am sobbing and crying,
19.	*Au momoli ana-mak*	I have turned into an orphan
20.	*Ma au dadadi falu-ina.*	And I have become a widow.
21.	*Au ina tebengo ta*	I have no true mother
22.	*Ma au te'ong hungo ta.*	And no origin aunt.

This is not a trivial difference. In ordinary discourse, a repetition of the phrase 'with whom will I speak, with whom will I talk' can be used to allude to this composition. In Termanu, no other lines are more evocative of this chant.

There are other stock formulaic phrases that one might expect in a *Suti Solo do Bina Bane* composition but that do not occur in Zet's composition. Old Meno, along with the other poets, often uses some variant of the formulaic phrase that asserts that something is 'good and proper'. This is not a formula that is distinctive to this composition. It is in fact a formulaic phrase that occurs in most compositions.

In Meno's composition, this formula is phrased as:

| *'De malole-la so* | 'These things are good |
| *Ma mandak-kala so.'* | And these things are proper.' |

In Seu Ba'i's recitation this phrase occurs as:

| *'De malole ndia so* | 'This is good |
| *Do mandak ndia so.'* | Or this is proper.' |

Malesi makes use of this formula in various ways; one such example is:

| *'Ah, malole la so* | 'Ah, that would be good |
| *Ma mandak kala so'* | And that would be proper' |

Mikael Pellondou's phrasing is:

| *'Boe ma malole lai ndia* | 'Such things would be good |
| *Ma mandak lai ndia'* | And such things would be proper' |

Joel Pellondou twice uses only the orphan line, which can be understood to invoke its pair:

| *Malole la so* | That is good |

Pak Pono has yet another variation on this recognisable formula:

| *Malole basa sila* | All this is good |
| *Ma mandak basa sila.* | And all this is proper. |

In Zet's recitation, this formula does not occur at all. The absence of this formula and other similar formulae, however, does not mean that Zet's recitation is completely without such standard formulaic phrasing. Zet, for example, utilises a common time-marking formula as follows:

| 86. | *De faik esa mate'ena* | But on one particular day |
| 87. | *Ma ledo dua ma nuni* | And at a certain time |

Some variation of this formula is used by several of the poets in their compositions.

In Meno's composition, this phrase occurs as:

| *Faik esa manunin* | On one certain day |
| *Ma ledok esa mateben* | And at one particular time |

In Mikael Pellondou's composition, he uses

| *De faik esa manunin* | At a certain day |
| *Do ledok esa mate'ena* | Or at a particular time |

Pak Pono begins his 2008 recitation with this formula:

| *Faik esa manunin* | On one particular day |
| *Do ledok esa mate'e-na* | Or one certain time |

Although Zet's composition has none of the familiar directives to the shells that punctuate the other versions of the *Suti Solo do Bina Bane* composition, he does, however, utilise the dyadic phrasing associated with the directive that returns the shells to the sea. Old Meno's directive is illustrative of how this extended formula is phrased with its metaphoric reference to two kinds of light wood like *balsa*—*boa* wood and *piko* wood—that float on the sea's surface. Meno's directive is as follows:

Fo ela fa oek ana mai	So that when the current's water arrives
Ma ela epo oek ana mai	And when the eddy's water arrives
Na bonu boa fo mu	That bobbing like *boa* wood, you may go
Ma ele piko fo mu,	And drifting like *piko* wood, you may go,
Leo sain dale mu	To the sea, you may go
Ma leo liun dale mu.	And to the ocean, you may go.

Zet uses similar phrasing to describe both the arrival of the shells and their return to the sea, thus shaping a recurrent refrain in his composition. At the beginning of his composition, Suti Solo do Bina Bane describe their condition as follows:

27.	*'Besak ia au bonu boa nai li poik*	'Now I bob like *boa* wood on top of the waves
28.	*Ma au ele piko nai tasi bafak,*	And I drift like *piko* wood on the sea's surface,
29.	*Au ele piko o nasakeduk*	I drift like *piko* wood, sobbing
30.	*Ma au bonu boa o namatanik'*	And I bob like *boa* wood, crying'

Much the same phrasing is used again 10 lines later:

40.	*'De au ele piko mai meti-ia*	'I have drifted like *piko* wood to this tidal site
41.	*Ma au bonu boa mai namo ia.*	And I have bobbed like *boa* wood to this harbour.
42.	*Sueka maeik lai se*	Who will have pity on me
43.	*Madalek lai se'*	And who will have sympathy with me'

And again this phrasing is used towards the end of the composition as the shells are returned to the sea:

121.	*Ana ele piko de neni leo liun*	That he may drift like *piko* wood to the ocean
122.	*Ma ana bonu boa de neni leo sain.*	And bob like *boa* wood to the sea.

123.	*De ana fali leo liun*	So that he may return to the ocean
124.	*Ma ana fali leo sain.'*	And that he may return to the sea.'

In the context of this composition, a more curious formula that Zet uses twice in his recitation is the invocation of sprouting rice and millet. The first use of this formula is combined with another formula that portrays the condition of being in an unfortunate or uncomfortable position—that is, literally being at 'twos and threes':

35.	*Au mole duanga*	My welfare is in twos
36.	*Ta tona kale hade*	Does not sprout like proper rice
37.	*Ma au soda telunga*	And my wellbeing is in threes
38.	*Ta le'a bu'u bete.*	Does not grow like good millet.

The same formula is used again to confirm that, on their return to the sea, the shells do indeed prosper.

125.	*Boe ma besaka ana le'a bu'u bete*	Now he sprouts like good millet
126.	*Ma ana tona kale hade.*	And grows like proper rice.[3]

It is not the case that Zet is less formulaic in his composition than the other poets, but rather that he is, as he has always tried to be, idiosyncratic. Although he adheres to the formal canons of dyadic composition, he does not use the formulae that are expected in such compositions nor does he follow the narrative schema of those compositions. From a Rotenese—or more specifically, a Termanu—perspective, he has never had ancestral training in these matters. He is what he is: a fluent outsider.

---

3 Literally, this expression refers to the fact the grains on a millet stalk stretch straight upward while the panicles of a rice stalk droop with grain.

11
Poetic Authority and Formulaic Composition

Termanu was among the first Rotenese domains given recognition by the Dutch East India Company in 1662 and, for most of the past 350 years, it has enjoyed a considerable degree of political autonomy under a continuing ruling dynasty. For centuries, even after the beginnings of Christianity in the domain, Termanu has been a single 'ritual' community with its organised succession of 'origin ceremonies'. This continuity in social and ritual life underlies a sharing of poetic traditions that are both rich and varied.

On an island with considerable linguistic diversity, Termanu is a single-speech community. The various versions of *Suti Solo do Bina Bane* presented with authority by recognised master poets in the previous chapters are a good illustration of the diversity of interpretative possibilities within this tradition. They cover a period of nearly 45 years from the first recitation to the last recitation and thus also give evidence of changes that have occurred in this period.

As a start, to appreciate this diversity, it is useful to review the narrative structures of the various chants. In this summary, I have followed a simple convention. I refer to all double-named chant characters in the singular but refer to Suti Solo do Bina Bane, who are differentiated as bailer shell and nautilus shell, in the plural.

Variations in the Narrative Structures of *Suti Solo do Bina Bane*

Version I: Old Meno's (Stefanus Adulanu's) *Suti Solo do Bina Bane*

Version I embeds its narrative within the ambit of an account of the 'origins' of things—the ritual telling of how things began in a world divided between the powers of the Heavens and Depths of the Sea. Version I begins with a genealogical introduction: the marriage of Hali Siku of the Woods//Manu Koa of the Forest with Bane Aka of the Ocean//Solo Bane of the Sea, a marriage that gives rise to Bina Bane//Suti Solo.

Bane Aka//Solo Bane holds a lively origin feast. Po'o Pau Ai//Latu Kai Do ('Mouldy Pau Tree'//'Withered Kai Leaves') comes to the feast and asks to dance with Suti Solo//Bina Bane. Suti Solo and Bina Bane reject her and Po'o Pau Ai//Latu Kai Do is deeply shamed. This causes the Heights to grow angry and the Heavens to rage. A storm strikes the sea. Suti Solo and Bina Bane flee and are washed away to a place called Tena Lai//Mai Oe.

On Rote, Manupui Peda//Kokolo Dulu wishes to hold an origin feast but the feast cannot be celebrated without an offering of two particular ritual fish: Dusu La'e//Tio Holu. The woman Nggiti Seti//Pedu Hange is sent out with her scoop-net to find these fish. Nggiti Seti//Pedu Hange is the wife of Holu Ama Daek//Bafa Ama Laik; their daughter is Lole Holu//Lua Bafa, who eventually becomes the close companion of Suti Solo do Bina Bane.

While fishing at Tena Lai//Mae Oe for the required ritual fish, Nggiti Seti//Pedu Hange encounters Suti Solo and Bina Bane. When she eventually agrees to scoop the shells up, Suti Solo and Bina Bane initiate a dialogue by asking what would happen if the leaf bucket in which they are being carried were to break. Nggiti Seti//Pedu Hange tells Suti Solo and Bina Bane that if this were to happen, to go with the syrup vat and rice basket. This sets off the symbolic journey of the shells from syrup vat and rice basket to the millet grains and ears of maize and from there to the lontar palm's shadow and the tree's shade, and further on to boundary tree and border stone and finally to the forest cuckoo and river watercock. This final move signals a return to the sea.

On their return to the depths of the seas, Suti Solo and Bina Bane discover Po'o Pau Ai//Latu Kai Do still dancing. The shells declare that Lole Holu//Lua Bafa is now their partner.

Following this it is Lole Holu//Lua Bafa's turn to search for the ritual fish for the celebration of Manupui Peda//Kokolo Dulu's feast. She is described as a skilled weaver of tie-dyed cloth and she makes her way into the sea to dance as partner to Suti Solo and Bina Bane.

The chant concludes with allusions to other key origin chants, particularly the chant known as *Pata Iuk ma Dula Foek*, which recounts the death of Shark and Crocodile that gives rise to the different patterns on Rotenese textiles.

Version II: Eli Pellondou's (Seu Ba'i's) Version of *Suti Solo do Bina Bane*

Version II begins with the Manupui Peda//Boko Dulu's origin feast, which cannot be properly performed. Nggiti Seti//Pedu Hange is sent to search for the two ritual fish required as ritual offerings. She goes to Tena Lai//Mai Oe but only encounters Suti Solo and Bina Bane. At this point, the narrative's progress of the chant is interrupted to offer a genealogy for Suti Solo and Bina Bane. (Bane Aka//Solo Bane marries Manu Koa//Hali Siko, who brings forth Suti Solo//Bina Bane.)

Suti Solo and Bina Bane beg Nggiti Seti//Pedu Hange to scoop them up. Nggiti Seti//Pedu Hange does so and brings them to the upper house and inner cooking fire of her house. Immediately, Suti Solo and Bina Bane begin to sob, calling for Lole Holu//Lua Bafa.

A dialogue is begun on where the two shells should be located. The first proposal is the syrup vat and rice basket (within the house). The boundary tree and border stone are invoked next. Then red *kumea* grass and the black *kuku* shrub are invoked, and this is followed by forest cuckoo and river watercock, which signal the onset of the monsoon and lead back to the sea.

Suti Solo and Bina Bane return to the sea where they bob and drift like *boa* wood and *piko* wood. In the depths of the sea, there is a feast at which Mila Ama Daik beats a drum and O Ana Selan strikes a gong. Suti Solo and Bina Bane are made to dance, though they are unable to do so; they are joined by the woman Po'o Pau Ai//Latu Kai Do and are shamed. This causes the Heights to rage and the Heavens to grow angry. And the two shells lose their insides.

This version appears to be an attempt to imitate Stefanus Adulanu's recitation. Its narrative structure is less well constructed and its ending is abrupt. The chief characters' names are the same as those in the Adulanu recitation, with the exception of Boko Dulu for Kokolo Dulu. Mila Ama Daik//O Ana Selak is a new named character who does not appear in the Adulanu version.

Version III: Petrus Malesi's Version of *Suti Solo do Bina Bane*

Version III begins with the storm that carries Suti Solo and Bina Bane to Tena Lai ma Mae Oe. At the time, Teke Hulu Hutu//Sio Pale Enge is preparing to hold a feast and has selected Lole Holu//Lua Bafa to perform the *peda-poi//fua-bafa* ritual. Sama Dai//Kuku Nou is designated to prepare a scoop-net and to go to search for the ritual fish required for the ceremony. She fashions the fishnet and goes in search of the Tio Holu//Dusu La'e fish at Tena Lai ma Mae Oe. She encounters Suti Solo and Bina Bane, who beg her to scoop them up. This initiates a dialogue. Sama Dai//Kuku Nou tells the shells to go to house post and floor beam and then, in succession, to the syrup vat and rice basket, boundary tree and border stone, *kumea* grass and *kuku* shrub, the forest cuckoo and river watercock and finally to the river's bank and the estuary's edge. Suti Solo and Bina Bane return to the sea, bobbing like *boa* wood and drifting like *piko* wood.

This version has various chant characters with different names from those of Versions I and II. Lole Holu//Lua Bafa is, however, specifically named, but her function is that of the ritual performer for the origin ceremony.

Version IV: Petrus Malesi's Second Version of *Suti Solo do Bina Bane*

Petrus Malesi began his recitation by recounting the storm that sets Suti Solo and Bina Bane bobbing in the sea. He then stopped and began his recitation again.

11. POETIC AUTHORITY AND FORMULAIC COMPOSITION

Version IV begins by recounting Kali Dulu//Kule Langa's plans to celebrate a feast. Sama Dai//Kuku Nou is sent to search for the ritual fish, Tio Holu//Dusu La'e, at Tena Lai ma Mae Oe. Sama Dai//Kuku Nou finds Suti Solo and Bina Bane and scoops them up. However, at a crossroads, three winding paths//two rounding roads, she throws them away. This initiates a dialogue between Sama Dai//Kuku Nou and Suti Solo do Bina Bane. Sama Dai//Kuku Nou advises Suti Solo do Bina Bane to go to the syrup vat and rice basket, then to the forest cuckoo//river watercock, then to the lontar palm's shadow//tree's shade, and to the river's bank//estuary's edge before finally returning to the sea.

After a few lines describing the shells being carried away in the sea, Malesi interrupted his recitation, and when he resumed, he redirected his narrative.

This redirected narrative introduces the woman Pasa Paku//Finga Fiti, the wife of Manupui Peda//Kokolo Dulu, whose gardens are planted with indigo and cotton. She goes to the sea, finds the two empty shells and brings them back. She uses Bina's shell as the base on which to mount the spindle for spinning cotton and she uses Suti's shell as a receptacle to hold indigo dye.

This narrative introduces the woman Kuku Dulu//Lima Le'u, who is able to dye cloth in indigo-blue and *morinda*-red. She goes in search of a woman who can weave.

She goes to eastern Rote, Dulu Balaha//Langa Mangaledo ('Tomorrow East'/'Dawning Head'), to the domain of Diu Dulu//Kana Langa to a place named Lata Nae//Pinga Dai, where she asks the woman Adu Pinga//Leo Lata if she is able to weave. When Adu Pinga//Leo Lata explains that she cannot weave, Kuku Dulu//Lima Le'u goes further east to where she encounters Menge Solu//Li Pota, who sits beside the *delas*//*nitas* trees of her father, Solu Oebau//Pota Popo. Kuku Dulu//Lima Le'u gives her dyed bundle of threads to Menge Solu//Li Pota, who weaves a woman's cloth with a *selu-kolo* pattern and a man's cloth with a *tema-nggik* pattern.

The narrative ends with a recitation of the ritual names of places (domains) in eastern Rote that retain this traditional pattern: Diu Dulu//Kana Langa (Diu), Bolo Tena//Soti Mori (Landu), Londa Lusi//Batu Bela (Ringgou), Tua Nae//Selu Beba (Ringgou), Fai Fua//Ledo Sou (Oepao), and Oe Manu//Kunu Iko (Bilba?).

Version IV is basically two versions of *Suti Solo do Bina Bane* in a single narrative: the first part of the recitation recounts the gathering of Suti Solo and Bina Bane and the progression of the shells through a variety of 'symbolic locations' back to the sea. This progression is not without its flaws: the recitation of locations should ideally, as in other chants, move from and through the house to the area around the house with its lontar palms and shade trees and then outward, eventually to forest cuckoo and river watercock, whose song signals the monsoon floods that flow to the sea. Malesi has these slightly out of sequence but in the end the narrative leads Suti Solo do Bina Bane back to the sea. This narrative is broadly similar to Versions I, II and III—Malesi's initial recitation of *Suti Solo do Bina Bane*. Lole Holu//Lua Bafa, however, is not mentioned and the woman who scoops the shells from the sea is named Sama Dai//Kuku Nou, not Nggiti Seti//Pedu Hange, as in Versions I and II.

When Malesi resumed his recitation, the narrative turned to reveal the traditional underpinnings of the *Suti Solo do Bina Bane* chant, whose original purpose was to provide a ritual basis to initiate the processes of spinning and dyeing. In this narrative, Suti Solo and Bina Bane are scooped from the sea to be used as the base for turning the spindle and as the receptacle for holding the indigo dye. This narrative introduces new chant characters. Pasa Paku//Finga Fiti is introduced as the wife of Manupui Peda//Kokolo Dulu. Manupui Peda//Kokolo Dulu, whose origin feast is recounted in Version I, is here cited for his gardens of cotton and indigo. A key figure is Kuku Dulu//Lima Le'u, who is able to do tying and dyeing of the cotton threads. Equally important is the weaver woman Menge Solu//Li Pota, the daughter of Solu Oebau//Pota Popo. (Also mentioned is the woman Adu Pinga//Leo Lata, who is unable to weave.) This part of Version IV fills out, in detail, elements that Meno only hints at in the conclusion of his version of *Suti Solo do Bina Bane*.

Version V: Mikael Pellondou's First Version of *Suti Solo do Bina Bane*

Version V introduces a slight name variation for its main chant character and provides a new setting for the narrative. The new chant character is the woman Fua Bafo//Lole Holu (instead of Lua Bafa//Lole Holu). Her millet and maize fields are the ones ripening and require a feast to celebrate the harvest. She prepares a scoop-net and then goes to fish for the ritual fish at a site, Fopo Sandika//Teli Noe Mina, on the coast of

Termanu (rather than at Tena Lai ma Mai Oe in Landu at the eastern end of the island). When she encounters Suti Solo and Bina Bane, the shells tell her to gather them up and fasten them to wood and stone so that they may be shaken to drive away the monkeys and pigs that are eating the millet and maize in her fields. When the fields are harvested, she urges the shells to go home, telling them first to go to *kumea* grass and *kuku* shrub and then to *titi'i* shrub and *kai-hule* bush and then with the *dini* grass (*dini* grass is not paired). Finally, Fua Bafo//Lole Holu tells the shells to go with the woman Po'o Pau Ai//Latu Kai Do at the river's lip and the estuary's edge. The shells take this advice to return to the sea: to bob like *boa* wood and float like *piko* wood. They descend into the sea where an origin celebration is under way (apparently at Nggusi Bui//Pinga Dale). The women of the sea are dancing but they shame the two shells, who return once more to the domain at the western end of Rote, Dela Muli ma Ana Iko. There Suti Solo and Bina Bane acquire a friend and companion, Ka Lau Ao//Tena Hu Dulu, and decide to remain in Delha.

Version VI: Mikael Pellondou's Second Version of *Suti Solo do Bina Bane*

Version VI is similar to Version V with similar chant characters and a similar narrative structure. Version VI begins with Fua Bafo//Lole Holu, whose ripening millet and maize fields are being attacked by pigs and monkeys. She prepares a scoop-net and goes to fish for Tio Holu//Dusu La'e at Fopo Sandi-kala//Teli Noe Mina. There she encounters Suti Solo and Bina Bane, who ask her to scoop them up and attach them to rock and wood so that they can serve as clappers to drive away the pigs and monkeys that are eating her millet and maize. (Here at the outset of the dialogue sequence with the shells, Mikael Pellondou mentions the names Po'o Pau Ai//Latu Kai Do instead of Fua Bafo//Lole Holu but reverts to the use of Fua Bafo//Lole Holu just a few lines later.) Fua Bafo//Lole Holu suggests a number of directives: to go with *titi'i* bush and *kai-hule* shrub, then to go with *dini* grass and then with the red *kumea* grass and black *kuku* shrub, and finally with the forest cuckoo and river watercock, whose song follows the monsoon flood to the sea. Then she tells the shells to go to meet Po'o Pau Ai//Latu Kai Do at the river's lip and the estuary's edge. Suti Solo do Bina Bane return to the sea, bobbing like *boa* wood and drifting like *piko* wood. There is a celebration in the sea at which women dance but they shame the shells, who return to Dela Muli ma Ana Iko at the western end of Rote. There Suti Solo and Bina Bane gain a companion (who, in this version, is not named).

In addition to the slight change in the main female character's name—Fua Bafa instead of Lua Bafa—these two versions break with other earlier versions in situating the place of encounter with the shells in Termanu rather than at Tena Lai//Mai Oe. Version VI includes a sequence of dialogue directives and the eventual return of the shells to the sea. It mentions the shaming of the shells at the feast in the sea and their return to Delha in the west of the island.

Version VII: Joel Pellondou's Version of *Suti Solo do Bina Bane*

Version VII offers yet another name for the chief chant character who fishes Suti Solo and Bina Bane from the sea. In Version VII, which is a particularly short version of the chant, the woman Ole Masi//Bisa Oli takes up her scoop-net and goes in search of the ritual fish, Tio Holu//Dusu La'e. She encounters only the two shells, who ask to be scooped up. She tells them that she will give them to the woman Titi Letek//Huule Mok ('Titi of Hill'//'Huulu of the Field'). Suti Solo and Bina Bane insist they will be lonely on hill and field, so Ole Masi//Bisa Oli directs them to red *kumea* grass and black *kuku* shrub. Thereafter, she directs them to the woman Po'o Pau Ai//Latu Kai Do at the mouth of the river and edge of the estuary and then to the river watercock and forest cuckoo, who follow the monsoon floods to the sea. Suti Solo and Bina Bane return to the sea, bobbing like *boa* wood and floating like *piko* wood.

Version VIII: Esau Pono's First (2008) Version of *Suti Solo do Bina Bane*

Version VIII and Version IX are similar. Version VIII introduces the woman Mo Bisa//Ole Masi as the woman who takes up her scoop-net and goes to fish for Tio Holu//Dusu La'e. She gathers up Suti Solo and Bina Bane. When she comes to where two roads circle and three paths cross, the two shells begin to speak, asking to be cared for as human beings.

The shells address Mo Bisa//Ole Masi as mother and aunt and ask to be taken home. However, Mo Bisa//Ole Masi directs the shells first to where two roads circle//three paths cross, then to the lontar's shadow and tree's shade, then to syrup vat and rice basket, then to the high hills//wide fields, then to the river's edge and the estuary's side, and finally to the forest cuckoo and river watercock to descend with the monsoon floods to the sea. When Suti Solo and Bina Bane return to the sea, they bob like *boa* wood and float like *piko* wood. The chant recounts that the shells are never found with any content but only as empty shells.

Version IX: Esau Pono's Second (2009) Version of *Suti Solo do Bina Bane*

Version IX is a close approximation of Version VIII but it offers yet another name for the woman who scoops Suti Solo and Bina Bane from the sea: instead of Mo Bisa//Ole Masi, the woman is named Mo Bisa//Masi Tasi. Mo Bisa//Masi Tasi scoops up the shells, who ask to be taken home; instead Mo Bisa//Masi Tasi proposes leaving them where two roads cross and three paths circle, then directs them to the lontar's shadow and tree's shade, then to rice basket and syrup vat, then to long field and mountain ridge, then to the side of the river bank and the edge of the estuary, then to follow the forest cuckoo and the river watercock to the sea. They bob like *boa* wood and drift like *piko* wood in the sea. They are washed back to land and made into the base for spinning and a vessel for indigo dye.

Version X: Zet Apulugi's Version of *Suti Solo do Bina Bane*

Masi Bisa//Bisa Oli goes to fish for Dusu La'e//Tio Holu and encounters Suti Solo and Bina Bane. (The location of this encounter is not mentioned.) Most of this recitation is taken up with discussion of the distressed situation of the shells. Masi Bisa//Bisa Oli scoops them up, stating in a long reply that she does not know how to relieve their distress. The shells answer in a long reply, claiming that they will be better on land than at sea if they have someone to care for them. They add that they expect to be returned to the sea. Finally, Masi Bisa//Bisa Oli realises that it would be better to return the shells to the sea. She explains in another

14 lines that though they may be companions, the shells have no affinity with the earth and would be better in the sea. On return to the sea, the shells are said to prosper.

The Pattern of Development in *Suti Solo do Bina Bane* Compositions in Termanu

If one recognises that the first of these recitations was gathered in 1965 and the last of them in 2009 and that these 10 recitations have been arrayed in a sequence spanning nearly 45 years, it is possible to discern a development in their composition. The earliest recitations—particularly those by Old Meno and his understudy Seu Ba'i, but also those by Pe'u Malesi—are told primarily as origin chants that allude to and describe relations with the humans on the earth and creatures in the ocean. For example, Old Meno's recitation describes two origin feasts: one on the land, the performance of which requires two ritual fish, Tio Holu//Dusu La'e, and another in the depths of the sea, which determines Suti Solo and Bina Bane's fate. It is the interrelation between these worlds that is crucial to the narrative structure of the recitation. Seu Ba'i's recitation is a less coherent rendering of this same origin account. Similarly, Pe'u Malesi's two recitations both give initial emphasis to the need for Tio Holu//Dusu La'e fish for the performance of an origin feast. And as in the versions by Old Meno and Seu Ba'i, these fish must be gathered at the ritual site Tena Lai//Mai Oe. Pe'u Malesi, in his second recitation, goes on to link the shells to the dyeing required in the weaving process—an aspect of Old Meno's recitation that is only alluded to. To do this, the shells must once more be scooped from the sea after having returned to the ocean.

A major change in the telling of *Suti Solo do Bina Bane* comes with Mikael Pellondou's recitations. His recitations, like most others, mention the search for Tio Holu//Dusu La'e but he shifts the ritual site for this search from Tena Lai//Mai Oe to Fopo Sandika//Teli Noe Mina on the coast of Termanu. At their conclusion, his recitations describe an origin feast held in the sea depths; it is at this feast that the shaming of the shells occurs, providing the occasion for the return of the shells to Rote. Although not entirely coherent, his versions still maintain a degree of connection with the origin format of this chant.

Joel Pellondou's rendition of *Suti Solo do Bina Bane* is relatively short. He retains mention of the search for Tio Holu//Dusu La'e but there is no further connection with any origin chant. In the end, the shells simply return to the sea. In comparison, Esau Pono's two recitations are somewhat longer. They both mention the search for Tio Holu//Dusu La'e and the return of the shells to the sea. The second of Esau Pono's recitations does mention that the shells are washed ashore again and used as a base for spinning and as a vessel for indigo. Finally, Zet Apulugi's recitation, though it mentions the search for the ritual fish, consists of an extended dialogue between the shells and the woman who scoops them up.

Except for Zet Apulugi's recitation, all of the other Termanu recitations feature a dialogue in which the shells are directed to different symbolic locations. These 'dialogue directives' are as much a part of Old Meno's recitation as they are of other recitations. However, progressively, these dialogue directives tend to dominate the narrative structure of the composition to the point that they constitute most of the narrative structure. By the time of Esau Pono's recitation, little remains of its underpinnings as an origin chant. Both recitations consist primarily of a dialogue with a succession of directives.

The clearest expression of the detachment of the *Suti Solo do Bina Bane* narrative from its original embedding in an ancestral origin narrative is the progressive diminution of the number of ritual chant names. Old Meno's recitation cites nine ritual chant characters including Suti Solo and Bina Bane; Seu Ba'i's version has seven; and Malesi's second version has nine along with Suti Solo and Bina Bane. Thereafter the citation of ritual chant characters diminishes: in addition to Suti Solo and Bina Bane, Mikael Pellondou cites just two or three ritual chant characters; Joel Pellondou three; and Esau Pono and Zet Apulugi both just one—the woman who fishes the shells from the sea.

The Second Return of the shells

All of the recitations of *Suti Solo do Bina Bane* recount the arrival of the shells from the sea and their return to the sea, but a number of recitations provide a sequel to the return of the shells to the sea that involves a second return of the shells to land.

Old Meno's recitation is ambiguous on this second return. The shells return to the sea depths, where they declare that Lole Holu//Lua Bafa is their partner. The recitation then asserts that Lole Holu//Lua Bafa: 1) is a skilled weaver; 2) is tasked with carrying out a new search for the ritual fish; and 3) enters into the sea to dance with Suti Solo do Bina Bane. Seu Ba'i's recitation, which closely resembles that of Old Meno, recounts that after the return of the shells to the sea, there is a feast in the ocean at which the shells are shamed but there is no mention of their second return to Rote. Pe'u Malesi makes no mention of a second return of the shells in his first recitation but in his second, the chant character, Sama Dai//Kuku Nou, scoops up the empty shells and makes them into a spinning base and an indigo vat. Mikael Pellondou's two recitations make explicit what Old Meno and Seu Ba'i hint at in their recitations. In his account, the shells return to the sea, where they are shamed and therefore return to Delha at the far end of Rote, where they acquire a new companion. None of the other Termanu recitations makes any mention of a second return, though Esau Pono does offer the observation that when the empty shells are found they are made into a base for spinning and a container for indigo dye.

As is evident, only the earlier recitations—those that purport to be origin chants—touch on the idea of a second return of the shells. This feature is significant in the telling of *Suti Solo do Bina Bane* in other domains on the island.

Dialogue Directives

The dominant—and perhaps the most memorable—feature of the recitations from Termanu is the sequence of 'dialogue directives'. These directives are formulaic and the different poets call on many of these directives. They all designate a significant symbolic space and, because they are formulaic, they can be identified by their constituent dyadic sets.

There are roughly 12 formulae that serve as directives—one of which is just a slight variant on another. Most poets cite five directives in their compositions; Mikael Pellondou has either three or four, while Esau Pono has six directives. In the recitations by Old Meno and Seu Ba'i, the woman who shames Suti Solo do Bina Bane is Po'o Pau Ai//Latu Kai Do ('Mouldy Pau Trees'//'Withered Kai Leaves'). Curiously, in his recitations, Mikael Pellondou directs the shells to go to the woman Po'o Pau Ai//Latu Kai Do, who lives near the shore, before they re-enter the sea. Joel Pellondou also directs the shells to go to the woman Titi Letek//Huule Mok, as if this were a kind of location.

The most popular of the directives is the one that enjoins the shells to go with the 'rice basket and the syrup vat' and the one, just before the shells descend into the sea, that directs them to go with the 'forest cuckoo and river watercock'. (Mikael Pellondou is the only poet not to use this directive in one of his recitations.) Table 3 gives an idea of the range of these directives and their use in different recitations.

Table 3: Dialogue Directives in *Suti Solo do Bina Bane* Compositions in Termanu

	I	II	III	IV	V	VI	VII	VIII	IX
[*Titi Letek//Huule Mok*]							x		
Three Paths//Two Roads (*Enok Telu//Dalak Dua*)				x				x	x
Timi Post//Lungu Beam (*Timi Di//Lungu Tua*)			x						
Rice Basket//Syrup Vat (*Neka Hade//Tua Bou*)	x	x	x	x				x	x
Millet Grain//Ear of Maize (*Bete Pule//Pela Po'o*)	x								
Lontar Shadow//Tree Shade (*Sa'o Tua//Mafo Ai*)	x				x			x	x
Boundary Tree//Border Stone (*Peu Ai//To Batu*)	x	x	x						
Red *Kumea*//Black *Kuku* (*Pila Kumea//Nggeo Kuku*)		x	x			x	x	x	
Titi'i Shrub//*Kai-Hule* Bush (*Titi'i Letek//Kai-Hule Mok*)						x	x		
High Hills//Wide Fields (*Lete Nalu//Mo Loa*)								x	x
[*Po'o Pau Ai//Latu Kai Do*]						x	x		
Forest Cuckoo//River Watercock (*Doa Lasi//Koloba'o Le*)	x	x	x	x		x	x	x	x
Estuary's Edge//River's Bank (*Oli Titian//Le Tatain*)				x				x	x
Estuary's Edge//River's Lip (*Oli Tatain//Le Bibia/Bifa*)					x	x	x		

On the Semantics of Oral Composition in Termanu

The formulaic directives are certainly among the most prominent features of the recitations, but there are other key dyadic sets that are used in all of the recitations. These sets are intimately connected with the telling of the chant. They include any number of familiar sets such as *fai//ledo* ('day'//'sun'), *feto//ina* ('girl'//'woman'), *dede'a//kokola* ('to speak'//'to talk'), *liun//sain* ('ocean'//'sea') and *ndai//seko* ('to scoop'//'to scoop fish'). All of these sets and hundreds like them in these compositions can be described by the simple formula: *(a, b)*. Similarly, where two sets are linked to form a formula, this can be described as: *(a + b, c + d)*. Examples of such formulae are numerous. In addition to the formulae of the directives, such as *neka hade//tua bou* ('rice basket'//'syrup vat') or *pila kumea//nggeo kuku* ('red *kumea* grass'//'black *kuku* shrub'), a frequent double-set formula is *dae bafok//batu poik* ('earth'//'world': literally, 'face/mouth of the earth'//'pointed rocks'), Dusu La'e//Tio Holu ('Dusu La'e fish'//'Tio Holu fish'), or the verbal pair *dei-dongo//nene-fino* ('stand and wait'//'stop and listen'). Some of these formulae can be 'deconstructed' into their constituent elements. For example, *dae//batu* can occur separately but not with the meaning of *dae bafok//batu poik*. The formulaic expression for the ceremony involving the ritual fish, *fua bafa//peda poi*, can be literally deconstructed as 'to place on the mouth'//'to set on the top', but many of the identifying formulae for textiles, *pana dai//tola te* or *busa-ei//pana-dai*, cannot.

Most formulae consist of a combination of two distinct dyadic sets but occasionally some formulae can be considered to be made up of three sets: *(a + b + c, d + e + f)*. An example of this might be the formula *pila kumea letek//nggeo kuku telas* ('the red *kumea* grass on the hill'//'the black *kuku* in the underbrush'). Another example might be *dala dua bobongo//eno telu tia-lolo* ('two roads that circle'//'three paths that cross'). In my writings, I have referred to all of these formulae—whether longer or shorter—as 'complex sets'. They are variously formed and need to be considered in the context of their production.

The combinatorial semantics of dyadic language is, however, more complex than these examples might indicate. It is possible for a semantic element to combine with more than one other semantic element. Thus, one can encounter: *(a, b), (a, c), (a, d)* ... This capacity of any particular semantic element to combine with other elements, I describe as the 'range' of that element. Most semantic elements have a limited range. In fact, the majority of semantic elements in dyadic language combine with only one other element—in other words, form only a single set and hence have a range of one.

The 10 recitations in the first half of this volume, all of them recounting a similar chant, can provide only a limited conspectus of the full range of the semantics of Rotenese ritual language. Nevertheless, the dyadic sets from the current recitations provide numerous examples of the formation of sets with a range of one. Consider, for example, the dyadic set *seko*//*ndai*. This is a set used in all of the recitations. *Seko* in this pair is the verb 'to fish with a scoop net'; *ndai* is the noun for 'fishnet' but is used in ritual language as a suitable verbal pair with *seko*. The dyadic set *seko*//*ndai* is a highly specific, similar, if not synonymous pair; neither of its constituent elements forms a set with any other element. It is thus a good example of a dyadic set with a range of just one. Other examples abound: *babi*//*sulu*, *bonu*//*ele*, *daehena*//*hataholi*, *hapa*//*heta*, *lu*//*pinu*, *mafo*//*sa'o*, *sao*//*tu*, *uma*//*lo* and more.

A significant number of semantic elements (or lexical terms) out of a total ritual language vocabulary have a range greater than one. In the recitations, for example, the semantic element *lete* ('hill, mountain') forms a set with both *mok* ('field') and *telas* ('underbrush'). The occurrence of *lete* in a large corpus of other Termanu chants appears to confirm that *lete* combines only with *mok* and *telas*; hence it has a simple range of two.

Consider the relationships among numerals in Rotenese ritual language. Interestingly, *dua* ('two') forms a set with both *esa* ('one') and *telu* ('three'); in turn, *telu* forms a set with *dua* ('two') and *ha* ('four'), whereas *ha* forms a set only with *telu* and not with *lima* ('five'), while *lima*, as a numeral, forms a set with *ne* ('six'). (The fact that *lima* also refers to 'hand' means that it has a wide semantic range of connections forming sets from *langa*, 'head', to *eik*, 'foot', and more.) In ritual language, the numerical pairing of semantic elements follows a strict pattern: *hitu*//*falu* ('seven'//'eight') form a dyadic set, as do *falu*//*sio* ('eight'//'nine'). Generally, *hitu*//*falu* is an inauspicious number set while *falu*//*sio* is a particularly auspicious set, representing 'totality'. *Natu* ('hundred') forms a set with *lifu* ('thousand'). Basically, therefore, while some numbers have a range of two, other key numbers form only single pairs. Knowing the rules of lexical pairing is essential. These relationships can be represented as follows. (The symbol > means 'forms a set with'.)

Formal Relationships among Numerals in Rotenese Ritual Language

esa > dua   (1 > 2)
dua > esa, telu   (2 > 1, 3)
telu > ha   (3 > 4)
lima > ne   (5 > 6)
hitu > falu   (7 > 8)
falu > hitu, sio   (8 > 7, 9)
natu > lifu   (100 > 1,000)

This is a disjunctive semantic field in which (*esa – dua – telu – ha*) form a mini-network, while (*hitu – falu – sio*) form yet another distinct network. Neither *lima//ne* nor *natu//lifu* are linked with either of these networks.

Another simple example of semantic connectivity can be illustrated with the word *tasi* ('sea'). In the recitations of *Suti Solo do Bina Bane*, it forms a dyadic set with *li* ('wave'), with *meti* ('tide'), with *namo* ('harbour') and with *oli* ('estuary'). As such, it has a range of four.

In the *Suti Solo do Bina Bane* recitations, *bafi* ('pig') forms a set with *kapa* ('water buffalo') and with *kode* ('monkey'), but based on more extensive textual evidence, *bafi* also forms a set with *manu* ('chicken') and *kue* ('civet cat'). Thus, on the evidence of a large corpus of compositions, *bafi* can be shown to have a semantic range of four. Each of these pairings, however, casts the significance of 'pig' in a different light. With buffalo, pig is a form of wealth; with monkey, 'wild pig' is implied. With chicken, pig is used as a signifier in a formula to mark the feeding time at the end of the day; whereas paired with 'civet cat', pig takes on special ritual significance in the most important of Rotenese origin chants.

It is possible to extend this analysis and consider the more complex network associated with *bafi* ('pig'). This semantic network encompasses all of the animals associated with household life as well as the main categories of domestic wealth including various forms of gold objects. The network in which these elements form a recognisable cluster links, link this cluster to a larger network of semantic relationships.

Formal Relationships Associated with the Semantic Element *Bafi* ('Pig')

bafi > kapa, kode, kue, manu	(pig > buffalo, monkey, civet cat, chicken)
kapa > bafi, bi'i, lilo, manu	(buffalo > pig, goat, gold, chicken)
kode > bafi, kue, teke	(monkey > pig, civet cat, lizard)
kue > bafi, fani, kode, meo	(civet cat > pig, bee, monkey, cat)
manu > bafi, kapa, busa, koa	(chicken > pig, buffalo, dog, cock's comb)
bi'i > kapa	(goat > buffalo)
lilo > kapa, besi, habas, lusi, pota, tena, batu	(gold > gold, iron, braided gold, copper, gold bead, large livestock, rock)
teke > kode, lafa	(lizard > monkey, mouse/rat)
fani > kue, bupu	(bee > civet cat, bumblebee/wasp)
meo > kue	(cat > civet cat)
busa > asu, manu	(dog > 'dog' [synonym], chicken)
koa > manu, pau	(cock's comb > chicken, chin hair/goat's beard)
besi > lilo, leti(k), ai	(iron > gold, hard/stiff, tree)
habas > lilo, lidak	(braided gold > gold, gold string)
lusi > lilo	(copper > gold)
pau > koa	(chin hair/goat's beard > cock's comb)
pota > lilo	(gold bead > gold)
tena > lilo, bote	(large livestock > gold, small livestock)
lafa > teke	(mouse/rat > lizard [gecko])
bupu > fani	(bumblebee/wasp > bee)
asu > busa	(dog > dog [synonymous pair])
bote > tena	(small livestock [goats] > large livestock [buffalo])

The arrangement of these semantic elements and their linkages to one another highlight a feature of Rotenese ritual language. The arrangement shows clearly the variable range of the semantic connections of different semantic elements. It is notable that the elements of the same dyadic set may each have a different range. For example, for the dyadic set *bi'i*//*kapa* ('goat'//'buffalo'), *kapa* has a semantic range of four whereas *bi'i* has a semantic range of one, forming a set only with *kapa*. Similarly, for the dyadic set *kue*//*meo* ('civet cat'//'cat'), *kue* has multiple semantic links—a range of four—while *meo* forms a set only with *kue*. *Lilo* ('gold') has an even wider semantic range but its pairing with 'copper' is unique. Whereas many of the terms for key animals—pig, buffalo, chicken and civet cat—have a range of four and include links to one another, the category *lilo* ('gold') has a range of seven and thus creates yet wider associations. The linkage of *lilo* to *batu*, which, on Rote, is a category of measurement for gold, and of *batu* to *ai* ('tree') links the semantic field focused on animals and wealth to a much wider network of relationships.

Many semantic elements that have multiple links with other elements can interlink with one another to form wider networks of relationships, which can be considered as interrelated semantic fields.

A small group of semantic elements—like *batu* ('rock') and *ai* ('tree'), but also *dae* ('earth') and *tua* ('lontar palm'), among others—has an extended range. These particular elements with their extended range of semantic linkages connect not just with other elements but with one another as well. They thus form an interconnected core network within a larger network of semantic relations.

The following are some of the links among these four basic elements.

ai > *batu, besi, boa, dae, di, do(k), na'u, oe, tali, tua* …	tree > rock, iron, fruit, earth, post, leaf, grass, water, rope, lontar palm …
batu > *ai, dae, lilo, lutu, nesuk, te, tena*	rock > tree, earth, gold, rock pile, mortar, spear, large livestock …
dae > *ai, batu, dale, de'a, dulu, loe, muli, oe, tua* …	earth > tree, rock, inside, outside, east, lower, west, water, lontar palm …
tua > *ai, bete, dae, feto, hade, masi, meti, le, tasi* …	lontar palm > tree, millet, earth, female, rice, salt tide, river, sea …

Thus, for example, in the *Suti Solo do Bina Bane* recitations, *ai* forms a set with *batu* ('rock') and *tua* ('lontar palm'). In other ritual language compositions, it pairs with *boa* ('fruit'), with *dok* ('leaf'), with *na'u* ('grass'), with *oe* ('water') and with *dae* ('earth'). *Ai* has one of the widest ranges of semantic connectivity in ritual language; it includes among its linkages other basic terms—*batu* ('rock'), *tua* ('lontar'), *boa* ('fruit'), *na'u* ('grass'), *oe* ('water') and *dae* ('earth')—with similarly wide semantic connectivity.

At the present stage of an analysis based on the steady compilation of a *Dyadic Language Dictionary* (for Termanu), networks emerge that are of varying sizes. Among them is one network of semantic relationships that is larger than the rest, consisting of 470 connected vertices. At an earlier stage in this analysis, I attempted to identify a 'core' to this emerging network of semantic relations in ritual language (see Fox 1975; 2014: 162–64). I did this by taking those semantic elements with the widest semantic range and tracing the linkages they had to each other. The diagram of this earlier network can be seen in Fox (1975; 2014: 164). Subsequent analysis has only heightened and focused on the 'core' of this network. Since deciding just how widely to draw this core may be arbitrary, for present purposes, I have chosen to present the set of 18 semantic elements that has remained at the centre of that network. This core is represented in Figure 11.1.

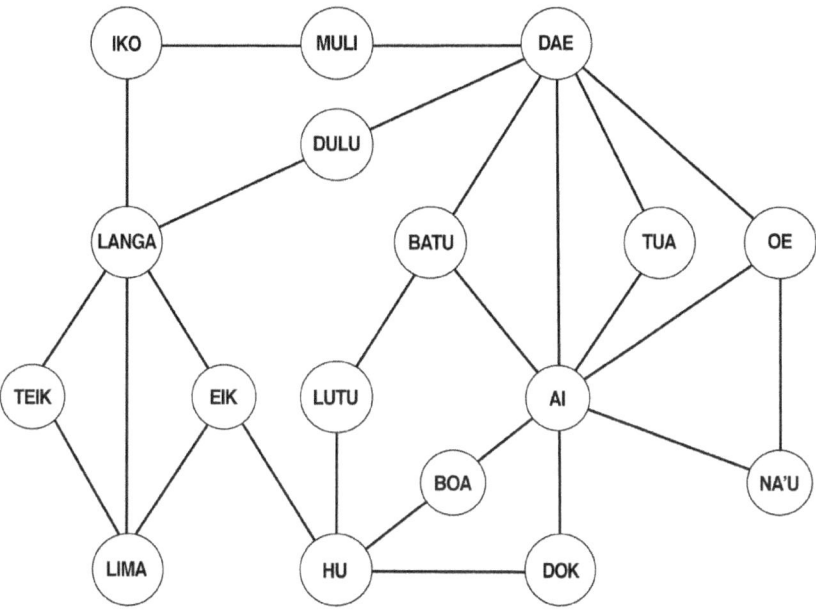

Figure 11: Core Semantic Categories in Termanu Ritual Language
Source: © The Australian National University CAP EMS 15-207 JS

The semantic elements in this core network highlight the cosmological nature of Rotenese ritual language. These elements include the following interrelated sub-clusters:

1. Basic elements: rock (*batu*), tree (*ai*), earth (*dae*), water (*oe*), lontar palm (*tua*), fruit (*boa*), leaf (*dok*), grass (*na'u*), trunk (*hu*) and piled rock (*lutu*)

2. Orientation + body parts: east (*dulu*), west (*muli*), head (*langa*) and tail (*iko*), stomach/inside (*tei*), hand (*lima*), foot (*eik*)

Although the *Suti Solo do Bina Bane* chant is just one among a large corpus of ritual texts, it would be expected that even in the recitations of this single chant, most of the basic core terms would tend to appear. An assessment of the entire array of dyadic sets used by the different poets of Termanu in their compositions reveals the following list of eight dyadic sets with both core terms: *ai//batu, ai//tua, batu//dae, dulu//langa, ei//lima, hu//lutu, iko//langa, iko//muli*.

Oral Formulaic: The Dyadic Sets Used in the Compositions of *Suti Solo do Bina Bane*

The 10 Termanu versions of *Suti Solo do Bina Bane* are composed of a total of 227 dyadic sets. At the end of this chapter, I have attached the full list of these dyadic sets as used in each of the Termanu recitations. Here I want to focus on those sets that occur in at least nine versions of the chant.

The whole idea of the 'formulaic' depends on the recurrent use of identical linguistic forms and there can be no better evidence of this formulaic usage than the recurrent use of a host of similar dyadic sets. Not surprisingly, the most frequently used dyadic sets reflect the content of the narrative. Nonetheless, the recourse of all the poets to these same dyadic sets highlights their formulaic use of ritual language.

One dyadic set that is used in all the recitations is *dede'a//kokola*, the formulaic expression for 'speaking' and 'talking'. Another set in all the recitations is *fai//ledo*, the expression for 'time' or 'day/sun'. Yet another

11. POETIC AUTHORITY AND FORMULAIC COMPOSITION

set in all recitations is *feto//ina*, the expression for 'girl' and 'woman'. Still another set in all recitations is *liun//sain*, the formula for the 'ocean' and 'sea'.

Other dyadic sets that occur in almost all recitations relate to the specifics of the search that leads to the discovery of the shells. These sets include names for the ritual fish, Dusu La'e//Tio Holu, the verbal pair *ndai//seko* (for 'scoop-net and scoop-net fishing'); paired terms *le//oli* (for 'river' and 'estuary'); and sets such *hamu//tei* and *besi//lilo*, used to describe the scoop-net: *seko ma-tei besik ma ndai ma-hamu lilok* ('scoop-net with iron-weighted insides and a fishnet with a gold-weighted belly'). These sets also include the complex formulae *bonu boa ma ele piko* ('to bob like *boa* wood and drift like *piko* wood').

Altogether there are 35 dyadic sets that are used in five or more recitations. Taken in reference to the entire Termanu corpus, all of the dyadic sets that occur in *Suti Solo do Bina Bane* are formulaic; all of them occur in other recitations and are part of the stock-in-trade by which poets create chants in ritual language.

The List of Dyadic Sets Used Five or More Times in the Compositions from Termanu

1)	*ai//batu*	'tree'//'rock'
2)	*bafa//poi*	'mouth'//'top, point'
3)	*ba'o//doa*	'*ba'o*'//'*doa*': the sound of two birds
4)	*besi//lilo*	'iron'//'gold'
5)	*bete//pela*	'millet'//'maize'
6)	*bifa//tai*	'edge'//'side'
7)	*boa//piko*	'*boa*'//'*piko*': two kinds of tree
8)	*bonu//ele*	'to bob'//'to drift'
9)	*bu'u//kalen*	'joint'//'knob, top'
10)	*dasi//hala*	'voice'//'word'
11)	*dede'a//kokola*	'to speak'//'to talk'
12)	*doa//kolobao*	'*doa*'//'*kolobao*': two kinds of bird
13)	*dua//telu*	'two'//'three'
14)	*dulu//langa*	'east'//'head'
15)	*Dusu La'e//Tio Holu*	'*Dusu La'e*'//'*Tio Holu*': two kinds of fish

16)	-edo//-toko	'exudes'//'expels, throws away'
17)	fak//timu	'(west) monsoon'//'east monsoon'
18)	fa//uda	'monsoon'//'rain'
19)	fai//ledo	'day'//'sun'
20)	feto//ina	'girl'//'woman'
21)	hamu//tei	'belly' of a fishnet//'inside' of a scoop-net
22)	isi//nggi	'inside'//'pods'
23)	-kedu//-tani	'to sob'//'to cry'
24)	kuku/kumea	'*kuku*'//'*kumea*': two kinds of wood shrub
25)	lasi//le	'forest'//'river'
26)	le//oli	'river'//'estuary'
27)	lek//lifu	'waterhole'//'harbour'
28)	lete//telas	'hill'//'wood'
29)	liun//sain	'ocean'//'sea'
30)	-lole//-nda	'good'//'proper'
31)	meti//tasi	'tide'//'sea'
32)	nalu//tua	'long'//'large'
33)	ndai//seko	'to scoop fish'//'to fish with a scoop-net'
34)	ndano//toko	'to catch, to thrust'//'to throw'
35)	nggeo//pilas	'black'//'red'

Table 4: Dyadic Sets in All Versions of *Suti Solo do Bina Bane* from Termanu

Dyadic sets	I	II	III	IV	V	VI	VII	VIII	IX	X
aba//do	x	x	x	x						
ae//lole		x			x	x	x			
ae dasi//lole hala		x			x					
ae-ana//fui-ana									x	x
afi//du'a									x	x
ai//batu	x	x	x		x	x				
ai//nula						x				
ai//tua	x			x				x	x	
alu//langa	x				x	x				
ana-ma//falu-ina	x							x	x	x
ane//teli	x	x			x					

11. POETIC AUTHORITY AND FORMULAIC COMPOSITION

Dyadic sets	I	II	III	IV	V	VI	VII	VIII	IX	X
ane-ana (?)//hataholi										x
ate-lasi//oba-tula										x
bafa//fude	x	x								
bafa//poi	x	x	x	x						x
babi//sulu	x									
bafi//kapa	x									
bafi//kode	x	x			x	x				
-bani//-hena	x								x	
ba'o//do(a)		x	x				x	x	x	
batu//dae						x				x
batu//enggak						x	x	x	x	
bebi//tato	x									
beku-te//lol										x
bela-bui//kokolo		x								
bengo//toto						x				
bengu//kolo						x				
besi//lilo	x	x	x	x	x	x	x	x	x	
bete//hade										x
bete//pela	x	x	x	x	x	x				
Beu//fe'e							x			
bi//mae	x	x			x	x				
bifa//tai	x	x			x	x	x			x
boa//piko	x	x	x	x	x	x	x	x	x	x
bolu//dopo										x
bongi//lae	x	x							x	x
bongo//lona										
bonu//ele	x	x	x	x	x	x	x	x	x	x
bou//neka		x	x						x	x
bou//soka	x	x							x	x
bote//tena										
busa-ei//pana-dai	x									
buluk//(na)-lelak						x				
bu'u//kalen		x	x		x	x				x
bu'u//langa							x			
-da'a//-nggela									x	

Dyadic sets	I	II	III	IV	V	VI	VII	VIII	IX	X
dadi//tola	x									
daehena//hataholi						x	x	x	x	
dala//eno								x	x	x
dale//lai		x			x	x				
dale//tei										x
dasi//hala		x	x	x	x	x	x	x		
dao//lai	x									
dea//lutu	x	x		x						
dede'a(k)//kokola(k)	x	x	x	x	x	x	x	x	x	x
dedein//mata-boa		x								
dei-dongo//nene-fino	x	x								
delu//sali		x								
deta//sama		x			x	x				
dilu//loe	x			x				x	x	
-dilu//-sesu	x	x	x			x				
dipo//ifa	x									
do(n)//pena		x								
-doa//-ba'o						x				
doa//koloba'o	x	x	x			x	x	x	x	
do-se//oku-bolu		x			x	x				
-doto//-se	x	x				x				
dua//esa						x				
dua//telu dudua//telu	x		x	x	x			x	x	x
dula kakaik//sidi soti	x									
dulu//langa	x	x	x	x	x	x				
dusu//tio	x	x			x	x		x	x	x
dusu la'e//tio holu	x	x	x	x	x	x	x	x	x	x
du'u//eke										x
du'u lalu//eke nggeto										
edo//pode				x					x	
-edo//-toko	x	x	x		x	x	x	x		
ei//lima	x	x								
eke//lalu									x	
eki//hika	x									

11. POETIC AUTHORITY AND FORMULAIC COMPOSITION

Dyadic sets	I	II	III	IV	V	VI	VII	VIII	IX	X
elo//tolesi						x				
fa//epo	x									
fak//timu		x	x	x	x	x	x			
fa//uda	x	x			x	x	x			
fada//nosi	x									
fai//ledo	x	x	x	x	x	x	x	x	x	x
fali//tule						x			x	
fal//-na'a (?)										
feto//ina	x	x	x	x	x	x	x	x	x	x
foki//hopo		x								
fua//peda	x	x	x	x						
fua bafa//peda poin	x	x	x	x						
hade//tua								x	x	
hai-pai//lepa-sola	x									
hamu//tei	x	x	x	x	x	x	x	x	x	
hapa//heta								x	x	
hene//kae								x	x	
henge//tenu	x									
heok//hiluk								x	x	
-hilu//-keko	x		x							
holu//lai?	x	x	x	x	x	x	x	x	x	x
-hope//-seti		x								
hu(s)//lipa					x					
hu//lutu	x	x								
hu(s)//sio	x	x								
hu//tebe		x								
hu'a//silu	x	x								
huka//si						x	x			
huka//silu						x				
huka//si'u							x	x	x	
huka papa//si unu						x	x		x	
huas//nakas	x									
ifa//souk	x									
iko//langa										x
iko//muli										x

221

MASTER POETS, RITUAL MASTERS

Dyadic sets	I	II	III	IV	V	VI	VII	VIII	IX	X
ina//te'o								x	x	x
isa//pa'u					x					
isi//nggi	x	x	x		x	x	x	x	x	
ka'a//ketu	x	x								
kai-hule//titi'i					x					
kai-tio//ko-boa										
-kako//-lua	x	x								
kani batu//lea te	x									
kedi//pena	x	x	x							
-kedu//-tani	x	x	x	x						x
ketu//na'a						x				
ki//kona	x									
kila//koasa	x									
kolo//seko						x				
kokolo//seko-bui (balu-bui)	x	x								
kuku//kumea		x	x		x	x	x			
labu//meko	x	x								
(na-)lai//tolomu	x				x					
lalo//sapu										x
lao//uma		x								
lao dale//uma lai		x								
lapu//pela						x				
lasi//le	x	x	x			x	x	x	x	
lasi//nula	x	x								
le//oli	x	x	x	x	x	x	x	x	x	
lek//lifu	x	x			x	x	x	x	x	x
lek//namo								x		
le'a//tona										
lelu//lipa						x				
lena//sali	x					x				
leno//foti						x				
leno//pela	x	x			x	x				
lepa//nalu									x	
lete//mok						x	x	x	x	
lete//telas		x	x		x	x	x			

11. POETIC AUTHORITY AND FORMULAIC COMPOSITION

Dyadic sets	I	II	III	IV	V	VI	VII	VIII	IX	X
li//tasi										x
-li//-mu	x									
lili//neka										x
lima-ku'u//pu-lete	x									
lima//lolo		x			x					
lipa//mete										x
liun//sain	x	x	x	x	x	x	x	x	x	x
lo//uma						x		x	x	
loa//lu'a										x
loa//nalu									x	
loe//soko										x
(ma-)lole//(ma-)nda	x	x	x	x	x	x	x	x	x	
lolek//ine	x									
lole hala//selu dasi			x	x						
longe//pela	x	x			x					
longe//sodo		x								
losa//nduku		x				x		x	x	
lu//pinu										
luli//sangu	x		x	x						
lunu//tono	x	x	x							
lutu//sopu						x				
mada//meti										x
mafo//sa'o	x			x				x	x	
masu ndalu//pila nuli								x	x	
mata-dale//setele	x		x							
mau//pole	x	x								
meti//namo			x							x
meti//tasi		x		x	x	x	x	x	x	x
mole//soda										x
molo//tabu								x	x	
monu//tuda	x									
-mula//-nae						x				
na//ndia									x	
-na'a//-pena	x									
nale//ua	x									

MASTER POETS, RITUAL MASTERS

Dyadic sets	I	II	III	IV	V	VI	VII	VIII	IX	X
-nalu//-sesu						x				
-nalu//-tua		x	x	x	x	x				x
namo//tasi								x	x	
-nasa//nggele	x	x		x						
na'u//tela										x
-neda//-ndele						x		x	x	
neka hade//tua bou	x	x								
neka hade//bou tua			x	x						
nene-fino//dei-dongo	x	x								
-nosi//-titi										x
nda//soa						x				
nda//tongo		x			x	x				
ndae//su'u	x				x	x				
ndai//seko	x	x	x	x	x	x	x	x	x	x
ndano//solu						x				
ndano//toko	x	x			x		x	x	x	x
-ndu//-sa'a		x								
nggafu//sodo						x				
-nggao//dama	x									
nggao//tenga							x	x	x	
nggama//tenga		x								
nggape//sodo	x									
nggeo//pilas		x	x	x	x	x	x			
-nggeo//-tana										x
nggolo//tadu						x				
oli//tasi										x
pana-dai//tola-te	x									
papa//unu						x	x			
peu//to	x	x	x							
po'o//pule	x									
posi//unu	x									
pou//lafa	x			x						
pou//sidi	x									
sao//tu	x	x		x						
seli//sudi	x									

11. POETIC AUTHORITY AND FORMULAIC COMPOSITION

Dyadic sets	I	II	III	IV	V	VI	VII	VIII	IX	X
sena//tia	x				x	x				x
soti//leu	x									
tai//tia								x	x	
-talada//-ton		x								
(ma)-te'ek//(man)-unin						x	x	x		x
(ma)-teben//(man)-unin	x	x								

PART II

Figure 12: Group photo taken on 13 June 2009 after the fourth Bali recording session
Back Row: James Fox, Jonas Mooy, G. A. Foeh, Anderias Ruy, Frans Lau and Esau Pono
Front Row: Alex Koan, Benjamin Sah, Esau Nalle and Lintje Pellu

12
Historical Diversity and Dialect Differences on Rote

A Brief History of the Rotenese Domains (*Nusak*)

Rote is a relatively small island located off the south-western tip of West Timor. The island measures roughly 83 km in length from south-west to north-east, while, at its widest point, it is 25 km across. It covers an area of approximately 1,670 sq km, which includes a number of tiny islands scattered along its coast. Rote is a low-lying island with stretches of savannah and occasional limestone hills on its southern flank.

Despite its diminutive size, Rote is remarkably diverse—linguistically, socially and in its political history. In the mid-eighteenth century, after a number of devastating reprisals for opposing the Dutch presence, local rulers on Rote sought to establish close relations with the Dutch East India Company. In 1662, the first group of four local rulers gained Dutch recognition of their domains. These were the rulers from Termanu, Dengka, Bilba and Korbaffo. Within a few years, in 1690, another eight local rulers officially pledged their loyalty to the Company. This second group came from Landu, Ringgou, Oepao, Bokai, Loleh, Lelain, Thie (Ti) and Oenale.

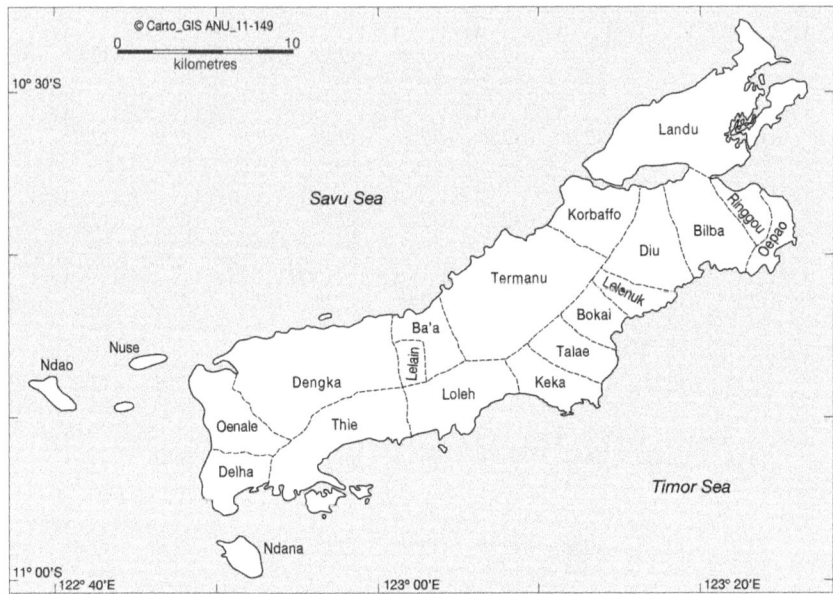

Figure 13: Map of the Domains (*Nusak*) of Rote
Source: © The Australian National University CartoGIS

Thus, even before the beginning of the eighteenth century, Rote was divided among a dozen small polities, each with its own ruler and ruling dynasty. But this did not put an end to the creation of further polities on the island. Indeed the Dutch archives of the period mention quite a number of local areas clamouring for recognition and their own political autonomy. The first of these was the domain of Ba'a, which was split from Lelain by Dutch agreement in 1700. Also mentioned at the time was the domain of Diu, which only succeeded in obtaining recognition in 1756. Following Diu, the domains of Lelenuk, Keka and Talae were separated from Termanu in 1772.

Whereas at the beginning of the eighteenth century, Rote was divided among 13 polities, by the nineteenth century, the number of these official domains had increased to 17, with yet another domain, Delha, to be split from the larger domain of Oenale and to be given official recognition sometime in the early nineteenth century. At this point, the Dutch policy of fostering ever more divisions on the island came to an end. Instead, under colonial government policy, dissident local populations were transported to Timor to form a buffer around the Dutch settlement at Kupang.

In the twentieth century, the Dutch Government attempted, for purposes of governance, to amalgamate various domains. These efforts did not lessen the social reality of the separate domains nor did the Indonesian Government when initially it made the whole of Rote a single political entity (*kecamatan*). With the policy decentralisation after 2002, Rote has become a higher-order political entity (*kabupaten*) and has been divided into a number of *kecamatan*. Among these new *kecamatan*, the large domains of Landu, Termanu, Dengka and Thie have been accorded autonomy, while other domains have been grouped with neighbouring domains. The domain structure established in the seventeenth century continues to this day on Rote.

On Rote, each of the domains originally recognised by the Dutch is referred to as a *nusak*. Each *nusak* was and remains the focus of long-standing social identity. Although Dutch recognition may go back more than 350 years, the oral narratives of these domains claim a distinct ancestral past that extends well before the arrival of the Dutch. These oral narratives recount the coming of the earliest ancestors but also successive developments in the formation of the domain. For most domains, this has been a development of relations among the constituent clans of the domain.

For one domain, Landu, once among the largest of Rote's domains, this development was aborted. In 1756, in retaliation for opposition to the East India Company, Landu's population was devastated. Some of its population was able to flee while others were either slaughtered or sold into slavery. For decades thereafter, Landu became a no man's land. When in the nineteenth century Landu was gradually resettled, it never regained its previous integrity. By contrast, despite dismemberment in 1772 of the domains of Talae and Keka on its southern coast, Termanu retained a privileged position on the island, occupying a considerable area of central Rote with a port on its north coast that was used by the Dutch as the primary entry to the island. From the beginning of relations with the Company, the Dutch tended to deal with Termanu among the domains of Rote.

Each domain on Rote was a diarchy with rule divided between a superordinate 'male' lord (*manek*) and a subordinate 'female' lord (*fettor*). Each domain was defined by its local court, situated in the chief settlement of the male *lord*. This settlement as the centre of the domain with the court as its focus was also referred to as *nusak*. The court was presided over by the male ruler, who was supported by the heads of the clans of the domain. Disputes were regularly heard at court and decided on by the ruler in deliberation with its clans (see Fox 2007b). This dispensation of traditional justice based on local customary practice provided a focus of intense interest and a prime forum for argument, debate and litigation—the disputation and taking sides that, for Rotenese, are among the great joys of life.

All domains are made up of clan groups that are distinctive to that *nusak*. There is no island-wide network of clans to unite the island. Clans are arrayed as either noble or commoner, with one or more clans recognised as the original ritual custodians of the earth. The ordered arrangement among clans differs from domain to domain. Termanu, for example, has a subtle hierarchy of lineages particularly within its large royal clan. In turn, this royal clan is linked to the other clans of the domain according to their derivation or initial affiliation and incorporation within the domain. By contrast, all the clans of Thie are divided into one or another moiety: Sabarai and Taratu. Sabarai was presided over by the male lord and Taratu by the female lord (see Fox 1979a, 1980). Clan groups intermarry with one another so that the overwhelming majority of all marriages are contracted within one's domain.

All *nusak* were also, once, distinct ritual communities whose integrity was affirmed in a series of 'origin' ceremonies performed by the constituent clans of the domain. Ceremonies of the life cycle were also performed in a distinctive manner. These ceremonies—of birth, marriage and death, along with the rituals associated with house-building, tie-dyeing, weaving and planting and harvesting—were carried out by reference to chants that invoked the 'origin' of these activities.

Changes to the ceremonial life of the *nusak* began in 1729 with the conversion to Christianity of the first ruler of a domain, the domain of Thie. This was followed by the conversion of other rulers from smaller domains in south-central Rote, who together claimed Dutch protection as sovereign Christian states. Coupled with conversion came a request for Malay schoolteachers to establish *nusak*-schools. By the middle of the eighteenth century, the prestige of having a school and the rivalry among the *nusak* led to the establishment of numerous schools, but the costs demanded by the Company eventually favoured the larger domains, most of which did not have Christian rulers (see Fox 1977: 106–12).

In time, a tradition of schooling in Malay and of adherence to Christianity became part of Rotenese life. Schooling and Christianity went hand-in-hand but both progressed slowly. Towards the end of the nineteenth century, Rote had 34 local schools with more than 3,000 students, but after more than 170 years of Christianity, only one-fifth of the population of the island was estimated to be Christian. In the words of a Dutch missionary, the Rotenese wore Christianity as 'Sunday apparel' over their heathen interiors (see Fox 2014: 321 ff.).

Only in the twentieth century were there dramatic changes to the ceremonial lives of the different *nusak* on Rote. These changes came with the use of Rotenese and Rotenese ritual language, instead of Malay, for the preaching of Christianity. Gradually, the *nusak* abandoned their origin (*hus//limba*) ceremonies. Thie, the first domain to become Christian, was one of the last to cease to perform its origin ceremonies. Today one village in Dengka still performs an origin ceremony but this ceremony is limited to a small community of that village.

Similarly but more slowly, the ceremonies of the life cycle began to change and were either combined with or gradually replaced with Christian ceremonies. In the process, ritual language developed a second lease on life and an extensive new vocabulary as it was used increasingly in the services of the Protestant Church, particularly in sermons and especially in rendering the Bible into elevated Rotenese. As a result, the knowledge of origins and the memory of many traditional rituals exist alongside the creative use of ritual language blending in a Christian vein.

The Languages of the Different Domains (*Nusak*)

Throughout Rote, it is categorically asserted that each *nusak* has its own 'language'. Superficially this is undeniable. The local geography of each domain is unique: place names and clan names are distinctive as are other identifying features of the domain. Behind the assertion about the different, distinct languages of the domains lies the recognition of considerable dialect diversity across the island.

Rote consists of a dialect chain of related languages. Speakers in neighbouring domains are generally able to understand one another, but for speakers in domains separated from one another intelligibility is reduced. Domains at a distance from one another find mutual intelligibility difficult or impossible. Based on these criteria, Rotenese consists of more than one language.

Various attempts have been made to distinguish the dialects of Rote. In the nineteenth century, a Rotenese schoolteacher, D. P. Manafe, proposed a grouping of nine dialects based mainly on phonological (Indonesian: *lagu*) criteria. His grouping, based on a native acquaintance with the languages of the island, is pertinent.

His group of nine dialects is the following:

1) Eastern Dialect: Landu, Ringgou and Oepao
2) East-Central Dialect: Bilba, Diu and Lelenuk
3) Korbaffo Dialect: Korbaffo
4) Central Dialect: Termanu, Keka and Talae
5) Bokai Dialect: Bokai
6) South-Central Dialect: Ba'a and Loleh
7) North-East Dialect: Dengka and Lelain
8) South-West Dialect: Thie [Ti]
9) Western Dialect: Oenale and Dehla

Despite decades of research on the Rotenese language, the Dutch linguist J. C. G. Jonker never ventured a definitive grouping for the dialects of Rote. When he published his *Rottineesch-Hollandsch Woordenboek* (1908) based on the Termanu dialect, he was acutely aware of dialect variation. As a consequence, for many Termanu lexical items, he included variant forms listed according to specific domains. At the end of his dictionary, he also included a long list (103 pages) of 'alternative forms and words from other dialects'. Subsequently, he published an extended article on the dialects of Rote, 'Bijdragen tot de kennis der Rottineesche tongvallen' (Jonker 1913). Most of the article consists of similar texts in different dialects, but as an introduction, Jonker offered comments on the dialect situation on Rote. His comments, which begin with a consideration of Manafe's earlier assessment of dialects, are instructive but inconclusive. For the most part, Jonker simply summarises the variety of phonological differences among dialects. He disagrees with some of Manafe's distinctions—on the one hand, pointing to differences among dialects that Manafe grouped together, and on the other hand, noting the continuous variations among dialects that Manafe separated. A major point that he does emphasise is that putting aside phonological criteria and looking instead at grammatical criteria, there is a significant difference between the languages of Dengka and Oenale in the west and the languages of eastern Rote, with Thie situated in a kind of intermediary position. Many of the distinctive features of Dengka and Oenale are similar to those of Timorese.

When I embarked on my attempt to record and translate ritual language compositions across the dialects of Rote, I had to my advantage the previous work by Manafe and Jonker, but not until I was already launched into my recording sessions did I come to appreciate the complexity of variation among Rotenese dialects. As a basic aid to my own understanding, I drew up a list of the principal sound variations in the main dialects that I came to focus on. Although this list is by no means complete, it provides a starting point for comprehending the sound variations one encounters in the ritual languages of Rote.

Table 5: Principal Sound Variations in Rotenese Dialects

Termanu values:	Ringgou	Bilba	Termanu	Thie	Dengka	Oenale
Initial	0	k	k	k	0	0
[k]	ona	kona	kona	kona	ona	ona
Medial	0	k	k	k	k	k
[k]	se'o	seko	seko	seko	seko	seko
Initial	d	d	d	d	l	r
[d]	dale	dale	dale	dale	lala	rala
Initial	k	ng	ngg	ngg	ngg	ngg
[ngg]	kia	ngia	nggia	nggia	nggia	nggia
Medial	k	ng	ng	ngg	ngg	ngg
[ng]	boki	bongi	bongi	bonggi	bonggi	bonggi
Initial	r	l	nd	nd	nd	nd
[nd]	rai	lai	ndai	ndai	ndai	ndai
Medial	n	n	n	nd	nd	nd
[n]	tane	tane	tane	tande	tande	tande
Initial	b	b	b	b	f	f
[b]	bafi	bafi	bafi	bafi	fafi	fafi
Initial	p	p	p	mb	mb	mb
[p]	peda	peda	peda	mbeda	mbeda	mbeda
Medial	p	p	p	mb	mb	mb
[p]	hapu	hapu	hapu	hambu	hambu	hambu
Initial	l	l	l	l	r	l
[l]	ledo	ledo	ledo	ledo	lelo	ledo

Termanu values:	Ringgou	Bilba	Termanu	Thie	Dengka	Oenale
–	r	l	l	r	l	r
Medial	r	l	l	r	r	r
[l]	hara	hala	hala	hara	hara	hara

Note: In relation to Termanu dialect, 0 = 'absence of'.

As a further means of distinguishing these dialects, I drew up another chart of the pronominal system of the different dialects. This chart gives some indication of Jonker's observation about differences between eastern and western Rote.

Table 6: Pronominal Systems of the Different Dialect Areas on Rote

	I	II	III	IV	V	VI
	Ringgou	Bilba	Termanu	Thie	Dengka	Oenale
1st p. sg.	au	au	au	au	au	au
2nd p. sg.	o	ko	o	o	ho	ho
3rd p. sg.	ria	ndia	ndia/ana	ana	eni	eni
1st p. pl. (excl.)	kita	kita	ita	ita	hita	hita
1st p. pl. (incl.)	ami	ami	ami	ai	hai	hai
2nd p. p.l	emi	kemi	emi	ei	hei	hei
3rd p. pl.	ara	ala	ala	ara	ala	ara

Finally, on the basis of my recordings and my understanding of the dialects I recorded, I ventured to draw a map to provide a geographical dimension to distinguish among the dialects of Rote. This map in many respects follows Manafe's language groupings. To produce it, I have 'lumped' related dialects rather than 'differentiating' them in the attempt to reduce Manafe's nine dialect groups to six, each of which is focused on a major domain. This reflects the fact that in my recording efforts, I was unable to find poets from many of the small domains of Rote and had therefore to rely on poets from larger domains.

This map distinguishes six 'Dialect Areas':

I. An *Eastern Dialect Area* centred on Ringgou but including much of Landu and all of Oepao. A majority of the population to resettle Landu after it was depopulated in 1756 came from Ringgou and these Ringgou speakers are more densely settled on the south-eastern coast of the domain.

II. An *East-Central Dialect* Area centred on the domain of Bilba but including the domains of Diu, Lelenuk and Korbaffo, with some influence on Landu because of migration to this domain.

III. A *Central Dialect Area* centred on the domain of Termanu but including the domains of Keka and Talae with extended influence to Bokai and to Ba'a and Loleh.

The *Central and East-Central Dialect* gives evidence of continuous variation among the different domains included within these areas. Hence the map shows no sharp line of demarcation across these two dialect areas. These two areas make up the most internally diverse yet related dialects of the island.

IV. A *South-Western Dialect* area centred on the domain of Thie.

V. A *North-Western Dialect* area centred on the domain of Dengka.

VI. A *Western Dialect* area centred on the domain of Oenale including the domain of Delha, which was politically separated from Oenale in the nineteenth century.

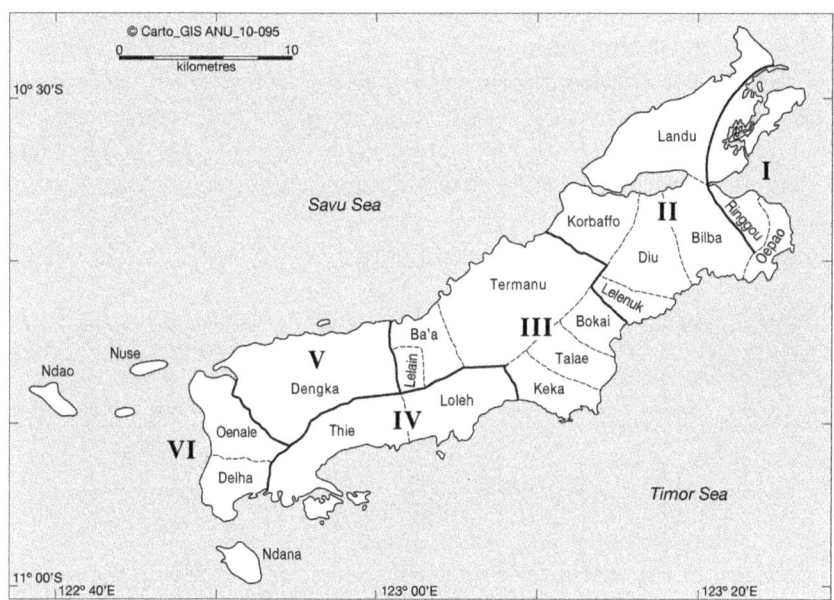

Figure 14: A Tentative Map of the Dialects of Rote
Source: © The Australian National University CartoGIS

Dialect Diversity and the Semantics of Ritual Language

Rote's dialect diversity is a prime resource for the elaboration of the island's ritual language. Numerous word pairs in ritual language are composed of one term drawn from the local speech community and another term from some other dialect. These pairings are formal and are recognised as the established dyadic sets for that speech community. This is a process common to all the different speech communities of Rote, involving a combination of a local term and a dialect term, though not the same dialect term among the different domains.

What term belongs originally to the local speech community and what term derives from elsewhere can only be determined by reference to the usages within the local community. In a previous paper based on my earlier research centred on Termanu, I listed more than a dozen dyadic sets composed of a term from Termanu's speech community combined with a dialect term from outside (Fox 1974: 80–83; 2014: 143–46). I also tried to specify the domain from which the 'outside' term originated and to categorise it as belonging either to eastern or to western Rote. In many cases, this designation was too domain-specific since subsequent research has indicated that 'outside' words generally have a wider 'dialect area' provenance. Nevertheless, a list of 10 of these dyadic sets is illustrative of the basic process of combining a common ordinary language term with one from outside that speech community.

Table 7: Dialect Terms in the Formation of Termanu's Dyadic Sets

Termanu speech community	Outside dialect term	Gloss
lea(k)	lua(k)	'cave, grotto'
li	nafa	'wave, breaker'
henu	sofe	'enough, sufficient'
lain	ata	'heaven, sky, above'
longe	pela	'to dance'
ka	kiki	'to bite'
sele	tane	'to plant'
lo	nggou	'to call out loudly'
tenga	nggama	'to take up, to grasp'
pu	oku	'to shout, to scream'

A good example of dialect diversity is the dyadic set for 'human being', *hataholi//daehena*—an example that is iconic of the process of combining local and dialect terms. *Hataholi* is the term for 'human being' in Termanu and is regularly used as such in ordinary speech. *Daehena*, by contrast, is a dialect borrowing, which is considered to have come from eastern Rote. The linguistic reality is, however, more complex when seen from the perspective of the island as a whole. Each of the main dialect areas of Rote has a different variation of this dyadic set:

I	Ringgou	*hataholi//lahenda*
II	Bilba	*hataholi//dahena*
III	Termanu	*hataholi//daehena*
IV	Thie	*hatahori//andiana*
V	Dengka	*hataholi//andiana*
VI	Oenale	*hatahori//andiana*

Perhaps, interestingly, the distribution of this particular dyadic set is divided between eastern and western Rote with *hataholi/hatahori* as the common element in all dialect sets, though not the common local term for 'human being' in all dialects. The distribution of other dyadic sets across the dialects is not so neatly bifurcated.

In a closely related process, a speech community may adopt a pair of similar terms for a particular concept. Both may be terms that occur in that speech community, but given the dialect diversity on Rote, a combination of other pairs may be used in a different speech community but may, by analogy, be recognised widely across the island. Examples of these processes are numerous. Three particular instances—all of them of common dyadic sets—illustrate this process as seen from the perspective of the island as a whole.

In Termanu, the dyadic set for 'name' is *nade//tamo*. *Nade* is the general term for a person's 'name' while *tamo* refers to a secret ancestral name, the name of a person's ancestral guardian. Similarly, in Termanu the dyadic set for dry field or garden is *tina//osi*. It is composed of terms for different kinds of fields: *osi* is the term for a distant dry field while *tina* refers to a field in close proximity to the house. As a third example, the dyadic set *tada//ba'e*, which refers to the ritual distribution of goods, is composed of *tada*, which in Termanu dialect has the sense of 'dividing', and *ba'e*, which has the sense of 'distributing'.

The distribution of the equivalent dyadic sets in the different dialect areas is as follows:

Table 8: An Illustration of the Concatenation of Dyadic Sets Across Dialect Areas

	Dialect area	'Name'	'Field/garden'	'To distribute'
I	Ringgou	nade//bo'o	tine//oka	pala//bati
II	Bilba	nade//bo'o	tine//oka	pala//bati
III	Termanu	nade//tamo	tina//osi	tada//ba'e
IV	Thie	nade//bo'o	tine//lane	ba'e//bati
V	Dengka	nade//tola	osi//mamen	pala//ndu
VI	Oenale	nade//nara	tine//osi	banggi//ba'e

The result of these processes, for the island as a whole, is a concatenation of pairs with varying components in different dialect areas. Importantly, however, whatever one's position in the chain of Rotenese dialects, this concatenation of pairs represents 'recognisable variation' that serves two functions. It promotes intelligibility across divergent dialects and it enhances each dialect's claim to be distinctive.

Dialect Versions of *Suti Solo do Bina Bane*

The second half of this volume is replete with a great variety of dialect concatenation. It includes nine separate versions of *Suti Solo do Bina Bane* composed by poets from all of the six dialect areas I have identified, from the eastern end of the island to its western end. The narrative of the chant varies far more than the versions of *Suti Solo do Bina Bane* in Termanu, as do the ritual contexts for these recitations. Perhaps most striking is the change of gender that the shells undergo from male in eastern and central Rote to female in western Rote. The shells also undergo a name change: in western Rote, Suti Solo do Bina Bane becomes known as Suti Saik do Bina Liuk.

As in the first half of the volume, in the second half the focus is on the parallelism of ritual language usage: the variety and continuity of formulaic expressions that continue to be maintained across the island of Rote. Despite phonological differences, there is clearly recognisable a core of shared dyadic sets that persists from one end of the island to the other. However, intermingled with this core of shared sets are distinct dialect variants that flavour each composition.

The nine versions of this chant come from the following master poets: Alex Mada of Landu and Anderias Ruy from Ringgou (Dialect Area I); Kornalius Medah from Bilba (Dialect Area II); Laazar Manoeain from Ba'a (Dialect Area III); N. D. Pah, Samuel Ndun and Jonas Mooy from Thie (Dialect Area IV); Simon Lesik and Frans Lau from Dengka (Dialect Area V); and Hendrik Foeh from Oenale (Dialect Area VI). Most of these compositions were recorded in gatherings on Bali as part of the Master Poets Project between 2006 and 2013. However, I gathered Laazar Manoeain's composition during fieldwork on Rote in 1963 and the joint composition by the poets N. D. Pah and Samuel Ndun during fieldwork in 1973.

In the presentations of these various versions, I have tried to follow a roughly similar format. In presenting each composition, I provide background and exegesis to understand it. Following the translation of the chant, I initially try to identify the island-wide dyadic sets used in its composition—both those that are similar to the recognisable dyadic sets from Termanu and those sets that have undergone phonological change according to the dialect used in their composition. Thereafter I try to identify the dyadic sets and formulae that are distinctive to the dialect in question and compare these usages with usages in other ritual language compositions. At the beginning, comparisons are necessarily with ritual language usages in Termanu but once enough different dialect usages have been presented, comparison can be directed to a variety of dialect usages on Rote.

13

Suti Solo do Bina Bane: A Version from the Domain of Landu

I recorded this version of *Suti Solo do Bina Bane* from the poet Alex Mada from Landu during the second recording session on Bali in October 2007. Although it was hard to gauge his age, Alex Mada is, I suspect, the oldest Rotenese poet whom I have recorded—probably even older than Old Meno. Small and sprightly and without his teeth, he spoke with a quiet, clear voice. His trip from Landu on Rote to Sanur in Bali was for him, an extraordinary adventure. He confided to me that flying above the clouds in the plane that brought him to Bali was like travelling to heaven. He was an enthusiastic participant and was particularly happy to offer his version of *Suti Solo do Bina Bane*.

The traditions of Landu are somewhat problematic among the domains of Rote. In 1756 in a bitter dispute with the Dutch East India Company, Landu's population was ravished. Its settlements were destroyed and hundreds of men, women and children were captured and sold into slavery. Those who escaped this onslaught dared not return to their homes. Landu became, for decades, a no man's land and only began to be resettled in the nineteenth century. Gradually, Landu's dynasty re-established itself and re-established the domain with settlers from many other domains— from as far away as Dengka but predominantly from its own remnant population and that of the neighbouring domains of Ringgou and Korbaffo. Its traditions reflect this history.

Figure 15: Alex Mada

My student Lintje Pellu, who was born in Termanu, wrote her ANU PhD thesis on Landu in 2008. This thesis, 'A Domain United, A Domain Divided: An Ethnographic Study of Social Relations and Social Change among the People of Landu, East Rote, Eastern Indonesia', is a critical ethnography that documents the tragic history and eventual reconstitution of Landu. During Lintje's fieldwork, Alex Mada became one of her key informants and she was able to record a version of *Suti Solo do Bina Bane* from him, which she included in her thesis. This version is a slightly longer recitation of this same chant.

Suti Solo do Bina Bane

The Rice and Millet Ripen in the Fields

Alex Mada's recitation begins by naming the woman Noa Bafo and the girl Lole Ora. She guards her ripening fields. The women are considered a pair who speak to each other, preparing for the harvest that will require a *fua poi*//*peda bafa* offering.

1.	*Ina Noa Bafo*	The woman Noa Bafo
2.	*Ma feto a Lole Ora*	And the girl Lole Ora
3.	*Feto ma-nea tine*	A girl who watches her field
4.	*Ma ina ma-sala rene*	And the woman who guards her garden
5.	*Ina ma-nea rene*	The woman who watches her garden
6.	*Ma feto ma-sala tine*	The girl who guards her field
7.	*Na-nea neu tine*	She watches over her field
8.	*Ma na-sala neu rene.*	And she guards her garden.
9.	*Boe ma mete i no ona*	She looks north and south
10.	*Ma relu dulu no muri*	And she spies east and west
11.	*Bete-ka kaboa*	The millet puts forth grains
12.	*Fo kaboa e'etu*	Grains ready to be plucked
13.	*Ma hade-ka modo peda*	And the rice grows green tips
14.	*Fo modo peda o'oru.*	Green panicles to be harvested.
15.	*Tehu, duas dede'a leo*	But the two talk with each other
16.	*Ma telus o'ola leo:*	And the three speak with each other:
17.	*'Kaboa e'etu*	'Grains ready to be plucked
18.	*Ma modo peda o'oru*	And panicles ready to be harvested
19.	*Tehu fua poi bei ta'a*	But the *fua poi* ritual has not been held
20.	*Ma peda bafo bei ta'a.'*	And the *peda bafo* ceremony has not been done.'

Lole Ora and Noa Bafo prepare their scoop-nets with lontar leaf stalks and Ndaonese cotton.

Lole Ora and Noa Bafo Make their Fishing Nets

21.	*Beka rae: tua esa nai Safu*	They say: a lontar on Savu
22.	*Fo beba esa nai Safu*	With its leaf-stalk on Savu
23.	*Ma rae: abas esa nai Rao*	And they say: a cotton plant on Ndao
24.	*Fo pena esa nai Rao.*	With its cotton tufts on Ndao.
25.	*Boe ma besak ka*	Now then
26.	*Fetok ka Lole Ora*	The girl Lole Ora
27.	*Ma inak ka Noa Bafo*	And the woman Noa Bafo
28.	*Tati neni beba esa*	She cuts a leaf-stalk
29.	*Ma sesa neni laka esa*	And slices its head
30.	*Teri kokondo rai*	She ties tightly a scoop-net
31.	*De rai ea aba don*	A scoop-net of cotton
32.	*Ma ane bubui se'o*	And she binds closely a fishnet
33.	*De se'o bui fepa dean.*	A fishnet of thick lontar leaf.
34.	*Se'o bui a dadi*	The scoop-net is made
35.	*Ma rai ea mori.*	And the fishnet is ready.

Before dawn, the two women go to the sea and begin their fishing—throwing and thrusting their nets, then scooping up their contents. In the process, they scoop up Suti Solo and Bina Bane.

Lole Ora and Noa Bafo Go Fishing in the Tidal Waters

36.	*Boe ma rae:*	So they say:
37.	*Meti bei koa kako*	The tide before the rooster crows
38.	*Ma tasi bei dulu pila*	And the sea before the east reddens
39.	*Feto a Lole Ora*	The girl Lole Ora
40.	*Ma ina Noa Bafo*	And the woman Noa Bafo
41.	*Neu nama rai rarano*	Goes to thrust and fish
42.	*Ma nama-se'o toto'o*	And to throw and to scoop
43.	*Nama-se'o toto'o*	To scoop by throwing

13. A VERSION FROM THE DOMAIN OF LANDU

44.	*Ma nama-rai rarano.*	And to fish by thrusting.
45.	*De rae:*	They say:
46.	*Tasi bei koa kako*	The sea before the friarbird sings
47.	*Ma meti bei dulu pila*	And the tide before the east reddens
48.	*De sua se'o neu laka*	She mounts the scoop-net on her head
49.	*Ma rae rai neu aru*	And she rests the fishnet on her shoulder
50.	*Nama-se'o toto'o*	To scoop by throwing
51.	*Ma nama-rai rarano*	And to fish by thrusting [in]
52.	*Meti leo lifu dale*	The tide like a water pool
53.	*Na mada nama-tutu*	As it dries steadily
54.	*Ma tasi leo nusa lai*	And the sea becomes like raised land
55.	*Na meti nama-sesele*	As the tide recedes
56.	*Se'o to'o, se'o to'o*	Scoop throw, scoop throw
57.	*Ma rai rano, rai rano*	Fish thrust, fish thrust
58.	*Rai ra Suti Solo*	She fishes Suti Solo
59.	*Ma se'o na Bina Bane*	And she scoops Bina Bane
60.	*Se'o toto'o heni*	Scoops and throws away
61.	*Ma rai rarano heni.*	Fishes and thrusts away.
62.	*Rali lifu ma pinda meti*	Shifts pool and changes tides
63.	*Tehu leo na ko se'o a*	But even as she scoops
64.	*Nama-se'o toto'o*	She scoops and throws
65.	*Ma nama-rai rarano*	And she fishes and thrusts
66.	*Se'o na Bina Bane*	She scoops Bina Bane
67.	*Ma rai na Suti Solo*	And she fishes Suti Solo
68.	*Se'o toto'o heni*	She scoops and throws away
69.	*Ma rai rarano heni.*	And she fishes and thrusts away.

Suti Solo do Bina Bane speak, telling Lole Ora and Noa Bafo not to throw them away but to take them home.

The Beginning of the Dialogue with Suti Solo do Bina Bane

70.	*Boe ma Suti Solo dede'a*	So Suti Solo speaks
71.	*Ma Bina Bane nafada, nae:*	And Bina Bane talks, saying:

72.	*'Boso se'o toto'o heni*	'Don't scoop and throw [me] away
73.	*Ma boso rai rarano heni*	And don't fish and thrust [me] away.
74.	*Uma tala uma teu*	Let us go to your house
75.	*Ma lo tala lo teu.*	And let us go to your home.
76.	*Boe ma uma rala uma*	Houses are houses
77.	*Ma lo rala lo.'*	Homes are homes.'

The dialogue begins with Suti Solo do Bina Bane. Lole Ora and Noa Bafo suggest that the two shells go with sea refuse and ocean flotsam; the shells consider this but decline the offer.

The First Dialogue Directive

78.	*Boe ma nae:*	It is said:
79.	*Lole Ora nafada*	Lole Ora talks
80.	*Ma Noa Bafo dede'a, nae:*	And Noa Bafo speaks, saying:
81.	*'Mo tere tasi leo*	'Go with the sea refuse
82.	*Ma mo hambau leo.'*	And go with the flotsam.'
83.	*Boe ma Suti Solo nafada*	So Suti Solo talks
84.	*Ma Bina Bane dede'a, nae:*	And Bina Bane speaks, saying:
85.	*'Tere tasi o,*	'Oh the sea refuse
86.	*Malole la boe*	May be fine
87.	*Ma hambau o*	And the flotsam
88.	*Mara a boe*	May be proper
89.	*Te leo timu rasa-rua dulu*	But if the monsoon comes again to the east
90.	*Fo koka heni hambau*	To sweep away the flotsam
91.	*Ma fa rasa fali laka*	And the west monsoon returns to the head
92.	*Fo fa heni tere tasi,*	To flood away the sea refuse
93.	*Ma au asaedu o bea*	Then with whom will I sob
94.	*Ma au amatani o bea?'*	And with whom will I cry?'

Lole Ora and Noa Bafo then propose that the shells go with the harbour crabs and shore molluscs. But the harbour crabs and shore molluscs are the target of night-time fishing so, weepingly, Suti Solo do Bina Bane again decline this possibility.

The Second Dialogue Directive

95.	*Boe ma Lole Ora dede'a*	So Lole Ora speaks
96.	*Noa Bafo nafada, nae:*	Noa Bafo talks, saying:
97.	*'Sona mu mo ni namo*	'Then go with the harbour crabs
98.	*Ma mu mo kuma dae.'*	And go with the shore molluscs.'
99.	*Boe ma Suti Solo dede'a leo*	So Suti Solo speaks forth
100.	*Ma Bina Bane nafada leo, nae:*	And Bina Bane talks out, saying:
101.	*'De tata pele laka namo*	'Then if the fishing torch is unwound
102.	*Ma [Fo] loti heni ni namo*	To torch-fish away the harbour crabs
103.	*Ma fule no do dae*	And coconut leaves are unbound
104.	*Fo pele heni kuma dae*	To night-fish away the shore molluscs
105.	*Na u o bea bali?'*	Then with whom will I be once more?'
106.	*Suti nasa-edu boboto*	Suti sobs weepingly
107.	*Ma nama-tani bobolu*	And cries tearfully.

Lole Ora and Noa Bafo then propose that they go with the *boa* trees in the harbour and the *pi'o* (*piko*) trees in the estuary. These soft-wooded trees are easily split apart by the monsoon, so again Suti Solo and Bina Bane decline this proposal.

The Third Dialogue Directive

108.	*Boe ma Lole Ora nafada*	So Lole Ora talks
109.	*Ma Noa Bafo dede'a, nae:*	And Noa Bafo speaks, saying:
110.	*'Sona mu mo boa namo*	'Go with the *boa* trees in the harbour
111.	*Ma mu mo pi'o oli.'*	And go with the *piko* trees in the estuary.'
112.	*Boe ma Suti nafada bali*	So Suti talks once more
113.	*Ma Bina dede'a bali, nae:*	And Bina speaks once more, saying:
114.	*'Te leo pi'o oli malole so*	'The *piko* trees in the estuary are fine
115.	*Ma o boa namo mara a so*	And the *boa* trees in the harbour are proper
116.	*Te leo timu rasa-rua dulu*	But if the monsoon comes again to the east
117.	*Fo seki heni boa namo*	To split apart the *boa* trees in the harbour
118.	*Ma fa rasa-fali laka*	And the west monsoon returns to the head

119.	*Fo hea heni pi'o oli*	To pull apart the *piko* trees in the estuary
120.	*Au o u bea bali?*	With whom will I be once more?
121.	*Au ama-tani o bea?*	With whom will I cry?
122.	*Ma au asa-edu o bea?'*	And with whom will I sob?'

Lole Ora and Noa Bafo then propose that they go with the house post and old beam. These lines appear to conflate house post//old beam with syrup vat//millet basket. As a result, there are four lines here that, though paired, do not make clear sense.

The Fourth Dialogue Directive

123.	*Boe ma Lole Ora nafada*	So Lole Ora talks
124.	*Ma Noa Bafo dede'a nae:*	And Noa Bafo speaks, saying:
125.	*'Sona mu mo timi di*	'Then go with the house post
126.	*Sona [mu] mo balo tua.'*	Then go with the old beam.'
127.	*Boe ma [Suti] nae:*	So Suti says:
128.	*'O balo tua a malole a so*	'Oh the old beam is good
129.	*Ma timi di ho mara so*	And the house post is proper
130.	*Te leo bou tua hene lo**	But if the lontar vat ascends the home*
131.	*Ma fati bete ae uma**	And the millet basket rises in the house*
132.	*Seki heni bou tua**	And splits apart the lontar vat*
133.	*Te [hea] heni balo tua**	And tears apart the old beam*,
134.	*Na o u bea bali?'*	Then with whom will I be once more?'

These next lines correct the preceding lines (130–33): Lole Ora and Noa Bafo tell the shells to go with the lontar (syrup) vat and the millet (not the rice) basket, but if visitors come and take from the vat and basket, it will be emptied.

The Fifth Dialogue Directive

135.	*Boe ma Lole Ora nafada*	So Lole Ora talks
136.	*Ma Noa Bafo dede'a, nae:*	And Noa Bafo speaks, saying:
137.	*'Sono mu mo fati bete*	'Then go with the millet basket
138.	*Ma mu mo bou tua.'*	And go with the lontar vat.'
139.	*Boe ma [Suti] nae:*	So Suti says:

13. A VERSION FROM THE DOMAIN OF LANDU

140.	*'Te leo pa'u raonda mai*	'But if visitors arrive
141.	*Ma fui na ranoko mai*	And strangers come
142.	*Fo hai heni bou tua*	To take [from] the lontar vat
143.	*Ma hai heni fati bete*	And take [from] the millet basket
144.	*Ma au u bea bali?'*	Then with whom will I be once more?'

Lole Ora and Noa Bafo tell the shells to go with the border stone and boundary tree, but if a hundred goats and a thousand buffalo come, they will kick over the boundary tree and trample the border stone, leaving the shells on their own.

The Sixth Dialogue Directive

145.	*Boe ma sona, Lole Ora nafada*	So then Lole Ora talks
146.	*Ma Noa Bafo dede'a nae:*	And Noa Bafo speaks, saying:
147.	*'Mu mo to batu*	'Go with the border stone
148.	*Ma mu mo peu ai.'*	And go with the boundary tree.'
149.	*Boe ma Suti nafada leo*	So Suti talks out
150.	*Ma Bina dede'a leo, nae:*	And Bina speaks forth, saying:
151.	*'Te leo bulan bibi nara mai*	'But if the moon's goats come
152.	*Fo bibi natu ara mai*	A hundred goats come
153.	*Fo fetu heni peu ai*	To kick over the boundary tree
154.	*Ma ledo apa nara mai*	And the sun's buffalo come
155.	*Fo apa rifun nara mai*	A thousand buffalo come
156.	*Fo hake heni to batu*	To trample the border stone
157.	*Na o bea bali?'*	Then with whom will I be once more?'

Again, Lole Ora and Noa Bafo make another proposal: that the shells go to sacred forest groves—the *huta* of the wood//*luli* of the forest. But if these are cut down, the shells will be alone once more.

The Seventh Dialogue Directive

158.	*Boe ma nafada bai*	So she talks again
159.	*Lole Ora dede'a*	Lole Ora speaks
160.	*Ma Noa Bafo nafada:*	And Noa Bafo talks:
161.	*'Sona mu mo nura huta*	'Then go to the sacred grove

162.	*Ma mu mo lasi luli.'*	And go to the forbidden forest.'
163.	*Boe ma Bina Bane nafada*	So Bina Bane talks
164.	*Ma Suti Solo dede'a nae:*	And Suti Solo speaks, saying:
165.	*'Au u o nura huta*	'I will go to sacred grove
166.	*Ma o lasi luli*	And to the forbidden forest
167.	*Te leo atu asa oli*	But if the sharpened chopping knife
168.	*Na lo'o heni nula huta*	Cuts down the sacred grove
169.	*Ma sosa do tei sina na*	And the adze with its Chinese blade
170.	*Huka heni lasi luli*	Opens up the forbidden forest
171.	*Na o bea bali?'*	Then with whom will I be once more?'

Once again, the women make a proposal. This time, they urge the shells to go with the people of the land and clansmen of the mountain, but if these people shift, the shells will again be abandoned.

The Eighth Dialogue Directive

172.	*Boe ma ana dede'a bali, nae:*	So she speaks once more, saying:
173.	*'Sona mu mo nusa iku*	'Go with the people of the land
174.	*Ma mu mo lete leo.'*	And go with the clansmen of the mountain.'
175.	*Nae:*	[Suti] says:
176.	*'Au o lete leo o malole a so*	'My going with the clansmen of the mountain is good
177.	*Ma au o nusa iku o mara a so*	And my going with the people of the land is proper
178.	*Tehu leo lete leo a hiru*	But if the clans of the mountain shift
179.	*Ma nusa iku a hai*	And the people of the land move
180.	*Na u o bea bali?'*	Then with whom will I be once more?'

Finally, Lole Ora and Noa Bafo propose that the shells go to be joined with a *gewang* (Corypha palm) trunk and a lontar (Borassus palm) stalk and set in fields to serve as clappers to drive away birds that attack the growing fields. With this suggestion, the recitation comes to an end.

The Ninth Dialogue Directive

181.	*Boe ma Lole Ora nafada*	So Lole Ora talks
182.	*Ma Noa Bafo dede'a, nae:*	And Noa Bafo speaks, saying:
183.	*'Sona mo isi tula*	'Then go with the *gewang* trunk
184.	*Ma mu mo londa fepa*	And go with the lontar stalks
185.	*Fo era etu mu londa fepa*	To be bound with the lontar stalks
186.	*Ma puru mo isi tula*	And attached to the *gewang*'s trunk
187.	*Nai tine a dale*	Within a dry field
188.	*Ma nai rene a dale.'*	And within an irrigated field.'

The poem ended with Alex Mada's follow-up explanation that the shells were to become 'clappers' to drive away the birds (*manea manupui ra*).

Analysis of Alex Mada's Version of *Suti Solo do Bina Bane*

Alex Mada's version of *Suti Solo do Bina Bane* consists of 69 dyadic sets. This number includes several formulaic sets that cannot be decomposed into simpler dyads. Of these 69 dyadic sets, a majority are dyadic sets shared with Termanu and would appear to belong to a widespread—possibly island-wide—core of ritual pairs. Many of these sets are basic and are recognisable despite phonological differences in the dialects of the two domains.

Some of these dyadic sets with similar phonology that are immediately recognisable are, for example: 1) *bete*//*hade* ('millet'//'rice'); 2) *bulan*//*ledo* ('moon'//'sun'); 3) *dua*//*telu* ('two'//'three'); 4) *fa*//*timu* ('west wind/monsoon'//'east wind'); 5) *feto*//*ina* ('girl'//'woman'); 6) *lifu*//*meti* ('pool'//'tide'); 7) *lo*//*uma* ('home'//'house'); 8) *loti*//*pele* ('[to fish] by torchlight'//'[to fish] by leaf-torch'); 9) *meti*//*tasi* ('tide'//'sea'); 10) *namo*//*oli* ('harbour'//'estuary').

Other sets, which may be less easily recognised because of Landu's dialect phonology, still form part of this wider core of shared ritual terms. They are the same terms as used in Termanu. Some examples of these dyadic sets are the following—for example, in contrast to Termanu, Landu lacks initial 'k'. Hence the following transformations:

Table 9: Termanu–Landu Dialect Comparisons I

Termanu		Landu	Gloss
kapas//tua	>>	abas//tua	'cotton'//'lontar'
ketu//kolu	>>	etu//oru	'to pick'//'pluck'
kedu//tani	>>	edu//tani	'to sob'//'weep'
ki//kona	>>	i//ona	'left'//'right'

Landu also lacks medial 'k', while on the other hand, Landu retains certain medial consonants that Termanu lacks:

Table 10: Termanu–Landu Dialect Comparisons II

Termanu		Landu	Gloss
boa//piko	>>	boa//pi'o	'*boa* tree'//'*piko* tree'
kapa//bi'i	>>	apa//bibi	'water buffalo'//'goat/sheep'

Medial 'ng' in Termanu becomes 'k' in Landu, while some initial and some medial 'l' become 'r'; hence these transformations:

Table 11: Termanu–Landu Dialect Comparisons III

Termanu		Landu	Gloss
alu//langa	>>	aru//laka	'shoulder'//'head'
ane//teli	>>	ane//teri	'tie'//'bind/plait'
dadi//mori	>>	dadi//moli	'happen'//'occur/become'
dulu//langa	>>	dulu//laka	'east'//'head'
dulu//muli	>>	dulu//muri	'east'//'west'
leo//ingu	>>	leo//iku	'clan'//'land'
natu//lifu	>>	natu//rifu	'hundred'//'thousand'
nula//lasi	>>	nura//lasi	'wood'//'forest'

Medial 'nd' in Termanu becomes 'r' in Landu:

Table 12: Termanu–Landu Dialect Comparisons IV

Termanu		Landu	Gloss
ndae//sua	>>	rae//sua	'to rest on shoulder'//'mount on head'
ndai//seko	>>	rai//se'o	'to scoop'//'fish with scoop-net'

Despite these phonological differences, the semantic value of these dyadic sets is retained across both dialects. It is possible—though admittedly sometimes difficult—for speakers of one dialect to adjust to the sound shape of the other dialect and thus follow a ritual recitation.

More significant are the dyadic sets in which there occurs a shift in semantic terminology.

It is with these sets that we encounter levels of difference between ritual recitations in Landu and Termanu.

It is useful to focus on a few clear examples.

One example is the slight difference between Landu and Termanu in reference to the offerings that are supposed to be made at origin/harvest ceremonies. Where Termanu has *peda poi//fua bafa*, Landu has *fua poi// peda bafa*—a simple reversal of the terms *fua//peda* ('to lift'//'to place').

Another example of a minor difference is in the terms for the house: Malesi uses the expression *timi di//lungu tua* ('house post'//'cross-beam'), while Landu has *timi di//balo tua* ('house post'//'old beam'). There is, in fact, variation among the naming of house parts in different domains and, as a consequence, variations among poets on the island in their references to parts of the house.

Another good example is where several poets of Termanu use the expression *bou tua//neka hade* ('lontar syrup vat'//'rice basket'), while Landu has *bou tua//fati bete* ('lontar syrup vat'//'millet basket'). Termanu is noted for its rice fields; Landu for its extensive millet cultivation.

In reference to growing rice and millet, Mikael Pellondou uses the formulaic expression *hade la modo peda//betekala dio hu'u* ('the rice is green-tipped'//'the millet has ripened grains'), whereas Alex Mada's expression is *hade-ka modo peda//bete-kaboa* ('the rice grows green tips'//'the millet puts forth grains').

In Termanu, *ni//poek* ('crab'//'shrimp') form a pair; in Landu *ni//kuma* ('crab'//'mollusc') form a pair. They appear to be used in similar contexts.

Other differences occur but may appear to be less immediately apparent.

Table 13: Termanu–Landu Dialect Comparisons V

Termanu	Landu	Gloss
osi//tina	*rene//tine*	'two kinds of fields'//'gardens'
bobolu//dodopo	*bobolu//boboto*	'weeping'//'sobbing'
taka//tala	*atu//sosa*	'axe'//'adze' (machete)
seseko//kokolo	*bubui//kokondo*	'tightly'//'closely'

A Succession of Distinctive Formulaic Expressions

There occurs in Alex Mada's recitation a succession of distinctive formulaic expressions that would resonate and be recognised by speakers of Termanu dialect but would not necessarily be considered part of Termanu's oral phraseology.

Twice—in lines 37–38 and again in lines 46–47—Alex Mada uses the formulaic expression to describe the seascape in the early dawn:

| *Tasi bei koa kako* | The sea before the friarbird sings |
| *Ma meti bei dulu pila.* | And the tide before the east reddens. |

By contrast, both Meno and Seu Ba'i describe the dawn with this expression:

| *Siluk bei ta dulu* | When morning is not yet in the east |
| *Ma hu'ak bei ta langa.* | And dawn is not yet at the head. |

Equally common, in Termanu, is the expression that links the dawn to the sound of the friarbird and parrot:

| *Boe-ma koa bei timu-dulu-la* | Friarbirds still in the dawning east |
| *Ma nggia bei sepe-langa-la* | And green parrots still at the reddening head |

Alex Mada's expression beautifully blends the physical appearance of the dawn with the song of the friarbird.

In Alex Mada's recitation, the woman Lole Ora//Noa Bafo offers nine separate directives in her dialogue with the shells. Several of these directives given to the shells are distinctive. Thus, for example, initially Lole Ora//Noa Bafo tells the shells:

'Mo tere tasi leo	'Go with the sea refuse
Ma mo hambau leo.'	And go with the flotsam.'

These words would be understood in Termanu but no poet of Termanu uses this formula as one of his directives. (As will be seen, however, this expression is used in other domains, particularly Bilba.)

Again, in her second directive, Lole Ora//Noa Bafo urges the shells:

'Sona mu mo ni namo	'Then go with the harbour crabs
Ma mu mo kuma dae.'	And go with the shore molluscs.'

This, too, is a distinctive directive.

Similarly, Loe Ora//Noa Bafo tells the shells:

'Sona mu mo boa namo	'Go with the *boa* trees in the harbour
'Ma mu mo pi'o oli.'	And go with the *piko* trees in the estuary.'

In Termanu, virtually all versions of *Suti Solo do Bina Bane* allude to the shells floating in the sea like *boa* and *piko* driftwood but in no recitation is there a directive to the shells to join these two soft-wooded coastal trees.

The fourth directive, 'house post and old beam', and the fifth directive, 'lontar syrup vat and millet basket', are variants on Termanu's directives; the sixth directive, 'border stone and boundary tree', is a common formulaic expression in Termanu. The seventh directive, '*huta* stand and *luli* grove' in the forest, is distinctive, while the eighth directive could be considered a variation on various formulaic expressions in Termanu.

The final directive is that the shells attach themselves to *gewang* palm trunk and lontar palm stalk to become a kind of sounding clapper to drive away birds and animals from the fields. This is reminiscent of some of the dialogue in Mikael Pellondou's recitation and will occur again in Ande Ruy's recitation from Ringgou.

14
Suti Solo do Bina Bane: A Version from the Domain of Ringgou

This version of *Suti Solo do Bina Bane* was recorded from the master poet Ande Ruy during the first recording session held in Bali in July 2006. I had travelled earlier in the year to Rote to meet Ande and to persuade him to join the first group invited to Bali. He agreed and joined all subsequent recording sessions.

When we met, Ande Ruy's reputation was already considerable. He is the best-known chanter (*manahelo*) on Rote. A farmer in his ordinary day-to-day activities in the domain of Ringgou, Ande is a natural and enthusiastic performer: energetic, talented and versatile. He is able to recite, to sing, to chant to the accompaniment of the drum and to play the Rotenese *sesandu*. All of these talents have made him the first choice among the chanters on Rote at government functions, at official performances and cultural competitions.

Unlike most other poets on the island, Ande Ruy has had wide experience: he has travelled to, and performed in, different parts of Indonesia including Jakarta. Despite this experience, he remains deeply traditional. When we first met, we talked about the restrictions on recitation that he felt applied to key segments of the traditional canon. After many years of recording him, he has not yet revealed more than a portion of his ritual knowledge.

In our recording sessions over the years, Ande Ruy's approach to the exegesis of his recitations has expanded. Initially, for him, explication involved further ritual elaboration of what he had already said. Gradually, however, in the course of his participation with other poets, particularly Esau Pono, Ande developed a wider view of Rotenese ritual language and could begin to offer clearer explication of his performances in relation to others.

Initially, I struggled to understand Ande's recitation of *Suti Solo do Bina Bane*. It was my first serious encounter with the dialect of Ringgou and it took many sessions with Ande Ruy to comprehend his recitation properly. After the first rough transcription of his performance by Lintje Pellu and joint work on a preliminary translation, I continued to work with him, checking and correcting this recitation. After recording and translating this version in 2006, I worked through the translation with Ande when we met again in October 2007 and again worked further with him in June 2009. By 2009, I had recorded many other of his recitations and had slowly begun to understand his performance style and incredible command of ritual language.

This recitation consists of 182 lines. It begins with a standard formula that locates the narrative in the distant past and then goes on to describe Oli Masi ma Bisa Oli's search for the two ritual fish, here identified as Tio Holu//Dusu Lake. In their search, Oli Masi ma Bisa Oli find Suti Solo and Bina Bane, who immediately voice their plea, insisting that they are 'widow and orphan'. They beg to be taken up by Oli Masi and Masi Oli as 'aunt and mother'.

14. A VERSION FROM THE DOMAIN OF RINGGOU

Figure 16: Ande Ruy

Figure 17: Ande Ruy reciting

Oli Masi and Bisa Oli Encounter Suti Solo do Bina Bane

1.	*Hida bei leo hatan*	At a time long ago
2.	*Ma data bei leo dona*	At a period long past
3.	*Ina a Oli Masi*	The woman Oli Masi
4.	*Ma feto a Bisa Oli*	And the girl Bisa Oli
5.	*Neu nama-rai rarano*	Goes to thrust her fishnet
6.	*Ma neu nama-se'o toto'o,*	And goes to throw her scoop-net,
7.	*Nama-rai saka Tio Holu*	To fish forth Tio Holu
8.	*Ma nama-se'o saka Dusu Lake.*	And to scoop up Dusu Lake.
9.	*Tehu nama-rai nala le esa,*	She net-fishes in one tidal pond,
10.	*Na rai na Suti Solo*	But only nets Suti Solo
11.	*Ma nama se'o nala lifu esa,*	And she scoop-fishes in one pool,
12.	*Na se'o na Bina Bane.*	But only scoops Bina Bane.
13.	*Boe ma ina Oli Masi*	So the woman Oli Masi

14. A VERSION FROM THE DOMAIN OF RINGGOU

14.	*Ma feto a Bisa Oli*		And the girl Bisa Oli
15.	*Lole harana neu*		Raises her voice
16.	*Ma selu dasi na neu:*		And lifts her words:
17.	*'Tute hata leo hata*		'What is amiss
18.	*De Suti Solo masa-edu*		That you, Suti Solo, sob
19.	*Ma sala hata leo hata*		What is wrong
20.	*De Bina Bane mama-tani?'*		That you, Bina Bane, cry?'
21.	*Boe ma Suti Solo lole haran*		So Suti Solo raises his voice
22.	*Ma Bina Bane selu dasin:*		And Bina Bane lifts his words:
23.	*'Ami ia ana ma*		'We here are orphans
24.	*Ami ia falu ina.*		We here are widows.
25.	*Awe, ami inam o ta'a*		Awe, our mother is no more
26.	*Ma ami amam o ta'a,*		And our father is no more,
27.	*Ami tiam o ta'a*		Our friend exists no more
28.	*Ma senam o ta'a.*		Our companion exists no more.
29.	*De ami tesa tei bei ta'a*		Our contentment is no more
30.	*Ma ami tama dale bei ta'a.*		And our satisfaction is no more.
31.	*De mama-tani meu dua*		We cry forth together [as two]
32.	*Ma masa-edu meu telu.*		And we sob in unison [as three].
33.	*De o ina ko nou*		You, dear mother
34.	*Ma o te'o ko nei,*		And you, dear aunt,
35.	*Ifa muni ami leo*		Lift and carry us away
36.	*Ma o'o muni ami leo*		And cradle and carry us away
37.	*Fo saka fe ami tesa tei*		To give us contentment
38.	*Ma tuka fe ami tama dale*		And provide us satisfaction
39.	*Nai te'ok oen*		In an aunt's water
40.	*Ma nai inak daen.'*		And in a mother's land.'

Oli Masi and Bisa Oli carry the shells home and then issue the first directive to go with the 'rice basket and syrup vat'. Suti Solo and Bina Bane question the permanence of this option because the 'rice will be doled from the basket and syrup scooped from the vat'.

First Directive: To Go with the Rice Basket and Syrup Vat

41.	*Boe ma ina a Oli Masi*	So the woman Oli Masi
42.	*Ma feto o Bisa Oli o*	And the girl Bisa Oli
43.	*O'o neni Suti Solo*	Cradle Suti Solo
44.	*Ma ifa neni Bina Bane*	And lift Bina Bane
45.	*Leo lon mai*	Bringing them to their home
46.	*Ma leo uma mai.*	And bringing them to their house.
47.	*Mai losa lo na*	They come to the home
48.	*Mai ru'u uma na.*	They come to the house.
49.	*Boe ma ina Oli Masi*	Then the woman Oli Masi
50.	*Ma feto a Bisa Oli*	And the girl Bisa Oli
51.	*Nadasi neu Suti Solo*	Speaks to Suti Solo
52.	*Ma nahara neu Bina Bane:*	And says to Bina Bane:
53.	*'Iku fo mo nea hade*	'Your land is with the rice basket
54.	*Ma leo fo mo bou tua.'*	And your lineage is with the syrup vat.'
55.	*Tehu Suti Solo lole haran*	But Suti Solo raises his voice
56.	*Ma Bina Bane selu dasin:*	And Bina Bane lifts his words:
57.	*'Ami iku fo mo ne'a hade*	'Our land is with the rice basket
58.	*Ma ami leo fo mo bou tua, tebe!*	And our lineage is with the syrup vat, indeed!
59.	*Tehu fai esa nai na*	But on some day
60.	*Ma ledo esa nai ria,*	And at some time,
61.	*Ne'a sasau hade,*	[If] the basket continually doles out rice,
62.	*Sau heni nea hade*	This will dole the rice basket empty
63.	*Ma rui kokola tuan,*	And [if] the vat continually scoops syrup,
64.	*Rui heni bou tua.*	This will scoop the syrup vat clean.
65.	*Na ami iku fo mo be a*	Then with whom will our land be
66.	*Ma ami leo fo mo be a?*	And with whom will our lineage be?
67.	*Te [bei] ta tesa tei*	This is not yet contentment
68.	*Ma bei ta tama dale.*	And not yet a satisfaction.
69.	*Hu fo fai bea ma*	For from time to time

70.	*Fui hene lo*	Outsiders climb up into the home
71.	*Ma pa'u ae uma*	And strangers ascend to the house
72.	*Na neuko sau heni nea hade*	Then rice will be doled from the basket
73.	*Ma rui heni bou tua.'*	And syrup will be scooped from the vat.'

The second directive is to go with the 'rice field's wide embankment and the dry field's long boundary'. The directive highlights a contrast between two kinds of field and their respective boundaries. Suti Solo and Bina Bane question the permanence of this option because both boundaries can be washed by flooding rain.

Second Directive: To Go to the Rice Field's Wide Embankment and Dry Field's Long Boundary

74.	*De la'o fo tarali*	So they go forth
75.	*Ma lope fo tahi.*	And they walk out.
76.	*Boe ma lope tarali dae*	They walk forth through the land
77.	*Ma lao tahi oe.*	And they go forth through the waters.
78.	*De reu losa opa loa ara*	They go to the rice field's wide embankment
79.	*Ma reu ru'u e naru ara.*	And they go to the dry field's long boundary.
80.	*Oli Masi lole haran*	Oli Masi raises her voice
81.	*Ma Bisa Oli selu dasin:*	And Bisa Oli lifts her words:
82.	*'Nea mo opa loa*	'Shelter with the wide embankment
83.	*Ma tama mo e naru.'*	And join with the long boundary.'
84.	*Tehu Suti Solo selu dasin*	But Suti Solo lifts his words
85.	*Ma Bina Bane lole haran:*	And Bina Bane raises his voice:
86.	*'Fai esa nai na*	'Yet some day
87.	*Ma ledo esa nai ria*	And at some time
88.	*Uda te mai lasi*	The rain will spear through the forest
89.	*Fo fa rama henu le*	So the flood fills the river
90.	*Fo seki heni opa loa*	So washes away the wide embankment

91.	*Ma sea heni enaru.*	And carries away the long boundary.
92.	*Na ami iku fo mo be a*	Then with whom will our land be
93.	*Ma ami leo fo mo be a?*	And with whom will our lineage be?
94.	*Te tesa tei bei ta'a*	There is no contentment there
95.	*Ma tama dale bei ta'a.'*	And there is no satisfaction there.'

The third directive, to go with the raised horns and waving tails, is a proposal to take refuge with buffalo and goat herds. For Suti Solo and Bina Bane, these animals could die and leave them abandoned.

Third Directive: To Go with the Raised Horns and Waving Tails

96.	*De lope tarali dae*	So they walk forth through the land
97.	*Ma lao tarali oe.*	And go forth through the waters.
98.	*Boe ma reu losa mo tale hade a*	They go to the dry rice field
99.	*Ma reu ru'u lete batu lau.*	And to the hill's rocky grassland.
100.	*Boe ma ina a Oli Masi*	So the woman Oli Masi
101.	*Ma feto a Bisa Oli nae:*	And the girl Bisa Oli says:
102.	*'Sana nea mo sura mana mamasua*	'Your shelter will be with the raised horns
103.	*Ma iku fo mo iko mana fefelo a.'*	And your land with the waving tails.'
104.	*Tehu Suti Solo lole haran*	But Suti Solo raises his voice
105.	*Ma Bina Bane selu dasin:*	And Bina Bane lifts his words:
106.	*'Fai esa nai ria*	'On some day like this
107.	*Ma ledo esa nai na,*	And at some time like that,
108.	*Roe apa a mai*	The water buffalo disease will come
109.	*Sapu heni tena apa*	So that the water buffalo herds die
110.	*Ma lalo heni bote bibi.*	And the goat flocks perish.
111.	*Na ami iku fo be a*	Then with whom will our land be
112.	*Ma ami leo fo mo be a?*	And with whom will our lineage be?
113.	*De ami tetum bei ta'a*	For us, there is yet no order
114.	*Ma ami temam bei ta'a.'*	And for us, there is yet no integrity.'

14. A VERSION FROM THE DOMAIN OF RINGGOU

The fourth directive is not voiced but only responded to by the shells: neither the lontar palm nor the harvested rice offers any permanence or fellowship.

A Fourth Directive: To Go with the Lontar Palm and Rice Field

115.	*De lope tarali oe*	So they walk forth through the waters
116.	*Ma lao tarali dae,*	And they go forth through the land,
117.	*Te tesa tei bei ta'a*	There is yet no contentment
118.	*Ma tama dale bei ta'a.*	And yet no satisfaction.
119.	*Boe ma reu peu tua*	They go to tap the lontar
120.	*Ma reu lele hade a.*	And they go to harvest the rice fields.
121.	*Tehu Suti Solo selu dasin*	But Suti Solo raises his voice
122.	*Ma Bina Bane lole haran:*	And Bina Bane lifts his words:
123.	*'Fai esa nai ria*	'On some day like this
124.	*Ma ledo esa nai na*	And at some time like that
125.	*Tua rama loe suma*	The lontar lower the tapping baskets
126.	*Ma modo [hade?] rama pelu polo*	And the rice has its panicles cut
127.	*Na ami iku fo mo be a*	Then with whom will our land be
128.	*Ma ami nea fo mo be a?*	And with whom will our shelter be?
129.	*De bei ta tesa tei*	Yet no contentment
130.	*Ma bei ta tama dale.'*	And yet no satisfaction.'
131.	*De lope tarali oe*	So they walk forth through the waters
132.	*Ma lao tarali dae.*	And they go forth through the land.
133.	*Tetun bei ta'a*	There is yet no order
134.	*Ma teman bei ta'a.*	And there is yet no integrity.

The fifth directive is to go with boundary stone and border tree and the response is that these markers can be trampled and shifted by the 'moon's buffalo and the sun's goats'. Hence, there is still no permanence—no contentment or satisfaction.

267

Suti Solo and Bina Bane Go among Boundary Stone and Border Tree

135.	*Boe ma reu losa to batu*	So they go to boundary stone
136.	*Ma reu ru'u peu ai.*	And they go to border tree.
137.	*Tehu Suti Solo lole haran*	But Suti Solo lifts his words
138.	*Ma Bina Bane selu dasin:*	And Bina Bane raises his voice:
139.	*'Fai esa nai na*	'On some day like that
140.	*Ma ledo esa nai ria,*	And some time like this,
141.	*Bulan apa nara mai*	The moon's buffalo will come
142.	*Fo hake heni to batu*	To change the boundary stone
143.	*Ma ledo hote nara mai*	And sun's goats will come
144.	*Fetu heni peu ai.*	To shift the border tree.
145.	*Na ami iku mo be a*	Then with whom is our land
146.	*Ma ami leo mo be a?*	And with whom is our lineage?
147.	*De tesa tei bei ta'a*	There is yet no contentment
148.	*Ma tama dale bei ta'a.'*	And yet no satisfaction.'

Finally and perhaps somewhat abruptly, Suti Solo and Bina Bane's quest comes to an end. They find rest at the base of the *ko-nau* tree, a bidara or Indian plum tree (*Ziziphus mauritana*), and in the shade of the *nilu-foi* tree, a tamarind tree (*Tamarindus indica*). Both species are fruit-bearing dryland trees and their steady production of fruit is an attraction for the shells. One has only to pick and eat, pluck and consume the abundant fruit. For the shells, there is no return to the sea, no indication of the symbolic significance of these trees and no explanation (in this recitation) of why the shells find their rest among these trees.

Suti Solo and Bina Bane Find Rest at the *Ko-Nau* Tree and *Nilu-Foi* Tree

149.	*Lope tarali oe*	So they walk through the waters
150.	*Ma lao tarali dae.*	And they go through the land.
151.	*Boe ma reu to telu*	They go to the three markers
152.	*Ma reu lane dua.*	And go to the two boundaries.

153.	*Boe ma ina a Oli Masi*	The woman Oli Masi
154.	*Ma feto a Bisa Oli*	And the girl Bisa Oli
155.	*Fai neu huru manu*	When the day turns to the roosting chicken
156.	*Ma ledo neu hani bafi.*	And the time comes to feed the pigs.
157.	*De mai ko-nau laon*	They arrive at the *ko-nau* tree's shade
158.	*Fo iku mo ko-nau*	A place with the *ko-nau* tree
159.	*Ma mai nilu-foi hun*	And they come to the *nilu-foi* tree's base
160.	*Fo nea mo nilu-foi*	A shelter at the *nilu-foi* tree's base
161.	*Leo fo tatai*	A lineage in which to stay
162.	*Ma iku fo dodo.*	And a land in which to ponder.
163.	*Boe ma Suti Solo selu dasin*	Then Suti Solo raises his voice
164.	*Ma Bina Bane lole haran:*	And Bina Bane lifts his words:
165.	*'Ina sue o nei*	'O dearly loved woman
166.	*Ma feto lai o nei*	And much beloved girl
167.	*Tule diu dua leo*	Go back, turn away
168.	*Ma fali soro lele leo*	And return, turn round
169.	*Te ra dale a so*	This is pleasing here
170.	*Ma to'e tei a so.*	And this is satisfying here.
171.	*Hu fo fai na neu fai*	For when day passes day
172.	*Ma ledo na neu ledo*	And time passes time
173.	*Ko-nau na boa*	The *ko-nau* tree bears fruit
174.	*Na ami here hao, here hao*	Then we will pick, pick and eat
175.	*Ma nilu-foi na petu*	And the *nilu-foi* tree puts forth fruit
176.	*Na ami etu folo, etu folo.*	Then we will pluck, pluck and consume.
177.	*De ra dale a so*	It is pleasing here
178.	*Ma to'e tei a so.'*	And it is satisfying here.'
179.	*Losa fai ia,*	To this day
180.	*Ma ru'u ledo ia*	And until this time
181.	*Suti Solo bei nai ko-nau hun*	Suti Solo remains at the base of the *ko-nau* tree
182.	*Ma Bina Bane bei nai nilu-foi la'on.*	And Bina Bane remains in the *nilu-foi*'s shade.

An Analysis of Ande Ruy's Ritual Language Usage

This recitation by Ande Ruy has 182 lines and is composed of 66 dyadic sets. Its compositional structure is roughly in proportion to the recitation by Alex Mada, which has 188 lines and is composed of 69 dyadic sets. Sound changes in Ringgou are similar to those in Landu. Both domains form part of a broadly similar dialect area: Dialect Area I. The two recitations would be easily intelligible to members of these domains but would present some problems of comprehension to speakers of dialects in central and western Rote. As in the case with the Landu recitation, the majority of dyadic sets form part of an island-wide core.

Some examples of dyadic sets whose phonology would be recognisable to Termanu speakers are: 1) *ai//batu* ('tree'//'rock'); 2) *ama//ina* ('father'//'mother'); 3) *dale//tei* ('inside, heart'//'stomach'); 4) *dae//oe* ('earth'//'water'); 5) *fa//uda* ('monsoon'//'rain'); 6) *fai//ledo* ('day'//'sun'); 7) *hade//tua* ('rice'//'lontar palm juice'); 8) *le//lifu* ('river'//'waterhole, pool'); 9) *ina//te'o* ('mother'//'father's sister'); 10) *sena//tia* ('friend'//'companion'); 11) *lo//uma* ('house'//'home'); 12) *lai//sue* ('to have affection for'//'to care for').

Other dyadic sets show sound changes that are prominent in both Ringgou and Landu. Like Landu, Ringgou lacks initial 'k' and medial 'k'; 'ng' occurs as 'k'; 'nd' as 'r', while some medial 'l' also occur as 'r'. Hence, for example, the variety of transformations of these following common dyadic sets:

Table 14: Termanu–Ringgou Dialect Comparisons

Termanu	Ringgou	Gloss
kae//hene	ae//hene	'climb'//'step'
kapa//bote	apa bote	'water buffalo'//'small livestock'
ifa//ko'o	ifa//o'o	'to lift'//'to cradle'
bou//neka	bou//ne'a	'vat'//'basket'
losa//nduku	losa//ru'u	'up to'//'until'
na//ndia	na//ria	'this'//'that'
ndano//toko r	ano//to'o	'to thrust'//'to throw'
ndui//sau	rui//sau	'to ladle'//'to scoop out'
sanga//tunga	saka//tuka	'to seek'//'to search, follow'

Refrain and Counter-Refrain

Ande Ruy's composition is made particularly poignant by the use of refrain and counter-refrain. He combines this use of refrains with further repeated rephrasing of Suti Solo and Bina Bane's quest. This is all part of his performance style.

Suti Solo and Bina Bane's initial request (lines 37–38) is phrased as a plea:

Fo saka fe ami tesa tei	To give us contentment
Ma tuka fe ami tama dale	And provide us satisfaction

This quest for 'contentment and satisfaction' (*tesa tei//tama dale*) becomes a recurrent refrain that runs through the whole of the recitation. The expression *tesa tei//tama dale* is a formulaic expression that has wide currency in eastern Rote: it connotes a sense of inner peace and tranquility—an emotional state that is defined as a social ideal.

In the lines that propose the first directive, Suti Solo and Bina Bane's quest is phrased as a search for 'land and lineage' (*iku//leo*)—a phrasing that is also repeated in later lines. In lines 53–54, Oli Masi and Bisa Oli reply to Suti Solo and Bina Bane, saying: 'Your land is with the rice basket and your lineage is with the syrup vat.'

In the passage that offers the second directive (lines 94–95), Suti Solo and Bina Bane's quest is voiced as a negative refrain:

Te tesa tei bei ta'a	There is no contentment there
Ma tama dale bei ta'a.	And there is no satisfaction there.

And at the end of the passage with the third directive (lines 113–14), another critical refrain is introduced. Instead of the refrain based on the set *tesa//tama*, the new refrain is based on *tema//tetu*. Whereas the *tesa//tama* refrain is common in eastern Rote, this refrain is more common in central Rote.

Suti Solo and Bina Bane voice this negative refrain in reference to themselves:

De ami tetum bei ta'a	For us, there is yet no order
Ma ami temam bei ta'a.	And for us, there is yet no integrity.

As the recitation proceeds to the passage that offers the fourth directive, both refrains occur (the primary refrain in lines 117–18, and secondary in lines 133–34). This only increases the momentum of the disappointment of the shells:

Te tesa tei bei ta'a	There is yet no contentment
Ma tama dale bei ta'a.	And yet no satisfaction.
Tetun bei ta'a	There is yet no order
Ma teman bei ta'a.	And there is yet no integrity.

By the time of the fifth directive (lines 147–48), there is again a repetition of the primary refrain of the recitation:

De tesa tei bei ta'a	There is yet no contentment
Ma tama dale bei ta'a.	And yet no satisfaction.

In the end, however, Suti Solo and Bina Bane do find a resting place: 'a lineage in which to stay and a land in which to ponder.' This place of rest is described by another distinctive expression—this one based on the dyadic formulae *to'e tei*//*ra dale* (in contrast with *tesa tei*//*tama dale*):

De ra dale a so	It is pleasing here
Ma to'e tei a so.	And it is satisfying here.

Suti Solo and Bina Bane's Journey through the Landscape

While most Termanu versions of *Suti Solo do Bina Bane* trace the journey of the shells in a cycle from sea back to sea, both Landu and Ringgou versions focus on a journey that passes predominantly across a fixed landscape. In Ande Ruy's version, the shells are literally carried by Oli Masi and Basi Oli, who are described as 'walking' through the land and its waters. This journey through the landscape begins as soon as the shells are scooped from the sea: it is first explicitly spoken of in lines 76–77 and the lines that recount this walk are repeated four more times in similar lines: 96–97, 115–16, 131–32 and 149–50.

Boe ma lope tarali dae	They walk forth through the land
Ma lao tahi oe.	And they go forth through the waters.

This journey through the landscape is dotted with sites whose descriptions are distinctively phrased in the dialect of Ringgou. Some of these expressions are the following:

In lines 78–79, there occurs this formulaic expression:

De reu losa opa loa ara	They go to the rice field's wide bund
Ma reu ru'u e naru ara.	And they go to dry field's long boundary.

Opa loal/e naru are a specific dyadic formula that describes the boundaries of different kinds of fields.

In lines 98–99, this formulaic expression is used:

Boe ma reu losa mo tale hade a	They go to the dry rice field
Ma reu ru'u lete batu lau.	And to the hill's rocky grassland.

The dyadic components of this formula are *mo tale hade//lete batu lau*.

Similarly, in lines 119–20, there occurs this phrase:

Boe ma reu peu tua	They go to tap the lontar
Ma reu lele hade a.	And they go to harvest the rice fields.

In all of these instances, although elements are similar, there are no precise equivalent formulae in Termanu.

The Shells' Journey's End and its Significance

Suti Solo and Bina Bane's journey ends at the foot of the *ko-nau* tree and in the shadow of the *nilu-foi* tree. These two trees are large fruit-bearing trees. The consumption of the fruit of these trees is emphasised at the conclusion to this recitation.

In the interpretations of all his recitations, Ande Ruy is decidedly a 'literalist'. In his view, this narrative, like his other narratives, recounts events that occurred in the past—in his words: 'at a time long ago, at a period long past.' Hence, at the conclusion of the recitation he insisted that if one goes to a certain field on the border between Ringgou and

Bilba, it would be possible to find the remains of the shells. For Ande Ruy, his recitation prompts no symbolic interpretation and he can become irritated if any such interpretation is proposed.

Other poets, particularly Esau Pono, my closest collaborator from Termanu, Jonas Mooy from Thie, Frans Lau from Dengka and Hendrik Foeh from Oenale—and indeed most other poets—are less inclined to a literalist interpretation of each other's compositions. They are responsive to the significance of the particular use of expressions, particular pairs and the symbolic arrangement and direction of a composition.

After the first couple of recording sessions, I had accumulated the beginnings of a growing corpus of recordings that had been duly transcribed and which—between recording sessions—I struggled to understand and translate. In each subsequent session, in addition to continuing the recording of new compositions, my task was to check the transcriptions and my initial attempts at a translation for compositions that had already been recorded. I generally did this with the poet himself, but often after the first or second pass at a particular composition, other poets would join the discussion out of personal interest and with a concern that I get things right.

I made several attempts to work through Ande Ruy's version of *Suti Solo do Bina Bane*. It had been one of the earliest compositions I recorded on Bali. However, I kept coming back with further questions in successive sessions. One of my questions was why in this version from Ringgou, the shells came to rest at *ko-nau* and *nilu-foi* trees. Although Ande Ruy resisted any idea of symbolism in the significance of these trees, Jonas Mooy commented that the trees were of great significance. In Rotenese belief, there was a period in their most ancient history when they practised tree burial and the specific trees that they choose for such burials were the *ko-nau* and *nilu-foi*. If this were the case then the journey of the shells concludes at a place of tree burial. It is like so many other versions of this chant: a journey through life to death.

If this version of *Suti Solo do Bina Bane* involves a journey of the shells chiefly through a landscape, the next version of *Suti Solo do Bina Bane*, from Bilba, offers a narrative contrast, which focuses significantly on the shells' drifting journey at sea. In this version from Bilba, like that of Ringgou, the journey's end for the shells occurs at the *ko-nau* and *nilu-foi* trees.

15
Suti Solo do Bina Bane: A Version from the Domain of Bilba

When I set out to bring poets from different parts of Rote to Bali for recording in 2006, I was entirely uncertain of whom I would be able to attract and, more importantly, what the abilities of these various poets would be. Initially I had to rely on two master poets who were critical to the project from the beginning: Esau Pono from Termanu and Ande Ruy from Ringgou. In turn, they relied on what they could learn about the reputations of other poets in different domains. I insisted that we endeavour to invite poets from all the domains—or at least all the larger domains—thus prompting them to seek out a range of able poets. In the second recording session that I held, we invited some notable poets from Landu and one distinguished elder poet from Bilba, who unfortunately came down with malaria and was able to provide only a limited number of recitations. It was not until the fifth recording session, in October 2009, that I was able to invite another three able poets from Bilba. Among these poets was Kornalius Medah, who turned out to be a poet of exceptional ability: able, versatile and fluent, with a considerable and distinctive repertoire. His recitation of *Suti Solo do Bina Bane* is the longest I recorded and is certainly one of the most elaborate. Although it resembles, in many recognisable features, recitations of *Suti Solo do Bina Bane* from Termanu, it is distinctive and remarkable.

The Narrative Structure of Kornalius Medah's *Suti Solo do Bina Bane*

Like other versions of *Suti Solo do Bina Bane*, Kornalius Medah's narrative recounts a journey. This journey follows a cycle that eventually returns to where it began. The narrative begins and ends in Dulu Oli//Langa Le ('East Estuary'//'Headland River'). Suti Solo and Bina Bane leave Dulu Oli//Langa Le, enter the sea and begin their journey in search of a place of 'certainty and security' where they hope to be able to find a 'true mother' (literally, 'a birth mother': *ina bongi*) and a 'true father' (literally, 'a birth father': *ama bongi*). At one point, this sought-after kin attachment is also referred to as a 'lineage aunt' (*te'o leo*) and 'land mother' (*ina ingu*).

On their journey, Suti Solo and Bina Bane experience various 'encounters', each of which in the end proves unfulfilling. These encounters are personalised and designated by distinct person/place names. Each name reveals the nature and condition of the encounter. Initially, Suti Solo and Bina Bane find contentment in the sea: the rolling waves and meandering sea (*pela oe leleu//tasi oe lalama*).

In the sea, the shells experience three encounters:

1. *tele tasi//hamu le*   'sea refuse'//'river dregs'
2. *engga lima//latu koko*   'Seaweed *Lima*'//'Waterweed *Koko*'
3. *le naluk//lifu loak*   'long river'//'wide pool'

Only after this sea journey does the girl 'Tomorrow's Tide' and the woman 'Dawning Sea' (Meti Balaha//Tasi Dulupila) scoop the two shells from the sea. They, in turn, place the shells within the house, but the shells shift from one place within the house to another:

4. *timi di//nata tuak*   'house post'//'lontar beam'
5. *bou tua//neka hade*   'lontar vat'//'rice basket'

When neither of these places proves satisfactory, they shift progressively further from the house to:

6. *tua timu//hade safu*   'east lontar (season)'//'*savu* rice (harvest)'
7. *nita lete//dela mo*   'mountain *nitas* (tree)'//'field *delas* (tree)'
8. *tuli tini//kaba osi*   'pigeon pea garden'//'cotton field'

15. A VERSION FROM THE DOMAIN OF BILBA

Figure 18: Kornalius Medah

They then make a decision to return to Dulu Oli//Langa Le and there set forth on a specifically named path (*eno//longe*) that is identified as that of:

9.   *Hena Le//I Lasi*   'Pandanus River'//'Jasmine Forest'

This path leads them to:

10. *Nilu Neo//Ko Nau*   'The Nilu Neo Tree'//'The Ko Nau Tree'

Nilu Neo//Ko Nau become their 'true mother' and 'true father' (*ina bongi// ama bongi*), where they rest 'content' and 'satisfied' (*tesa teik//tama dalek*).

As such, Kornalius Medah's *Suti Solo do Bina Bane* is more of a ritual lament about the nature of life than an origin chant. After the departure of the shells from Dulu Oli//Langa Le and until their return, each episodic encounter follows a similar formulaic development that begins with initial contentment but quickly turns to disappointment and leads to a departure in search of yet another encounter.

For presentation's sake, I have arranged this recitation into separate sections beginning in Dulu Oli//Langa Le, followed in turn by a succession of encounters, concluding with the return to Dulu Oli//Langa Le and the Pandanus//Jasmine path leading to Nilu Neo//Ko Nau.

Kornalias Medah's recitation begins with the shells in East Estuary and Headland River with both their mother and their father. They wake their parents to seek for peace and well-being (*soda-molek*), recognising that there are inner satisfaction and heartfelt contentment with both mother and father in East Estuary and Headland River. Yet this condition is neither certain nor lasting.

Suti Solo and Bina Bane in East Estuary (Dulu Oli) and Headland River (Langa Le)

1.   *Tene-tu ana mak Le Naluk*   Hasten the orphan Le Naluk
2.   *Ma hae-lai falu ina Oli Loak.*   And hurry the widow Oli Loak.
3.   *Faik lia nasa-kendu Le Lain*   On this day, Le Lain sobs
4.   *Ma ledok na nama-tani Oli Dale*   And at this time, Oli Dale cries
5.   *Sama leo Suti Solo*   Just like Suti Solo

15. A VERSION FROM THE DOMAIN OF BILBA

6.	*Ma deta leo Bina Bane.*	And similar to Bina Bane.
7.	*Te hu faik lia Suti ma-no ina bongik*	But on this day Suti has a birth mother
8.	*Ma ledok na Bina ma-no ama bongik,*	And at this time Bina has a birth father,
9.	*Suti no ina na ma Bina no ama na.*	Suti with his mother and Bina with his father.
10.	*Hu no tepok lia Suti natane sodak ka*	At that time Suti seeks well-being
11.	*Ma lelek na Bina teteni molek ka.*	And at the moment Bina asks for peace.
12.	*Lia na foa kela ina bongi na*	He wakes his true mother
13.	*Ma lako kela ama bongi na,*	And to greet his true father,
14.	*Mai de tena neuk Dulu Olin*	To descend to Dulu Oli
15.	*Ma monu neuk Langa Len, lae:*	And go down onto Langa Le, saying:
16.	*'Tesa teik Dulu Oli*	'There is inner satisfaction in Dulu Oli
17.	*Ma tama dalek Langa Le.'*	And heartfelt contentment in Langa Le.'
18.	*Te hu tean tak Dulu Olin*	Yet nothing is certain at Dulu Oli
19.	*Ma mepen tak Langa Len*	And nothing is permanent at Langa Le.

The shells descend into the sea where they continue to find contentment and satisfaction in the rolling waves but they are no longer with their parents. These lines, as is so often the case in ritual language recitations, shift between singular and plural in reference to the shells.

Suti Solo and Bina Bane Descend into the Rolling Waves and Meandering Seas

20.	*Faik lia dilu liu na neu*	On this day, he goes down into the ocean
21.	*Ma ledok na loe sain na neu*	At this time, he descends into the sea
22.	*Neu no pela oe leleu ka*	To go with the rolling waves
23.	*Ma neu no tasi oe lalama ka.*	And to go with the meandering seas.
24.	*Neu [no] pela oe leleu ka,*	To go with the rolling waves,
25.	*Hika boe setele*	Laughing loudly

26.	*Ma neu tasi oe lalama*	In the meandering seas
27.	*Eki boe lata-dale.*	Shouting gaily.
28.	*Lia na lae:*	So they say:
29.	*Tesa teik pela oe leleu na*	Satisfaction in the rolling waves
30.	*Ma tama dalek tasi oe lalama na.*	Contentment in meandering seas.
31.	*Tehu noi-tuv leo lia*	Yet however one strives
32.	*Ho tunu-hai leo lia*	There is trouble there
33.	*Ma sanga-tao leo na*	And however one seeks
34.	*Ho kelo-kea leo na.*	There is difficulty there.
35.	*Lia na dadi neuk Suti Solo*	This happens to Suti Solo
36.	*Ma na moli neuk Bina Bane*	And this arises for Bina Bane
37.	*Ho ina o tak ma ama o tak.*	With no mother and with no father.

A storm arises and the shells lose their inner pods. They bob like *boa* wood and drift like *piko* wood, speaking and crying to themselves.

Suti Solo and Bina Bane are Carried Away by Storm and Cyclone

38.	*Faik lia luli dulu fafae na*	On day a storm arises in the waking east
39.	*Ma ledok na sangu langa titipa na.*	And at one time a cyclone blows at the thrusting head.
40.	*Boe ma li sio lasa-ngengeli*	Nine waves rage
41.	*Ma nafa falu laka-tutulek*	And eight crests heave
42.	*Pode ketu Suti ate na*	Cutting loose Suti's liver
43.	*Ma lui ketu Bina ngi na.*	Pulling out Bina's pods.
44.	*Suti bonu-bonu,*	Suti bobs and bobs,
45.	*Bonu boa no ao na*	Bobs like *boa* wood on his own
46.	*Ho nama-tani no ao na.*	Crying on his own.
47.	*Bina ele-ele,*	Bina drifts and drifts,
48.	*Ele piko no ao na*	Drifts like *piko* wood on his own
49.	*Ho nama-tani no ao na.*	Crying on his own.
50.	*Boe ma Suti de'a-de'a no Bina*	Then Suti speaks with Bina

51.	*Ma Bina kola-kola no Suti:*	And Bina talks with Suti:
52.	*'Tia Suti nga ko*	'Suti, my friend
53.	*Ma sena Bina nga ko,*	And Bina, my companion,
54.	*Tean o tak ma mepen o tak.*	Nothing is certain and nothing permanent.
55.	*Pode hini ita ate na*	Our liver is cut away
56.	*Lui hini ita ngi na*	And our pod is pulled out
57.	*De bonu boa to ao tala*	We bob like *boa* wood on our own
58.	*Ma ele-ele to ao tala,*	And we drift and drift on our own,
59.	*Tehu ma-uak ka dei*	But with fortune still
60.	*Ma-nalek ka bali.'*	And with luck yet.'

Suti Solo and Bina Bane begin their encounters, the first of which is with sea refuse and river dregs. Rather than being directed to these encounters, each encounter marks the movement of the shells. An encounter begins in optimism and ends with recognition of that encounter's impermanence and of the need to continue the journey.

Suti Solo and Bina Bane Encounter Sea Refuse and River Dregs

61.	*Faik lia tele tasi bobonu na*	This day the sea's refuse comes bobbing
62.	*Ma hamu le e'ele na.*	And the river's dregs drift by.
63.	*Suti tepa noi tele tasi*	Suti meets the sea's refuse
64.	*Ma Bina kala noi hamu le.*	And Bina strikes the river's dregs.
65.	*Luku no hamu le*	Squats on the river's dregs
66.	*Ma sake no tele tasi,*	And snuggles with the sea's refuse,
67.	*Hika no setele*	Laughing loudly
68.	*Ma eki ho lata dale.*	And shouting with joy.
69.	*Boe ma dua dea-dea*	Then the two speak
70.	*Ma dua kola-kola*	And the two talk
71.	*'Tean nai hamu le so*	'Certainty lies in the river's dregs
72.	*Mepen nai tele tasi so.*	And security rests in the sea's refuse.
73.	*De hika boe-boe setele*	To laugh out loud

74.	*Ma eki boe-boe lata-dale.*	And shout out with joy.
75.	*Tehu noi-tao leo lia*	Yet however one strives
76.	*Tean tak hamu le*	There is no certainty in the river's dregs
77.	*Ma sanga-tao leo na*	And however one seeks
78.	*Mepen tak tele tasi.'*	There is nothing lasting in the sea's refuse.'
79.	*Faik lia luli dulu fafae seluk*	One day a storm arises again in the waking east
80.	*Ma ledok na sangu langa titipa seluk.*	And at one time a cyclone blows again at the head.
81.	*Boe ma li lasa-ngengeli*	The waves rage
82.	*Ma nafa laka-tutulek.*	And the crests heave
83.	*Li tipa hini Suti*	The waves push Suti away
84.	*Ma nafa sonu hini Bina.*	And the crests thrust Bina away.
85.	*De bonu-bonu no ao na*	He bobs and bobs on his own
86.	*Ho nasa-kedu no ao na*	While sobbing on his own
87.	*Ma ele-ele no ao na*	And he drifts and drifts on his own
88.	*Ho nama-tani no ao na.*	While crying on his own.
89.	*Li tipa nini mai*	The waves push forward
90.	*Ho tipa nini Suti mai*	Pushing Suti forward
91.	*Ma nafa toko nini mai*	And the crest thrusts forward
92.	*Ho toko nini Bina mai.*	Thrusting Bina forward.
93.	*Ma-uak neu Suti Solo*	Luck is with Suti Solo
94.	*Ma-nalek neu Bina Bani.*	And good fortune is with Bina Bane.

The next encounter is with seaweed and waterweed. The shells join with this seaweed but its vulnerability to heat and rain makes it particularly fragile. So, crying to themselves, the shells move onward.

Suti Solo and Bina Bane Encounter Seaweed *Lima* and Waterweed *Koko*

95.	*Faik lia tepa noi Engga Lima*	One day they meet Seaweed *Lima*
96.	*Ledo na kala noi Latu Koko.*	At one time they encountered Waterweed *Koko*.

15. A VERSION FROM THE DOMAIN OF BILBA

97.	*Suti de'a-de'a no ao na*	Suti speaks to himself
98.	*Ma Bina kola-kola no ao na,*	And Bina talks to himself,
99.	*'Dua topa teuk Engga Lima leo*	'Let us two befriend Seaweed *Lima*
100.	*Ma dua tai teuk Latu Koko leo.'*	And let us two be close to Waterweed *Koko.*'
101.	*Boe ma luku lo Engga Lima*	So they squat with Seaweed *Lima*
102.	*De tesa teik Engga Lima*	And are satisfied with Seaweed *Lima*
103.	*Ma sake lo Latu Koko*	And they snuggle with Waterweed *Koko*
104.	*De tama dale Latu Koko.*	And are content with Waterweed *Koko.*
105.	*Lae: 'Tean na nai lia so.'*	They say: 'Certainty is here.'
106.	*Ma lae: 'Mepen na nai na so.'*	And they say: 'Permanence is here.'
107.	*Tehu noi-tao leo lia*	Yet however one strives
108.	*Ho tunu-hai leo lia*	There is trouble there
109.	*Ma sanga-tao leo na*	And however one seeks
110.	*Ho kelo-kea leo na.*	There is difficulty there.
111.	*Faik na uda te Engga Lima*	One day the rain spears Seaweed *Lima*
112.	*Ma lelek lia ledo ha Latu Koko.*	And one time the sun heats Waterweed *Koko.*
113.	*De tean ta Engga Lima*	So no certainty with Seaweed *Lima*
114.	*Ma mepen tak Latu Koko.*	And no security with Waterweed *Koko.*
115.	*Uda te Engga Lima*	The rain spears Seaweed *Lima*
116.	*De kou heni Engga Lima*	Causing Seaweed *Lima* to disappear
117.	*Ma ledo ha Latu Koko*	And the sun heats Waterweed *Koko*
118.	*De noe heni Latu Koko*	Causing Waterweed *Koko* to dissolve
119.	*Dadi neu te'o leo*	To [cease] to become a lineage aunt
120.	*Ma moli neuk ina ingu.*	And [cease] to be a domain mother.
121.	*Lasakedu lo ao nala*	They sob to themselves
122.	*Ma lamatani lo ao nala.*	And cry to themselves.

The shells drift to Long River and Wide Pool where again they recognise the precariousness of their situation.

Suti Solo and Bina Bane Encounter Long River and Wide Pool

123.	*Boema bonu-bonu lo ao nala*	So they bob and bob on their own
124.	*Bonu boa lo ao nala*	Bob like *boa* wood on their own
125.	*Ma ele-ele lo ao nala*	And drift and drift on their own
126.	*Ele piko lo ao nala.*	Drift like *piko* wood on their own.
127.	*Faik lia noi-tao leo lia*	On this day, however one strives
128.	*Ho tunu-hai leo lia*	There is trouble there
129.	*Ma ledok na sanga-tao leo na*	At this time, however one seeks
130.	*Ho kelo-kea leo na.*	There is difficulty there.
131.	*Faik lia bonu-bonu no ao*	One day bobbing on his own
132.	*Na tepa noi le naluk*	He meets with long river
133.	*Ma ledok na ele-ele no ao*	One time drifting on his own
134.	*Na te kala noi lifu loak.*	He encounters wide pool.
135.	*Bina luku no lifu loak*	Bina squats in wide pool
136.	*Ma Suti tai no le naluk.*	And Suti meets with long river.
137.	*Boema dua de'a-de'a lo ao nala*	The two speak with each other
138.	*Ma dua kola-kola lo ao nala.*	And the two talk with each other.
139.	*Ita tean tak le naluk*	Our certainty is not in long river
140.	*Ma ita mepen tak lifu loak.*	And our security is not in wide pool.
141.	*Boe ma noi-tao leo lia*	But however one strives
142.	*Ho tunu-hai leo lia*	There is trouble there
143.	*Ma sanga-tao leo na*	And however one seeks
144.	*Ho kelo-kea leo na.*	There is difficulty there.

At this point, Tomorrow's Tide (Meti Balaha) and Dawning Sea (Tasi Dulupila) are introduced by their ritual names. They prepare their scoop-nets and then set out to fish for two required ritual fish—in this case, Moka Holu and Kuku Lake. Meti Balaha and Tasi Dulupila scoop up Suti Solo and Bina Bane from the middle of Long River and Wide Pool. The shells beg Meti Balaha and Tasi Dulupila to be their mother and father to protect and shelter them.

15. A VERSION FROM THE DOMAIN OF BILBA

Tomorrow's Tide and Dawning Sea
Scoop-net Suti Solo and Bina Bane

145.	*Feto Meti Balaha na*	The girl Tomorrow's Tide
146.	*Ma ina Tasi Dulupila na*	And the woman Dawning Sea
147.	*Ane bubui ho seko*	She braids and twines a scoop-net
148.	*Seko bui na fepa deak*	A scoop-net of heavy lontar leaf
149.	*Teli kokono ho lai*	She strings and twists a fishnet
150.	*Lai ke na kabak dok.*	A fishnet with cotton thread.
151.	*Dua leu lama-seko totoko*	The two go to cast their scoop-net
152.	*Ma dua leu lama-lai lalano.*	And the two go to throw their fishnet.
153.	*Leo seko sanga Moka Holu*	Scoop-netting for Moka Holu
154.	*Ho kelak seko la Moka*	To scoop forth Moka fish
155.	*Na Moka la-holu ao.*	For the Moka protects itself.
156.	*Leu lai tunga Kuku Lake*	Fishing for Kuku Lake
157.	*Ho kelak lai la Kuku*	To fish forth Kuku fish
158.	*Na Kuku lasa-lake ao.*	For the Kuku guards itself.
159.	*Faik lia loe neuk metik*	One day they go down to the tidal shore
160.	*Ledok na dilu neuk namo*	One time they descend to the estuary
161.	*Tehu tepa lo noi Suti Solo*	But they meet with Suti Solo
162.	*Ma kala lo noi Bina Bane*	And they encounter Bina Bane
163.	*Bonu-bonu no ao na*	Bobbing on his own
164.	*Ho nai lifu loak ka dale so*	In the middle of wide pool
165.	*Ele-ele no ao na*	Drifting on his own
166.	*Ho nai le naluk ka dale.*	In the middle of long river.
167.	*Tek lai na neu*	To be scooped into the fishnet
168.	*Ma suma seko na neu.*	And lifted into the scoop-net.
169.	*Feto Meti Balaha*	The girl Tomorrow's Tide
170.	*Mo ina Tasi Dulupila*	And the woman Dawning Sea
171.	*Lai neni Suti Solo mai*	Fish and take Suti Solo
172.	*Ma seko neni Bina Bane mai.*	And scoop and take Bina Bane.
173.	*Suti de'a-de'a no na*	Suti speaks with her
174.	*Ma Bina kola-kola no na:*	And Bina talks with her:

Figure 19: Woman with scoop-net

'The girl, Tomorrow's Tide
And the woman, Dawning Sea
Fish and take Suti Solo
And scoop and take Bina Bane.'

175.	*'O, feto mama-seko nga ko*	'Oh, girl, scoop me up
176.	*Ma o ina mama-lai nga ko*	And oh, woman, fish me up
177.	*Muni au ia Suti Solo*	Take me here, Suti Solo
178.	*Ma mini au ia Bina Bane.*	And take me here, Bina Bane.
179.	*Tehu ma-sulu au*	But shelter me
180.	*Sama leo au ama bongi*	Like my birth father
181.	*Ma ma-hapa au*	And protect me
182.	*Deta leo au ina bongi.'*	Like my birth mother.'

Meti Balaha and Tasi Dulupila carry the shells to their house, placing them at the *timi* post and lontar beam. At first, they feel satisfied and content but then realise the impermanence of their new location and seek again for another mother and father.

Suti Solo and Bina Bane are Placed on the *Timi* Post and Lontar Beam

183.	*Dua leni nana mai*	The two carry them forth
184.	*Fua neu timi di*	Place them on the *timi* post
185.	*Fe Suti no timi di*	Allocate Suti to the *timi* post
186.	*Ma bati Bina no nata tuak.*	And assign Bina to the lontar beam.
187.	*Tesa teik timi di*	Satisfied at the *timi* post
188.	*Ma tama dale nata tuak.*	And content at the lontar beam.
189.	*Hika ho boe setele*	Laughing out loud
190.	*Ma eki ho boe latadale.*	And shouting with joy.
191.	*Dua de'a-de'a lo ao nala*	The two talk to themselves
192.	*Ma dua kola-kola lo ao nala:*	And the two speak to themselves:
193.	*'Ita nai na-sulu uda te ka*	'We are sheltered from the piercing rain
194.	*Ma ita nai nahapa ledo ha ka.'*	And we are protected from the scorching sun.'
195.	*Dua boe de'a-de'a lo ao nala*	The two again talk to themselves
196.	*Ma dua boe kola-kola lo ao nala.*	And the two again speak to themselves.
197.	*Lae: 'Tesa teik.'*	They say: '[We are] satisfied.'

198.	*Ma lae: 'Tama dale.'*	And they say: '[We are] content.'
199.	*Tehu noi-tao leo lia*	Yet however one strives
200.	*Ho tunu hai leo lia*	There is difficulty there
201.	*Ma sanga-tao leo na*	And however one seeks
202.	*Ho kelo kea leo na.*	There is trouble there.
203.	*Faik lia uda te timi di*	One day the rain spears the *timi* post
204.	*De sengi heni timi di*	It snaps the *timi* post
205.	*Ma tepok na ledo ha nata-tua*	One time the sun heats the lontar beam
206.	*De pulu heni nata tuak.*	It splits the lontar beam.
207.	*Suti de'a-de'a no ao na*	Suti talks to himself
208.	*Ho nasakedu no ao na*	While sobbing to himself
209.	*Ma Bina kola-kola no ao na*	And Bina speaks to himself
210.	*Ho namatani no ao na:*	While crying to himself:
211.	*'Tean tak timi di*	'No certainty in the *timi* post
212.	*Ma mepen tak nata tuak.*	And nothing lasting in the lontar beam.
213.	*Ta ina teu bea bali*	No mother for us to go to
214.	*Ma ta ama teu bea dei*	No father for us to go to
215.	*Mai teu teteni seluk ina bongi ka*	Let us again request a birth mother
216.	*Ma teu tatane seluk ama bongi ka.'*	And let us again ask for a birth father.'

The shells go next to the lontar vat and rice basket but again realise the impermanence of their situation. (Lines 244 and 245 are translated as they were spoken. These lines, however, would make more sense if they were not in the negative. Without the negative '*tak*', they might read: 'Let us go where there is certainty and let us go where there is permanence.')

Suti Solo and Bina Bane Shift to the Lontar Vat and the Rice Basket

217.	*Dua dilu leu*	The two go down
218.	*Ho dilu leu bou tuak*	Go down to the lontar vat
219.	*Ma dua loe leu*	And the two descend
220.	*Ho loe leu neka hade.*	Descend to the rice basket.

15. A VERSION FROM THE DOMAIN OF BILBA

221.	*Dua de'a-de'a lo ao nala*	The two talk to themselves
222.	*Ma dua kola-kola lo ao nala:*	And the two speak to themselves:
223.	*'Tean nai bou tuak so*	'There is certainty in the lontar vat
224.	*Ma mepen nai neka hade so.*	And there is permanence in the rice basket.
225.	*Lole tama-hena*	Let us well hope for
226.	*Neu ina bongi ka leo*	A birth mother
227.	*Ma lena taka-bani*	And let us fondly expect
228.	*Neu ama bongi ka leo.*	A birth father.
229.	*Tehu noi-tao leo lia*	Yet however one strives
230.	*Ho dadi neuk te'o leo*	For someone to become a lineage aunt
231.	*Ma sanga-tao leo na*	And however one seeks
232.	*Ho moli neuk ina ingu*	For someone to be a clan mother
233.	*Ho bengu bafa ka dadi*	Word of mouth reports
234.	*Ma lali ma ka moli*	And wagging of tongues reveal that
235.	*Soke sasau neka*	Scooping and ladling the basket
236.	*Soke sau basa neka hade*	Scoops and ladles all the rice from the basket
237.	*Ma kola lului tua*	Drawing and draining the lontar syrup
238.	*Lui heni basa bou tua.'*	Drains all the lontar vat.'
239.	*Suti nasakedu seluk*	Suti sobs again
240.	*Ma Bina namatani seluk.*	And Bina cries again.
241.	*'Tean tak ma mepen tak.*	'No certainty and no permanence.
242.	*He, tia Suti nga ko*	He, my dear friend Suti
243.	*Ma he, sena Bina nga ko,*	And he, my dear companion Bina,
244.	*Ita teu bea tean tak*	Let us go where there is (no) certainty
245.	*Ma ita teu bea mepen tak.*	And let us go where there is (no) permanence.
246.	*Teu teteni bea balik*	Let us go ask for someone again
247.	*Ho lia dadi neuk ina bongi*	Who may become a birth mother
248.	*Ma teu tatane bea dei*	And let us go request someone once more
249.	*Ho na moli neuk ama bongi.'*	And who may be a birth father.'

In the next lines, the shells move out of the house and into the fields where the lontar palm is tapped and rice is harvested. The time for tapping and harvesting with its accompanying celebrations is brief and thus also impermanent so the shells are left to themselves to cry and sob.

Suti Solo and Bina Bane Shift to the East Lontar Season and Savu Rice Harvest

250.	*Teu tateni tua timu*	Let us go ask the lontar-tapping season
251.	*Ma teu leo tatane hade safu*	And let us go request the *Savu* rice harvest
252.	*Ho tua timu lesu ngi*	Lontar palms put out their inflorescences
253.	*Na dua ngata dadi tasafali ao*	Let us two renew ourselves
254.	*Ma hade safu tona kale*	And *Savu* rice bends at the head
255.	*Na dua ngata moli tasafali ao tala.'*	Then let us restore ourselves.'
256.	*Faik lia leu*	One day they go to
257.	*Tua timu lesu ngi*	The budding lontar inflorescences
258.	*Ho kiki tua la-dopo*	Where the tapping of the cleaning brush
259.	*Na dadi neuk koa tua*	Gives rise to great celebration
260.	*Ma nesu ingu langu*	And mortar's heavy pounding
261.	*Ho manu ingu na*	With its squabbling chicken
262.	*Dadi neu ngia sina.*	Gives rise to great exuberance.
263.	*Luku lo nesu ingu*	Squatting with the great mortar
264.	*Ma sake lo tua timu*	And snuggling with the lontar tapping
265.	*Hika ho setele*	Laughing out loud
266.	*Ma eki ho latadale.*	And shouting with joy.
267.	*Lae: 'Tean liak so.'*	They say: 'Something certain is here.'
268.	*Ma lae: 'Mepen liak na so.'*	And they say: 'Something lasting is here.'
269.	*Tehu ledok esa nai lia*	But then at one time
270.	*Na lengu heni nesu ingu*	The great mortar is cast aside
271.	*Ma faik esa nai na*	And on one day
272.	*Na hulu heni tua timu*	The lontar season comes to an end
273.	*Hu uda te tua timu*	Because the rain spears the lontar tapping
274.	*Na tua lama loe suma.*	The lontar baskets are lowered.

15. A VERSION FROM THE DOMAIN OF BILBA

275.	*Te tean tak ma mepen tak.*	Nothing certain and nothing permanent.
276.	*Dua boe lasakedu*	The two sob again
277.	*Ma dua boe lamatani.*	And the two cry again.

The shells move further afield to find a place with mountain *nitas* tree and the field *delas* tree. Both are large trees that have a marked flowering season. They join with these trees but when the rain puts an end to their flowering period, the shells are left to themselves as orphan and widow.

Suti Solo and Bina Bane Move to the Mountain *Nitas* Tree and the Field *Delas* Tree

278.	*Dua leu lateteni seluk*	The two go in search again
279.	*Lateni neuk nita lete*	In search of the mountain *nitas* tree
280.	*Ma dua leu latane seluk*	And the two go in quest again
281.	*Latane neuk dela mo.*	In quest of the open field *delas* tree.
282.	*Leu dei,*	They go,
283.	*Laneta lo nita lete*	They encounter the *nitas* of the mountain
284.	*Nita lete nabuna*	The mountain *nitas* is in bloom
285.	*Ma latonggo lo dela mo,*	And they meet the open field *delas*,
286.	*Dela mo napena*	The *delas* is flowering
287.	*Dadi latafali ao na*	Renewing itself
288.	*Ma moli laleo ao na.*	And restoring itself.
289.	*Dadi leu koa tua*	These things give rise to great celebration
290.	*Ma moli leu ngia sina.*	And give forth great exuberance.
291.	*Sake lo nita lete*	They snuggle up to the mountain *nitas*
292.	*Ho lo nita lete buna na*	And with the blossoms of the mountain *nitas*
293.	*Ma luku lo dela mo*	And they squat with the field *delas*
294.	*Ho lo dela mo pena na*	And with the field *delas*'s flowers
295.	*Hika ho setele*	Laughing loudly
296.	*Ma eki ho latadale.*	And shouting for joy.
297.	*'Tia Suti nga ko*	'My friend, Suti

298.	*Ma sena Bina nga ko*	And my companion, Bina
299.	*Tean tak nai ia*	There is nothing certain here
300.	*Ma mepen tak nai ia.'*	And there is nothing lasting here.'
301.	*Tehu noi-tao leo lia*	Yet however one strives
302.	*Ho tunu-hai leo lia*	There is difficulty there
303.	*Ma sanga-tao leo na*	And however one seeks
304.	*Ho kelo-kea leo na.*	There is trouble there.
305.	*Tean bei tak*	There is yet nothing certain
306.	*Ma mepen bei tak.*	And there is yet nothing permanent.
307.	*Faik lia timu lasa-lua dulu*	One day the monsoon widens in the east
308.	*Ma ledok na fa lasa-fali langa.*	One time the west winds return to the head.
309.	*Ani dulu fifiu*	The east wind blows
310.	*Lefa heni nita bunan*	Letting drop the *nitas* blossoms
311.	*Ma uda te dela pena*	And the rains strike the *delas* flowers
312.	*Kono heni dela pena.*	Letting fall the *delas* flowers.
313.	*Tehu be ana ma*	But what of the orphan
314.	*Ho ana ma lasakedu lo ao*	The orphan sobs with himself
315.	*Be ina falu*	What of the widow
316.	*Ho falu ina lamatani lo ao na.*	The widow cries with herself.
317.	*Dua de'a-de'a lo ao na*	The two talk to each other
318.	*Ma dua kola-kola lo ao na:*	And the two speak to each other:
319.	*'Tean tak nita lete*	'No certainty with the mountain *nitas* tree
320.	*Ma mepen tak dela mo.'*	No permanence with the field *delas* tree.'

The shells move on again, this time to the pigeon pea garden and cotton field, whose harvest is late in season and affected by the wind and rain, leaving them alone.

Suti Solo and Bina Bane Shift to the Pigeon Pea Garden and the Cotton Field

321.	*Faik lia lae:*	One day they say:
322.	*Dua leu teteni leo*	The two go to seek

15. A VERSION FROM THE DOMAIN OF BILBA

323.	*Ma ledok na lae:*	And one time they say:
324.	*Dua leu tatane leo*	The two go to quest
325.	*Leu de tepa loi tuli tini*	They go to meet the pigeon pea garden
326.	*Ma kala loi kaba osi*	And to encounter the cotton field
327.	*De luku lo kaba osi pena*	Snuggling with the cotton field boll
328.	*Ma sake lo tuli tini buna.*	And squatting with pigeon pea garden flowers.
329.	*Hika ho setele*	They laugh out loud
330.	*Ma eki ho latadale*	And shout with joy
331.	*Luku lo kaba osi*	Snuggling in the cotton field
332.	*Ma latadale neu tuli tini.*	And happy in the pigeon pea garden.
333.	*Tehu bei tean tak*	But there is yet no certainty
334.	*Ma bei mepen tak.*	And yet no permanence.
335.	*Faik lia uda te tuli tini*	One day the rain strikes the pigeon pea garden
336.	*Ma ledok na ani fiu kaba osi*	One time the wind blows the cotton field
337.	*Kono heni tuli buna*	Letting fall the pigeon pea flowers
338.	*Ma lapu heni kaba pena.*	And lifting away the cotton bolls.

Suti Solo do Bina Bane come to recognise the uncertainty and impermanence of the world. They recognise that the human condition is to be orphaned and widowed. They resolve therefore to return to where they began at East Estuary and Headland River and there follow the Pandanus River and the Jasmine Forest.

Suti Solo and Bina Bane Follow Pandanus River Road and Jasmine Forest Path

339.	*Dua de'a-de'a lo ao na*	The two talk with each other
340.	*Ma dua kola-kola lo ao na:*	And the two speak with each other:
341.	*'Teu teteni ina bongik ka leo*	'Let us go in search of a birth mother
342.	*Te tean tak dae bafok*	For there is no certainty on earth
343.	*Ma teu tatane ama bongik ka leo*	Let us go in quest of a birth father
344.	*Te mepen tak batu poik ka.*	For there is no permanence in the world.

345.	*Teu tatane*	Let us go in search
346.	*Teu bea o tean tak*	Let us go where there is no certainty
347.	*Ma teu teteni*	And let us go in quest
348.	*Teu bea o mepen tak.*	Let us go where there is no permanence.
349.	*Ita dua dadi ana ma*	Let us two become orphaned
350.	*Ho ana ma Le Lai*	With the orphan Le Lai
351.	*Tasakedu to ao tala*	That we may sob with each other
352.	*Ita dua dadi falu ina*	Let us two become widowed
353.	*Ho falu ina Oe Bolo*	With the widow Oe Bolo
354.	*Tamatani to ao tala*	That we may cry with each other
355.	*Tasakedu to ao tala*	Let us sob with each other
356.	*Ho nai Dulu Oli*	In Dulu Oli
357.	*Ma tamatani to ao tala*	And let us cry with each other
358.	*Ho nai Lange Le.*	In Langa Le.
359.	*Au ia, ana mak Suti Solo*	Here I am, the orphan Suti Solo
360.	*Ma au ia, falu ina Bina Bane.*	And here I am, the widow Bina Bane.
361.	*Falu ina ko fali*	I am a widow going back
362.	*Ma ana ma ko tulek.*	And an orphan returning.
363.	*De ana ma teteni*	The orphan quests
364.	*Ho Suti Solo mu teteni*	Suti Solo, you go in quest
365.	*Ma falu ina tatane*	And the widow searches
366.	*Ho Bina Bane mu matane*	Bina Bane, you go in search
367.	*Teteni Hena Le*	In quest of Hena Le [Pandanus River]
368.	*Ho tabu tunga Hena Le*	Treading along Hena Le
369.	*Ma tatane I Lasi*	In search of I Lasi [Jasmine Forest]
370.	*Ho nama tunga I Lasi enok.*	Following the I Lasi path.
371.	*Nama osok maketu na*	Hold on without letting go
372.	*Ma molo Hena Le eno*	And step on the Pandanus River road
373.	*Molo osok mabasan.*	Step along without stopping.
374.	*Teteni Hena Le eno*	Seek the Pandanus River path
375.	*Ma tatane I Lasi dala*	And quest for Jasmine Forest road
376.	*Ho kelak molo tunga Hena Le enon*	To step along Hena Le's path
377.	*Ma nama tunga I Lasi dala.*	And follow along I Lasi's road.

The shells arrive at East Estuary and Headland River and then begin to follow the steps and ladder that lead up the Pandanus River road and Jasmine Forest path.

Suti Solo and Bina Bane Arrive at East Estuary and Headland River

378.	*Ita dua tena Dulu Oli*	So that we two arrive at Dulu Oli
379.	*Ma ita dua monu Langa Le*	And we two enter Langa Le
380.	*Fali seluk Dulu Oli*	Come back again to Dulu Oli
381.	*Ma tulek seluk Langa Le.*	And return again to Langa Le.
382.	*Teu dulu*	Let us go east
383.	*Lada edak losa nateke na*	The ladder leads upward
384.	*Ma teu langa*	Let us go to the head
385.	*Ho nasalai kakae losa nabasan*	The steps lead to the top
386.	*Molo tunga Hena Le eno*	Step along the Pandanus River road
387.	*Ma nama tunga I Lasi longe*	And follow along the Jasmine Forest path
388.	*Molo na tak nabasa na*	Step upward without stopping
389.	*Ma nama na tak naketu na.'*	Hold on without ending.'
390.	*De'a-de'a lo aon na*	They talk to themselves
391.	*Ma kola-kola lo ao na.*	And they speak to themselves.

This is a symbolic return: a return to mother and father, who are represented by the Nilu Neo tree and the Ko Nau tree, the same two trees—the tamarind (*Tamarindus indica*) and the *bidara* or Indian plum tree (*Ziziphus mauritana*)—that Suti Solo and Bina Bane find shelter with in Ande Ruy's recitation from Ringgou.

Suti Solo and Bina Bane Come to Rest at the Nilu Neo Tree and the Ko Nau Tree

392.	*'Fali seluk leo ina bongi ka teu*	'Going back to the birth mother, we go
393.	*Ma tulek seluk leo ama bongi ka teu.*	Returning to the birth father, we go.

394.	*Ina bongi lia Nilu Neo*	To the birth mother, Nilu Neo
395.	*Ma ama bongi lia Ko Nau.*	And to the birth father, Ko Nau.
396.	*Nai tema sio dei*	In the fullness of nine
397.	*Ma nai bate falu dei*	And in the abundance of eight
398.	*Ko Nau naboa nai na*	The Ko Nau fruits there
399.	*Ma Nilu Neo napetu nai na*	And the Nilu Neo sprouts there
400.	*Teu ho ketu kolu*	Let us go to pick and pluck
401.	*Ho tesa teik nai na*	Inner satisfaction is there
402.	*Ma teu ho hele hao*	And let us go to choose and eat
403.	*Ho tama dale nai na*	Heartfelt contentment is there
404.	*Ho kelak losa do na neu*	That goes on forever
405.	*Ma kelak sekunete na neu.*	And that does not end.

Kornalius Medah's Recurrent Use of Refrain

No less than Ande Ruy, Kornalius Medah relies on the use of a distinctive refrain and counter-refrain to move his recitation forward. His use of one particular refrain based on the dyadic set *tean//mepen* is emphatic. This set is used no less than 20 times in the course of the recitation: positively to express Suti Solo and Bina Bane's vain hope and more frequently to announce the failure of all such hopes.

The dyadic set *tean//mepen* is difficult to translate. It has a concrete and specific sense while connoting a more general quality or condition of being. *Tea(n)* can mean 'hard, strong, firm' and most frequently applies to the hard, inner core of a tree; *mepen* (seemingly related to the verb *nepen*) means 'to hold tight, to grip, to fix'. Together the set denotes what is 'hard' and 'held tight' and, by extension, what is 'certain and lasting'. This set is, in some ways, the equivalent in Bilba's ritual language to the recurrent dyadic set used in Termanu based on *tetul//tema*.

Thus, early in the recitation (lines 18–19), Kornalius Medah sets the scene for the departure of the shells from Dulu Oli//Langa Le:

Te hu tean tak Dulu Olin	Yet nothing is certain at Dulu Oli
Ma mepen tak Langa Len.	And nothing is lasting at Langa Len.

A more literal translation might be: 'But nothing holds firm at Dulu Oli and nothing holds tight in Langa Len.'

Kornalius used this set in separate lines and, often as well, in single lines. Thus, in lines 54, 241 and 275, the set *tean//mepen* is used in a single line:

Tean o tak ma mepen o tak.	Nothing is certain and nothing permanent.

Combined with this steady refrain is a further equally distinct and idiomatically difficult set of lines. These lines in their full form recur six times (lines 31–34, 107–10, 141–44 and 301–04), each time following a phrasing of the major refrain:

Tehu noi-tao leo lia	Yet however one strives
Ho tunu-hai leo lia	There is trouble there
Ma sanga-tao leo na	And however one seeks
Ho kelo-kea leo na.	There is difficulty there.

They also appear in truncated form as, for example, in lines 75/77 and 128/130:

Tehu noi-tao leo lia ...	Yet however one strives ...
Ma sanga-tao leo na.	And however one seeks.

This refrain is composed of the double dyadic sets *noi-tao//sanga-tao* and *kelo-kea//tunu-hai*. *Noi-tao//sanga-tao* indicates a 'striving, struggling or searching'. In Termanu, the near equivalent combines the terms *sanga// tunga*. *Kelo-kea//tunu-hai*, on the other hand, connotes 'difficulties, problems, setbacks'. Its closest equivalent in Termanu is *toa//pia*.

The use of these particular dyadic sets serves as Kornalius Medah's key signature, and the interweaving of complementary refrains is an expression of his mastery of Bilba dialect.

An Analysis of Kornalius Medah's Ritual Language Usage

This recitation by Kornalius Medah, in Bilba dialect, has 405 lines and is composed of 107 dyadic sets. Bilba's dialect belongs to Dialect Area II, which falls between Ringgou and Landu in the east and Korbaffo and

Termanu in the central-west of Rote. As a dialect, it is closer to the language of Termanu than to the language of Ringgou. For Termanu speakers, it presents less of a challenge than Ringgou's dialect.

The majority of the dyadic sets in Bilba's ritual language are sets shared through most of the island. Some examples of sets that are identical to those in Termanu are the following: 1) *bafa//ma* ('mouth'//'tongue'); 2) *dela//nita* ('*delas* tree, *Erythina spp.*'//'*nitas* tree, *Sterculia foetida*'); 3) *deta//sama* ('like'//'as'); 4) *eki//hika* ('to scream, shout'//'to laugh'); 5) *-hapa//-sulu* ('to protect'//'to shelter'); 6) *loak//naluk* ('broad'//'long'); 7) *liun//sain* ('ocean'//'sea'); 8) *luli//sangu* ('storm'//'cyclone'); 9) *li//nafa* ('wave'//'wave crest'); 10) *molo//tabu* ('step'//'tread').

There are, however, a number of sound changes that distinguish Bilba's dialect from Termanu's. Most notably, initial 'nd' in Termanu becomes 'l' in Bilba (as opposed to 'r' in Ringgou). Similarly, initial 'ngg' in Termanu becomes 'ng' in Bilba (as opposed to 'k' in Ringgou). Medial 'd' in Termanu becomes 'nd' in Bilba. These sound changes yield the following transformations of shared dyadic sets:

Table 15: Termanu–Bilba–Ringgou Dialect Comparisons

Termanu	Bilba	Ringgou	Gloss
na//ndia	*na//lia*	*na//ria*	'this'//'that'
ndui//sau	*lui//sau*	*rui//sau*	'to ladle'//'to scoop out'
ndai//seko	*lai//seko*	*rai//se'o*	'to scoop'//'to net-fish'
ndano//toko	*lano//toko*	*rano//to'o*	'to throw'//'to thrust'
-nggeli//-tulek	*-ngeli//-tulek*	–	'to rage'//'to heave'
-kedu//-tani	*-kendu//-tani*	*-edu//-tani*	'to sob'//'to weep'

Bilba has a range of specific sets with terms that distinguish these sets from those of Termanu and Ringgou or Landu. For example, Bilba has a different set of terms for house post and beam (*nata-tuak//timi-di*) than Landu (or Ringgou) (*balo-tua//timi-di*) or Termanu (*lungu-tua/timi-di*). Similarly, Bilba has the set *hamu-le//tele-tasi*, whereas Landu has *hambau//tere-tasi*. The verbs *teteni//tatane* ('to seek'//'to quest') are distinctive in their use in Bilba dialect.

There are other distinctive usages. For example, in lines 38–39:

Faik lia luli dulu fafae na	One day a storm arises in the waking east

15. A VERSION FROM THE DOMAIN OF BILBA

Ma ledok na sangu langa titipa na.	And at one time a cyclone blows at the thrusting head.

The density of these lines is notable. Whereas generally poetic lines may contain three or four dyadic sets, these lines contain five dyadic sets: *faik//ledo*, *lia//na*, *luli//sangu*, *dulu//langa* and *fae//tipa*, which occurs in reduplicated form as *fafae//titipa*. Although analysable in separable sets, the combination *dulu fafae//langa titipa* constitutes a formula. *Fae* as a verb means to 'to shake, to wake', while the verb *tipa* means 'to push, to shove'. When these verbs with similar meanings are applied to east//head, they describe an early dawning, an opening to the east. This same formula is repeated in lines 79–80 when a storm again arises in the east:

Faik lia luli dulu fafae seluk	One day a storm arises again in the waking east
Ma ledok na sangu langa titipa seluk.	And at one time a cyclone blows again at the thrusting head.

Another idiomatic expression occurs (in singular format using *neu*) in lines 259/262 and again (in plural format using *leu*) in lines 289–90:

(1)

Na dadi neuk koa tua	Gives rise to great celebration
Dadi neu ngia sina.	Gives rise to great exuberance.

(2)

Dadi leu koa tua	These things give rise to great celebration
Ma moli leu ngia sina.	And give forth great exuberance.

The combination of *koa tua//ngia sina* in Bilba signifies a 'celebration, rejoicing, a show of exuberance'. However, if translated literally, this combination of terms means 'old, large friarbird'//'Chinese parrot'. This particular idiomatic usage is not an expression used (or possibly even understood) in Termanu.

Kornalius Medah's Recitation as a Christian Parable

With its recurrent refrains, the narrative progression of Kornalius Medah's recitation is relatively clear and easy to follow. Its intent, however, may be more difficult to fathom. Unlike some versions of *Suti Solo do Bina Bane*, this version is not revelatory: it does not link the shells' journey to specific events in any origin chants. Instead its insistent theme focuses on the uncertainty, impermanence and transitory nature of life.

As is emphatically stated in lines 342/344 towards the end of the recitation:

Te tean tak dae bafok	For there is no certainty on earth
Te mepen tak batu poik ka.	For there is no permanence in the world.

Like numerous other mortuary chants, this recitation reiterates a basic Rotenese conception of the human condition: that all human beings in the world are ultimately like orphans and widows. However they may live, they are born and die as widows and orphans.

As the shells prepare to embark on the Pandanus River road and Jasmine Forest path, they enunciate this fundamental view of themselves:

'Au ia, ana mak Suti Solo	'Here I am, the orphan Suti Solo
Ma au ia, falu ina Bina Bane.	And here I am, the widow Bina Bane.
Falu ina ko fali	I am a widow going back
Ma ana ma ko tulek.'	And an orphan returning.'

This view of the human condition is explicitly voiced in some of the oldest and most traditional mortuary chants from Rote (see Fox 1988: 161–201, particularly pp. 166–69), but it can also be tinged, in various chants, with clear Christian sentiments. Kornalius Medah's recitation offers hints of these Christian sentiments in its use of certain key words. At the beginning of the recitation (lines 10–11), it is announced that:

Hu no tepok lia Suti natane sodak ka	At that time Suti seeks well-being
Ma lelek na Bina teteni molek ka.	And at the moment Bina asks for peace.

The dyadic set *soda//mole*, drawn from the vocabulary of the Christian canon, implies a state of heavenly grace. These paired terms, *Soda-Molek*, are used as a Christian greeting and their use in this context, at the outset of the recitation, signals the potential direction for the recitation.

The return to East Estuary and Headland River and the ascent along the Pandanus River road and Jasmine Forest path to the two prolific fruiting trees, the Ko Nau and the Nilu Neo, can be interpreted as a Christian parable that traces a path from birth to death.

16

Suti Solo do Bina Bane: A Version from the Domain of Ba'a

I met the blind poet Laazar Manoeain only once, in 1966. Most of the research during my first fieldwork in 1965–66 was carried out in the domain of Termanu and in Korbaffo to the east of Termanu. Old Manoeain lived in the domain of Ba'a to the west of Termanu. During my time on the island, I was frequently told of his great fluency as a poet and also of his power as a preacher. As was not uncommon at this time and in the past, Manoeain's reputation was based on his knowledge and abilities to recite traditional compositions and to use this knowledge and skill in his sermons as a minister (*pendeta*) in the main church in Ba'a. He was a member of a generation of Rotenese ministers, inspired by the Dutch missionary G. J. L. Le Grande, who urged the use of Rotenese ritual language, rather than Malay, in the preaching of Christianity. What made Old Manoeain's reputation particularly notable was the fact that although he had gone blind, he had continued in his two roles as preacher and poet—and, as most Rotenese would contend, his skills increased after he lost his sight.

On a short visit to Ba'a in 1966, I made an effort to meet him, walking to his house just outside the administrative town of Ba'a. I found him alone in his house. He welcomed me and told me that he had heard of my presence. What struck me most about him was the gentleness of his voice. He was then perhaps in his late 70s, probably slightly older than Old

Meno but of the same generation. We talked for a while and I explained to him that I wanted to record him on my tape recorder[1] but had not brought the machine with me.

His response was immediate. He had time and he would recite slowly so that I could write down his chanting as he went along. True to his word, he recited slowly, clearly and was willing to repeat lines to make things easy for me. As a result, Old Manoeain was the only poet whose recitations I transcribed directly and for which I have no sound recording.

We only recorded a couple of recitations, one of which was *Suti Solo do Bina Bane*, which I specially requested. His version of this chant came to only 117 lines. It is my suspicion that he shortened the telling of this version purposely to simplify my transcription of it. He may also have tried to cast his recitation in a kind of Termanu dialect because, when we met, he could tell that I only knew that dialect.

The domain of Ba'a is located between the domains of Dengka to its west and Termanu to its east and, in one or two features, its dialect appears to be a halfway house between the dialects of its larger neighbouring areas. This is particularly true of what is initial and medial 'p' in Termanu. In the dialect of Dengka, this is 'mb', whereas in Ba'a, this initial consonant sounds more like 'mp'. (However, this is variable for non-initial 'p'. In some words, Ba'a retains a 'p' like that in Termanu.) On the other hand, the 'ng' in Termanu becomes 'ngg' in Ba'a, which is closer to its neighbours to the west. In other respects, however, Manoeain's recitation more closely resembles recitations in Termanu than in other domains to the west.

Manoeain's version of *Suti Solo do Bina Bane* has few of the revelatory features of an origin chant. He gives an origin to the shells, mentioning the loss of their 'father', Bane Aka//Solo Bane, but he does not elaborate on this genealogy. The shells are described as drifting to the shore but there is no mention of the place where they are encountered, nor any mention of a search for the ritual Dusu La'e//Tio Holu fish, nor any identification of the women who encounter the shells and initiate a dialogue with them.

---

[1] For all my recordings in 1965–66, I relied on a sturdy but somewhat bulky Uher spool tape recorder. Since I travelled almost everywhere on horseback, it was not always easy to carry my tape recorder. So when I knew that I would have the chance to record a poet, I would walk to a particular destination and carry the tape-recorder with me. On this particular trip to Ba'a, where I had gone for supplies, I had not brought my tape recorder.

The emphasis from the start of the composition is on being a widow and an orphan. The composition consists chiefly of four dialogue directives. These formulaic dialogues are interesting because each is different from those of Termanu. Finally, the return of the shells to the sea leads to their being transported to Timor, where they experience a demise that transforms them into distinct cultural objects.

Suti Solo do Bina Bane

A storm arises that carries Suti Solo do Bina Bane from the depths of the ocean to the shore.

The Storm and Arrival of Suti Solo and Bina Bane

1.	*Sanggu nala liun*	A storm strikes the ocean
2.	*Luli nala sain.*	A cyclone strikes the sea.
3.	*Neni Bane Aka Liun*	It carries away Bane Aka of the ocean
4.	*Ma Solo Bane Sain.*	And Solo Bane of the sea.
5.	*De la'o ela Suti Solo Bane*	They depart, leaving Suti Solo Bane
6.	*Ma Bina Bane Aka.*	And Bina Bane Aka.
7.	*Boe ma duas-sa bomu bina*	The two of them bob like *bina* wood
8.	*Ma ele mpiko.*	And drift like *mpiko* wood.
9.	*Leo soloka'ek ke haba-na mai*	Coming to where the sand is banded with gold braid
10.	*Ma tasi-oe mpesi lilon-na mai.*	And to where the sea is splashed with gold.

A woman and girl scoop-fishing in the sea find the shells, who are crying, and ask them what is wrong. They reply that they have lost their father and mother and are now left alone in the sea.

The Encounter and Initial Dialogue

11.	*Boe ma ina mana-seko meti-la*	A woman scooping in the tide
12.	*Ma feto mana-ndai tasi-la*	And a girl fishing in the sea
13.	*Ala mai nda Bina Bane no Suti Solo.*	They meet Bina Bane or Suti Solo.

14.	*Mpinu lama-tuda idu*	Snot falls from [their] nose
15.	*Ma lu lama-sasi mata.*	And tears pour from [their] eyes.
16.	*Boe-ma la-tane lae:*	They ask, saying:
17.	*'Te sala hata leo, hatak*	'What wrong like this
18.	*Ma singgo hata leo hatak*	And what mistake like this
19.	*De ei duang nge lu sasi mata*	That you two have tears pouring from the eyes
20.	*Ma mpinu tuda idu?'*	And snot falling from the nose?'
21.	*Boe ma lae:*	So they say:
22.	*'Sanggu nala liun*	'A storm struck the ocean
23.	*Ma luli nala sain.*	And cyclone struck the sea.
24.	*De neni ai amam ma ai inam,*	It carried away our father and our mother,
25.	*Bane Aka Liun*	Bane Aka of the ocean
26.	*Ma Solo Bane Sain.*	And Solo Bane of the sea.
27.	*De la'o ela ai dadi neu*	They departed, leaving us to become
28.	*Ana-ma manu ma kisa kapa.*	An orphan chicken and lone buffalo.
29.	*De ai ta hampu*	We have no one
30.	*Mana-fali oli*	Who will help us in the estuary
31.	*Ma mana-toa tasi.'*	And who will provide for us in the sea.'

The women propose that the shells go with 'creaking wood and scraping forest' to hide themselves in the forest. They reply that if a cyclone uproots the trees and liana of the forest, there will be no order or integrity there for them.

The First Dialogue Directive

32.	*Boe ma ina mana-seko meti-la*	The woman scooping in the tide
33.	*Ma feto mana-ndai tasi-la*	And the girl fishing in the sea
34.	*La-fada lae:*	Speak, saying:
35.	*'Meu mo nula kekek*	'Go with the creaking wood
36.	*Ma lasi nggio-nggiok*	And with the scraping forest
37.	*Fo nabi nula*	To hide yourself in the wood
38.	*Ma keke lasi.'*	And conceal yourself in the forest.'

16. A VERSION FROM THE DOMAIN OF BA'A

39.	*Boe ma lae:*	So they say:
40.	*'Luli mai fafae*	'[If] a cyclone comes to shake
41.	*Ma sanggu mai fofoi*	And a storm comes to uproot
42.	*Na latuk ai do nula la*	Then the yellowed tree leaves of the wood
43.	*Monu mai hun-na*	Will fall to the foot of the tree
44.	*Ma hi'i po'o ai lasi la*	And the mouldy liana cords of the forest
45.	*Kono mai okan.*	Will drop to their roots.
46.	*De tetun ta ndia boe*	Order is not there then
47.	*Ma tema ta ndia boe.'*	And integrity is not there then.'

The women then propose that they go with the 'wild pig and forest monkey' to conceal themselves in caves and holes. They reply that if the pig were hunted and the monkey flushed out of their hiding place, there would again be no order or integrity for them.

The Second Dialogue Directive

48.	*Boe ma lae:*	So they say:
49.	*'Te nana meu mo bafi fui*	'Go, then, with the wild pig
50.	*Ma kode lasi*	And forest monkey
51.	*Fo keke nai leak*	To conceal yourself in caves
52.	*Ma nabi nai luak.'*	And hide yourself in holes.'
53.	*Boe ma lae:*	So they say:
54.	*'Tebe te mbu bafi nama-hana*	'True, but if the pig is hunted heatedly
55.	*Ma oka kode naka-doto.*	And the monkey is flushed noisily.
56.	*Na bafi fui sapu boe*	Then the wild pig will die too
57.	*Ma kode lasi lalo boe.*	And the forest monkey will perish too.
58.	*De tetun ta ndia boe*	Order is not there then
59.	*Ma teman ta ndia boe.'*	And integrity is not there then.'

The women then propose that the shells go with river shrimp and the grassland cuckoo to hide deep in the grass or deep in a waterhole. But they reply that if the river's water ceases to flow and the grass dries, there will once more be no order and integrity there.

The Third Dialogue Directive

60.	*Boe ma lae:*	So they say:
61.	*'Te nana meu mo mpoe le*	'But go, then, with the river shrimp
62.	*Ma meu mo koko na'u*	And go with grassland cuckoo
63.	*Fo nabi nai na'u dale*	To hide yourself deep in the grass
64.	*Ma keke nai lifu dale.'*	And conceal yourself deep in a water hole.'
65.	*Boe ma lae:*	So they say:
66.	*'Tebe te le lama-ketu meti*	'True, but when the river ceases its ebb
67.	*Na mpoe le lai aon*	Then the river shrimp pities itself
68.	*Ma na'u lama-tu tongo*	And the grass dries on the blade
69.	*Na koko na'u sue aon.*	Then the grassland cuckoo sorrows for itself.
70.	*De tetun ta ndia boe*	Order is not there then
71.	*Ma teman ta ndia boe.'*	And integrity is not there then.'

The women then propose that the shells enter the surf and plunge into the waves and make their way to 'Helok and Sonobai'. These are names for the islands of Semau and Timor based on terms for the major populations on these islands. Semau is seen as populated by the Helong people while Timor is identified with the once great ruler of the Atoni population, Sonbait. Taken together, these names define a place to the east of Rote. The shells follow this advice and are carried to the shore of Helok//Sonobai.

The Fourth Dialogue Directive

72.	*Boe ma lae:*	So they say:
73.	*'Te nana sida li fo meu*	'But, then, shear through the surf to go
74.	*Ma susi nafa fo meu*	And plunge through the waves to go
75.	*Leo Helok Sonobai meu.*	To Helong and Sonobai.
76.	*Te dae sodak nai ndia*	For the land of well-being is there
77.	*Ma oe molek nai na.'*	And the waters of peace are there.'
78.	*Boe ma Bina Bane*	So Bina Bane
79.	*Ma Suti Solo*	And Suti Solo
80.	*Ala sida li*	They shear through the surf
81.	*Ma susi nafa.*	And plunge through the waves.

82.	*De leu Helok Sonobai,*	They go to Helong and Sonobai,
83.	*Leo losa solokaek ke haba-na*	To where the sand is banded with gold braid
84.	*Tasi-oe mpesi lilo na.*	And where the sea is splashed with gold.

There the woman of Helong and the girl of Sonobai encounter them, as they cry along the shore. They ask them what is wrong and the shells tell them that they have lost their mother and father in a great storm. They are alone and looking for someone to help them.

The Encounter on Timor: Suti Solo and Bina Bane's Lament

85.	*Boe ma ina Helok-ka mai nda duas*	A woman of Helong meets the two
86.	*Ma fetok Sonobai mai tonggo duas-sa.*	And a girl of Sonobai encounters the two.
87.	*Lu la-sasi mata*	Tears pour from [their] eyes
88.	*Ma pinu la-tuda idu.*	And snot falls from [their] nose.
89.	*Boe ma lae:*	So they say:
90.	*'Sala hata leo hatak*	'What wrong like this
91.	*Ma singgo hata leo hatak?*	And what mistake like this?
92.	*De ei mpinu idu*	This snot from your nose
93.	*Ma lu mata.'*	These tears from your eyes.'
94.	*Boe ma lae:*	So they say:
95.	*'Ai dadi neu kisa kampa*	'We have become a lone buffalo
96.	*Ma ana-ma manu,*	And an orphan chicken,
97.	*Hu sanggu neni ai amam*	Because a storm has carried away our father
98.	*Ma luli neni ai inam.*	And a cyclone has carried away our mother.
99.	*De se fali oli ai*	Who in the estuary will help us
100.	*Ma toa tasi ai.'*	Who in the sea will provide for us.'

The woman of Sonobai and the girl of Helong invite them to their house. When they arrive, the women carve them to make haircombs and file them to make earrings. This is done badly and they perish.

The Demise of Suti Solo and Bina Bane

101.	*Boe ma ina Sonobai*	So the woman of Sonobai
102.	*Ma feto Helok-ka lae:*	And the girl of Helong say:
103.	*'Tungga ai leo uma teu*	'Follow us to our house
104.	*Ma lo teu.'*	And to our home.'
105.	*Boe ma Bina Bane*	So Bina Bane
106.	*No Suti Solo tungga.*	Or Suti Solo follow [them].
107.	*De losa.*	They arrive there.
108.	*Boe ma ina Sonobai*	So the woman Sonobai
109.	*No feto Helok-ka*	Or the girl Helong
110.	*Hai lala Bina Bane*	Pick up Bina Bane
111.	*De ala sein neu sua*	They cut incisions in him to make hair combs
112.	*Ma hai lala Suti Solo*	And pick up Suti Solo
113.	*De folan neu falo.*	They file him to make earrings.
114.	*De fola falo la salan*	They file the earrings badly
115.	*Ma se sua la singgon*	And they incise the hair combs inexactly
116.	*Boe ma Bina Bane sapu*	So Bina Bane dies
117.	*Ma Suti Solo lalo.*	And Suti Solo perishes.

Comparisons with Termanu

For someone from Termanu, there is nothing in this composition that would be unintelligible or even difficult to understand, yet it would be recognised as a composition that was not from Termanu. Putting aside the pronunciation of a few words, there are other subtle differences in this composition that mark it as 'not from Termanu'. Some are notable and do not relate to the composition's dyadic form. Thus, for example, the two-word phrase *tebe te* in lines 54 and 66, which means 'true, indeed', would probably not occur in a Termanu dialect text. The equivalent would be '*te'ek*'. Similarly, the use of pronominal terms in Ba'a dialect identifies this recitation—thus, for example, the pronominal *ai*, meaning 'we, us', occurs where Termanu would use *ami*.

Most significant is the fact that this version of *Suti Solo do Bina Bane* has been given no genealogical foundation. Poets in Termanu and elsewhere may differ in the genealogical foundations that they offer in support of the authority of their recitations but all of them insist on providing some kind of genealogical basis for their recitations. This lack of a genealogical foundation may be an artefact of the way I collected this chant: with Manoeain on his own and without any demanding Rotenese audience who might have insisted on such basic background.

Equally different are the various directives proposed to the shells. None of these is the familiar directive (of Termanu) that proposes to locate the shells within the house or in the surrounding fields.

1)	*nula kekek//lasi nggio-nggiok*	'creaking wood'//'scraping forest'
2)	*bafi fui//kode lasi*	'wild pig'//'forest monkey'
3)	*mpoe le//koko na'u*	'river shrimp'//'grassland cuckoo'
4)	*Helok//Sonobai*	Helong//Sonobai

Pig and Monkey, for example, form a familiar set in other versions of *Suti Solo do Bina Bane* but these creatures always appear as the marauders and destroyers of gardens and fields. The common expression in Termanu is *Kode ketu betek//Bafi na'a pelak* ('The monkey plucks the millet and the pig eats the maize'). Neither monkey nor pig is ever proposed as a companion for the shells.

Intriguingly in this version of *Suti Solo do Bina Bane*, there occur formulaic lines that resonate with Termanu's traditions. These lines (42–45), formed around the formulaic pair *latu ai do//hi'i po'o ai*, are as follows:

Na latuk ai do nula la	Then the yellowed tree leaves of the wood
Monu mai hun-na	Will fall to the foot of the tree
Ma hi'i po'o ai lasi la	And the mouldy liana cords of the forest
Kono mai okan.	Will drop to their roots.

In Termanu, the somewhat similar formulaic set is used exclusively as a name, Latu Kai Do//Po'o Pau Ai, for the woman in the ocean whom Suti Solo do Bina Bane reject and with whom they refuse to dance.

An Analysis of Laazar Manoeain's Use of Ritual Language

This recitation with its 117 lines is composed of some 49 dyadic sets. As in all of the other recitations, the majority of the dyadic sets used in the composition are the same as those that occur elsewhere throughout the island. Among these basic dyadic sets, which are identical to those in Termanu, are the following: 1) *bafi*//*kode* ('pig'//'monkey'); 2) *dae*//*oe* ('earth'//'water'); 3) *haba*//*lilo* ('braided gold'//'gold'); 4) *hu*//*oka* ('trunk'//'root'); 5) *idu*//*mata* ('nose'//'eye'); 6) *kono*//*monu* ('to fall down'//'to fall off'); 7) *lasi*//*nula* ('forest'//'wood'); 8) *lo*//*uma* ('home'//'house'). To these may be added sets, also shared with Termanu, that are marked by the sound change p > mp: 1) *lu*//*mpinu* ('tears'//'snot'); 2) *ke*//*mpesi* ('braided, banded'//'splashed, thrown together'); 3) *koko na'u*//*mpoe le* ('grassland cuckoo'//'river shrimp').

This version of *Suti Solo do Bina Bane* uses various complex formulaic sets that are like those in Termanu: *soloka'ek ke haba-na*//*tasi-oe mpesi lilon-na* ('the sand banded with gold braid'//'the water of the sea splashed with gold'), *lu sasi mata*//*mpinu tuda idu* ('tears pouring from the eyes'//'snot falling from the nose') or *ana-ma manu ma kisa kapa* ('an orphan chicken and lone buffalo'). However, there are other usages that are distinctive and unlike the formulaic expressions in Termanu or other dialect areas. Instead of the familiar *bonu boa*//*ele piko* ('bob like *boa* wood'//'drift like *piko* wood'), this version has a variant form: *bomu bina*//*ele mpiko* ('bob like *bina* wood'//'drift like *mpiko* wood'). In Termanu, the set meaning to hunt by shouting or flushing out animals is *pu*//*oku*; here it is *mpu*//*oka*. In Termanu, *latu* forms a set with *po'o*, meaning 'ripe, mouldy'; in Ba'a, this set is *hi'i*//*latu*. These slight variations in form are what distinguish one dialect's recitation from another.

17
Suti Solo do Bina Bane: Version I from the Domain of Thie

The Canon of Origins: Relations between the Sun and Moon and the Lords of the Sea

This recitation, which I recorded in 1973, is remarkable not just as another version of *Suti Solo do Bina Bane* but also as a composition that locates the initial cause of the shells' distress in the context of one of the most important episodes in the origin narratives of the Rotenese. This episode, which serves to introduce the recitation, recounts the attack of the Sun and Moon, Ledo Horo and Bula Kai, and their children on the Lords of the Ocean and Sea, Manetua Sain and Danga Lena Liun. In the course of this attack, Suti Solo and Bina Bane are tainted with the spilled blood of battle and this sets the shells adrift in the sea. Thereafter the recitation is concerned with the fate of the shells.

The introduction to this recitation gives a glimpse of the drama of the origin narratives, all of which recount the successive involvement and intimate engagement of the Sun and Moon with the Lords of the Ocean and Sea, who are identified as Shark and Crocodile. Their field of interaction is on earth as much as in the heavens or sea.

On a trip to the village of Oe Handi in Thie in 1973, I recorded this version of *Suti Solo do Bina Bane* together with a wealth of other chants from the two master poets at that time: N. D. Pah, who was invariably referred to as Guru Pah ('Teacher Pah'), and his close friend and companion, Samuel Ndun. These chants included a long and detailed version of the foundation chant that recounts the discovery of fire and cooked food in the sea and another chant about the origin of the house built with tools obtained from the sea. In addition, the two poets provided other chants, including two extended mortuary chants. My week's stay in Oe Handi was the most intensive and productive period of my second fieldwork on Rote.

In retrospect, I realise that the version of *Suti Solo do Bina Bane* that I was offered was intended as an integral component of the other origin chants I recorded. It is critical therefore to introduce this recitation by reference to the other origin chants that provide the 'cosmological' context for this version of *Suti Solo do Bina Bane*. In Thie, *Suti Solo do Bina Bane* is itself a vital origin chant—one that was previously recited at one of the major origin ceremonies of the domain.

The origin narratives of Thie begin with the heavenly marriage of Pua Kende and No Rini to Ledo Horo and Bula Kai, the Lords of the Sun and Moon. The first sons of this marriage are Adu Ledo and Ndu Bulan. As young men, they set out to hunt 'pig and civet cat'. During their hunt, they meet the sons of the Lords of the Ocean and Sea, Tio Dangak and Rusu Mane, and agree to join each other in the hunt.

When eventually they catch a 'woodland civet and a forest pig', the sons of the Sun and Moon propose that they divide their catch. Instead, Tio Dangak and Rusu Mane invite Adu Ledo and Ndu Bulan to their realm beneath the sea. There in the ocean's depths, the sons of Sun and Moon discover the immense wealth of the Shark and Crocodile. More importantly still, they discover fire for the first time and the delicious taste of cooked food. The taste is so extraordinary that Adu Ledo and Ndu Bulan hide a portion of their meal and take it back to their father, Ledo Horo and Bula Kai.

17. VERSION I FROM THE DOMAIN OF THIE

Figure 20: Samuel Ndun

Figure 21: N. D. Pah — 'Guru Pah'

What follows is a debate about how the Sun and Moon can acquire the full bounty of the sea. The first inclination is to make war on the sea but this proves futile. Eventually Ledo Horo and Bula Kai decide to divorce their daughters Sa'o Ledo and Mani Bulan from their husbands and offer these women in marriage to Tio Dangak and Rusu Mane. In return, they demand an immense bridewealth, which consists of a litany of objects that they desire. Besides gold and livestock, particularly water buffalo, they demand the means for making fire—a flint set and fire drill—but also an array of tools for building a house, as well as axe and adze for clearing fields for planting.

Among their specific demands is the 'mortar whose thudding shakes its base and a pestle whose thrust blisters the hand'. When they have concluded their marriage alliance and obtained a bridewealth of useful objects, the Lords of the Sun and Moon have gained for themselves the implements for planting, for pounding grains and for cooking but they lack the 'seeds' to plant. These seeds originate in the sea. This version of *Suti Solo do Bina Bane* recounts the origin of these seeds.

Recording and Interpreting this Version of *Suti Solo do Bina Bane*

In 1966, many years before my 1973 visit, I journeyed to the settlement of Oe Handi in Thie to meet 'Guru Pah'. As a young man, he had assisted the Swiss researcher Alfred Buehler in his study of textiles and gained a wide reputation throughout Rote as one of the most knowledgeable authorities on Rotenese traditions. He was noted as a brilliant Christian preacher, a fine singer and versatile player of the Rotenese *sesandu*—a tradition that continued in subsequent generations of his family.

On my arrival, Guru Pah's first question to me was why had it taken so long for me to pay him a visit. He felt that I was wasting my time doing research in Termanu, whereas, in his opinion, research in Thie would have been far more productive.

I was able to stay only a few days in Oe Handi but during that time I recorded two long chants of remarkable beauty associated with the celebration of origins in Thie.

Like my first visit to Oe Handi, my second visit in 1973 was brief. It lasted for only a week. At the time, Guru Pah was involved in a variety of ritual activities including both a funeral and a large-scale wedding. He was prepared to continue his recitations but he invited another poet, Samuel Ndun, to join him. The two were almost inseparable and made themselves available for my recording. They would confer with each other about each particular recitation and then take turns at reciting, commenting on and correcting their recitations. Because of their mutual efforts, I have designated the set of recordings that I did at this time as joint compositions.

Although I never learned a great deal about Pak Sam, he gave his recitations with authority and enthusiasm. While I was in Oe Handi, he was also involved in officiating at a wedding. I remember that when he arrived to conduct the ritual, he asked whether the family wanted a Christian or traditional ceremony. He was willing and capable of performing either.

While I was in Oe Handi, I tried to work through each recitation, identifying new dyadic sets and annotating difficult lines. Despite these efforts at understanding, Thie's dialect has always presented difficulties for me. Hence, over the years, I have turned to other knowledgeable speakers from Thie to check my transcriptions and assist me with my understanding and my translations.

Years later, I sought help on understanding this recitation from Guru Pah's daughter, Ibu Guru Ena Pah, who was by that time a respected teacher in Kupang, and also from Paul Haning, who had a deep knowledge of the ritual language of Thie. Even after having properly transcribed and worked out an initial literal translation, I was still uncertain of the meaning of certain key passages in this recitation. Like many of the most important Rotenese chants, this recitation is challengingly elusive, with references to places whose significance is not immediately apparent. Years later, for further elucidation, I sought the help of the master poet Jonas Mooy, who carefully and patiently assisted me to understand more of the metaphoric expressions in this version.

The Narrative Structure of the Pah–Ndun Version of *Suti Solo do Bina Bane*

This recitation begins with a peroration of some seven lines that acknowledge the rule borne by the Heavens and the Earth. These lines foreshadow the concluding five lines of the recitation, which extol the rule and bounty of the Heavens. After this peroration, 49 lines launch immediately into a crucial episode from the canon of the origin chants. They give an account of the lead-up to the war waged by the Sun and Moon on the Lords of the Ocean and Sea. These lines also provide the genealogical background to the key members of the Heavenly Realm. Ledo Horo//Bula Kai is Lord of the Sun and Moon; his wife is Pua Kende//No Rini, the daughter of Kende Bei Sama//Rini Bala Sama. Some of Ledo Holo//Bula Kai's children, who bear the first half of the name of their father—Bulan and Ledo—are mentioned in this recitation: 1) Patola Bulan//Mandeti Ledo, 2) Tuti Leo Bulan//Si Lete Ledo, 3) Ninga Heu Bulan//Lafa Lai Ledo, and 4) Hundi Hu Bulan//Tefu Oe Ledo. The names of other children of the Sun and Moon, however, are missing from the initial lines of this version. Neither the son who first descends into the sea to taste cooked food, Adu Ledo//Ndu Bulan, nor the daughter who marries Tio Dangak//Rusu Mane, Sa'o Ledo//Mani Bulan, is cited in this recitation.

The Lords of the Sea, Manetua Sain//Danga Lena Liun, are mentioned along with various sea creature warriors. These sea creatures, Ain Bo'o Bai//Etu Asa Siru and Bara Kota Nau//Pila Mengge Mea, are specifically named, but with the exception of Pila Mengge Mea ('Red Snake of the Sea'), these names do not clearly indicate what creatures they represent. The fighting occurs at Lau Mara//Leme Niru. All of this is provided as the prelude to the introduction of the shells.

Ledo Horo and Bula Kai Declare War on the Lords of Ocean and Sea

1.	*Hida bei fan na*	At a time long ago
2.	*Dalu bei don na*	At a period long past
3.	*Lalai ma na te dae bafok*	The Heavens and the Earth
4.	*Neni parinda ma neni koasak*	Carry rule and carry power
5.	*Neni ko'o ifak*	Carry it lifting and cradling it
6.	*Neni nekeboik*	Carry it with care
7.	*Ma neni nesemaok.*	And carry it with concern.
8.	*Faik esa no dalen*	Then on a certain day
9.	*Ledo esa no tein*	At a particular time
10.	*Touk kia Bula Kai*	The man Bula Kai
11.	*Ta'ek esa Ledo Horo*	The boy Ledo Horo
12.	*Ana dea-dea no tun*	He speaks with his wife
13.	*Ma na te ana kola-kola no saon*	And he addresses his spouse
14.	*Kende Bei Sama anan*	Kende Bei Sama's child

15.	*Inak kia Pua Kende*	The woman Pua Kende
16.	*Ma Rini Bala Sama anan*	And Rini Bala Sama's child
17.	*Fetok kia No Rini.*	The girl No Rini.
18.	*Ana dea-dea no anan nara*	He speaks with his children
19.	*Mandeti Ledo bali*	Mandeti Ledo
20.	*Ma Patola Bulan bali*	And Patola Bulan
21.	*Kola-kola no anan nara*	Addresses his children
22.	*Si Lete Ledo bali*	Si Lete Ledo
23.	*Tuti Leo Bulan bali*	Tuti Leo Bulan
24.	*Ana kola-kola no anan nara*	He addresses his children
25.	*Ningga Heu Bulan*	Ninga Heu Bulan
26.	*Lafa Lai Ledo*	Lafa Lai Ledo
27.	*Hundi Hu Bulan bali*	Hundi Hu Bulan
28.	*Tefu Oe Ledo bali ma nae:*	Tefu Oe Ledo and says:
29.	*'Tetenda tafa langga*	'Sharpen the sword blade
30.	*Ma seseru siro nggoe*	And set the flintlock trigger
31.	*Sain dale miu dei*	We are going into the sea
32.	*Ma liun dale miu dei.'*	And we are going into the ocean.'
33.	*Ela leo be na,*	So let it be,
34.	*Rani falu rai liun*	Eight warriors in the ocean
35.	*Ma meru sio rai sain.*	And nine defenders in the sea.
36.	*Ma na te tetenda tafa langga dei*	Strike their sword heads
37.	*Ma seseru siro nggoe dei.*	Set their flintlocks' triggers.
38.	*Hu na te ara konda sain dale mai*	So they descend into the sea
39.	*Ma ana konda liun dale mai*	And descend into the ocean
40.	*Ratonggo ro liun meru nara*	To meet the ocean's defenders
41.	*Ma na te randa ro sain rani nara,*	And to meet the sea's warriors,
42.	*Manetua Sain rani nara*	The Lord of the Sea's warriors
43.	*Ma Danga Lena Liun meru nara*	And Hunter of the Ocean's defenders
44.	*Ain Bo'o Bai ma Etu Asa Siru*	Ain Bo'o Bai and Etu Asa Siru

45.	*Bara Kota Nau sain*	Bara Kota Nau of the sea
46.	*Ma Pila Mengge Mea sain*	And Pila Mengge [red snake] of the sea
47.	*Ara tonggo ro*	They meet them
48.	*Ma ara nda ro*	And they encounter them
49.	*Rain falu ma meruk sio*	The eight warriors and nine defenders
50.	*Ruma sain bei Lau Mara*	In the sea at Lau Mara
51.	*[Ruma liun] bei Lema Niru bali*	And in the ocean at Lema Niru too
52.	*Tonggo langga reu tonggo*	They meet head to head
53.	*Tetenda tafa langga*	Strike their sword blades
54.	*Ma seseru siro nggoen.*	Fire their cocked flintlocks.
55.	*Hu na de ara siro la'e Lau Mara*	Thus they fire at Lau Mara
56.	*Ma ara tati la'e Leme Niru.*	And they slash at Leme Niru.

It is during the fighting at Lau Mara//Leme Niru that Suti Solo and Bina Bane are touched by the blood of battle, put forth their pods and are carried to Loko Laka Fa//Tebu Tipa Re. The lines that explain this also introduce the shells by way of their paternal genealogy. They are the children of Bane Aka Liun and Solo Bane Sain. This genealogical identification is the same as that recognised in Termanu (in both Meno's and Eli Pellondou's recitations). Rotenese genealogies that cite such a succession of generations—Bina Bane from Bane Aka Liun and Suti Solo from Solo Bane Sain—provide no indication of the gender of the succeeding generation. Other commentary is required to provide this information. In Termanu, the tradition is strong and clear: Suti Solo and Bina Bane are male. However, outside Termanu, in Thie and elsewhere in western Rote, tradition asserts that the shells are female. This recitation, however, offers no indication of the gender of the shells.

The Blood of Battle Falls on Suti Solo and Bina Bane and They Flee

57.	*Dan, ana nonosi*	Blood, it pours out
58.	*Ma oen, ana tititi.*	And water, it drips out.
59.	*Ana tititi la'e*	It drips on

60.	*Bane Aka Liun anan ia*	Bane Aka Liun's child
61.	*Bina Bane*	Bina Bane
62.	*Ma ana nosi la'e*	And it pours out on
63.	*Solo Bana Sain anan*	Solo Bana Sain's child
64.	*Suti Solo.*	Suti Solo.
65.	*Faik esa no dalen*	In the course of one day
66.	*Boe ma Suti rama-roko isi*	Suti puts forth his insides
67.	*Ma Bina reu-edo nggi*	And Bina extends his pods
68.	*Hu na ara la latu, de mai*	So they drift like seaweed
69.	*Ma ara bonu engga, de mai.*	And they bob like seagrass.
70.	*De ara mai Loko Laka Fa lain*	They come to Loko Laka Fa
71.	*Ma ara mai Tebu Tipa Re lain*	And they come to Tebu Tipa Re
72.	*Isi nara haradoi*	Their insides cry out
73.	*Ma na te nggi nara kurudo.*	And their pods are in pain.

The Woman Bui Len and Girl Eno Lolo Encounter Suti Solo and Bina Bane

74.	*Neu faik ka boe,*	On that day,
75.	*Na te Nggonggo Inggu Lai tun*	Nggonggo Ingu Lai's spouse
76.	*[Leu] Le Dale anan*	[Leu] Le Dale's child
77.	*Ma na te Bui Len.*	Bui Len.
78.	*Neu faik ka boe,*	On that day,
79.	*Rima Le Dale saon*	Rima Le Dale's wife
80.	*Ma na te Lolo Dala Ina anan*	Lolo Dala Ina's child
81.	*Eno Lolo*	Eno Lolo
82.	*Eno Lolo na te Bui Len*	Eno Lolo and Bu Len
83.	*Nggonggo Inggu Lai saon*	Nggonggo Ingu Lai's wife
84.	*Ma Leu [Rima] Le Dale tun*	And Leu [Rima] Le Dale's spouse
85.	*Ana ha'i nala ndai tasi*	She takes her sea scoop-net
86.	*[Ana] tengga nala seko metin*	Lifts up her tidal fishnet
87.	*Reu meti manggatitiri nara*	Goes to the receding tide
88.	*Ma mada manggaheheta nara.*	And to the drying sea.

89.	*Ana nda no Bina nggin*	She encounters Bina's pods
90.	*Ma ana tonggo no Suti isin.*	And she meets Suti's insides.
91.	*Ara haradoi numa Loko Laka Fa*	They cry out at Loko Laka Fa
92.	*Ma ara kurudo numa Tebu Tipa Re.*	They are in pain at Tebu Tipa Re.
93.	*'Soro meni nggai dei*	'Lift us up
94.	*Ma ndai meni nggai dei.'*	And scoop us up.'
95.	*'Ai belu Bina mia se*	'With whom will we attach Bina
96.	*Ma ai toto Suti mia se?'*	And with whom will we fit Suti?'
97.	*Boe ma ko'o reni sara mai*	So they cradle them away
98.	*[Ifa] reni sara [mai].*	And [carry] them away.
99.	*'Ai ndae ei miu be?*	'Where should we hang you?
100.	*Ma ai fua ei miu be?'*	And where should we place you?'

Suti Solo and Bina Bane's first request to Bu Len and Eno Lolo is to be placed on *ufa* and *bau* trees when they are in blossom. Both of these trees produce beautiful flowers. The *ufa* tree is otherwise known as the Malabar plum tree, rose apple or Malay apple tree (*Syzygium jambos*), while the *bau* tree is the hibiscus tree (*Hibiscus tiliaceus*). But almost immediately this proves unsatisfactory.

Suti Solo and Bina Bane Ask to be Carried to *Ufa* and *Bau* Trees

101.	*Boe ma rae: 'Fua ai miu*	So they say: 'Place us on
102.	*Ufa mabuna henu [kara]*	The *ufa* tree full of gold-bead flowers
103.	*Ma Bau malusu lilok kara.'*	And on the *bau* tree with golden blossoms.'
104.	*Fai esa no dalen*	On one day
105.	*Ara bei ta ratetu*	They still do not feel right
106.	*Ma bei ta randa.*	And still do not yet feel proper.

Suti Solo and Bina Bane's next request is to be carried into the house and placed on two of the major beams of the house. These are the places where sacrifices are carried out in the traditional house in Thie.[1]

Suti Solo and Bina Bane Ask to be Carried to the Sema Kona and Lunggu Lai

107.	*Ara dea-dea ro Nggonggo Inggu Lai tun*	They address Nggonggo Ingu Lai's spouse
108.	*Inak ia Eno Lolo*	The woman Eno Lolo
109.	*Ana kola-kola ro Rima Le Dale saon*	They speak to Rima Le Dale's wife
110.	*Fetok ia Bui Len:*	The girl Bui Len:
111.	*'Ma ha'i falik ai dei*	'Carry us back
112.	*Ma tengga falik ai dei*	And take us back
113.	*Ndae ai miu Sema Kona*	Hang us on the Sema Kona
114.	*Fua ai miu Lunggu Lai*	Place us on the Lunggu Lai
115.	*Fo ama bara manu Sema Kona*	To sacrifice chickens at the Sema Kona
116.	*Na te ama langge lilo Lunggu Lai.'*	And to place gold at the Lunggu Lai.'
117.	*Hu na de ara fati bete sara*	They offer millet there
118.	*Ma ara hao hade sara,*	And they consume the rice there,
119.	*Faru kapa ma na te mina bafi.*	Water buffalo horns and pig's fat.
120.	*Faik esa no dalen*	Then on one day
121.	*Ledok esa no tein*	And at one time
122.	*Bei ta ratetu*	They still do not feel right
123.	*Ma bei ta randa.*	And still do not feel proper.

Suti Solo and Bina Bane then ask to be carried eastward so that at dawn they may be placed at the boundary stone and field's border. It is at this point that the lines occur: 'So let it be: a hundred rise and a thousand mount at the rice field dike and the dry field boundary.' These metaphoric lines signal the planting of the shells as the first seeds of rice and millet and foretell the harvests ('a hundred rise//a thousand mount' refers to

---

1   See Fox (1993) for drawings of the internal architecture of a traditional house.

the myriad stalks in the fields) that will come from them. This is stated again in the lines in which the shells are described as giving rise to the 'Planting at the Boundary Stone' (*Tanek To Batu*) and 'Sowing at the Field Boundary' (*Selek Lane Ai*).

Suti Solo and Bina Bane Ask to be Carried to the East and to the Headland

124.	*Ana de'a-de'a ro Bui Len*	He talks to Bui Len
125.	*Ma kola-kola ro Eno Lolo*	And speaks to Eno Lolo
126.	*Nggonggo Inggu Lai tun*	Nggonggo Ingu Lai's spouse
127.	*Ma Rima Le Dale saon ma rae:*	And Rima Le Dale's wife, and says:
128.	*'Keko ai dulu miu dei*	'Shift us to the east
129.	*Ma lali ai langga miu dei*	And transfer us to the headland
130.	*Fo ai Timu Dulu miu dei*	So that we may be in the Dawning East
131.	*Ma ai Sepe Langga miu dei.*	And at the Reddening Headland.
132.	*Mbeda ai miu to batu*	Take us to the border stone
133.	*Ma na te ndae ai miu lane tiner.*	And carry us to the field's border.
134.	*Fo ela leo be na:*	So let it be:
135.	*Natun kae ma rifun hene*	A hundred rise and a thousand mount
136.	*Nai omba hade dei*	At the rice field dike
137.	*Nai lane tiner dei.*	And the dry field boundary.
138.	*Fo ela leo be na*	So let it be that
139.	*Ai makaboi miu ana mar*	We are cared for as orphans
140.	*Ma ai masamao miu falu inar*	And are treated as widows
141.	*Bonggi tanek To Batu*	Giving birth to planting at To Batu
142.	*Ma bonggi selek Lane Ai*	And giving birth to sowing at Lane Ai
143.	*Ruma Timu Dulu Sepe Langga.'*	At Timu Dulu Sepe Langga.'

The next three lines appear to be an interjection—a comment on an imagined Biblical homeland in the Dawning East and at the Reddening Headland (Timu Dulu//Sepe Langga). Thereafter, the women Bui Len// Eno Lolo carry the shells westward to a succession of named places: Deras//Le Lena, Mundek//Na'u Dalek, Rote//Kode Ana, Oe Batu//Bau

Foe, Kone Ama//Sai Fua and onward to Nggonggoer//Lasi Lai and Liti//Sera Dale. Each of these places is a recognised field in Thie or on the border with Thie and Dengka, which is planted with either rice or millet.

Suti Solo and Bina Bane Are Carried to a Succession of Fields Where They Are Planted

144.	*Neu na au ba'ing Ibrahim*	At the time my ancestor Ibrahim
145.	*Ana leo numa Timu Dulu Sepe Langga*	He lives in Timu Dulu Sepe Langga
146.	*Nusak Urkasdin*	The Land of Urkasdin
147.	*Faik na ana ko'o nala sara*	That day she cradles them
148.	*Ma na te ana ifa nala sara*	And she lifts them
149.	*Natun kae o kae*	A hundred to rise and rise
150.	*Ma rifun hene o hene*	And a thousand to mount and mount
151.	*Kae, ara muri mai*	Rising, they go to the west
152.	*Hene, ara iko mai*	Mounting they go to the tail
153.	*Ara mai Deras no Lelena*	They come to Deras and Le Lena
154.	*Ara mai Mundek no Na'u Dale*	They come to Mundek and Na'u Dale
155.	*Leo na, ara mai Rote no Kode Ana*	Then they come to Rote and Kode Ana
156.	*Oe Batu no Bau Foe*	Oe Batu and Bau Foe
157.	*Kone Ama ma Sai Fuan*	Kone Ama and Sai Fuan
158.	*Ara hene, ara kona reu*	They mount, they descend
159.	*Reu Nggonggoer ma reu Lasi Lai*	To Nggonggoer and Lasi Lai
160.	*Liti ma Sera Dale.*	Liti and Sera Dale.

In the concluding lines of this recitation, Suti Solo and Bina Bane are declared to be 'orphan and widow'. In virtually every other version of this chant, this designation is mentioned early and often. Here it appears once at the very end of the recitation. As 'orphan and widow', Suti Solo do Bina Bane take their rest in the fields of Thie from whence their descendants (*tititin*//*nonosin*) continue to spread throughout the world. The final lines reiterate the initial lines of the recitation that assert the power that the Heavens and the Heights exert on the Earth.

Suti Solo and Bina Bane as Orphan and Widow Achieve Their Rest in the Fields of Thie

161.	*Natun kae ma rifun hene*	A hundred rise and a thousand mount
162.	*Natun kae nai be*	One hundred rise to where
163.	*Ana mar reu suru*	The orphan goes to rest
164.	*Ma na te rifun hene nai be*	And a thousand mount to where
165.	*Ma falu inar reu tai.*	The widow goes to cling.
166.	*Boe te Suti oen tititin*	So Suti's descendants
167.	*Ma nate Bina oen nonosin*	And Bina's successors
168.	*Ndule basa dae bafok ledo sa'ak*	Cover all the world and sunlit Earth
169.	*Ki boe, kona boe*	North also and south also
170.	*Dulu boe, muri boe.*	East also and west also.
171.	*Lain bati malole*	The Heights distribute the good
172.	*Ma ata ba'e mandak*	The Heavens allocate the proper
173.	*Ruma mana parinda kisek mai a*	From them is a single rule
174.	*Numa tema sion mai*	From the fullness of nine
175.	*Numa bate falu mai ooo …*	From the completeness of eight …

Thie's Version of *Suti Solo do Bina Bane* in Relation to Other Versions

This version of *Suti Solo do Bina Bane* from Thie recounts the origin of rice and millet. It is the only version of a *Suti Solo do Bina Bane* chant for which, we are told, there was a specific ritual setting—one of the two annual origin ceremonies known as *Limbe* (or as *Limba* in some dialects) previously celebrated in Thie. The key to understanding this chant occurs in the lines (134 ff.) that proclaim:

Fo ela leo be na:	So let it be:
Natun kae ma rifun hene	A hundred rise and a thousand mount
Nai omba hade dei	At the rice field dike
Nai lane tiner dei.	And the dry field boundary.

There is no explanation that the phrase *natun kae ma rifun hene* ('a hundred rise and a thousand mount') is a ritual expression that alludes to waving grains in a field. The sense of these lines and their subsequent repetition (lines 149–52) and (161–65) would appear elusive. Significantly the chant acknowledges a ritual order of precedence in planting: the first planting of the seeds of rice and millet was not in Thie but at Dawning East// Reddening Headland (*Timu Dulu//Sepe Langga*), which, in this version, is given a Christian interpretation and identified as the land of the ancestor Ibrahim.

There are other elements of this chant that are elusive, particularly the invocation of specific places. The cause for the expulsion of the shells from beneath the sea is also different from other versions of the chant. However, in other respects, this version follows the standard pattern of most *Suti Solo do Bina Bane* chants: 1) an initial expulsion from the sea, 2) a tidal encounter with women who fish them from the sea and bring them onto land, and 3) a quest for an appropriate resting place phrased as a search by an 'orphan and widow'. Although some versions end with a return to the sea, others conclude with a resting place on Rote. In a truncated fashion, for example, the conclusion of this version of *Suti Solo do Bina Bane* resembles the conclusion of Kornalius Medah's version of *Suti Solo do Bina Bane* from Bilba. Instead of the Pandanus River road and the Forest Jasmine path leading to the Nilu Neo and Ko Nau trees, complete with 'the fullness of nine and the abundance of eight' (*tema sio// bate falu*), the shells in this version come to rest as seeds in fields that continue to produce their harvests—an order that presides over the Heavens and Heights 'in the fullness of nine and in the abundance of eight' (*tema sio//bate falu*).

17. VERSION I FROM THE DOMAIN OF THIE

An Analysis of the Ritual Language Usage of Ndun–Pah's *Suti Solo do Bina Bane*

This composition of 175 lines is composed of just 60 dyadic sets. In addition, the composition cites 14 distinct dyadic personal names and 10 dyadic place names. As with other compositions, a majority of the sets that make up this composition are common to most of the speech communities of the island. Thus, for example, the following basic dyadic sets are immediately recognisable: 1) *bete*//*hade* ('millet'//'rice'); 2) *ki*//*kona* ('north, left'//'south, right'); 3) *de'a*//*kola* ('speak'//'talk'); 4) *falu*//*sio* ('eight'//'nine'); 5) *da*//*oe* ('blood'//'water'); 6) *ta'ek*//*touk* ('boy'//'man'); 7) *fua*//*ndae* ('to place'//'to let hang down'); 8) *henu*//*lilo* ('golden beads'//'gold'); 9) *ata*//*lain* ('heights'//'heavens'); 10) *malole*//*mandak* ('good'//'proper').

A similar range of basic dyadic sets is also recognisable despite the various sound changes that occur in Thie dialect. Thus the 'p' in Termanu becomes 'mb' in Thie; 'ng' becomes 'ngg'; and some (but not all) 'l' in Termanu become 'r' in Thie. Thie dialect also appends a final 'r' to give emphasis to particular nouns. An illustrative list of these basic dyadic sets is: 1) *dulu*//*muri* ('east'//'west'); 2) *dulu*//*langga* ('east'//'head'); 3) *iko*//*muri* ('tail'//'west'); 4) *natun*//*rifun* ('hundred'//'thousand'); 5) *tafa*//*siro* ('sword'//'flintlock'); 6) *tati*//*siro* ('cut, slash'//'fire a flintlock'); 7) *langga*//*nggoe* ('head'//'snout'); 8) *mbeda*//*ndae* ('place'//'let hang down'); 9) *nda*//*-tonggo* ('meet'//'encounter'); 10) *ha'i*//*tengga* ('take, seize'//'lift, grasp'); 11) *ana mar*//*falu inar* ('orphan'//'widow'); 12) *rani*//*melu* ('warrior'//'defender').

In this composition, there are surprisingly few dyadic sets whose semantic elements are distinctive to Thie. One such set is *haradoi*//*kurudo*, which refers to 'problems, difficulties and sufferings'. The nearest equivalent in Bilba is *kelo-kea*//*tunu-hai* and in Termanu the dyadic set *toa*//*pia*.

There are, however, many grammatical features that distinguish this recitation as a composition in the dialect of Thie. The use of pronominals defines it as Thie dialect: thus where Termanu uses *ami* for the third-person plural inclusive, Thie uses *ai*; where Termanu uses *emi* for the second-person plural, Thie uses *ei*; and where Termanu uses *ala* for the third-person plural, Thie uses *ara*. Equally distinctive are the verbal forms *numa* (singular) and *ruma* (plural), indicating 'action from'. Termanu uses *neni* and *leni*.

A Comparison of Distinctive Refrains from Different Dialects

Although this recitation places less emphasis on dialogue directives, it highlights the initial plight of the shells and their search for a place of rest. Crucial to this version, as in other versions, is the decisive moment when they are scooped from the sea and brought onto dry land. The women Bui Len and Eno Lolo ask the shells:

'Ai ndae ei miu be?	'Where should we hang you?
Ma ai fua ei miu be?'	And where should we place you?'

The dyadic set used to indicate this placement is *ndae*//*fua* ('to hang'//'to place').

In reply, the shells ask to be placed in two trees:

'... *Fua ai miu*	'... Place us on
Ufa mabuna henu [kara]	The *ufa* tree full of gold-bead flowers
Ma Bau malusu lilok kara.'	And in the *bau* tree with golden blossoms.'

This location in the *ufa* and *bau* trees does not satisfy the shells, and their discomfort is indicated by a set refrain:

Ara bei ta ratetu	They still do not feel right
Ma bei ta randa.	And still do not yet feel good.

The shells then ask to be placed on two specific beams within the house:

'Ndae ai miu sema kona	'Hang us on the *sema kona*
Fua ai miu lunggu lai'	Place us on the *lunggu lai'*

This location also proves unsatisfactory and their discomfort is again indicated by the same refrain:

Bei ta ratetu	They still do not feel right

Ma bei ta randa.	And still do not feel proper.

Such refrains are indicative of each domain's (or each poet's) formulaic discourse. Here this refrain is based on the dyadic set *tetu//nda*. The two terms have a range of meanings but in this context, they indicate what is 'right' and 'proper' or 'fitting'. A similar refrain in Termanu relies on *tetu// tema*:

De tetun ta ndia boe	Order is not there then
Ma teman ta ndia boe.	And integrity is not there then.

Often this refrain is expressed in universal terms:

Tetun ta nai batu poik	Order is not of this world
Teman ta nai dae bafok	Integrity is not of this earth.

In Ringgou, the most common refrain based on the dyadic set *tesa//tama* (or *tesa tei//tama dale*) is:

Te tesa tei bei ta'a	There is no contentment there
Ma tama dale bei ta'a.	And there is no satisfaction there.

The equivalent refrain in Bilba is based on the dyadic set *tean//mepen*:

Tean o tak ma mepen o tak.	Nothing is certain and nothing lasting.

The 'Origin' Traditions of Thie and Their Significance

Although I gathered this version of *Suti Solo do Bina Bane* in 1973 and, with the help of Ena Pah and Paul Haning, was reasonably confident of its transcription and literal translation, I gained further understanding of its significance only after discussions with Jonas Mooy, who joined the Master Poets Project in 2011 and came again as a participant in 2013 and 2014. It was in discussing the chants in my earlier collection from Thie that I discovered that another of my long chants, *Masi Dande ma Solo Suti*, gathered in 1966 from Guru Pah—a chant of more than 550 lines— is the foundation for the other 'origin ceremony' of Thie. In addition, I have another chant from Guru Pah, *Bole Sou ma Asa Nou*, which also recounts the origin of rice and millet and, in its narrative, resembles this version of *Suti Solo do Bina Bane*. It is clear in retrospect that Guru Pah was concerned to impart to me in our brief encounters as much of the traditional knowledge of 'origins' as he could. The purpose here has been to situate Thie's version of *Suti Solo do Bina Bane* in relation to a wide range of other versions of this 'same' chant from the different domains and different ritual communities of Rote. At the same time, this telling of *Suti Solo do Bina Bane* needs to be considered in relation to the rich ritual traditions of Thie. It is appropriate that I was able to gather another version of *Suti Solo do Bina Bane* from Thie—this one by Jonas Mooy. In a ritual sense, though not in any strict compositional sense, these two recitations are the 'same chant'.

18
Suti Solo do Bina Bane: Version II from the Domain of Thie

I recorded this version of *Suti Solo do Bina Bane* from Jonas Mooy on 25 October 2011. The recording was done during the seventh recording session in Bali of the Master Poets Project. This was the second session of the project that Jonas Mooy attended. Earlier, in 2009, Pak Mooy, as I usually referred to him, had come to Bali with a group of four poets from Thie, three of whom were capable poets. Of these poets, one died before he could be invited back to Bali for more recording. In the end, it was Pak Mooy who was able to return for another recording session, at which he offered his version of *Suti Solo do Bina Bane*. Thereafter he joined the recording sessions in 2013 and 2014.

From the outset, Jonas Mooy was something of a curiosity for me. Perhaps the most avid and earnest of all the poets, Pak Mooy did not fit the pattern of any of the other poets. He was curiously 'bookish': always taking notes on the other poets and especially the genealogies they evoked in their recitations. He would invariably be scribbling in his notebook or on a piece of paper during our recording sessions. Gradually, I came to realise that he, in his curious way, was much like my colleague Esau Pono with whom I had worked for years. He took an interest not just in his own traditions of Thie but also in all of the diverse traditions of the island. He could and would reflect on Rote's different traditions and on the different recitations by his fellow poets, interpreting and comparing their significance. In time, I came to rely on him for insights on some of the more cryptic passages in recitations from different domains.

Pak Mooy explained to me that, as a young man, he wanted to become a teacher but instead he married early and settled down to ordinary Rotenese life. In time, he became a respected elder and began to master the use of ritual language. Although he never displayed the innate fluency of some master poets, his recitations were clear and coherent. He used our recording sessions to develop his skills. Thus, for example, Pak Mooy was particularly taken by the skills of Yulius Iu from Landu, whose speciality was to retell passages from the Bible in strict parallelism. He told me that, as a church elder, he would on occasion deliver sermons in the local church but these sermons were never in ritual language. However, during the fourth session with the group, he took up the challenge that I posed to him and he gave his own recitation: the Biblical passage of the Sermon on the Mount in strict, formal parallelism.

In 1966 and again in 1973, on visits to Oe Handi in Thie, I had recorded a corpus of chants, first from Guru Pah, and then from Guru Pak and his companion Sam Ndun. Initially, I read one or another of these chants to Pak Mooy, but when I came to realise his depth of understanding of his traditions, I shared most of this original corpus from Thie with him, asking him to give me his translation and interpretation of the texts.

Jonas Mooy's recitation of *Suti Solo do Bina Bane* was done before I had the chance to share with him the Pah–Ndun version of *Suti Solo do Bina Bane* that I had recorded in 1973. I showed him this version and my translation of it in 2014 because there were a number of puzzling elements. He was able to elucidate many passages and certainly correct some of my misinterpretations. More significantly, he insisted that his version was the same telling of *Suti Solo do Bina Bane* as that of Guru Pah and Sam Ndun. By this, he did not imply an identity of recitation but rather that his recitation was intended to cover the same cast of events and was told for the same ritual purposes: the celebration of the origin of rice and millet in Thie. It is critical to recognise in Pak Mooy's version the points of juncture that make the two versions the 'same' ritual chant.

The final lines in this recitation describe the ancestral establishment of one of the two *limba* or 'origin' ceremonies in Thie whose celebration, under pressure from the church, has long ceased to be performed. These lines contain references to important ritual elements of the ceremony.

18. VERSION II FROM THE DOMAIN OF THIE

Figure 22: Jonas Mooy

Suti Solo Liun Ma Bina Bane Saik

Suti Solo and Bina Bane Arrive at the Reef's Base and Sea's Edge

1.	*Bei hida fan na*	At a time long ago
2.	*Ma bei dalu don na*	And in an age long past
3.	*Lurik neu nala liun*	A cyclone strikes the ocean's depths
4.	*Ma sanggu neu tao sain*	And a storm strikes the sea's depths
5.	*Te inak ia Suti Solo sain*	The woman Suti Solo of the sea
6.	*Ma fetok ia Bina Bane liun*	And the girl Bina Bane of the ocean
7.	*Ara rama roko isi*	They exude their insides
8.	*Ma ara rama ketu nggi.*	And they cut loose their pods.
9.	*De rama tani sira nggin nara*	They cry for their pods
10.	*Ma rasa kedu sira isin nara*	And they sob for their insides
11.	*Ruma posi pedan ma unuk hun.*	At the sea's edge and reef's base.
12.	*Tehu ina mana-adu lolek*	The woman who creates beautifully
13.	*Ma feto mana-doki ladak*	And the girl who designs wonderfully
14.	*De rama tani unuk hun*	They cry at the reef's base
15.	*Ma bele halu posi pedan.*	And they are sad at the sea's edge.

The next lines introduce the women Lutu Koe and Rema Ko, who scoop in the sea and fish in the tide. They hear the shells calling and are told of their sad condition. The shells beg to be scooped up and placed on the edge of the shore.

The Woman Lutu Koe and the Girl Rema Ko Encounter Suti Solo and Bina Bane

16.	*Boe ma neu faik ia dalen*	Then on a particular day
17.	*Ma ledok ia tein*	And at a certain time
18.	*Feto mana-ndai tasi*	The girl who scoops in the sea
19.	*Fetok nade Lutu Koe*	The girl named Lutu Koe
20.	*Boema inak mana-seko meti*	And the woman who fishes in the tide
21.	*Inak nade Rema Ko*	The woman named Rema Ko

22.	*Ara su seko neu langgan*	They rest the fishnet on their heads
23.	*Ma ara ndae ndai neu arun.*	And they hang the scoop-net on their shoulders.
24.	*De ara loe mada loak reu*	They descend to the wide drying area
25.	*Ma ara loe meti naruk reu*	And they descend to the long tidal area
26.	*Ara losa posi pedan ma unuk hun*	They arrive at the sea's edge and reef's base
27.	*Boema ara rama-nene dasik kara ra-nggou*	They hear a voice shouting
28.	*Ma harakara haru kara ralo'o*	And they discern a tongue calling
29.	*Dua de'a-de'a dua*	The two speak with one another
30.	*Ma telu kola-kola telu:*	And the three talk with each other:
31.	*'Ai mama ketu nggi*	'We have cut our pods
32.	*Ma ai mama roko isi ia*	And exuded our insides
33.	*De ai mamatani ai nggi*	We are crying for our pods
34.	*Ma ai masakedu ai isin ia*	And sobbing for our insides
35.	*Hu sanggu ana tao ai*	A storm has done this to us
36.	*Ma lurik ana tao ai.*	And a cyclone has done this to us.
37.	*De torano dua nggarene*	My two relatives
38.	*Ma takadena dua nggarene,*	And my two companions,
39.	*Mai ndai tasi mini ai*	Come fish us from the sea
40.	*Ma seko meti mini ai dei*	And scoop us from the tide
41.	*Mbeda ai miu nembe hun dei*	Place us at the shore's edge
42.	*Ma tao ai miu oli su'un dei.'*	And put us at the estuary's mouth.'

The women agree to scoop up the shells and leave them near two trees along the shore. The shells ask that they come back and visit them at their resting place.

The Shells are Scooped Up and Placed Near Two Trees at the Edge of the Estuary

43.	*Boe ma dua sara rahik rala.*	So the two agree.
44.	*Ara seko meti reni sara*	They fish them up
45.	*Ma ara ndai tasi reni sara*	And they scoop them up
46.	*Tehu bei ra-ndeni aru*	But they are heavy on the shoulder

47.	*Ma bei ra-ta'a langga*	And weighty on the head
48.	*De ara losa nembe hun*	They come to the shore's edge
49.	*Ma oli su'un [bifin].*	And to the estuary's mouth.
50.	*Boema ara dua de'a-de'a dua ma rae:*	The two speak with each other and say:
51.	*'Ela ei mai ia leo*	'Let us set you here
52.	*Boema ai mbeda ei mai ia leo.*	Let us place you here.
53.	*Tehu ai helu ela ei duangga*	But we promise you two
54.	*Ai fedu ai sauk neu*	We will bend the *ai sauk* tree
55.	*Ma tumbu lenggu-ha'ik neu*	And we load the *lenggu-hai'k* tree
56.	*De ama rada mai ia leo*	That you may lean here
57.	*Ma ama tia mai ia leo.'*	And that you may attach here.'
58.	*Boe ma rae:*	So they say:
59.	*'Ei ela ai duangga mai ia*	'If you leave the two of us here
60.	*Do tehu, mai la'o ladi ai dei*	Do still come stop and see us
61.	*Ma mai lope tule ai dei*	And come swing past and visit us
62.	*Tehu ai mai bengga lada mbeda*	For we come to offer delicious nourishment
63.	*Ma ai mai tou lole heu ia.*	And we come to provide fine attire here.
64.	*Ai tu'u sara sira*	We can hold ourselves here
65.	*Ai mbeda sara sira*	We can place ourselves here
66.	*Ara reu de ara losa uma.'*	When you leave and return to your house.'
67.	*Boe ma ara rama nene*	They listen
68.	*Ma ara raka-se'e bebenggu*	And they are noisy as horses' bells
69.	*Ma ara raka-doto kokoro,*	And they are as lively as *kokolo* birds,
70.	*Numa olik su'un ma nembe hun.*	At the edge of the estuary and shore's base.

The ancestral founders of Thie, Tola Mesa and Le'e Lunu, go to see what has happened after the storm. They arm themselves but they only encounter the two shells, who plead with them not to fire their flintlocks or draw their swords. The shells ask to be wrapped in cloth and taken to the house.

Tola Mesa and Le'e Lunu Encounter Suti Solo and Bina Bane

71.	*Boe ma bai ia baing Tola Mesa*	Our grandfather of grandfathers, Tola Mesa
72.	*Ma ai soro ia sorong Le'e Lunu*	And our ancestor of ancestors, Le'e Lunu
73.	*Ara hengge bosan nara reu*	They tie their pouch
74.	*De ara ndae tafa nara reu*	And they hang their sword
75.	*De rae fama kate*	They then consider
76.	*Lurik mai tao sira*	The cyclone comes to strike them
77.	*Do sanggu mai tao sira*	And the storm comes to strike them
78.	*De reu mete ma reu suri.*	They go to look and go to see.
79.	*Reu de ara sudi sira su'u reu sara*	They go, ready to fire their flintlocks
80.	*Ma ara ndae tafa dale reu sara*	And set to draw out their swords
81.	*Ara rahara ma rae:*	They answer and say:
82.	*'Boso sudi sira su'u ai*	'Don't fire your flintlocks at us
83.	*Ma boso ndae tafa dale ai.*	And don't draw your swords at us.
84.	*Te ai mini lole heu rai ia*	For we bring fine attire here
85.	*Ma ai mini lada mbeda rai ia.*	And we bring delicious nourishment here.
86.	*De ei lai ai*	Have sympathy for us
87.	*Boe ma ei sue ai boe*	And have care for us
88.	*Na pa'a pou su'u mini ai dei*	Wrap us in a sarong and take us
89.	*Ma hengge bosa dale mini ai dei*	Tie us in a pouch and take us
90.	*Miu ndae ai miu fara tanar dei*	Hang us on the door post
91.	*Ma mbeda ai miu lulutu nasun dei.'*	And place us at the fence's base.'

The shells instruct Tola Mesa and Le'e Lulu to take up a flat stone from the harbour and cut a tree from near the shore and bring them, along with the shells, to become the focus for the first origin feast. These critical ritual instructions include preparation for the 'coconut-holding post'.

The Ancestors are Instructed to Obtain the 'Rock and Tree' for the Origin Ceremony

92.	*Boe ma bai-ia baing Tola Mesa*	So my grandfather of grandfathers, Tola Mesa
93.	*Ma soro ia sorong Le'e Lulu rae:*	And my ancestor of ancestors, Le'e Lulu say:
94.	*'Mete ma leonak*	'If this is so, then
95.	*Na ma hehere fo ita la'o*	Fold it so that we may go
96.	*Do ma bebenda fo ita la'o.'*	Or save it so that we may go.'
97.	*Ara pa'a pou su'u reu sara*	They wrap a woman's sarong around them
98.	*Ma ara mboti lafa una neu sara*	And they fold a man's cloth around them
99.	*Ma ara ra selu reu sara rae:*	They reply, saying:
100.	*'Mete ma ei pa'a pou*	'If you wrap the sarong
101.	*Ma hengge bosa meni ai*	And strap the pouch to take us
102.	*Na tati ai nia nembe dei*	Then cut the tree near the shore
103.	*Ma ei hengge bosa muni ai*	And strap with the belt to take us
104.	*Na ko'o batu bela namo dei*	Cradle a flat stone by the harbour
105.	*Fo mu tian neu tu'u batu*	Balance it as a resting stone
106.	*Ma ama fara neu rai ai*	And plant it as a standing pole
107.	*Fo ai masa-rai dei*	For us to lean upon
108.	*Ma ai mangga-tu'u dei.*	And for us to rest upon.
109.	*Boe ma ama sau leli sara dei*	So we may comb ourselves gently
110.	*Ma ama tusi bangga na'us sara dei.'*	And we may rub ourselves softly.'
111.	*Boe ma ko'o reni batu bela namo*	Then they cradle a flat stone from the harbour
112.	*De reu de ara tao neu tu'u batu*	They go and make it a resting stone
113.	*De ana dadi neu oli do limba*	To be used for an origin and harvest ceremony
114.	*Boe ma ara ha'i rala ai nia nembe*	And they take a tree from the shore
115.	*De ara fara no tu'u batu*	They plant it with the resting stone
116.	*De ana dadi neu rai ai*	To make it a leaning post
117.	*Fo dadi neu fara no.*	To become the coconut-holding post.

The lines that follow indicate the performance of an initial ritual celebration intended to bring the rains and prepare the earth for the planting of seeds. The instructions for the ceremony centre on the coconut that will 'distribute the dew and allot the rain' to prepare the earth for planting. When, after the ceremony, the rains have fallen, the shells give instructions for their own planting at particular named fields.

A Celebration Brings the Rains and Prepares the Earth for the Planting of Seeds

118.	*De ara hene Tola Mesa non*	They climb Tola Mesa's coconut
119.	*Ma ketu Le'e Lulu non*	And they pluck Le'e Lulu's coconut
120.	*De ara leli sau neu sara.*	They soften and cool them.
121.	*Boe ma ara bamba lololo neu sara*	They beat the drum steadily
122.	*De ana ba'e dinis mai dae*	It distributes the dew upon the earth
123.	*Ma ana bati udan mai lane.*	And it allots the rain upon the fields.
124.	*Boe ma rae:*	So they say:
125.	*'Udan dai dae ena*	'If the rain is sufficient for the earth
126.	*Ma dinis konda lane ena*	And the dew falls upon the fields
127.	*Tehu ai mini bini buik nai ia*	Then we bring the basic grains with us here
128.	*Ma mbule sio nai ia.*	And the nine seeds with us here.
129.	*De mete-ma ei mai pake do hambu*	If you want to use them and have them
130.	*Na keko seluk ai dei*	Then move us again
131.	*Ma lali seluk ai dei*	And shift us again
132.	*Fo ela neu lada mbeda*	To become delicious nourishment
133.	*Ma ela neu lole heu.*	And become fine attire.
134.	*De mete ma ei mae leo nak*	If you agree to this
135.	*Na keko ai miu*	Then move us
136.	*Fafa'e Tali Somba dei*	To Fafa'e Tali Somba
137.	*Fo tande ai miu na*	To plant us there
138.	*Boema lali ai miu*	And shift us
139.	*Teke Me Re'ik Oen dei*	To Teke Me Re'ik Oen
140.	*Fo sele ai miu na.'*	To sow us there.'

Following instructions from the shells, the planting is begun and the seeds sprout. The first fields in Thie where the seeds are planted are: 1) Fafa'e Tali Somba; 2) Teke Me Re'ik Oen; 3) Mundek Na'u Dale; and 4) Nggonggoer No Lasi Lain. Thereafter, these plants are spread throughout Rote. The place name Ledo So'u//Anda Iko indicates an area that extends from the east to the west of Rote, while the place name Pena Pua//Rene Kona connotes an area from the north to the south of Rote. Significantly, it is emphasised that orphans and widows are the ones to consume the harvest of rice and millet.

The Planting of the Seeds Begins in Fields in Thie and Thereafter Throughout Rote

141.	*Ara sele neu*	They sow them
142.	*Fafa'e Tali Somba*	At Fafa'e Tali Somba
143.	*Ma ara tande neu*	And they plant them
144.	*Teke Me Re'ik Oen.*	At Teke Me Re'ik Oen.
145.	*Boe ma ara do dua*	They form two leaves
146.	*Ma ara beba telu*	And form three stalks
147.	*De mbule na tatali*	Seeds with sprouts
148.	*Ma don na sese'i*	And leaves with spikes
149.	*Boe ma ara dadi reu lada mbeda*	They become delicious nourishment
150.	*Ma ara moli reu lole heu.*	And they turn into fine attire.
151.	*Boema ara keko neu*	They move them
152.	*Mundek Na'u Dale*	To Mundek Na'u Dale
153.	*Boema ara lali neu*	They shift them
154.	*Nggonggoer No Lasi Lain.*	To Nggonggoer No Lasi Lain.
155.	*De ana ndule losa Ledo So'u*	It spreads to Ledo So'u
156.	*Ma ana losa nala Anda Iko*	And to Anda Iko
157.	*Ki losa Pena Pua*	North to Pena Pua
158.	*Ma kona losa Rene Kona.*	And south to Rene Kona.
159.	*De ana mar ara fati hade*	The orphans consume rice
160.	*Ma ina falur ra ara hao bete*	And the widows eat millet
161.	*Ela lole heur bali*	Enjoy fine attire
162.	*Ma lada mbeda bali.*	And delicious food.

The next stage in this recitation marks the 'institutionalisation' of the origin ceremony. A sacred space is created around a 'sitting stone and standing tree' where there is dancing and the beating of drums and gongs to bring cooling rain down on the earth. Although initially rice and millet are planted, the chant expands its designation of what is planted, referring to 'the nine seeds and the basic grains, the nine children of Lakamola'. This is a ritual designation for all of the seeds that Rotenese plant in their fields.

The Perpetuation of the *Limba* Ceremony in Thie

163.	*De ara tia neu tu'u batu*	They create a sitting stone
164.	*De ara tao neni rai ai*	They make a standing tree
165.	*De mete ma fain na-nda*	So that when the day comes
166.	*Ma ledo na-tetu*	And the time arrives
167.	*Na ha'i nala babamba mba'u bibi rouk*	They take a drum sounding with goat's skin
168.	*No meko riti fani oen*	And a gong whose beat is sweet as bees' honey
169.	*Fo mu lutu mbatu lain*	To climb on top of piled stone
170.	*Fo bamba mbaun kurudo*	To drum with a begging sound
171.	*Ma dali sole hara doe*	And dance with a requesting voice
172.	*Ma lo neu Mana Adu Lain*	Calling upon the Creator of the Heaven
173.	*Fo Mana Adu Deti Ledo*	The Creator who shaped the Sun
174.	*Ma Mana Sura Ndu Bulan*	And who drew the Stars and Moon
175.	*Ma lo neu Mana Adu Lalai*	Calling to the Creator Above
176.	*Ma dae bafok*	For the surface of the earth
177.	*Tasi oe no isin*	The sea with its contents
178.	*Ma hatahori do andi ana*	Mankind and humankind
179.	*Fo ana monu fei*	To let fall
180.	*Ha'u dini makasufuk*	A gentle dampening dew
181.	*Ma uda oe makarinik*	And cooling rain water
182.	*Fo ana tolite batu poik*	To pour upon the world
183.	*Ma ana bibiru dae bafak.*	And to cool the earth.
184.	*Boe ma ana totoli laner*	It pours upon the rice fields
185.	*Ma ana tete tiner*	And it drips upon the dry fields

186.	*Fo tande mpule sio neun*	To plant the nine seeds
187.	*Ma sele bini bui'k neun.*	And sow the basic grains.
188.	*Fo Laka Mola anan sio.*	The nine children of Laka Mola.
189.	*Fo ela leo be na*	So it is thus
190.	*Ara rabuna fefeo*	They carry flowers that wind round
191.	*Na ra fefeo rifuk*	Wind a thousandfold
192.	*Na deta leo rifu ana tali do*	Like a thousand winding cords
193.	*Boe ara rambule roroso*	They set seeds that spread round
194.	*Na ra roroso natu*	Spread round a hundredfold
195.	*Na leo natu ana bolao.*	Like a hundred tiny spiders.
196.	*Fo ha'i malan fo mu'a*	Take them to eat
197.	*Fo tengga malan fo pake*	Grab them to use
198.	*Ma lo neu falu inar*	And provide for the widows
199.	*Fo ita tesik be na*	For those of us present
200.	*Teik esa ma dalek esa*	One stomach and one heart
201.	*Boe ma ita hambu lada mbeda*	We have delicious food
202.	*Ma lole heu*	And fine clothing
203.	*Tuda ma monu mai dae bafok*	Fallen and descended upon the earth
204.	*Boe ma lenak Rote Ndao.*	Particularly on Rote Ndao.

Comparing the Two Versions of *Suti Solo do Bina Bane* as Origin Chants

There is a span of 38 years between my recording of the first version of *Suti Solo do Bina Bane* and my recording of the second version. Guru Pah and Sam Ndun, from whom I recorded the first version, were among the oldest members of their community in 1973 and had undoubtedly seen, and possibly participated in, the origin celebration for which their recitation provides a cosmological foundation. Yet there is no mention of the origin ceremonies in their recitation; their composition is an account of the origins of the planting of rice and millet in Thie.

By contrast, for Jonas Mooy, who was 63 at the time of my recording in 2011, Thie's origin ceremonies could only be a memory; yet his recitation is concerned both with the planting of rice and millet and with the establishment of the first origin ceremonies.

A most interesting contrast between the two versions of *Suti Solo do Bina Bane* from Thie and most other versions is that almost from the moment the shells are fished from the sea, they begin issuing instructions about precisely where they should be placed and how they should be treated. There is no dialogue in their interaction with those who carry them from the sea.

It is also interesting to compare the ritual sites named in the first version with those in the second version. The first version recounts a succession of seven named sites; by contrast, the second version names only three sites, two of which are, however, the same as in the first version.

Table 16: Ritual Sites in Thie's Two Versions of *Suti Solo do Bina Bane*

First version:	Second version:
	1) Teke Me//Re'ik Oen
1) Deras//Le Lena	
2) Mundek//Na'u Dalek	2) Mundek//Na'u Dale
3) Rote//Kode Ana	
4) Oe Batu//Bau Foe	
5) Kone Ama//Sai Fua	
6) Nggonggoer//Lasi Lai	3) Nggonggoer No//Lasi Lain
7) Liti//Sera Dale	

The second version goes on to extend the planting of rice and millet—and of seeds in general—from Thie to the rest of the island. The ritual names Ledo So'u//Anda Iko and Pena Pua//Rene Kona are not actual place names but are dyadic sets that Jonas Mooy has created (from well-known domain names) to indicate the whole of the island. Ledo So'u is taken from the name of the domain of Oepao, Fai Fua ma Ledo Sou, at the eastern end of the island; Anda Iko from the name of the domain of Delha, Deli Muri ma Anda Iko, at the western end of Rote; Pena Pua from the name of the domain of Ba'a, Pena Pua ma Maka Lama, on the northern coast; while Rene Kona comes from one of the names for Thie, Tada Muri ma Rene Kona, on the southern coast.

The Role of the Coconut in the Origin Ceremony of Thie

In the second version, there is a particular emphasis on the coconut that the ancestors must gather and bring to the ceremony. Although it is not made explicit, this coconut is the focus of the origin ceremony: it brings 'gentle dampening dew and the cool rainwater' that pour down upon the earth.

In 1921, the Dutch colonial officer B. Koopmans, at the end of his tour of duty, wrote a long report on Rote, *Memorie van Overgave*, for his successor. In this *Memorie*, he describes an origin ceremony, which he apparently observed in Thie. His observations are, however, brief and inserted in a rambling disquisition on the comparative religions of the world, which makes up almost one-quarter of his transfer report.

According to these observations, an uneven number of women would first form a row by locking arms across each other's backs and then would dance in a circle around a pole that was less than 1m high on which was placed a young coconut. As they circled the pole, one of the dancers—the one who was the most decorated with golden ornaments—reached out and took the coconut and placed it three times between her legs. Thereafter all of the women adjourned to a nearby sacred house, where they were sprinkled with coconut water so that they would have as many children as 'the stars in the heavens and the sands on the beach' (Koopmans 1921: 18).

In Thie, the traditional marriage ceremony also centred on the use of a coconut whose fertility was invoked. This invocation gives some idea of the symbolism of the coconut:

No ia, tadak lima:	This coconut has five layers:
Mbunu holu so'en	The husk embraces the shell
So'en holu isin	The shell embraces the flesh
Isin holu oen	The flesh embraces the water
Ma oen holu mbolon.	And the water embraces the kernel.
De ela leo be na:	So let it be:
Ana touk ma ana inak-kia	That this boy and this girl
Ela esa holu esa	Let one embrace the other
Ma ela lili esa	And let one cling to the other

Fo ela numbu non ana dadi	That the sprout of the coconut may come forth
Ma sadu mbuan ana mori	And the core of areca nut may appear
Fo ela bonggi sio lai sio	That they may give birth to nine times nine
Ma rae falu lai falu.	And bring forth eight times eight.

Ritual Language Usage in Jonas Mooy's Version of *Suti Solo do Bina Bane*

Jonas Mooy's recitation of 204 lines is composed of 93 dyadic sets. This includes several formulaic sets that cannot be meaningfully analysed into component sets: 1) *data don//hida fan*; 2) *fara tanar//lulutu nasun*; or 3) *bini buik//mbule sio*. However, the majority of these dyadic sets, as in other versions of *Suti Solo do Bina Bane*, belong to a recognisable island-wide repertoire of similar dyadic sets. Given the similar focus of each of the texts, it is not surprising that these sets are familiar: 1) *liun//sain* ('ocean'//'sea'); 2) *fetok//inak* ('girl'//'woman'); 3) *lafa//pou* ('male cloth'//'female cloth'); 4) *fai//ledo* ('day'//'sun'); 5) *dale//tei* ('inside, heart'//'stomach'); 6) *-ndai//-seko* ('to fish with a net'//'to use a scoop-net'); 7) *meti//tasi* ('tide'//'sea'); 8) *ai//batu* ('tree'//'rock'); 9) *de'a//kola* ('to speak'//'to talk'); 10) *dua//telu* ('two'//'three'); 11) *ki//kona* ('left, north'//'right, south'); 12) *bete//hade* ('millet'//'rice').

Equally familiar are terms that reflect the sound changes that distinguish the dialect of Thie from that of Termanu. Among these differences are the use of 'r' in Thie where Termanu uses 'l'; the use of 'ngg' where Termanu has 'ng'; the use of 'mb' where Termanu has 'p'; and the use of final 'r' for emphasis where Termanu would use final 'k'. Examples of these sets are the following:

Table 17: Termanu–Thie Dialect Comparisons

Termanu	Thie	Gloss
alu//langa	aru//langga	'shoulder'//'head'
loa//naru	loa//naru	'wide'//'long'
lulik//sangu	lurik//sanggu	'storm'//'cyclone'
dasi//halu	dasi//haru	'song'//'voice'
bebengu//kokolo	bebenggu//kokoro	'to sound'//'to ring'
henge//pa'a	hengge//pa'a	'to tie'//'to bind, fence'
-lai//-tu'u	-rai//-tu'u	'to stand'//'to sit'

Termanu	Thie	Gloss
do//pule	do//mbule	'leaf'//'seed'
ana mak//falu inak	ana mar//falu inar	'orphan'//'widow'
natu//lifu	natu//rifu	'hundred'//'thousand'
feo//loso	fefeo//roroso	'to wind'//'to creep'
-linik//-sufuk	-rinik//-sufuk	'to cool'//'to make fresh'
bapa//meko	bamba//meko	'drum'//'gong'

Yet more interesting are the dyadic sets in Jonas Mooy's recitation that are distinctive to Thie: first among these expressions is the set *limba//oli*. This is a dyadic set used to designate Thie's origin ceremony; in Termanu, this ceremony is referred to by the dyadic set *hu(s)//sio*, which may be translated as 'the feast of origin'//'the celebration of nine'. Another set is *takadena//torano*, which is used to refer to a 'relative, close companion'; the equivalent in Termanu is *tola-tunga//dudi-no*. Both expressions relate to the term *tolano* (Thie: *torano*), which is used, in ordinary language, for a 'relative'. For 'human being or person', Thie uses the dyadic set *andiana//hatahori*. Thie also has a special expression for 'ancestors', *ba'i//soro*, which combines the terms for 'grandfather' and 'great grandfather'. Another set of particular relevance to this composition is *bini buik//mbule sio* ('the basic grains'//'the nine seeds'). There is no exact equivalent in Termanu but Ringgou's ritual language uses the set *pule sio//poko falu* ('the nine seeds'//'the eight kernels'); Dengka has *mbule sio//la'a mola* ('the nine seeds and eaten grains'). Finally, Thie utilises the set *lada mbeda//lole heu*, for which it is difficult to find an appropriate translation. This formula has as one of its components the well-known set *lada//lole*. *Lada* carries the notion of 'taste, good taste', while *lole* connotes what is 'beautiful, lovely, pleasant'. The only explanation that I was able to obtain for this formula as a whole is that it refers to the 'taste of food'//'attractiveness of clothing'.

The Formula for 'A Time Long Ago'

Some of the most recurrent formulae in ritual language are difficult to translate in any literal sense. In the first lines of his recitation, Jonas Mooy uses a formula of this kind:

Bei hida fan na	At a time long ago
Ma bei dalu don na	And in an age long past

This is a common formula with which to begin an origin narrative. To translate it literally makes little sense: 'still (how) much little'//'still long time'. More interesting is the variety of forms that this formula takes.

Guru Pah uses the following formula:

Hida bei fan na	At a time long ago
Dalu bei don na	At a period long past

But he also uses this formula in slightly abbreviated form:

Bei dalu don	Still in a former time
Do hida fan	Or in a bygone period

The poet Pe'u Malesi also uses this formula as follows:

Hida dodo bei leo fan	Once long ago

The poet A. Amalo, from Termanu, uses yet another variation on this formula:

Hida hatan ma data don-na	In a former period and a past time

Ande Ruy, in his version of *Suti Solo do Bina Bane*, uses the formula in this way:

Hida bei leo hatan	At a time long ago
Ma data bei leo dona	At a period long past

Each of these expressions is translated in a slightly different way to convey the range of variation in this formula. To some extent, each poet uses a slightly different variant as a personal signature of his style of composition.

19

Suti Saik ma Bina Liuk: Two Versions from the Domain of Dengka

For the third recording session in Bali—in the last week of October 2008—I was able to invite several poets from Dengka. Two of these poets, Simon Lesik and Frans Lau, proved to be true master poets, but were remarkably different in their approach to recitation.

Simon Lesik was a simple farmer and herdsman but a firm upholder of Rotenese traditions who seems not to have fully identified himself as a Christian. He was stunningly fluent and recited rapidly with personal authority and confidence. He completely dominated the recording session on Bali with his various recitations.

Simon Lesik's recitations were exuberant and revelatory, each casting a glimpse on Dengka's canonical traditions. The narrative of these recitations, however, was not particularly well structured. In fact, many of his recitations appeared to lack coherence because in the midst of a recitation he would go off on some interesting tangent. In his various recitations, Simon Lesik would proceed less by direct narrative and more by invoking elements of a tradition that he took for granted and assumed his listeners were aware of. His recitations consisted of bits of narrative with a succession of lines that variously alluded to different aspects of Dengka's oral traditions. These recitations were dense and difficult and I had to rely on Frans Lau, who had been a schoolteacher for most of his life, to assist me with the transcription, translation and exegesis of his outpourings. Simon Lesik saw no problem in offering two versions of the same chant, adding to his second version material that would seem to change the perspective of his earlier version. He did this in particular with his recitations of *Suti Solo do Bina Bane*.

Figure 23: Simon Lesik

19. TWO VERSIONS FROM THE DOMAIN OF DENGKA

In this chapter, I have included two recitations by Simon Lesik. The first of these versions is a fragment of a recitation that went off on a tangent to describe the illness and death of a particular chant character. After concluding, he recognised that this had happened and, for this reason, he recited a second version, which was slightly more focused. The two versions, at best, hint at an account that links the shells to their origin in the creation of the implements for dyeing.

In these versions, Suti Solo do Bina Bane undergo a name change—or, more precisely, the names of the shells are shortened: instead of Suti Solo do Bina Bane, they become Suti Saik do Bina Liuk ('Suti of the Sea or Bina of the Ocean'). More significantly, they are identified as female creatures.

Simon Lesik's First Version of *Suti Saik ma Bina Liuk*

This first version has various lines that are by no means clear. At the outset it offers specific references to chant characters whose significance is not explained elsewhere in the recitation. Thus, for example, references are made at the beginning of this recitation to the orphan Ola Oen and the widow Laba Daen, the orphan Ndule Daen and the widow Ndule Oen, but nothing more is spoken of them. Following this, the woman Tau Tenggu Bulan and the girl Kudu Henu Ledo are introduced. Although it is rare that ritual names are fully decipherable, most names contain elements that allude to that character's significance. In this case, the elements *Bulan*//*Ledo* ('Moon'//'Sun') indicate that these women are the heavenly children of the Sun and Moon (Ledo do Holo). More significant are the elements *Tau*//*Kudu* ('Indigo'//'*Morinda* Dye'). These terms identify Tau Tenggu Bulan//Kudu Henu Ledo as one of the chief characters involved in the chant of the origin of weaving and dyeing. In this first version, Tau Tenggu Bulan and Kudu Henu Ledo are the women who descend to the sea with their fishnets and scoop up Suti Saik and Bina Liuk.

1.	*Fai ia,*	This day,
2.	*Fai fua nafade*	Day dawns, they say
3.	*Ma ledo so'u nade'a.*	And sun rises, they speak.
4.	*Boe ma tonggo langga,*	They go to meet,
5.	*Ta tonggo*	But do not meet
6.	*Ma nda lima,*	They go to encounter,

7.	*Ta nda.*	But do not encounter.
8.	*Ala hahate falu-ina*	They remember the widows
9.	*Ma ala kokoni ana-ma.*	And they celebrate the orphans.
10.	*Ana-ma Ola Oen*	The orphan Ola Oen
11.	*Ma falu-ina Laba Daen,*	And the widow Laba Daen,
12.	*Ana-ma Ndule Dae boe*	The orphan Ndule Dae, too
13.	*Ma falu-ina Ndule Oe boe.*	And the widow Ndule Oe, too.
14.	*Na lele na ala e'o ina la*	At a time, they carry the women
15.	*Tau Tenggu Bulan*	Tau Tenggu Bulan
16.	*Ma feto a, Kudu Henu Ledo,*	And the girl Kudu Henu Ledo,
17.	*Ina mana ndai tasi*	A woman who fishes in the sea
18.	*Ma feto mana seko meti.*	And a girl who scoops in the tide.
19.	*Ha'i nala ndai tasi*	She takes her sea fishing net
20.	*Ma e'o nala seko metin*	And picks up her tidal scoop-net
21.	*Ndai mia unu*	To fish on the rocky reef
22.	*Mana maka-mu meko nala*	That sounds like a gong
23.	*Ma seko mia posi*	And to scoop at the sandy edge
24.	*Mana-mali labu.*	That pounds like a drum.

In these lines, when Tau Tenggu Bulan and Kudu Henu Ledo scoop up Suti Saik and Bina Liuk, there occurs a succession of lines that describe how the two shells danced before they were struck by the storm. Neither the dancing nor the cause of the storm is explained but instead the power of the storm is described: flattening everything especially coconut and areca palms and causing the shells to lose their insides.

25.	*Neu boe ma ana ndai nala.*	When she arrives there, she fishes.
26.	*Bina ma-edo nggi*	Bina, who exudes her pods
27.	*Ma solo nala*	And she scoops
28.	*Suti mana-loko isi.*	Suti, who issues forth her insides.
29.	*Te hu ana sole bebeu ein*	But she dances on her leg
30.	*Ma ana lendo lalai liman.*	And she turns quickly on her arm.
31.	*Tehu ana lendo nalesi sain*	But she turns outside the sea
32.	*Ma ana sole nalena liun.*	And she dances beyond the ocean.
33.	*Boe ma lae:*	So they say:
34.	*'To! Te ina bek ka ia?'*	'Oh! But what woman is this?'

35.	*De ana sole na lena liun*	She dances beyond the ocean
36.	*Ma ana lendo na lesi sain.'*	And she turns outside the sea.'
37.	*Sanggu nala liun dale*	A storm strikes the ocean's depths
38.	*Ma lulik nala sain dale.*	And a cyclone strikes the sea's depths.
39.	*Sanggu tao bela-bela*	The storm flattens everything
40.	*Ma lulik tao mefu-mefu.*	And the cyclone strikes everything.
41.	*Mbua ma-nggi lesu*	The areca palm with firm inflorescences
42.	*Ladi lesu na*	Snaps its inflorescence
43.	*Boe ma no ma-oka o*	The coconut with deep roots
44.	*Foi hun na boe.*	Uproots its trunk.
45.	*Suti Saik ko loko isin na*	Suti Saik exudes its insides
46.	*Ma Bina Liuk ko edo nggi na boe.*	And Bina Liuk turns out its pods.
47.	*Tehu Suti la-loko isin*	But Suti exudes its insides
48.	*Tehu ela Suti loun*	Leaving only Suti's shell
49.	*Ma Bina la-edo nggi nala*	And Bina turns outs its pods
50.	*Tehu ela Bina nggin.*	Leaving only Bina's pods.
51.	*Ala haladoi tungga namo*	They suffer, passing through the harbours
52.	*Ma sisi tungga meti.*	And are in pain, passing through the tides.

The next lines recount attempts to find shelter for the suffering shells. These lines resemble some of the 'placements' that occur in other versions of *Suti Solo do Bina Bane* where the location of each placement proves imperfect and therefore unsatisfactory. In these lines, however, Suti Saik ma Bina Liuk do not engage in extended dialogue, as is often the case in other versions of this chant. Instead they speak only once, indicating where they wish to be placed. The lines that describe the placement of the shells on the 'hill of black buffalo and the field of white goats' are in fact repeated. Following these lines, the shells are taken to the west of Rote, to the domain of Delha, Dela Muli ma Anda Kona.

53.	*Leo na ka boe ma*	Because of this then
54.	*Leu ndai lendi se [sia]*	They go, fish and carry them
55.	*Leu boe ma mbeda se [sia]*	And go and place them
56.	*Mia eno telu mandak*	On three appropriate paths
57.	*Ma dala dua i'ifan.*	And two cradled roads.

58.	*Tehu hataholi fe'a momolo*	But men still step [there]
59.	*Ma andiana fe'a tatabu.*	And people still tread [there].
60.	*Ala fe'a sisi*	They are still in pain
61.	*Ma ala fe'a hala doi.*	And they still suffer.
62.	*'Tendi sa lisi mok a leu*	'Let us be carried to the field
63.	*Ma lete a leu*	And to the hill
64.	*Ata bambi sa mok a.*	So that we may hide in the field.
65.	*Ta'a bambi sa Mbila Fume Lete*	Let us hide at Mbila Fume Lete
66.	*Ma ta'a sulu sa Nau Langga Loe Lesu.'*	And let us take cover at Nau Langga Loe Lesu.'
67.	*Tehu: fai nama tua dulu*	But the day grows great in the east
68.	*Ma ledo nama hana langga*	And the sun grows hot at the head
69.	*Boe ma Suti loun fe'a sisi*	Suti's shell is still in pain
70.	*Ma Bina nggi fe'a haladoi.*	And Bina's pod still suffers.
71.	*Boe te hu ala e'o selu fai*	So they shift them again
72.	*Lisi lete ngge-nggeo kapa*	Carrying them to the hill of black buffalo
73.	*Ma mo mumuti bi'in.*	And the field of white goats.
74.	*Lete nalu mana'a*	The hill is indeed high
75.	*Ma mo loa malole.*	And the field is truly wide.
76.	*Leu mbeda ma lete*	They go to place them on the hill
77.	*Ma mbeda ma mo.*	And place them on the field.
78.	*Boe nau langga napa lesu*	The tall grass withers
79.	*Do nama sesu neu bu'un na boe.*	Or bends toward its base.
80.	*Ala bambi ho.*	They hide you.
81.	*Fai nama tua dulu*	Day grows great in the east
82.	*Ma ledo nama nalu langga.*	And the sun grows long at the head.
83.	*Boe ma Suti lou na fe'a sisi*	Suti's shell is still in pain
84.	*Ma Bina nggi na fe'a haladoi.*	And Bina's pod still suffers.
85.	*Boe ma ala e'o selu sala*	They move them badly again
86.	*Lete ngge-nggeo kapa nala*	The hill is black with water buffalo
87.	*Ma mo mu-muti bi'in.*	And the field is white with goats.
88.	*Na letek ia, lete nalu mana'a*	This hill is indeed a high hill
89.	*Ma mok ia, mo loa malole.*	And this field is truly a wide field.

90.	*De leu mbeda ma lete*	They go to place them on the hill
91.	*Ma mbeda ma mok.*	And place them in the field.
92.	*Tehu fai na ala hahate*	But one day they realise
93.	*Lete ma nggeo kapa*	The hill of black water buffalo
94.	*Ma mok mumuti bi'i.*	And the field of white goats.
95.	*De bote bi'in fe'a fefetun*	The flock of goats still treads
96.	*Ma tena kapan fe'a hahangge.*	And the herd of buffalo still tramples.
97.	*Boe ala fe'a sisi ma hala doi.*	They still suffer and are in pain.
98.	*Deide ala e'o sala ma ala lali*	They lift them and shift them
99.	*Ala lali sala lisi Dela Muli*	They transfer them to Dela Muli.

Simon Lesik's Second Version of *Suti Saik ma Bina Liuk*

Simon Lesik's second version of *Suti Saik ma Bina Liuk* takes an entirely different direction in the telling of this chant. The intersection of the two versions occurs in Delha with the woman Seu Dela and the girl Fale Anda. The first version can be considered as the prelude to the second; however, the retrieval of the shells from the sea is done by another two women.

This second version begins, somewhat confusingly, with the birth of the woman Sina Kona and the girl Koli Mola, whose mother, it is mentioned, is Seu Dela. She is described as a woman who prepares cloth and who dyes thread. (The short genealogy is, however, flawed because lines 8–9 do not provide a proper succession of names—from father to daughter.) In any case, it is the mother, Seu Dela ma Fale Anda, who becomes the focus of the recitation.

In this telling, Sina Kona and Koli Mola go directly to the house of the Great Lord of the Sea, Langga Lena Liu and Manatua Sain, and there they scoop up Suti Saik and Bina Liuk and bring them to Delha.

1.	*Tehu touk ia mana bonggik*	But this man, he begets
2.	*Ma ta'ek ia mana laek*	And this boy, he brings forth
3.	*Ana lae ela Sina Kona*	He brings forth Sina Kona
4.	*Ma ana bonggi ela Koli Mola.*	And he begets Koli Mola.
5.	*Ana bonggi nala ina esa Sina Kona*	He brings forth the one woman, Sina Kona

6.	*Ma feto ia Koli Mola.*	And this girl, Koli Mola.
7.	*Ma ala hahate*	And they celebrate
8.	*Anda Kona anan*	Anda Kona's child
9.	*Boema Sina Kona na*	And Sina Kona's [child]
10.	*Inan na Seu Dela*	Whose mother is Seu Dela
11.	*Ina ma bo'a lafe*	A woman who prepares cloth
12.	*Ma feto mana futu abas.*	And a girl who dyes threads.
13.	*De fain na neu ndai tasi*	One day she goes to fish in the sea
14.	*Ma ledo na neu seko meti*	And one time she goes to scoop in the tide
15.	*Ala seko ma mia Langga Lena Liu loan*	They scoop at Langga Lena Liu's home
16.	*Ma Manatua Sain umen na.*	And at Manatua Sain's house.
17.	*Leu boema ala seko lala Suti Saik*	There they scoop up Suti Saik
18.	*Ma ndai lala Bina Liuk*	And they fish forth Bina Liuk
19.	*Ndai lendi Bina Liuk*	Fish and carry Bina Liuk
20.	*Ma seko lendi Suti Saik.*	And scoop and carry Suti Saik.
21.	*Boema lendi se leu.*	They carry them and go.
22.	*Te hu Bina na, bina madait*	But Bina is a restricted bailer shell
23.	*Ma Suti na, suti manoit.*	And Suti is a prohibited nautilus shell.
24.	*Leu losa daen henda.*	They go to the human land.
25.	*Boema ladai do la noi.*	They are restricted or prohibited.
26.	*Boema ala tu'u sa lisi Dela Muli*	They take them to Dela Muli
27.	*Ma ala lali sa lisi Anda Kona leu.*	And they move them to Anda Kona.
28.	*Hu Bina madait.*	But Bina is restricted
29.	*Ma Suti manoit.*	And Suti is prohibited.

Suti Saik and Bina Liuk initially ask to be used as a kind of noise-maker, knocking against rock and wood, to drive away pigs and monkeys. But when the shells speak again, they assert their prohibited status and so, instead, they are carried to Delha, where they meet Seu Dela ma Fale Anda.

30.	*Le na, Suti Saik nafade ma nae:*	Then Suti Saik speaks and says:
31.	*'Mendi au fo tende au u ai.'*	'Take me to knock against some wood.'
32.	*Boema Bina Liuk nafade:*	Then Bina Liuk speaks:
33.	*'Mendi au fo toto au u batu*	'Take me to bump against some rock
34.	*Fo au bengu-benggu no fatu*	So that I sound with the rock
35.	*Fo o tine to no sa be*	So where your field boundary lies
36.	*Ma o lane dae na sa be na,*	And where your land border lies,
37.	*Kode afi neu hahai*	The monkey considers abandoning it
38.	*Ma bafi afi neu sosoi.'*	And the pig considers ignoring it.'
39.	*Tehu Bina Liuk nafade nae:*	But Bina Liuk speaks, saying:
40.	*'Au Bina madait.'*	'I am Bina, the restricted.'
41.	*Boema Suti saik nadea no nae:*	Then Suti Saik talks and says:
42.	*'Au ia Suti mano'it.'*	'I am Suti, the prohibited.'
43.	*Boema ala seu leni sa lesi Dela Muli*	So they bear them to Dela Muli
44.	*Ma ala e'o leni sa lesi Anda Kona*	And they carry them to Anda Kona
45.	*Ma tonggo langga leu tonggo*	And they meet head to head
46.	*Lo ina a Fale Anda*	With the woman Fale Anda
47.	*Ma feto a Seu Dela.*	And the girl Seu Dela.
48.	*Boema la dai fai*	They are still dangerous
49.	*Ma la noi fai.*	They are still threatening.

Suti Saik and Bina Liuk question Seu Dela about beautiful cloth patterns. The questioning is in fact repeated and leads to lines 67–68, which are crucial: 'Suti is made for indigo and Bina for dyeing threads.' Thereafter, the lines that follow are somewhat repetitive until the concluding lines of the recitation: 'The pattern comes out from the sea and goodness comes out from the ocean.' At a linguistic level, there is a verbal play in these lines using three different but related dyadic sets—*dula//lada*, *dula//lole* and *lole//lada*—to describe the beauty and attractiveness of the cloth patterns.

50.	*Te hu fai na nafade Seu Dela:*	But on that day she speaks to Seu Dela:
51.	*'Mala au enangga*	'Take me to
52.	*Fo dula bek ka*	Where there are patterns

53.	*Ma lole bek ka.'*	And where there is loveliness.'
54.	*Ana sia Seu Dela*	She goes to Seu Dela
55.	*Ma sia Anda Kona*	And to Anda Kona
56.	*Hu na ala hahate ina Fale Anda*	So they celebrate Fale Anda
57.	*Ma ala kokoni feto Seu Dela.*	And they commemorate Seu Dela.
58.	*'Lole ala sa na*	'There is loveliness
59.	*Boema na lada a sa na.'*	So is there attractiveness.'
60.	*Ina ma nendi dulak a sa*	The woman who brings the pattern
61.	*Ma feto mana nendi ladak*	And the girl who brings attractiveness
62.	*De feto ma nendi lole*	The girl who brings loveliness
63.	*Ma ina sa Seu Dela*	And the woman Seu Dela
64.	*De ala fe sa leu Seu Dela*	They give them to Seu Dela
65.	*Ma ala fe sa leu Fale Anda*	And they give them to Fale Anda
66.	*Fo ela leo be na*	And so it is that
67.	*Suti nala tau do na*	Suti is made for indigo
68.	*Ma Bina nala futu aba.*	And Bina for dyeing threads.
69.	*Hu na na*	Because of this
70.	*Boema soa neu feto se ka*	It is necessary for a girl
71.	*Liman nae adu lolek*	Her hand must create well
72.	*Ina beka nae sangga dula*	For any woman who seeks a patttern
73.	*Na leu sangga sa Dela Muli*	They must go to search in Dela Muli
74.	*Ma leu sangga sa Anda Kona*	And they must go to search in Anda Kona
75.	*Na dei fo ina mana futu aba*	For the woman who dyes threads
76.	*Ma feto mana tau do.*	And the girl who prepares indigo.
77.	*Hu na na*	Because of this
78.	*Basana lole ia la*	All this is good
79.	*Ma lada ia la.*	And [all] this is fine.
80.	*Mana nendi a*	The one who carries
81.	*Lendi sa de de sa leu*	Carrying, they go
82.	*Ina Fale Anda*	The woman Fale Anda
83.	*Ma lali sa leu*	Shifting, they go
84.	*Feto a Seu Dela.*	The girl Seu Dela.

85.	*Losa besa kia*	Up until now
86.	*Hu na dei be bea mesan mae:*	Whoever may say:
87.	*Bilba Ringgou hela leo be na*	Whether Bilba or Ringgou
88.	*Mita lole na heu*	Look at the goodness on offer
89.	*Mete lada na mbeda.*	Regard the attractiveness here.
90.	*Ai lili afi, misi ngganggo.*	Don't forget, don't be mistaken.
91.	*Dula ma sain nea*	The pattern comes out from the sea
92.	*Ma lole ma liun nea.*	And goodness comes out from the ocean.

The Language of Simon Lesik's Two Versions of *Suti Saik ma Bina Liuk*

Simon Lesik's first version of *Suti Saik ma Bina Liuk* has 99 lines and is composed of 51 dyadic sets; his second version has 92 lines and is composed of just 25 dyadic sets. The two versions share seven dyadic sets in common, so together these two recitations are made up of 69 dyadic sets. The shared sets are some of the most common sets found across the dialects of Rotenese ritual language: 1) *fai*//*ledo* ('day'//'sun'); 2) *feto*//*ina* ('girl'//'woman'); 3) *meti*//*tasi* ('tide'//'sea'); 4) *liun*//*sain* ('ocean'//'sea'); and 5) *ndai*//*seko* ('to fish'//'to scoop with a fishnet'). Other sets are in Dengka dialect: 6) *de'a*//*fade* ('to speak'//'to talk'); and 7) *hate*//*koni* (in semi-reduplicated form: *hahate*//*kokoni*) ('to remember, recognise'//'commemorate').

Although there is a variety of dyadic sets that identify these recitations as belonging to the dialect of Dengka—as, for example, *loa*//*ume* (where Termanu has *lo*//*uma* for 'home'//'house') or *andiana*//*hataholi* (where Termanu has *daehena*//*hataholi* for 'human'//'person')—the overwhelming majority of sets are recognisable as part of an island-wide dyadic repertoire.

What makes these recitations distinctively representative of Dengka dialect is the use of a variety of elements—what I have described as 'connectors'—that constitute the syntax of expression. Among these connectors is Dengka's use of *sia* or *sa* where Termanu has *nai* (singular) and *lai* (plural) for 'in or at'; Dengka's use of *fe'a* where Termanu has *bei(k)* for 'still'; and Dengka's reliance on different verbal connectors, as in the use of *mendi*, *nendi* and *lendi* in these recitations, where Termanu has *muni*, *neni* and *leni* ('to bring with, to carry with'). Similarly, the second recitation ends with a unique Dengka verbal connector, *nea*, meaning 'to come out', for which there is no Termanu equivalent.

These two recitations provide a glimpse of Dengka's canonical traditions concerning the origin of weaving and dyeing. However, neither version is entirely coherent and there would appear to be some discrepancies between versions—particularly regarding the woman who is credited with scooping the shells from the sea.

What these versions share in common is mention of the gathering of the shells from the sea and short accounts of their travails until they are eventually carried to Delha. The first version recounts the shells' placement on the 'hill of black buffalo and field of white goats'; the second version alludes to the shells being taken to the 'field boundary and land border'. It is instructive to consider and compare critical aspects of these two brief interludes in Simon Lesik's recitations with other similar versions of these passages.

In both of his recitations, Esau Pono invokes the image of the 'hill of buffalo and a field of goats'. This segment from Pono's first recitation, which includes a dialogue with the shells, offers an interesting point of comparison. Pono's version consists of the following 11 lines:

'Mu mo lete nalu kala	'Go be with the high hills
Mu mo mo loa kala.'	And go be with the wide fields.'
Boe ma nae:	So he [Suti] says:
'Ndia boe malole	'That would be good
Ma ndia boe o manda-kala	And that would be proper
Tehu neu fai-na fo bote-la mai	But some day a flock of goats will come
Ma neu ledo na tena-la mai	And at a certain time a herd of buffalo will come
Fo ala heheta [ami]	They will trample us into the mud
Ma hahapa ami	And they will tread us into the dirt
Na ami dede'ak mo se	Then with whom will we speak
Ma ami kokolak mo se?'	And with whom will we talk?'

Simon Lesik (in the first poem) initially creates the image of 'hill and field' in lines 72 ff. and then repeats this image again in lines 86 ff. Here are 11 lines (lines 86 through 96) of this passage, which can be compared with Pono's lines:

86.	*Lete ngge-nggeo kapa nala*	The hill is black with water buffalo
87.	*Ma mo mu-muti bi'in.*	And the field is white with goats.
88.	*Na letek ia, lete nalu mana'a*	This hill is indeed a high hill
89.	*Ma mok ia, mo loa malole.*	And this field is truly a wide field.
90.	*De leu mbeda ma lete*	They go to place them on the hill
91.	*Ma mbeda ma mok.*	And place them in the field.
92.	*Tehu fai na ala hahate*	But one day they realise
93.	*Lete ma nggeo kapa*	The hill of black water buffalo
94.	*Ma mok mumuti bi'i.*	And the field of white goats.
95.	*De bote bi'in fe'a fefetun*	The flock of goats still treads
96.	*Ma tena kapan fe'a hahangge.*	And the herd of buffalo still tramples.

Both compositions rely on a common core of similar dyadic sets: both refer to *lete*//*mo* ('hill'//'field') and both describe this 'hill and field', *nalu*//*loa* ('high and wide'). Simon Lesik uses the set *kapa*//*bi'i* for 'buffalo and goat', while Esau Pono uses the specific term 'flock' (*bote*), which applies to goats, and *tena* ('herd'), which applies to buffalo. In his concluding line, however, Simon Lesik also uses these collective terms: *bote bi'in*//*tena kapan*.

Simon Lesik's imagery is more striking. He uses the partially reduplicated forms for 'black' (*nggeo* > *ngge-nggeo*) and white (*muti* > *mu-muti*) to emphasise the colours of the buffalo and goats. Esau Pono uses the set *malole*//*mandak* in Suti Solo's reply to indicate what is 'good and proper'; Simon Lesik uses a similar set, *malole*//*mana'a*, to give emphasis to the height of the hill and the width of the field: *nalu mana'a*//*loa malole*. The two poets use verbs—both in semi-reduplicated forms—from their different dialects for 'treading and trampling': Pono uses *heta* > *heheta*//*hapa* > *hahapa*, while Lesik uses *fetu* > *fefetu*//*hangge* > *hahangge*. The comparison of these short passages provides a good illustration of the combination of common dyadic sets and distinctive dyadic sets that is at the core of different dialect recitations.

More interesting, from a comparative perspective, is the brief passage in lines 35–36 that mentions specific boundary markers in Simon Lesik's second recitation:

Fo o tine to no sa be	So where your field boundary lies
Ma o lane dae na sa be na	And where your land border lies

References to boundary markers occur in virtually all recitations of *Suti Solo do Bina Bane* but dialect terms for such markers vary from domain to domain. Such references occur in various versions from Termanu. Thus, for example, in one of Pe'u Malesi's recitations, this directive is simply expressed:

'Mu mo peu ai	'Go with the boundary tree
Ma mu mo to batu.'	And go with the border stone.'

Alex Mada from Landu has the same directive in his recitation of the chant:

'Mu mo to batu	'Go with the border stone
Ma mu mo peu ai.'	And go with the boundary tree.'

In Ande Ruy's recitation from Ringgou, this directive has a different phrasing:

'Nea mo opa loa	'Shelter with the wide embankment
Ma tama mo e naru.'	And join with the long boundary.'

In the Pah–Ndun recitation from Thie, there occur two variants of this formula:

'Mbeda ai miu to batu	'Take us to the boundary stone
Ma na te ndae ai miu lane tiner	And carry us to the field's border …
Nai omba hade dei	At the rice field dike
Nai lane tiner dei.'	And the dry field boundary.'

Because these are complex sets, there is a double transformation that occurs:

Termanu	*to batu//peu ai*	*to//peu*	*batu//ai*
Landu	*to batu//peu ai*	*to//peu*	*batu//ai*
Thie	*to batu//lane tiner*	*to//lane*	*batu//tiner*
Dengka	*tine to//lane dae*	*to//dae*	*lane//tiner*
Thie	*omba hade//lane tiner*	*omba//lane*	*hade//tiner*
Ringgou	*opa loa//e naru*	*opa//e*	*loa//naru*

This simple example gives an indication of the continual minor variation that characterises ritual language usage across the dialects of Rote.

20
Suti Saik ma Bina Liuk: A Composition from the Domain of Dengka

Frans Lau was the older of the two master poets from Dengka who joined the recording session in October 2008. He was well-educated, a former schoolteacher and a civil servant who had spent much of his life involved in local political affairs. Compared with most of the other poets, Frans Lau had experience beyond the island of Rote. He had a host of connections established through his involvement with the Golkar Party and had passed these connections on to his son, who was a local representative of the party at the national level. When he joined the group in 2008, he took on the role of supporting Simon Lesik rather than putting himself forward as a speaker. In fact, his recitation of *Suti Saik ma Bina Liuk* consisted of hardly any narrative but was rather a commentary on the cosmology of Dengka's traditions and Simon Lesik's performances. Some of the lines from this short recitation provide an idea of his presentation:

Fai fe'a tetu-tetu	The day is still ordered
Ma ledo fe'a teme-teme	The time still harmonious
Na ala hahate do kokoni:	They remember and commemorate:
Ina mana nggao natu	The woman who holds a hundred
Ma feto mana ifa lifu …	And the girl who cradles a thousand …
Ala hahate do kokoni:	They remember and commemorate:
Ina mana nggiti ate	The woman who works the loom beams

Do mana ndolo selu	And who throws the shuttle
Ina mana sole sio	The woman who dances at the origin feast
Do feto mana foti limbe	And the girl who spins at the *limbe* feast
Ina mana lendo sai ala	The woman who dances in the sea
Ma ina Tau Tenggu Bulan	And the woman Tau Tenggu Bulan
Boema feto Kudu Hedu Ledo	And the girl Kudu Hedu Ledo
Ina mana sole sio sai ala	The woman who dances at the sea's origin
Inak Suti Sai do fetok Bina Liu	The woman Suti Sai and the girl Bina Liu
Ina mana o'o natu	The woman who lifts a hundred
Do mana ifa lifu …	Or who cradles a thousand …

While Simon Lesik's recitation links Suti Sai and Bina Liu to the creation and origin of textiles, particularly the patterns produced by the tying and dyeing of these cloths—a tradition that is widespread on Rote—Frans Lau's commentary seems to imply some association of these shells with the origins of rice and millet (as is the case in Thie). In his recitation, he twice refers to the 'woman who holds a hundred//who cradles a thousand'. As in Thie, this invocation of 'a hundred and a thousand' is a metaphoric reference to the flourishing of rice and millet. In another of his compositions, Frans Lau recounts the gathering of these seeds from the sea and the planting that enables them to grow:

Mbulen loloso	The buds creep forth
Loloso lifu hadek	Creep forth like a thousand rice plants
Kalen fefe o	The kernels spread round
Fefeo natu betek.	Spread round like a hundred millet stalks.

However, in that composition, he does not link Suti Sai and Bina Liu to these seeds.

Frans Lau, as an elder figure in his domain, may have been cryptic in his recitations, but he was someone who had reflected on Dengka's traditions and was concerned with their possible disappearance in his lifetime.

20. A COMPOSITION FROM THE DOMAIN OF DENGKA

Figure 24: Frans Lau

Figure 25: Frans Lau conferring with Simon Lesik

To our recording session in 2008, Frans Lau brought with him a personal notebook—a simple school notebook—that contained 18 compositions in ritual language, many of them shortened versions of much longer chants. This notebook offered an Indonesian translation and a commentary for each of his selected poems. These poems he described, in Indonesian, as the 'key' (*nada*) to understanding Rotenese originality and to appreciating Rotenese relations with the Heavens (*Lain//Ata*), the Earth (*Dae Bafok// Batu Poik*) and the Ocean and the Sea (*Sain//Liun*). Frans Lau had given considerable thought to his collection and, appropriately, he entitled it *Sastra Rote* ('Rotenese Literature').

Occasionally, he would refer to this notebook before launching into one of his oral recitations, but, on inspection of his notebook, I could see that his recitations had only a tenuous connection to his written notes. Like other Rotenese poets, Frans Lau was a genuine oral poet. The flow of words—his natural fluency—took over in his recitations and this had little to do with the written word.

Frans Lau lent me a copy of *Sastra Rote* so that I could make a xerox copy of it and use it to try to understand Dengka dialect. In the months that followed our recording session, this notebook proved an enormous help.

I worked through his various compositions and gradually managed to understand some of the main features of Dengka ritual language. From Frans Lau's notebook, I was able compile a word list of dyadic sets that are distinctive to Dengka dialect.

Among the poems in the collection, there was one (number 16) that was a kind of *Suti Saik ma Bina Liuk* chant. This composition had the engaging title 'Considering Death' (in Rotenese: *Ndanda Sapu Nitu*; in Indonesian: *Memikirkan Kematian*). Although the composition came to 63 lines, it was, in my judgement, a model of a Rotenese 'short poem' (*bini kekeuk*): a poem without narrative that consists of a succession of specific verbal images. The verbal images and short assertive statements that accompany them combine to convey an extended meaning. Such poems allude to other poems and demand knowledge of the wider poetic traditions. Often lines in these poems are in effect taken from other poems.

To begin to understand this poem, one must have an acquaintance with the *Suti Saik ma Bina Liu* traditions—not necessarily those revealed in the origin chants but rather the use of the idea of Suti and Bina's search for shelter and protection in a threatening and transient world.

To help the understanding of this composition, I have arranged the poem in terms of specific stanzas, most of which are four to six lines in length. The succession of these stanzas creates the impact of the poem. Some of the images in the poem require explanation to be understood properly and this is what I provide in my exegesis after the poem. I have numbered the stanzas for reference and will consider each of them in turn.

Considering Death: An Invocation of Suti Saik and Bina Liuk Frans Lau

I

1.	*Sanggu nala sain*	A storm strikes the sea
2.	*Lulik nala liun*	A cyclone strikes the ocean
3.	*Hu nitu hitu lele'an*	Caused by the seven grasping spirits
4.	*Hu mula falu nonolen.*	Caused by the eight snatching ghosts.

II

5.	*Nao saik lai bebelu aon*	*Nao*-pearl fish like to denigrate themselves
6.	*Nggoi liuk sue babala aon*	*Nggoi*-pearl fish care to lower themselves
7.	*Suti Saik si-si*	Suti Saik moans
8.	*Bina Liuk hala-doi.*	Bina Liuk is in pain.

III

9.	*Le'a nendi hataholi dae bafok*	Grasping humans on earth
10.	*Nole nendi andiana batu poi.*	Snatching people in the world.

IV

11.	*Sanggu nala Dae La'a*	A storm strikes the heartland
12.	*Lulik nala Sela Sue*	A cyclone strikes the ancestral land
13.	*Sapu nitu ala dadi*	The death of the spirit occurs
14.	*Lalo mula ala moli.*	The demise of the ghost appears.

V

15.	*Leu nda-nda mengge batu*	They consider the rock snake
16.	*Huna mengge batu olu-olu*	For the rock snake sheds its skin
17.	*Leu do-do lama na'u*	They reflect on the grasshopper
18.	*Huna lama nau selu lidan.*	For the grasshopper loses its wings.
19.	*Te hu …*	But yet …

VI

20.	*Ndefak lama-kea lutu batu*	If you overturn the rock pile
21.	*Mengge batu si-si*	The rock snake moans
22.	*Mengge batu o sapu boe.*	The rock snake dies too.
23.	*Dede lasapo na'u*	Burn away the grass
24.	*Lama nau hala-doi*	The grasshopper is in pain
25.	*Lama nau o lalo boe.*	The grasshopper dies too.

VII

26.	*Hataholi dae bafok lai bebelu aon*	Humans on earth like to diminish themselves
27.	*Andiana batu poi sue babala aon.*	People in the world care to lower themselves.
28.	*Sama leo nao saik*	They are like the *nao*-pearl fish
29.	*Deta leo nggoi liuk.*	Similar to the *nggoi*-pearl fish.

VIII

30.	*Suti Saik selu dasin*	Suti Saik raises her voice
31.	*Bina Liuk lole halan:*	Bina Liuk lifts her words:
32.	*Hai bambi mi be*	Where can we hide
33.	*Hai sulu mi be?*	Where can we shelter?

IX

34.	*Hai bambi mi to batu*	We can hide with the border stone
35.	*Tena kapa la hahangge*	Herds of buffalo trample there
36.	*Hai sulu mi lane ai*	We can shelter with the boundary tree
37.	*Bote bi'i la fefetu.*	Flocks of goats tread there.

X

38.	*Bambi mi sa'o ai*	Hide with the tree's shade
39.	*Sa'o ai mana lalalik*	The tree's shade that moves
40.	*Sulu mi mafo tua*	Shelter with the lontar's shadow
41.	*Mafo tua mana e'eok.*	The lontar's shadow that shifts.

XI

42.	*Ledo a hene dulu*	The sun climbs in the east
43.	*Sa'o ai la muli leu*	The tree's shadow moves west
44.	*Ledo a loe muli*	The sun descends in the west
45.	*Mafo tua la dulu neu.*	The lontar's shade moves east.

XII

46.	*Tetun ta nai dae bafok*	Order is not of the earth
47.	*Teman ta nia batu poik*	Integrity is not of the world
48.	*Mana sapuk mesa-mesan*	Those who die are everyone
49.	*Mana lalok mesa-mesan.*	Those who perish are everyone.

XIII

50.	*Hundi ma-sapo pedak o*	The banana is fertile with stems
51.	*Hundi sapu no nggin*	The banana dies with its fruit
52.	*Tule masa-lodo udok o*	The *gewang* rises straight upwards
53.	*Tule lalo no buan.*	The *gewang* perishes with its stalks.

XIV

54.	*Bambi mi namo tua*	Hide in a great harbour
55.	*Sulu mi teno dae.*	Shelter in a hole in the earth.

XV

56.	*Sadi masa-neda*	Remember, just remember
57.	*Sadi mafa-ndele*	Keep in mind, just keep in mind
58.	*Lutu batu neu langgan*	Pile rocks at the head
59.	*Fua dae neu ein.*	Raise earth at the foot.

XVI

60.	*Manu ai kakali*	Chickens scratch there
61.	*Bafi ai totofi.*	Pigs root there.
62.	*Dadi neu batu nenggetuk*	It becomes a stone to rest upon
63.	*Dadi neu ai nese laik.*	It becomes wood to lean upon.

The first stanza sets the tone of the poem with its announcement of the storm and cyclone (*lulik//sanggu*). The storm is a cosmological event and in the next two lines seems to be attributed to threatening spirits (*nitu//mula*).

The second stanza, 'the sea creatures stanza', offers the first reference to the distress and suffering of Suti and Bina. At the same time, however, it introduces a reference to two varieties of pearl fish without making clear the connection between these two references.

The pearl fish is a tiny, sinuous, translucent fish of the *Carapidae* family. The Rotenese describe the pearl fish as like a miniature eel. The larvae of the pearl fish are free-living but when they reach adulthood, they seek out habitats within various invertebrates. In the coastal waters of Rote, pearl fish find their habitat in sea cucumbers, entering via the creature's anus.

The pearl fish's actions have been carefully documented on many natural history sites.[1]

This symbiotic search for shelter is carefully noted and distinguished by the Rotenese. The *nao-saik* is the pearl fish that inhabits sea cucumber nearer the shore while the *nggoi-liuk* harbours in larger sea cucumber further from the shore. Together these pearl fish are seen as a complementary pair and cited as a dyadic set (*nao//nggoi*). However, the supposed security of their shelter in the anus of the sea cucumber is illusory because sea cucumbers (with their content) are regularly harvested from the seabed.

It is immensely difficult to find just the right translation for the reflexive verbal pair *bebelu//babala*, which is applied to the pearl fish in this context; both verbs describe a 'lowering, downward motion, a sinking action' that describes the pearl fish's behaviour but also, metaphorically, signals a general deprecation of self. By implication, it may imply a self-deception as well.

Stanza III consists of two lines. Although these lines have no specific subject, the use of the verbs *le'a//nole*, as in the first stanza, indicates that the spirits (*nitu//mula*) are the ones who are responsible for 'snatching' and 'grasping' the lives of men on earth.

Stanza IV alludes to Stanza I and makes explicit the implications of Stanza III. A storm strikes the Rotenese homeland, whose name is Dae La'a// Sela Sue (Termanu: Dae Laka ma Sela Sue). This is the mythic land from which the Rotenese claim to have originated—hence, as these lines assert, the origin of death (*sapu nitu//lalo mula*) began with the first ancestors.

---

1   See: *Pearlfish enters sea cucumber anus* (www.youtube.com/watch?v=Fw2DrbhOA-M).

Stanza V cites the snake and grasshopper—two putative icons of immortality. The snake is able to shed its skin and the grasshopper its wings, but both continue to live.

Stanza VI is prefaced by a 'but yet ...', which signals that the stanza is intended to take an opposing view to that of Stanza V. Neither snake nor grasshopper is immortal. Overturning the rock pile renders the snake vulnerable and burning the grass also renders the grasshopper vulnerable. Instead of appearing as icons of immortality, their situation is one of vulnerability and impermanence.

Stanza VII makes a direct comparison: human beings are like pearl fish, who lower themselves to seek illusory, self-deceiving shelter. The same verbal pair, *bebelu//babala*, is used in Stanza VII as in Stanza II.

Stanza VIII resumes the theme of Suti and Bina: the search for a place to hide and shelter. Stanzas IX, X and XI are all recognisable 'responses' to the shells' requests.

Stanza IX is cast in Suti and Bina's voice: they propose to find sanctuary with the border stone and boundary tree (*to batul//lane ai*). But this is where herds of buffalo and flocks of goats (*tena kapa//bote bi'i*) trample the earth. (Various comparative examples of this formulaic episode are examined in the previous chapter.)

Stanzas X and XI offer the possibility for the shells to 'hide and shelter' (*bambi//sulu*) with the 'tree's shadow and the lontar palm's shade' (*sao ai// mafo tua*), but this possibility is negated by the fact that the sun rises and falls and thus the protecting shade of the trees shifts.

Stanza XII is one of the most common refrains in ritual language discourse: that there is no (certain) order in the world or (complete) fulfilment in the world. From a linguistic perspective, Frans Lau uses the Termanu dyadic set (*tetu//tema*) rather than the Dengka dialect variant (*tetu//teme*). The next lines in this stanza are the assertion that everyone is subject to death—again, a common refrain in mortuary chants.

Stanza XIII presents two images of the possibility of death at the height of fertility. The first of these images is the banana that may die, even as it bears its last large cluster of fruit. More spectacular is the *gewang* palm that grows for a hundred years or more and then, suddenly, puts out a huge single-stalked inflorescence that surmounts the palm to several metres—and then dies. The Rotenese tap the lontar, a Borassus palm, on a regular basis because it puts out a succession of inflorescences; the *gewang* palm can only be tapped when it puts out its single inflorescence at the climax of its life cycle.

Stanza XIV's two lines are an urgent iteration of the need to 'hide and shelter' using the same verb pair, *bambi//sulu*, as in Stanzas IX and X.

Stanza XV offers the frequently enunciated ritual admonition 'to remember and keep in mind' (*masa-neda//mafa-ndele*), immediately followed by the injunction 'to pile rocks at the head' and 'to raise earth at the foot'—a reference to the creation of a burial mound.

Stanza XVI present an image of a neglected grave with chickens digging and pigs rooting at its headstone and wooden marker. However, in Frans Lau's Indonesian translation of these lines, he writes that this condition is to be avoided, *Jaga jangan* ('Be careful do not') and *Asallah agar tidak* ('Just so as not'). There is nothing in the Rotenese to indicate this. However, were one to translate these lines as Frans Lau indicates, they might read as follows:

Manu ai kakali	[Avoid] chickens scratching there
Bafi ai totofi.	Pigs rooting there.
Dadi neu batu ne-nggetuk	That it becomes a stone to rest upon
Dadi neu ai nese-laik.	That it becomes wood to lean upon.

The 63 lines of this composition are composed of 43 dyadic sets. Virtually all of these sets are part of the common island-wide repertoire.

21
Suti Sai ma Bina Liu from the Domain of Oenale

Thanks to the poet Ande Ruy, who joined the first recording session, invitations for subsequent sessions were initially extended to poets from eastern Rote, particularly Landu and Bilba. It proved relatively easy to find poets from these domains. Termanu was also represented from the beginning by Esau Pono and by other poets he brought to join the group. The goal from the outset, however, was to attract master poets from as many different dialect areas as possible. The third recording session was able to attract poets from Dengka and the fourth session had poets from Thie. It was harder, however, to find poets from other domains, particularly from the far west of Rote.

Fortunately for the seventh recording session, in 2011, we were able to attract a poet from the domain of Oenale. This poet, Hendrik Foeh, was remarkably capable. Unlike most other poets, however, he was quiet, almost self-effacing and hardly put himself forward as a notable Rotenese 'man of knowledge'. Yet his recitations were clear, coherent and linguistically beautiful. None of them was particularly long, nor were they reiterative. Instead they were focused and succinct. Moreover, he was able to provide reasonable exegesis on his recitations. His recitation of *Suti Sai(k) ma Bina Liu(k)*, recorded on 5 October 2011, is an excellent example of his style of composition.

Figure 26: Hendrik Foeh

Hendrik Foeh's recitation places Suti Sai and Bina Liu in an origin chant that recounts the creation of Rotenese cloths. Although it is not made explicit, Suti Sai and Bina Liu are female creatures. The recitation is an origin chant, but the poet emphasises from the beginning that this is also a 'widow and orphan' chant.

The first half of the recitation describes the shells' journey from the sea to the land and their quest for shelter and protection. Eventually they are taken to Delha. The arrival in Delha begins the second half of the recitation. The recitation does not name the chant characters who gather the shells and carry them to Delha nor does it identify the chant character who is responsible for the first weaving and patterning of the Rotenese cloth. It is a narrative of occurrence, not of named actors or agents.

In this first section, Suti Sai ma Bina Liu are carried by a storm from sea to land and, at 'the river's edge and the sea's boundary', they speak out with a plaintive cry, asking for shelter and protection.

Ina Falu Bina Liu Do Ana ma Suti Sai: Widow Bina Liu or Orphan Suti Sai

1.	*Ata ola-ola*	We speak of
2.	*Ina falu fo Bina Liu*	The widow Bina Liu
3.	*Ma ana ma fo Suti Sai.*	And the orphan Suti Sai.
4.	*Ana suru sia Mbia Liun na*	She takes cover in Mbia Liun
5.	*Do ana bambi sia Unu Sain*	Or she shelters in Unu Sain
6.	*Dadi neme-hena ma ne'e-bani.*	Offering hope and expectation.
7.	*Te hu sanggu sai na edo*	But a storm erupts in the sea
8.	*Ma ruli liun na eno*	And a typhoon makes its way in the ocean
9.	*De Bina ana edo nggi*	Bina, she puts forth her pod
10.	*Boe ma Suti ana roko isin.*	Then Suti lets loose her insides.
11.	*Ana lali hela sain*	She shifts from the sea
12.	*Ma ana keko hela liun*	And she moves from the ocean
13.	*Ana lalo no tere-tasi*	She is carried with the ocean refuse
14.	*Boe ma ana nggongga no hanu-lé*	And is moved with river debris

15.	*Ana losa ré pepisin*	She comes to the river's edge
16.	*Fo ndia ré retan*	There where the river ceases
17.	*Ana ndu'u tasi tatain*	She comes to the sea's boundary
18.	*Fo ndia tasi sun.*	There where the sea ends.
19.	*Ana na-lo*	She calls out
20.	*Do ana na-meli:*	Or she speaks:
21.	*'Au keko hela au daeng*	'I have moved from my land
22.	*Ma au lali hela au nggorongga.*	And I have shifted from my village.
23.	*Te touk sé tei telu*	What man will take pity
24.	*Ma ta'ek sé rala rua.*	And what boy will open his heart.
25.	*Au tuda u ana ma*	I have become an orphan
26.	*Ma au dadi u falu ina.*	And I have become a widow.
27.	*Sé ma tei telu*	Who will take pity
28.	*Ma sé ma dale dua*	And who will open his heart
29.	*Fo ana lai nala au*	Someone to love me
30.	*Ma ana sue nala au.*	And someone to care for me.
31.	*Ana dadi neu lane aon solo langga*	Someone to surround me like a wide hat
32.	*Ma ana foi aon nggeli tua*	And someone to cover me like a thatched roof
33.	*Fo ana na'a bambi nala au*	Someone to shelter me
34.	*Ma ana na'a suru nala au.'*	And someone to protect me.'

In this version, a young friarbird and a parrot are the ones to hear the shells' cry and carry them to Delha in the west.

35.	*Koa mana mete nggoro-a*	A friarbird who sees its village
36.	*Ma koa ma tei telu*	That friarbird has pity
37.	*Nggia mana suri inggu-a*	A parrot who spies its clan
38.	*Nggia ma dale dua,*	That parrot opens its heart,
39.	*Sama ona koa-ore ta'e tena*	Just like a still young friarbird
40.	*Ma deta leo nggia-mese tou landus.*	And just like an immature parrot.
41.	*Ana ninia nala Suti halan*	She hears Suti's voice

42.	*Ma ana nenene nala* *Bina dasin*	And she listens to Bina's words
43.	*Ana eko feo nala Bina*	She embraces Bina
44.	*De ana la'o losa Dela Muri*	Then she goes to Dela Muri
45.	*Ana lutu eko nala Suti*	She surrounds Suti
46.	*De nendin losa Ndana Ikon.*	Then bears her to Ndana Ikon.

The 'woman who spins and winds cotton' lives in Delha at the western end of Rote. She is engaged in producing cloths. Traditional cloths rely on two basic dyes: a blue-black dye derived from indigo and a red dye that comes from the roots of the *morinda* (*Morinda citrifolia*) plant. The Rotenese pair these dyes as a dyadic set: *tau*//*manukudu*. The passage describes the creation of such cloths. It implies that the very patterning of these cloths is based on these shells: 'the motif of the sea//the pattern of the ocean.' And, as a consequence, whoever wears these cloths carries 'Suti Sai's voice and Bina Liu's words'.

47.	*Te hu ina ia ina mana bindo inde,*	This woman is a woman who spins,
48.	*Te'o ia te'o mana lola kaba*	This aunt is an aunt who winds cotton
49.	*Ara losa Dela Murin*	They arrive at Dela Muri
50.	*Do ara ndu'u Ndana Ikon.*	Or they come to Ndana Iko.
51.	*Ana lolo kaba*	She winds cotton
52.	*Ma ana bindo inde*	And she spins
53.	*Ana sangga kaba sina*	She seeks *sina* cotton
54.	*Ana ta hambu*	She does not have any
55.	*Ana sangga fina koli*	She seeks *koli* thread
56.	*Ana ta nita.*	She does not see any.
57.	*Ana tao sa neu kaba sina*	She makes *sina* cotton
58.	*Fo ana lolo*	She lays out the loom
59.	*Ana tao sa neu fina koli*	She makes *koli* thread
60.	*Fo ana tenu.*	She weaves.
61.	*Ana seu kaba dae mbena*	She picks cotton bolls from the land
62.	*Fo ana hai fina koli* *Rote boan.*	She takes thread from the fruit of the *koli* tree.
63.	*Ana bindo inde*	She spins

64.	*Ma ana lolo kaba.*	And she lays out the cotton.
65.	*Ana lolo neu rambi*	She lays out a woman's cloth
66.	*Boe ma ana tenu neu lafe*	Then she weaves a man's cloth
67.	*Ana sangga nae tutu deta*	She wants to pound dyes
68.	*Fo mbila nggeo*	To make the red and black
69.	*Te hu ara ta hambu.*	But there are none.
70.	*Ana ketu tau ana tete don*	She cuts leaves of the small indigo
71.	*Boe ma ana kali manukudu lasi okan.*	Then she strips old roots of the *morinda* bush.
72.	*De ana tutu deta neu mbila nggeo*	She pounds to make the red and black
73.	*Fo ana adu dudula*	She creates a pattern
74.	*Fo lafe dulan.*	A pattern for a man's cloth.
75.	*De ana tao neu buna*	Then she makes a motif
76.	*Fo rambi bunan,*	A motif of a woman's cloth,
77.	*Fo rambi ra-buna*	A woman's cloth with a motif
78.	*Fo ra-buna saik*	A motif of the sea
79.	*Te lafe na-dula*	A man's cloth with a pattern
80.	*Te na-dula liu.*	A pattern of the ocean.
81.	*Hu Suti Sai nendi ma liu*	Because Suti Sai has been carried from the ocean
82.	*Ma Bina Liu nendi ma sain.*	And Bina Liu has been carried from the sea.
83.	*Ana na loa ma na naru.*	It is wide and long.
84.	*Sia dae mbenan ia sia Rote Ndao*	On the dry land here on Rote Ndao
85.	*Losa fai ia ma ndu'u fai ia.*	To this day and until this day.
86.	*Rote Ndao ana nalusa*	The people of Rote Ndao wrap it
87.	*Ma ana natai*	And wear it
88.	*Lafe fo dula sai ia*	A man's cloth with this sea pattern
89.	*Rambi fo dula liu ia*	A woman's cloth with this ocean pattern
90.	*Hu la'o mia Suti Sai ia*	Because it originates from Suti Sai
91.	*Ma la'o mia Bina Liu*	And originates from Bina Liu
92.	*Ana ma ma ina falu.*	The orphan and the widow.

93.	*No ia ana fe'a ndoe ndolu*	Those who still do not understand
94.	*Ma ana fe'a la'a lela*	And those who still do not comprehend
95.	*Te ta'e mana ma Rote Ndao ra*	The young men on Rote
96.	*Rendi Suti Sai haran*	They carry Suti Sai's voice
97.	*Boe ma rendi Bina Liu dasin na.*	And they carry Bina Liu's words.

This would seem to be the appropriate ending to this version of *Suti Sai ma Bina Liu*. However, as a good oral poet, Hendrik Foeh continued his recitation to provide a postscript that gave the context of his recitation. He made clear that his recitation was for me and that it was made on Bali but he then explained that this recitation was intended to be heard to affect people's hearts and convince them to provide for widows and orphans, especially on Rote Ndao.

98.	*Ne'e lolosan neu Pak Fox sa ia*	To this point for Pak Fox here
99.	*Sia Nusa Bali ia*	Here on the island of Bali
100.	*Fo ela leo bena*	So let it be that
101.	*Ndi'i don nenene*	The ear continually hears
102.	*Fo tao dalen leo be*	To affect the heart
103.	*Fo na-tetu ina falu*	To give order to widows
104.	*Ana tao tein leo be*	It affects the inner person
105.	*Fo na-lole ana ma*	To do good to orphans
106.	*Fo mana mia Rote Ndao nema.*	To those from Rote Ndao.

Hendrik Foeh's Recitation as a Distinct Example of a *Suti Solo do Bina Bane* Chant

Hendrik Foeh's recitation locates his version of *Suti Sai ma Bina Liu* within the context of an origin chant—one that recounts the origin of weaving, dyeing and the production of Rotenese tie-dyed textiles. In this respect, it is similar to Old Meno's recitation from Termanu and to Simon Lesik's recitation from Dengka, both of whose recitations link the shells to the origins of weaving. However, *Suti Sai ma Bina Liu* is a narrative without genealogical grounding. One of the features of most other versions of this chant is the insistence on particular named agents. Not only are these chant characters named, they also are often genealogically linked to one another. This version names no one except the shells (and no genealogy is given for these shells). It thus is a narrative without its embedding and as such lacks one of the critical features of an 'origin' chant.

This recitation conforms to the pattern of an 'orphan and widow' chant—one that recounts the expulsion of the shells from the depths of the sea, their arrival at the edge of the land, their identification as 'orphan and widow' and their plea for shelter and assistance.

Not a woman but a friarbird and parrot (*koa*//*nggia*) take pity on the shells and deliver them to a woman in Delha, who relies on them to create her cloths. Precisely what the shells are used for in this process is not explicit: in some versions, the shells become a vat for indigo and a base for spinning, but this is certainly not the case in this narrative. The final lines of the recitation are particularly evocative. They insist that though Rotenese men do not realise it, all the traditional textiles they wear 'carry Suti Sai's voice and Bina Liu's words'.

Language Use in Hendrik Foeh's *Suti Sai ma Bina Liu*

This recitation of just 106 lines is composed of some 52 dyadic sets. A relatively small number of these sets (less than one-fourth) are familiar, recognisable sets. The dozen or so of these sets are the following: 1) *liuk*//*saik* ('ocean'//'sea'); 2) *ana mak*//*ina falu* ('orphan'//'widow'; 3) *isi*//*nggi* ('insides'//'pod'); 4) *lali*//*keko* ('to move'//'to shift'); 5) *lai*//*sue* ('care for, to love'//'to have sympathy'); 6) *meti*//*tasi* ('tide'//'sea'; 7) *ta'e*//*tou* ('boy'//'man'); 8) *koa*//*nggia* ('friarbird'//'parrot'); 9) *deta*//*sama* ('like'//'similar'); 10) *ina*//*te'o* ('mother'//'father's sister'). The set *buna*//*dula* ('flower, pattern'//'design') is of interest because the lexical terms that make up this set are familiar but in this recitation, as a pair, they take on a metaphorical significance in reference to the patterning of Rotenese cloth.

Sound changes in Oenale are different from those in Thie and Termanu. One of the 'l' sounds in Termanu becomes 'r'. (This is not the same 'r' as in Thie—hence Oenale has *ruli* where Thie has *luri* and Termanu has *luli* for 'storm'.) Oenale also has 'r' where Termanu uses 'd'. Oenale uses 'ngg' where Termanu has 'ng' and 'mb' where Termanu has 'p'. Oenale also drops medial 'k' in some words. On the basis of these changes, there are many dyadic sets in Oenale that can be seen to belong to the island-wide repertoire:

Table 18: Termanu–Oenale Dialect Comparisons

Termanu	Oenale	Gloss
luli//sangu	ruli//sanggu	'storm'//'cyclone'
boa//pena	boa//mbena	'fruit'//'boll' (of cotton)
pila//nggeo	mbila//nggeo	'red'//'black'
dua//telu	rua//telu	'two'//'three'
dasi//hala	dasi//hara	'song'//'voice'
losa//nduku	losa//ndu'u	'up to'//'toward, until'
babi//sulu	bambi//suru	'shelter, cover'//'protect'

There are also dyadic sets that occur in this composition that are similar to sets in other dialects of Rote. For example, Hendrik Foeh uses the set *hanu-le*//*tere-tasi* for 'ocean refuse'//'river debris'; Alex Mada uses the expression *hambau*//*tere-tasi*; while Kornaluis Medah in his recitation uses the set *hamu-le*//*tele-tasi*. Another dyadic set that stands out in this composition is *lafe*//*rambi* as the terms for 'a man's cloth' and 'a woman's cloth'. In his recitation, Hendrik Foeh refers to these cloths as follows:

Ana lolo neu rambi	She lays out a woman's cloth
Boe ma ana tenu neu lafe	Then she weaves a man's cloth

In all other dialects, this pair is *lafa*//*pou*. Thus, for example, in Jonas Mooy's recitation, there occur the lines:

Ara pa'a pou su'u reu sara	They wrap a woman's sarong around them
Ma ara mboti lafa una neu sara	And they fold a man's cloth around them

Pe'u Malesi, in his recitation from Termanu, has these lines:

De ana tenu nan dadi pou	She weaves it to become a woman's cloth
Fo lae pou dula selu-kolo	They call this woman's cloth: the *selu-kolo* pattern
Ma ana tenu nan dadi lafa	And she weaves it to become a man's cloth
Fo lae lafa dula tema-nggik	They call this man's cloth: the *tema-nggik* pattern

There are also some puzzling usages in this recitation. For example, Henrik Foeh uses the pair *tei telu*//*rala rua* (literally: 'three stomach'//'two hearts') in lines 23–24. *Rala rua* (literally: 'heart two') is in Oenale dialect. In this context, this formula is an expression for 'taking pity'//'opening one's heart'.

Te touk sé tei telu	What man will take pity
Ma ta'ek sé rala rua.	And what boy will open his heart.

However, just a few lines later (lines 27–28) in the recitation, he shifts to the use of this same expression in what can only be interpreted as Termanu dialect:

Sé ma tei telu	Who will take pity
Ma sé ma dale dua	And who will open his heart

He then repeats this expression in lines 36 and 38:

Ma koa ma tei telu	That friarbird has pity
Nggia ma dale dua	That parrot opens its heart

Although this could be conceived of as some sort of exceptional dialect parallelism (the use of an expression in two dialects), it is more likely a lapse into the use of a Termanu literary standard of which the poet is well aware. The presence of other Termanu-speaking poets and the knowledge that I relied on the Termanu dialect as my comparative reference point may have influenced him.

Verbs in Oenale's ritual language have a different structure to verbs in Termanu. Despite these differences, they continue to retain the same semantic pairings in different dialectic grammars. Thus Oenale uses the third-person singular form *neme-hena*//*ne'e-bani* where Termanu has *nama-hena*//*naka-bani* for this expression ('to have hope'//'to have expectations'). Similarly, for the paired verbs 'to listen'//'to hear', Oenale uses the third-person singular form *nenene*//*ninia*, where Termanu has *nama-nene*//*nama-nia*.

There are also interesting differences. One example is the use of the verbs that describe the way the shells lose or expel their pods or insides.

21. *SUTI SAI MA BINA LIU* FROM THE DOMAIN OF OENALE

Old Meno in his recitation has the following:

Boe ma besak ka Suti lama-edo nggi	Now Suti exudes his pods
Ma Bina lamatoko-isi	And Bina puts out his insides

Esau Pono uses a similar verb pair in a slightly different format, *edo heni// toko heni*:

Boe ma liun na e'edo	The sea continually casts out
De ana edo heni Suti nggi	It casts forth Suti's pod
Ma ana toko heni Bina isin.	And it throws out Bina's contents.
Ana edo heni Suti nggi	It casts out Suti's pod
Ma ana toko heni Bina isin.	And throws out Bina's contents.

By contrast, Simon Lesik uses a lexically different verb, *-loko*, but one with a similar meaning to *-toko*, to pair with *-edo*:

Bina ma-edo nggi	Bina, who exudes her pods
Suti mana-loko isi.	Suti, who issues forth her insides.

Jonas Mooy offers a different pairing of verbs, combining *roko* (Dengka: *loko*) with *ketu* ('to cut'):

Ara rama roko isi	They exude their insides
Ma ara rama ketu nggi.	And they cut loose their pods.

Hendrik Foeh's verb pairing (*roko//edo*) is similar to that of Dengka:

De Bina ana edo nggi	Bina, she puts forth her pod
Boe ma Sui ana roko isin.	Then Suti lets loose her insides.

This chain of semantic relationships between *edo//toko* (T), *edo//loko* (D), *ketu//roko* (Th) and *edo//roko* (O) is yet another example of what I refer to as 'dialect concatenation'. Recognising the pervasiveness of dialect concatenation is a key to understanding how ritual language functions across the island of Rote.

22

Traditions of Oral Formulaic Composition across the Island of Rote

As a study of oral formulaic compositions, the first half of this book has focused on 10 versions of *Suti Solo do Bina Bane* from the domain of Termanu, examining in some detail the semantics of oral composition in a single speech community. The second half has focused on another 10 versions of this chant, from seven different domains of the island: Landu, Ringgou, Bilba, Ba'a, Thie, Dengka and Oenale. It has considered both the specific ritual semantics of these various speech communities and the general patterning of parallelism that allows communication across these speech communities. Since the second half of this study has had to proceed step by step to examine each speech community, the full extent of the semantics of oral composition can only begin to be grasped in relation to the traditions of the whole of the island.

It is apparent from the various versions of *Suti Solo do Bina Bane*, however distinctive, that these compositions share a common tradition. Similarities among versions of this chant are greater throughout eastern and central Rote but even in western Rote, where the shells change sex to become female, similarities in form of composition, in elements of the narrative and in the recurrence of many set formulae point to a shared tradition.

As at the end of the first half of this study, it is useful to review the narrative structures of these various versions.

Narrative Structures of the Dialect Versions of *Suti Solo do Bina Bane*

Version XI, Landu: Alex Mada's *Suti Solo do Bina Bane*

In Alex Mada's version of *Suti Solo do Bina Bane*, the woman Noa Bafo and the girl Lole Ora watch over their ripening fields. The fields are ready for harvest but the *fua poi* and *peda bafo* ceremony has yet to be held, so they prepare a scoop-net to go in search of the ritual fish. Before the friarbird sings and the east turns red, they make their way to the sea where they encounter Suti Solo and Bina Bane. At first they fish them up, then throw them away, but the shells beg them to take them home. The women begin a dialogue with the shells, telling them to go with the flotsam and sea refuse. When the shells decline this offer, the women tell them to go with the harbour crabs and shore molluscs. When they decline this possibility, the women propose that they go with the *boa* and *piko* trees that grow along the water's edge. The shells again refuse to accept this suggestion because these trees are vulnerable in the monsoon. The women then propose that they go with the house post and old beam. (The shells' formulaic answer confounds house post and old beam with syrup vat and millet basket.) This proposal is also declined. The women's next proposal is to go with the syrup vat and millet basket, but this is also declined. The women then urge the shells to go with border stone and boundary tree and when this is again declined, they propose they go to the sacred grove and forbidden forest. The shells reply that these forests could be cut down and they, the shells, would be abandoned. Finally, as the ninth dialogue directive of this recitation, the women propose that the shells join with the *gewang* (Corypha) palm and the lontar (Borassus) palm to serve as clappers to drive away birds. At this suggestion, the recitation ends.

Version XII, Ringgou: Ande Ruy's *Suti Solo do Bina Bane*

The woman Oli Masi and the girl Bisa Oli go to search for the fish Tio Holo and Dusu Lake, but they are only able to catch Suti Solo and Bina Bane in their nets. The shells explain that they are orphan and widow: without a companion, they seek a homeland. So the women take up the shells and bring them home, telling them that 'their land is the rice basket and their lineage the syrup vat'. Since these vessels can be depleted, the shells reject this proposal. So the women propose that they take shelter with the rice field's wide embankment and the dry field's long boundary. The shells reply that flooding rains could wash away the embankment and boundary and then they would not have 'contentment and satisfaction'. The women then propose that the shells take shelter with 'the raised horns and waving tails'. The shells answer that if disease strikes the buffalo and goats, there will be no 'order or integrity'. The women then direct the shells to the tapped lontar palms and to the harvested rice fields. In response, the shells say that when the lontar baskets are lowered at the end of the season and the rice is harvested from the fields, they will have no 'land and shelter', no 'contentment and satisfaction'. Next the women direct them to 'boundary stone and border tree', but these are liable to be trampled by 'the moon's buffalo and the sun's goats', leaving them no 'land or lineage'. Finally, as they continue on in the late afternoon, the women come upon a *ko-nau* (or *bidara*) tree and *nilu-foi* (or tamarind) tree under whose shade the shells are pleased to shelter. The shells are left to 'pick and eat, pluck and consume' the fruit of these trees.

Version XIII, Bilba: Kornalius Medah's *Suti Solo do Bina Bane*

The narrative begins in Dulu Oli ma Lange Le ('East Estuary'//'Headland River'). Suti Solo and Bina Bane leave the security and certainty of their homeland to embark on a sea journey. On their way, they try to find contentment in the 'rolling sea and meandering waves'. A storm arises in the east and a cyclone at the head; they lose their pods, and are carried bobbing like *boa* wood and drifting like *piko* wood. They utter the refrain 'nothing is certain and nothing lasting'. In the sea, they have various personified encounters, first with 'sea refuse and river dregs', then with 'seaweed *lima* and waterweed *koko*' and finally with 'long river and wide pool'. None of these encounters offers 'certainty and security'. At this point, the girl 'Tomorrow's Tide' (Meti Balaha) and the woman 'Dawning Sea' (Tasi Dulupila), who are fishing in long river and wide pool for the ritual fish Moka Holu and Kuku Lake, scoop the shells from the sea and take them to their home. The shells beg the women to be their father and mother to shelter and protect them. The women first assign the shells to the *timi* post and lontar beam within the house but if the rain spears the *timi* post and the sun heats the lontar beam, there can be no satisfaction there. The women next propose that the shells go with the lontar vat and the rice basket but these can be emptied so there is no certainty or permanence there. The women then direct the shells to the tapping of the lontar palms and the harvesting of fields of rice. Although there is celebration in these activities, they must come to an end when the lontar baskets are lowered and the great mortar for pounding rice is put aside. The shells move on to large flowering trees: the *nitas* (*kelumpang*) tree and the *delas* (*dedap*) tree. But when the monsoon rains end the flowering season of these trees, the shells are left to sob that there is no certainty with the mountain *nitas* tree and no permanence with the field *delas* tree. The shells move on to snuggle up in a pigeon pea garden and squat in a cotton field, but there, too, wind and rain blow away the cotton bolls and pigeon pea flowers. Unable to find certainty and permanence in the world, the shells resolve to return to East Estuary and Headland River by following the Pandanus River and the Jasmine Forest path. They recognise their condition as orphan and widow and join with the orphan Le Lai and the widow Oe Bolo on the path to East Estuary and Headland River. When they arrive there, they take the Nilu Neo (or tamarind) tree as their 'birth mother' and the Ko Nau (or *bidara*) tree as their 'birth father'. They are able to pick and pluck the fruits of these trees and there they are able to find inner satisfaction and heartfelt contentment.

Version XIV, Ba'a: Laazar Manoeain's *Suti Solo do Bina Bane*

A storm arises and carries away Bane Aka and Solo Bane, the father of Suti Solo do Bina Bane, leaving the shells abandoned, bobbing like *boa* wood and drifting like *piko* wood. Two women fishing along the shore scoop up the shells and direct them to go with the 'creaking wood' and with the 'scraping forest' to hide themselves in the wood and conceal themselves in the forest. But if a storm comes, the leaves and liana of the forest will fall from the trees. There is no order or integrity there. Next the women direct them to go with the 'wild pig' and the 'forest monkey' to conceal themselves in caves and hide themselves in holes. But the wild pig is hunted and the forest monkey is flushed out, leaving no order or integrity. So the women direct them to go with the 'grassland cuckoo' and the 'river shrimp' to hide themselves deep in the grass and conceal themselves deep in a waterhole. But the grass dries out and the river ceases its ebb, leaving the grassland cuckoo and the river shrimp in a pitiful state. Thus, once again there is no order or integrity. Finally, the women direct the shells to shear through the surf and plunge through the waves to make their way to Timor (Helok and Sonobai). They make their way to Timor and there meet the girl of Helok and the woman of Sonobai. Sobbing, they recount their plight, having become like a lone buffalo and an orphan chicken. The women tell them to follow them to their house, where they cut them badly into hair combs and file them poorly into earrings. And so the two shells perish.

Version XV, Thie: Samuel Ndun and N. D. Pah's *Suti Solo do Bina Bane*

This version of *Suti Solo do Bina Bane*, which recounts the origin of rice and millet, begins in the Heavens. The Sun and Moon, Bula Kai and Ledo Horo, inform their family that they intend to make war on the ocean and sea. They sharpen their swords and set their flintlocks and descend into the ocean to meet the Lord of the Sea's warriors and the Hunter of the Ocean's defenders. In the ensuing battle, blood drips down on Solo Bana Sain's child, Suti Solo, and on Bane Aka Liun's child, Bina Bane. They extend their pods and put forth their insides and drift away like seagrass, arriving at Loko Laka Fa and Tebu Tipa Re.

The woman Bui Len, the child of (Leu) Le Dale and wife of Nggongo Ingu Lai, and the girl Eno Lolo, the child of Lolo Dala Ina and wife of Rima Le Dale, take up their scoop-nets and go to fish in the receding tide at Loko Laka Fa and Tebu Tipa Re. There they encounter Suti Solo and Bina Bane, who beg to be scooped up. The women wonder where they might hang or attach these shells. The shells ask to be hung on the *ufa* (or Malay apple: *Syzygium jambos*) tree and *bau* (or Hibiscus: *Hibiscus tiliaceus*) tree. But this is soon considered not 'right and proper'. The shells then ask that they be hung on two sacrificial poles in the house, the Sema Kona and Lunggu Lai. But this, too, is considered not 'right and proper'. So the shells ask to be carried eastward and placed at the boundary stone and field's border. There they announce that at the rice field dike and the dry field boundary, they are to be cared for as orphans and to be treated as widows, giving birth to planting at To Batu and giving birth to sowing at Lane Ai. As the seeds of rice and millet, Suti Solo and Bina Bane are taken from field to field, where they are planted. One hundred plants rise to where the orphan goes to rest and a thousand stalks mount to where the widow goes to cling. So Suti's descendants and Bina's successors cover all the world and sun-lit earth.

Version XVI, Thie: Jonas Mooy's Version of *Suti Solo do Bina Bane*

This next narrative, like the preceding one, recounts the origin of rice and millet. It also makes explicit the 'western' Rotenese view that Suti Solo and Bina Bane are female. Presumably the shells, who become the rice and millet seeds in the previous narrative, are also to be regarded as female.

A storm strikes the ocean's depths and the woman Suti Solo and the girl Bina Bane exude their insides and cut loose their pods. They are left crying at the reef's base and the sea's edge. The woman Rema Ko and the girl Lutu Koe take up their scoop-nets and descend to the tidal reef. There they hear the voices of the shells begging them to scoop them up and place them at the shore's edge and the estuary's mouth. The women agree and carry the shells and hang them in two shoreline trees, the *ai sauk* and *lenggu-ha'ik* trees. The shells invite the women to come back and visit them because they offer the prospect of 'fine attire and delicious nourishment'. The shells are lively and happy to be in the trees along the shore.

The venerated ancestors of Thie, Tola Mesa and Lee Lunu, put on their sword and take up their flintlock to go to see what has happened after the storm. There they encounter the shells, who beg them not to harm them, again promising the prospect of 'fine attire and delicious nourishment'. The shells ask to be wrapped in a sarong and tied in a pouch and taken to be hung on the doorpost of the house and at the fence's base. The two ancestors wrap the shells up and then, following their instructions, cut a tree near the shore and cradle a flat harbour stone to plant as a resting stone and standing post for the shells to rest on. The stone and tree are to become the resting stone and 'coconut-holding' post for the performance of Thie's *limba* harvest ceremony. They then pluck the ancestral coconut, beat the drums and celebrate the first *limba*, bringing rain and dampening dew down upon the earth. The shells bear the 'nine seeds and the basic grains' and give instructions that they be planted in different fields in Thie. When the planting is done, the shells form leaves and stalks—seeds with sprouts and leaves with spikes. Orphans are able to eat rice and widows millet. The narrative then gives emphasis to its main revelation: the creation of the *limba* ceremony and the origins of rice, millet and other crops. This is repeated as follows: they create sitting stones and make a standing tree, drumming with a begging sound and dancing with a requesting voice, calling on the Creator of the Heavens to let fall gentle dampening dew and cooling rain to pour upon the fields that they may plant the nine seeds and basic grains. The narrative ends with a statement as spoken through the voice of the shells: 'We have delicious food and fine clothing fallen and descended upon the earth, particularly on Rote Ndao.'

Version XVII, Dengka: Simon Lesik's First Version of *Suti Saik ma Bina Liuk*

This narrative, which also identifies Suti and Bina as female, begins with a brief peroration remembering specific widows and orphans: Ola Oe and Laba Dae, Ndule Dae and Ndule Oe. It then introduces the woman Tau Tenggu Bulan and the girl Kudu Henu Ledo, a woman who fishes in the sea and a girl who scoops in the tide. They go to fish on the rocky reef and sandy edge and there encounter Suti Saik and Bina Liuk. The shells who once danced in the sea are struck by a storm. They exude their insides and turn out their pods. They suffer and are in pain, passing through the tides. The women take up the shells and place them on three paths and two roads but this proves unsatisfactory because human beings tread along these paths. The shells continue to suffer and are in pain. The shells ask to be carried to a specific hill and specific field: to hide at Mbila Fume Lete and to take cover at Nau Langga Loe Lesu. But they still suffer and are in pain so the women shift the shells to the hill of the black buffalo and the field of the white goats, but the buffalo trample there and the goats tread there. The shells still suffer and are in pain. So the women shift them to Dela Muli and Anda Kona at the western end of Rote. Here the narrative ends.

Version XVIII, Dengka: Simon Lesik's Second Version of *Suti Saik ma Bina Liuk*

This second narrative begins with a genealogical introduction to the woman Sina Kona and the girl Koli Mola, whose mother is Seu Dela (and Fale Anda). One day they go to fish at the home of the Lord of the Sea, Langga Lena Liu//Manatua Sain. There they scoop up Suti Saik and Bina Liuk and take them to Dela Muli and Anda Kona. At this point and at several other junctures, the shells proclaim their special status: 'I am Bina the restricted. I am Suti the prohibited.' The shells first ask to be taken to knock against wood and bump against rock to mark the field's boundary and the land's border and thus drive away monkeys and pigs. The shells are, however, carried on to Dela Muli and Anda Kona, and passed on to Seu Dela and Fale Anda, a woman who dyes threads and a girl who prepares indigo. They create patterns that are lovely and attractive. So it is that Suti is used for indigo and Bina for dyeing threads. The narrative ends with the observation that the pattern (for Rotenese cloth) comes out from the sea and goodness comes out from the ocean.

Version XIX, Dengka: Frans Lau's Invocation of *Suti Saik ma Bina Liuk*

This version of *Suti Sai ma Bina Liuk* is a poetic reflection on the inevitability of death. It is not a narrative but it has many of the aspects of other *Suti Solo do Bina Bane* narratives. As with most other narratives, this invocation begins with a storm—a storm caused ominously by 'seven grasping spirits and eight snatching ghosts'. The poem then invokes the pearl fish as a symbol of vulnerability because they hide themselves in the anuses of sea cucumbers. The poem invokes the pain of Suti Saik and Bina Liuk: 'Suti Saik moans'//'Bina Liuk is in pain.' The poem then returns to the theme that the initial lines pose. A cyclone strikes the ancestral land (of the Rotenese) and is the origin of death. Comparison is made with the snake that loses its skin but continues to live and the grasshopper that loses its wings but also continues to live. But this comparison is challenged because when a rock pile is overturned, the snake hiding beneath is exposed, suffers and dies. Similarly, when the grass is burnt, the grasshopper is exposed, suffers and dies. Humans are like pearl fish, seeking shelter from death in precarious places. Suti Saik and Bina Liuk also cry out, asking where they might hide and shelter. If they try to hide with the border stone, buffalo trample there and if they try to shelter with the boundary tree, goats tread there. If they try to hide in the tree's shadow, that shadow will move and if they try to shelter in the lontar's shade, that shade will move. Order is not of the earth, integrity is not of the world: everyone dies. The fertile banana eventually dies with its fruit; the *gewang* palm dies with its final great inflorescence. One can try to hide in a great harbour or shelter in a hole in the earth, but remember and keep in mind that the grave awaits with 'stones piled at its head' and 'earth raised at its foot', where 'chickens scratch' and 'pigs root', with only stone to rest on and wood to lean on.

Version XX, Oenale: Hendrik Foeh's Version of *Suti Saik ma Bina Liuk*

This narrative begins with the widow Bina Liuk and the orphan Suti Saik taking cover in Mbia Liun and sheltering in Unu Sain. A storm arises. Suti loses her insides and Bina puts forth her pod. They are carried with the ocean refuse and the river debris to the sea's boundary and the river's edge. They cry out for someone to take pity and open their heart to them. A friarbird and parrot hear their plea, take heart, embrace the shells and carry them to Dela Muri and Ndana Ikon. There is a woman who spins and winds cotton. She seeks what she needs for her work: *sina* cotton and *koli* thread, indigo blue and *morinda* red for dyeing. She creates a woman's cloth with a motif of the sea and a man's cloth with a pattern of the ocean. These designs originate from Suti Saik and Bina Liuk, the orphan and the widow. As a result, whether they know it or not, the population of Rote carries Suti Saik's voice and Bina Liuk's words.

Dialogue Directives and Other Encounters on the Journey of Suti Solo do Bina Bane

As in all of the versions of *Suti Solo do Bina Bane* from Termanu, the versions of this chant from among the dialect areas of Rote have as their most prominent and distinctive feature a succession of formulaic dialogue directives. In many instances, these directives involve a dialogue over the appropriate 'placement' of the shells between the women who scoop up the shells and the shells themselves. In other instances, as for example in the version of the chant from Bilba, these formulaic features occur as 'encounters' even before the shells are scooped from the sea. In yet other instances, as in the versions of the chants from Thie, the shells themselves direct their particular placement.

In the dialect versions of the chant, there is a far greater array of placements—both satisfactory and unsatisfactory—than in the versions from Termanu. There is also a significant overlap of formulae with the chants of Termanu, particularly in the case of the chants from eastern Rote. For example, the formula syrup vat//rice (or millet) basket occurs in the chants from Landu, Ringgou and Bilba. Variations on the formula Border Stone and Boundary Tree are used across dialect versions in Ringgou, Bilba, Thie and Dengka. Similarly, a formulaic expression for the house—in each case, citing different ritual poles or beams—is used in dialect versions in both eastern and western Rote: Landu, Bilba and Thie. Lontar Shade//Tree Shadow and Three Paths//Two Roads are both formulae shared between Termanu and Dengka.

In contrast with these formulae is a host of new formulae that are particular to one or another dialect tradition. While Sea Refuse//Flotsam (or River Dregs) occurs in the Landu and Bilba versions and the invocation of *ko-nau* tree//*nilu-foi* trees in Ringgou and Bilba versions, the rest of the formulae, with the exception of the place name for Delha, used in the dialogue directives appear in only a single dialect version of *Suti Solo do Bina Bane*. The domain of Delha, as in the case of several versions from Termanu, becomes a final resting place for the shells.

Whereas all versions of the chant in Termanu follow a progression from the sea back to the sea (and then a possible return to the domain of Delha), the journey of the shells in the dialect versions is far more varied. In Landu, the shells are joined with the *gewang* and lontar palms; in Ringgou and Bilba, they are joined with *ko-nau* and *nilu-foi* trees; in Ba'a, the shells make their way to Timor; in the two versions from Thie, the shells become the seeds of rice and millet and are planted in specific fields; in the Dengka and Oenale versions, the shells are moved to Delha where they are used for dyeing and weaving.

Table 19 provides a list of all the variant formulae (some 38 in total) used to chart the journey of the shells

Table 19: Encounters on the Journey of Suti and Bina in the Dialect Compositions of Rote

	I	II	III	IV	V	VI	VII	VIII	IX	X
Sea and shore										
Sea Refuse//Flotsam (*Tere-Tasi*//*Hambau*)	x									
Sea Refuse//River Dregs (*Tele Tasi*//*Hamu Le*)			x							
Seaweed *Lima*//Waterweed *Koko* (*Engga Lima*//*Latu Koko*)			x							
Harbour Crabs//Shore Shells (*Ni Namo*//*Kuma Dae*)	x									
Boa in Harbour//*Piko* in Estuary (*Boa Namo*//*Pi'o Oli*)	x									

22. TRADITIONS OF ORAL FORMULAIC COMPOSITION ACROSS THE ISLAND OF ROTE

	I	II	III	IV	V	VI	VII	VIII	IX	X
Shore's Edge//Estuary's Mouth (*Nembe Hun//Oli Su'un*)						x				
Long River//Wide Pool (*Le Naluk//Lifu Loak*)			x							
Pathway										
Three Paths//Two Roads (*Enok Telu//Dalak Dua*)							x			
House										
House Post//Old Beam (*Timi Di//Balo Tua*)	x									
House Post//Lontar Beam (*Timi Di//Nata Tuak*)				x						
(*Sema Kona//Lunggu Lai*)					x					
Door Post//Fence's Base (*Fara Tanar//Lulutu Nasun*)						x				
Vat and basket										
Syrup Vat//Millet Basket (*Bou Tua//Fati Bete*)	x									
Syrup Vat//Rice Basket (*Bou Tua//Ne'a Hade*) (*Bou Tua//Neke Hade*)		x	x							
Border and field										
Border Stone//Boundary Tree (*To Batu//Peu Ai*)		x	x							
Border Stone//Field's Boundary (*To Batu//Lane Tiner*)					x					
Wide Embankment//Long Boundary (*Opa Loa//E Naru*)			x							
Field Boundary//Land Border (*Tine To//Lane Dae*)								x		
Border Stone//Boundary Tree (*To Batu//Lane Ai*)									x	
Forest and trees										
Sacred Grove//Forbidden Forest (*Nura Huta//Lasi Luli*)	x									
Creaking Wood//Scraping Forest (*Nula Kekek//Lasi Nggi-Nggiok*)			x							
Ko-Nau Tree//*Nilu-Foi* Tree		x	x							
Ufa Tree//*Bau* Tree					x					
Ai-Sauk Tree//*Lenggu-Ha'ik* Tree						x				

	I	II	III	IV	V	VI	VII	VIII	IX	X
Mountain Nitas//Field Delas (Nita Lete//Dela Mo)			x							
Lontar Shadow//Tree Shade (Sao Ai//Mafo Tua)									x	
Gewang Trunk//Lontar Stalks (Isi Tua//Londa Fepa)	x									
Animals										
Raised Horns//Waving Tails (Sura Manamamasua//Iko Manafefelo)		x								
Wild Pig//Forest Monkey (Bafi Fui//Kode Lasi)				x						
River Shrimp//Grassland Cuckoo (Mpoe Le//Koko Na'u)				x						
Hills and fields										
Rice Fields//Tapped Lontar (Lele Hade//Peu Tua)		x								
Field//Hill (Mok//Lete)									x	
Black Buffalo Hill//White Goat Field (Lete Ngge-Nggeo Kapa//Mo Mumuti Bi'in)									x	
East Lontar Season//Savu Rice (Tua Timu//Hade Safu)				x						
Pigeon Pea Garden//Cotton Field (Tuli Timi//Kaba Osi)			x							
Pandanus River//Jasmine Forest (Henu Le//I Lasi)			x							
Other people/places										
Land People//Mountain Clansmen (Nusa Iku//Lete Leo)	x									
Semau//Timor (Helok//Sonbai)					x					
Dela Muli//Anda Kona							x	x		x

Notes: Identification of the 10 compositions covered in this table by poet: I: Alex Mada; II: Ande Ruy; III: Kornalius Medah; IV: Laazar Manoeain; V: Samuel Ndun and N. D. Pah; VI: Jonas Mooy; VII: Simon Lesik, version one; VIII: Simon Lesik, version two; IX: Frans Lau; X: Hendrik Foeh.

Comparisons across Different Dialect Traditions

This is principally a study of variations in the telling of a single ritual chant—one out of a large repertoire of other specifically named and distinctive ritual chants. The value of this study is its concentration on this single chant. However, because of this concentration of focus, the formulaic sets to be found in this chant represent a fraction of the total number of such sets used by poets within this tradition of composition. These sets are directed to the telling of a particular sort of narrative and do not cover the entire range of other forms of ritual composition—as for example, in the proliferation of mortuary chants—that make up this tradition.

Nonetheless, these various recitations of *Suti Solo do Bina Bane* can be said to provide a reasonable representation of this tradition of composition. Although by no means comprehensive, these recitations include a substantial number of the most common dyadic sets in ritual language. The 10 versions from Termanu definitely offer a wider glimpse of these forms of composition than do the one or two versions from the other dialects. On the basis of one or another dialect composition, there is little indication of the diversity of the ritual repertoire from which they derive. While it is possible to identify particular dialect variation, it is difficult to assert that the longer formulaic variations that occur in these dialect compositions are unique to just one particular dialect. Generally, there is subtle and considerable sharing across local traditions.

This is particularly the case in discussing the most basic of formulaic expressions that are in fact shared among the dialects of the island. In discussing these particular expressions, one must expand the purview of consideration and take into account a wider range of formulaic compositions available in different dialects.

The task is twofold: to identify what formulaic expressions form part of a common island-wide tradition and to identify what formulaic expressions are specific to particular ritual communities.

I begin with a long discussion of what are some of the most important formulaic expressions that are shared across the entire island.

Shared Dialect Expressions that Define the Quest for the 'Good Life'

At the heart of all the compositions of *Suti Solo do Bina Bane* is a quest for an imagined quality of life. In the different ritual compositions, the quality of life that the shells seek in their quest is given various expressions—frequently when the shells suffer disappointment in not achieving their goal. These expressions are generally repeated, both negatively and positively, to form a refrain. I call these formulae 'key expressions', and the dyadic sets that compose these expressions can be considered as 'signature sets'. They form a special class of frequently repeated formulae that punctate an entire composition.

The semantics of these expressions provides a starting point for considering the dialect variation across the island because these particular signature sets tend to be widely recognised throughout the island and many of the elements in them are used in multiple formulae.

The list of these signature sets that I propose to consider here is the following. Although each has been chosen from separate domains, my intention is to trace these signature sets among compositions in different dialects. While each of these signature sets needs to be considered in turn, they must also be considered in relation to each other. As a result, this discussion weaves its way among many related formulaic expressions.

Landu:	*Malole//Mara*
Ringgou:	*Tesa Tei//Tama Dale*
Bilba:	*Tean//Mepen*
Termanu, Ba'a:	*Tetu//Tema*
Thie:	*-Tetu//-Nda*
Dengka:	*Lole//Lada*
Oenale:	*Lole//Tetu*

Malole//Mara (Malole//Mandak)

Although the poet Alex Mada tends to express the loneliness of the shells ('with whom will I be once more') after each of the shells' successive disappointments, there is a passage near the beginning of his composition in which the shells voice the hope of the 'good life':

22. TRADITIONS OF ORAL FORMULAIC COMPOSITION ACROSS THE ISLAND OF ROTE

Tere tasi o	'Oh the sea refuse
Malole la boe	May be fine
Ma hambau o	And the flotsam
Mara a boe'	May be proper'

This signature set uses the paired terms *malole//mada* and is one of the most common signature sets to occur on Rote. In Termanu, this semantic pair is *malole//mandak*; it occurs frequently in various *Suti Solo do Bina Bane* compositions from Termanu—from Old Meno's recitation to that of the 2009 recitation by Esau Pono. In Meno's recitation (lines 144–45) are the lines:

'De malole-la so	'These things are good
Ma mandak-kala so.'	And these things are proper.'

While in Esau Pono's recitation, this expression is given even greater emphasis:

'Tete'ek ndia nde malole	'Truly, that would be good
Ma na nde mandaka'	And that would be proper'

Malole//mandak is equally common in other domains. In two of the most important origin chants of Thie, the two poets N. D. Pah and S. Ndun use this expression regularly. At the end of their recitation (lines 171–72), they have these lines:

Lain bati malole	The Heights distribute the good
Ma ata ba'e mandak	The Heavens allocate the proper

Similarly, in their chant on the origin of the house, they expound how at the beginning everything was arranged from on high:

Lain atur malole	The Heavens arrange things well
Ata atur mandak ia.	The Heights Above arrange things properly.

And in the course of a long chant on the origin of fire and of cooking, in the midst of difficulties, they state:

Mandan bei ta	Things are not yet proper
Ma malole bei ta dei.	And things are not yet good.

The formula *ma-lole*//*ma-nda(k)* is composed of two elements: *lole* ('good, lovely') and *nda(k)* ('proper, appropriate: that which meets, fits'). Both of these elements combine with other elements to form further significant sets.

Tesa Tei//Tama Dale

Ande Ruy from Ringgou uses the formulaic (double signature) set *tesa tei ma tama dale* no less than seven times in his recitation. Thus, for example, in lines 145–48, when the shells are disappointed by the possibilities offered by 'boundary stone and border tree', they utter these lines:

'Na ami iku mo be a	'Then with whom is our land
Ma ami leo mo be a?	And with whom is our lineage?
De tesa tei hei ta'a	There is yet no contentment
Ma tama dale bei ta'a.'	And yet no satisfaction.'

Tesa tei ma tama dale is no easy formula to translate. It combines *tesa*// *tama*, which carry connotations of being 'full, thick, tight, complete', with the paired terms *tei*/*dale* for 'stomach and inside'. In this context, I have ventured to translate this formulaic expression as 'contentment and satisfaction', although a fuller translation might be 'inner satisfaction and heartfelt contentment'.

Kornalius Medah of Bilba also makes frequent use of the formula *tesa tei ma tama dale* in his composition:

'Tesa teik Dulu Oli	'There is inner satisfaction in Dulu Oli
Ma tama dalek Langa Le.'	And heartfelt contentment in Langa Le.'

The shells, for example, find brief contentment within the house. They are described as:

Tesa teik timi di	Satisfied at the *timi* post
Ma tama dale nata tuak.	And content at the lontar beam.

Kornalius Medah also relies on the formula *tesa teik*//*tama dale* to conclude his recitation. When the shells come to rest with the Ko Nau and Nilu Neo trees, they utter these final lines:

'Teu ho ketu kolu	'Let us go to pick and pluck
Ho tesa teik nai na	Inner satisfaction is there

Ma teu ho hele hao	And let us go to choose and eat
Ho tama dale nai na	Heartfelt contentment is there
Ho kelak losa do na neu	That goes on forever
Ma kelak sekunete na neu.'	And that does not end.'

The set *tesa*//*tama* regularly occurs in Termanu compositions, as for example, in one of Pe'u Malesi's recitations (from 1977, lines 107–8) when he refers to the shells before the cyclone carries them away. They are:

Tama ota neu liun	Crowded together in the sea
Ma tesa bela [isi] neu sain.	And packed tightly in the ocean.

Although no Termanu compositions use the full formula *tesa tei ma tama dale*, Esau Pono, in one of his compositions (from 2009, line 123), offers a variation on this formula, *tesa tei*//*nda dalek*, which carries much the same meaning:

Ia sona nda dalek ma tesa teik.	This is pleasing and satisfying.

The replacement of *tama* with *nda* is of particular interest for the semantics of ritual language in that in Thie, *nda* replaces *tema* in the widely recognised set *tetu*//*tema*. *Tama* may itself be a variant of *tema* (see Jonker 1908: 592). Both share similar meanings.

Both Kornalius Medah from Bilba and the two poets S. Ndun and N. D. Pah from Thie use the element *tema* in another set, *tema*//*bate*, which generally forms the complex two-set formula *tema sio*//*bate falu*—a pairing that could qualify as a signature set. Generally, this set occurs towards the end of compositions to describe a kind of heavenly state of complete well-being; the numbers *falu*//*sio* ('eight'//'nine') are indicative of this state of completion. Thus, at the end of Kornalius Medah's recitation, when the shells finally arrive at the Nilu Neo and Ko Nau trees, these trees are personalised and described as the 'mother' and 'father' of the shells:

Ina bongi lia Nilu Neo	To the birth mother, Nilu Neo tree
Ma ama bongi lia Ko Nau.	And to the birth father, Ko Nau tree.
Nai tema sio dei	In the fullness of nine
Ma nai bate falu dei	And in the abundance of eight

Similarly, the Ndun–Pah recitation ends with the lines:

Lain bati malole	The Heights distribute the good
Ma ata ba'e mandak	The Heavens allocate the proper
Ruma mana parinda kisek mai a	From them is a single rule
Numa tema sion mai	From the fullness of nine
Numa bate falu mai ooo ...	From the completeness of eight ...

Tean//Mepen

Kornalius Medah makes use of the signature set *tean//mepen* more often than *tesa tei//tama dale*. He uses this expression no less than 19 times in his recitation. Most frequently, he follows each fleeting appearance of satisfaction with a long four-line phrase that sets the stage for the reversal of any hope of contentment:

Tehu noi-tao leo lia	Yet however one strives
Ho tunu hai leo lia	There is trouble there
Ma sanga-tao leo na	And however one seeks
Ho kelo kea leo na.	There is difficulty there.

This refrain is then followed by his invocation of *tean//mepen*:

Tean tak ma mepen tak	No certainty and no permanence

Perhaps most poignantly, just before the shells set out on the Pandanus River road and the Jasmine Forest path, they express their frustration with the world in general:

'Teu teteni ina bongik ka leo	'Let us go in search of a birth mother
Te tean tak dae bafok	For there is no certainty on earth
Ma teu tatane ama bongik ka leo	Let us go in quest of a birth father
Te mepen tak batu poik ka'	For there is no permanence in the world'

This use of *tean//mepen* to describe the world is not confined to Bilba. Ande Ruy uses the same signature set in one of his mortuary chants. The expression of this signature set is phrased to give particular emphasis to the negative:

Tean ta'a dae bafo	There is no certainty on earth
Ma mepen ta'a batu poi	And no permanence in the world

Although *tean//mepen* is not used in any of the other dialect compositions, the terms themselves are known widely. *Tepen* refers to what is 'hard or firm', as for example, the inner core of a tree, while *mepen* refers to what is held 'fast or firm'. These meanings are widely understood throughout Rote.

Tetu//Tema

Just as Kornalius Medah combines *tean//mepen* with *tesa tei//tama dale*, Ande Ruy relies on formulae combining *tesa tei//tama dale* with another signature set, *tetu//tema*—probably the best-known and most widely used signature set of its kind on Rote.

In Ande Ruy's composition, *tesa tei//tama dale* is explicitly used to allow the shells to voice their disappointment, whereas *tetu//tema* is offered as a comment on their situation:

'De bei ta tesa tei	'Yet no contentment
Ma bei ta tama dale.'	And yet no satisfaction.'
De lope tarali oe	So they walk forth through the waters
Ma lao tarali dae.	And they go forth through the land.
Tetun bei ta'a	There is yet no order
Ma teman bei ta'a.	And there is yet no integrity.

Along with *ma-lole//ma-ndak*, *tetu//tema* is a signature set used as a refrain in numerous ritual compositions in Termanu. It can be used in the same contexts as *tean//mepen*. Thus, for example, Old Meno, in one of his funeral chants, has these lines:

De teman ta dae-bafak	Integrity is not of this earth
Ma tetun ta batu-poi.	And order is not of this world.
Sadi madale hataholi	Just have a heart for mankind
Ma matei daehena	And sympathy for human beings

The domain of Ba'a follows a tradition similar to that of Termanu. In his recitation of *Suti Solo do Bina Bane*, at the end of the first, second and third dialogue directives (lines 46–47, 58–59 and 70–71), Laazar Manoeain allows the shells to voice the same plaintive observation:

'De tetun ta ndia boe	'Order is not there then
Ma teman ta ndia boe.	'And integrity is not there then.'

Frans Lau begins his short initial recitation of *Suti Saik ma Bina Liuk* by using the Dengka form of this same signature set, which is *tetu//teme*:

Fai fe'a tetu-tetu	The day is still ordered
Ma ledo fe'a teme-teme	The time still harmonious

However, in his longer composition (Stanza XII), he uses the more common (Termanu–Ba'a) form of this dyadic set:

Tetun ta nai dae bafok	Order is not of the earth
Teman ta nia batu poik	Integrity is not of the world
Mana sapuk mesa-mesan	Those who die are everyone
Mana lalok mesa-mesan.	Those who perish are everyone.

-Tetu//-Nda

The two poets from Thie, Samuel Ndun and N. D. Pah, use the set *-tetu//-nda* and give it a (plural) verbal form, *ra-tetu//ra-nda*, to describe the distress that the shells feel about their placement within the house.

Ara bei ta ratetu	They still do not feel right
Ma bei ta randa.	And still do not feel proper.

The element *-nda* is the same *-nda* as in *ma-ndak* (*ma-lole//ma-nda*) and in Pono's *nda dalek* (*tesa teik//nda dalek*). As such, it is intelligible throughout the island. In all these contexts, *nda* has the meaning of 'what fits, meets, has purpose' or is 'proper, fitting and appropriate'. It is a significant element in other formulaic sets. For example, Mikael Pellondou uses the set *nda//soa* to indicate 'purpose, meaning or gain'. Thus, in line 57 of his second recitation, the women Fua Bafa and Lole Holu ask the shells why they should scoop them instead of the ritual fish:

'Fo soa be ma o nda be?'	'For what purpose and what gain?'

Another notable example of this common formula—in this case, in reduplicated mode—occurs in the origin chant when the Lords of the Sea argue with the sons of the Sun and Moon on where they should go to sacrifice their pig and civet cat:

'Teu poin fina kue-na	'If we go to the Heights to eat the sacrifice of civet cat
Sosoan bei ta	This still has no purpose

Ma teu lain fati bafi-na	And if we go to Heaven to eat the offering of pig
Ndandan bei ta.	This still has no sense.
Dilu teu liun dalek	Let us turn and go down into the ocean
Ma loe teu sain dalek.'	And let us descend and go down into the sea.'

Nda also occurs in the formula *nda//tongo* ('to meet, to encounter'), another formulaic expression that is widespread on Rote. In Termanu, this formulaic expression is:

Boe ma lima leu la-nda	Their arms meet
Do langa leu la-tongo	Or their heads encounter

The equivalent usage in Thie is:

Reu ra-tonggo do ra-nda	They go to meet or encounter

Lole//Lada

Simon Lesik uses the signature set *lole//lada* in several different but related ways. For example, he uses this set to define the conditions of things in general, as for example, in lines 78–79 of his second recitation:

Basana lole ia la	All this is good
Ma lada ia la.	And [all] this is fine.

Towards the end of his second recitation (lines 88–89), Simon Lesik uses this signature set to describe the 'goodness and attractiveness' of the cloths. This usage is similar to the way that Jonas Mooy describes the 'goodness and attractiveness' (*lada mbeda//lole heu*) promised by the shells when they are planted as seeds:

Mita lole na heu	Look at the goodness on offer
Mete lada na mbeda.	Regard the attractiveness here.

Simon Lesik also uses this same set to describe the tie-dye patterns on Rotenese cloths that derive from the shells. He then goes on—possibly as a form of wordplay—to link this loveliness and attractiveness (*lole//lada*) explicitly with the patterns themselves (*dula*) by making a set of *lole//dula*:

'Lole ala sa na	'There is loveliness
Boema na lada a sa na …'	So is there attractiveness …'
Dula ma sain nea	The pattern comes out from the sea
Ma lole ma liun nea.	And goodness comes out from the ocean.

Simon Lesik also uses *lole* in another set, *ma-lole//ma-na'a* ('surpassing'), to emphasise the height and breadth (*nalu//loa*) of a particular hill and field (*lete//mok*):

Na letek ia, lete nalu mana'a	This hill is indeed a high hill
Ma mok ia, mo loa malole.	And this field is truly a wide field.

Both *lole//lada* and *ma-lole//ma-na'a* are commonly used dyadic sets. One of the most frequent uses of *lole//lada* is in the complex formulae that link three sets: *lole//lada* ('good'//'fine'), *faik//ledok* ('day'//'sun') and *dalen//tein* ('inside'//'stomach'). Most often this complex formulaic expression is used to begin a recitation:

Lole faik ia dalen	On this good day
Ma lada ledok ia tein na	And at this fine time

N. D. Pah provides a beautiful example of the use of this set in describing two young men:

Tou malole	Good-looking men
Ma ta'e mana'a.	And fine-looking boys.

One can trace the linkages among elements that form such sets. They do not, however, necessarily function as signature sets.

-Lole//-Tetu

Finally, it is necessary to consider the dyadic set *-lole//-tetu*, which the poet Hendrik Foeh uses at the conclusion of his recitation. He uses this set as a signature set to conclude his composition with an expression of hope:

Fo ela leo bena	So let it be that
Ndi'i don nenene	The ear continually hears
Fo tao dalen leo be	So that it affects the heart
Fo na-tetu ina falu	To give order to widows

Ana tao tein leo be	It affects the inner person
Fo na-lole ana ma	To do good to orphans
Fo mana mia Rote Ndao nema.	Especially to those from Rote Ndao.

This appears as an unusual pairing of *-lole//-tetu*. I can find no other example of this combination either in Hendrik Foeh's other compositions or in any other of the compositions. It may be a simple lapse, though it is clearly a pairing that is intelligible within the context of ritual language. It may be rare, unusual and idiosyncratic, but it falls within the overall semantic parameters of oral composition on Rote.

The Semantic Network of Key Terms

Signature sets form part of the semantic core of Rotenese ritual language. They extend beyond the confines of a single speech community—a single ritual community. Although these sets may vary in usage across different dialects, they are sufficiently connected to one another (and to other dyadic sets) to be recognised and intelligible throughout Rote. Critically, the elements that make up these sets relate to one another and most of these elements can be shown to belong to a relatively compact semantic cluster—a semantic field of significance that links the dialects of the island. This network consists of the following connections:

Lole	>	*nda, lada, tetu, na'a*
Nda	>	*lole, tetu, soa, tongo*
Lada	>	*lole*
Tesa	>	*tama, nda*
Tama	>	*tesa*
Tetu	>	*tema, nda, lole*
Tema	>	*tetu, bate*

It is notable that while elements of most of these signature sets can be shown to form part of a compact semantic field, the set *tean//mepen* does not form part of this network. As far as I can determine, the elements in this set have no links to other elements.

Figure 27 provides a diagrammatic representation of semantic relations among the terms that make up these key signature sets.

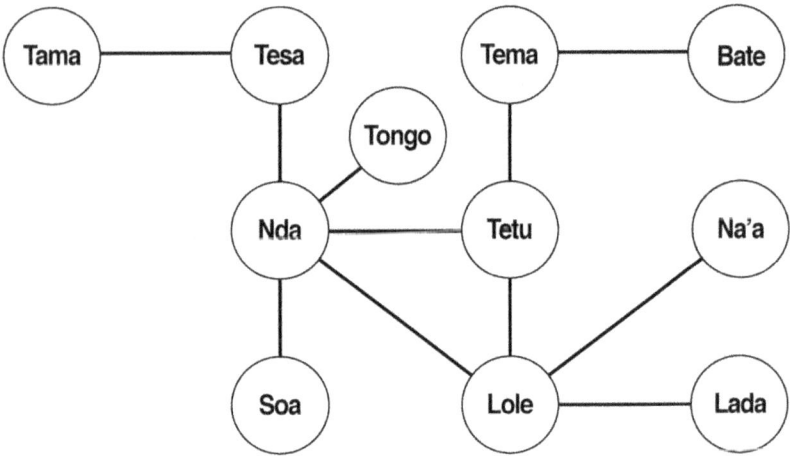

Figure 27: Diagram of Key Signature Terms

Ritual Language as Legacy

Ritual language is a legacy of the past. All the poets of Rote insist that they are speaking the language of their ancestors. Their duty as ritual masters is to preserve this language and the knowledge that it is used to convey. The issue here is the extent to which the various dialect versions of Rotenese language preserve a shared core of basic sets. At the end of each composition, I have pointed to: 1) dyadic sets that were recognisable (from the perspective of Termanu) as part of a shared core; 2) dyadic sets that were also part of this core, though their dialect sound shape made them less recognisable as such; and 3) dyadic sets that appeared to be distinctive to that dialect or closely related dialects but may not form part of a wider shared core. The difficulty in all of this is that the six dialects (or dialect areas) featured in this study are represented by either a single composition or by several short compositions, none of which can be considered to provide an adequate sample of those dialects' ritual language. We can at best only glimpse what might constitute a shared core of basic sets.

An appendix provides a complete list of all of the dyadic sets used in the compositions in the second half of this volume. The list is much longer than the comparable list drawn up for the compositions from Termanu. It

22. TRADITIONS OF ORAL FORMULAIC COMPOSITION ACROSS THE ISLAND OF ROTE

includes a large number of single-occurrence sets. These single-occurrence sets constitute the overwhelming majority of all such sets, as one might expect from such a small sample from each dialect.

The list groups sets that can be considered semantically the same set, even though the lexical representation of its elements may vary. Thus, for example, *dede'a*//*kokola* (Termanu: 'to speak'//'to talk') occurs in different compositions as: 1) *dede'a*//*o'ola*, 2) *de'a-de'a*//*kola-kola*, and 3) *de'a*//*kola*; *dulu*//*langa* (Termanu: 'east'//'head') occurs as *dulu*//*laka* and *dulu*//*langga*; *hambau*//*tere-tasi* (Landu: 'flotsam'//'sea's debris') occurs as *hamu-le*//*tele-tasi* and *hanu-le*//*tere-tasi*.

As a first approximation, it is possible to identify from this list those dyadic sets used in five or more dialect compositions. These sets are: 1) *ai*//*batu* ('tree'//'rock'); 2) *ana-ma*//*falu-ina* ('orphan'//'widow'); 3) *dale*//*tei* ('heart'//'stomach'); 4) *dua*//*telu* ('two'//'three'); 5) *fai*//*ledo* ('day'//'sun'); 6) *feto*//*ina* ('girl'//'woman'); 7) *liun*//*sain* ('ocean'//'sea'); 8) *loa*//*nalu* ('wide'//'long'); 9) *luli*//*sangu* ('storm'//'cyclone'); 10) *meti*//*tasi* ('tide'//'sea'); 11) *ndai*//*seko* ('to fish'//'to scoop'). All of these sets may be considered as part of a shared core but they also clearly reflect the narrative content of the ritual composition.

It is possible to go further and identify those sets that occur in four compositions. This yields another recognisable group of eight dyadic sets: 12) *dasi*//*hala* ('to sing, speak'//'to give voice'); 13) *dede'a*//*kokola* ('to speak'//'to talk'); 14) *dulu*//*langa* ('east'//'head'); 15) *isi*//*nggi* ('insides'//'pods'); 16) *-kedu*//*-tani* ('to sob'//'to cry'); 17) *keko*//*lali* ('to move'//'to shift'); 18) *lai*//*sue* ('to love'//'to have affection'); and 19) *lo*//*uma* ('house'//'home').

Going even further, one can identify those sets that occur three times in different dialects. There are 11 such sets: 20) *ama*//*ina* ('father'//'mother'); 21) *batu*//*dae* ('rock'//'earth') and 22) *bafo*//*poi* ('mouth'//'top, point'), which are both part of the formula *batu poi*//*dae bafo* ('the pointed rocks'//'the mouth, surface of the earth'—that is, 'the earth'); 23) *bete*//*hade* ('millet'//'rice'); 24) *edo*//*loko* ('to put forth'//'let loose, exude'); 25) *hambau*//*tere-tasi* ('flotsam'//'sea's debris'); 26) *ingu*//*leo* ('land, people'//'clan'); 27) *ki*//*kona* ('left, north'//'right, south'); 28) *lete*//*mo* ('hill'//'field'); 29) *ta'e*//*tou* ('boy'//'man'); and 30) *tema*//*tetu* ('integrity'//'order').

413

Going still further, it is evident from the Dyadic Dictionary that I have so far compiled for Termanu that at least three-quarters of the single-occurrence sets in this list of dialect dyadic sets has a recognisable equivalent in Termanu dialect and forms part of a shared core of dyadic sets used in oral composition. This issue has a further dimension since the legacy of ritual language is not confined to the island of Rote alone. As I have discussed elsewhere (2014: 378–79), many of the dyadic sets shared among the dialects of Rote have equivalent pairs in other ritual languages of the Timor region. Although they may have different lexical constituents, the canonical pairing of specific terms is the same. Rote's tradition of canonical parallelism is thus part of a larger regional tradition.

As evidence of this wider regional tradition, I provide here a short, select list of shared canonical pairs in Rotenese (Termanu dialect), Tetun (Lia Tetun) and Atoni (Uab Meto). These canonical pairs contain various shared lexical cognates since both Lia Tetun and Uab Meto are languages related to Rotenese.

Table 20: Rotenese, Tetun and Atoni Canonical Pairs

		Dede'a Lote	Lia Tetun	Uab Meto
1.	sun//moon	ledo//bulan	loro//fulan	manse//funan
2.	rock//tree	batu//ai	fatu//ai	fatu//hau
3.	trunk//root	hu//oka	hun//abut	uf//baaf
4.	areca//betel	pua//manus	bua//fuik	puah//manus
5.	seven//eight	hitu//walu	hitu//walu	hitu//faon
6.	eight//nine	walu//sio	walu//sio	faon//siwi
7.	pestle//mortar	alu//nesu	alu//nesung	alu//esu
8.	shame//fear	mae//tau	moe//tauk	mae//mtaus
9.	banana//sugar cane	huni//tefu	hudi//tohu	uki//tefu
10.	tuber//tales	ufi//talas	fehuk//talas	laku//nali
11.	lung//liver	ba//ate	afak//aten	ansao//ate
12.	thigh//navel	pu//puse	kelen//husar	pusun//usan
13.	turtle//dugong	kea//lui	kea//lenuk	ke//kunfui
14.	friarbird//parrot	koa//nggia	kawa//birus	kol ao//kit neno
15.	orphan//widow	ana ma//falu	oa kiak//balu	an anat//banu ina
16.	dedap//kelumpang	delas//nitas	dik//nitas	ensa//nitas
17.	waringin//banyan	keka//nunu	hali//hedan	nunuh//lete
18.	spear//sword	te//tafa	diman//surit	auni//suni

22. TRADITIONS OF ORAL FORMULAIC COMPOSITION ACROSS THE ISLAND OF ROTE

		Dede'a Lote	Lia Tetun	Uab Meto
19.	drum//gong	labu//meko	bidu//tala	kee//sene
20.	head//tail	langa//iku	ulun//ikun	nakan//ikon

This kind of comparative evidence points to a shared tradition that goes beyond—but historically links—the speech communities of the Timor area and of eastern Indonesia in general.

Postscript

This now concludes a project I began in 1965 but does not conclude my research on Rotenese ritual poetry. *Master Poets, Ritual Masters* merely marks a stage in this continuing work.

Suti Solo do Bina Bane, and its variant *Suti Saik do Bina Liuk*, is one ritual composition in the considerable Rotenese chant repertoire. It is considered an 'origin chant', but it has also been used as a mortuary chant. The knowledge of this composition throughout the island afforded me a superb opportunity to follow a lead in gathering variants of this chant and then to proceed to examine them, in comparative context, as an illustration of the art of oral composition among the master poets of Rote.

In my gathering of ritual language compositions on Rote from 1965 onwards, and, later, in my recording of the poets who joined me on Bali, *Suti Solo do Bina Bane* was, in fact, incidental to the larger effort of recording the full range of Rotenese poetry. Translating and analysing this large corpus of many hundreds of compositions are still in progress.

There is a danger in drawing general conclusions about the tradition on the basis of this single composition. *Suti Solo do Bina Bane* only hints at the extensive body of 'origin chants' that makes up the once revered traditional knowledge of the Rotenese. By this same token, *Suti Solo do Bina Bane* gives little idea of the even more extensive corpus of distinctive mortuary chants. Although some versions of *Suti Solo do Bina Bane* exhibit the influence of Christian ideas, no version of this chant portrays the new and developing repertoire of explicitly Christian chants (see Fox 2014: 317–64, for a discussion of this Christian canon). The full repertoire of possibilities within the Rotenese tradition remains to be documented.

It is precarious therefore to offer comment on the tradition as a whole. Since my arrival on Rote in 1965, I have been repeatedly told that the great master poets have died. Yet I encountered in my sessions on Bali several poets who were as capable as those I first recorded in 1965. The tradition has the capacity to throw up able individuals. Clearly, however, their numbers are diminishing.

It is not the ability of individuals that is in question but the knowledge that forms the basis for their recitations. The 'knowledge of origins' is definitely waning on Rote; occasions for the performance of the rituals of origins have ceased and what knowledge currently exists is steadfastly maintained by only a few older members of Rotenese society. For most Rotenese, such knowledge is considered of little ritual importance whereas the ideas of Christian origins are a matter of greater concern. More precarious is the knowledge of the numerous specific, stylised 'life-course' mortuary chants that make up an even larger component of the traditional repertoire. Although dirges are still performed in some domains, Christian funeral ceremonies have curtailed the recitation of most mortuary chants. The most prominent of these funeral chants are still remembered, as are origin chants, by key poets, but the former remarkable range of these individual chants has been progressively reduced.

As in the case of *Suti Solo do Bina Bane*, it is my present, pressing task to provide a record of these chants as evidence of a cultural tradition that has passed and in the hope that future generations of Rotenese may rediscover their value.

Appendix

Table 21: Dyadic Sets in Dialect Versions of *Suti Solo do Bina Bane*

Dyadic sets	1	2	3	4	5	6	7	8	9	10
-adu//-doki					x					
-adu//-sula					x					
ai//batu	x	x				x		x	x	
ai-do//poo-ai				x						
ai-sauk//nggu-haik						x				
ai//tua									x	
ale//bu'u							x			
[alu//langa] aru//laka aru//langga	x				x					
ama//ina		x	x	x						
ana-ma//falu-ina ana-mar//falu inar		x	x		x	x	x			x
ana-ma//kisa				x						
andiana//hataholi						x	x		x	
[ane//teli]	x		x							
ani//uda ane//teri asa oli//tei sina			x							
ata//lain					x					
[ate//nggi] ate//ngi			x							
atu//sosa	x									
ba'e//bati					x	x				
bafa//ma			x							
bafi//kode					x			x		

Dyadic sets	1	2	3	4	5	6	7	8	9	10
bafi//manu (bafi ais//manu ai)		x							x	
bafo//poi			x			x			x	
ba'i//soro						x				
bala//belu									x	
balo tua//timi di'i	x								x	
-bani//-hena			x							
bangga//leli						x				
[bapa//meko] bamba//meko						x				
bambi//sulu							x		x	x
-basan//-ketu			x							
bate//tema			x	x						
batu//dae			x			x			x	
batu//na'u										x
batu poi//dae bafok			x			x			x	
batu lau//tale hade		x								
bau//ufa					x					
beba//pena	x									
bebenda//hehere						x				
[bengu//kolo] bebengu//kokoro						x				
bela//mefu							x			
bengu//lali			x							
benggu//to benggu-benggu//toto								x		
beru//toto					x					
bete//hade	x				x	x				
bete//tua	x									
beu//lai						x				
bibi//fani						x				
[bibi//kapa] bibi//kappa							x			
[bibi louk//fani oen] bibi rouk//fani oen						x				
bina//mpiko			x							
bindo//lola										x

APPENDIX

Dyadic sets	1	2	3	4	5	6	7	8	9	10
bini buik//mpule sio						x				
[bini//pule] *bini//mpule*						x				
bibiru//toli						x				
-boa//-petu		x	x							
[boa//pena] *boa//mbena*									x	
[boa//piko] *boa//pi'o*	x		x							
boa lafe//futu aba							x			
bolao//talido						x				
bobolu//boboto	x									
-boi//-mao					x					
bonu//ele			x							
bomu//ele				x						
bonu//la					x					
[bongi//lae] *bonggi//lae*								x		
bosa//tafa						x				
bosa dale//pou su'u						x				
bote//tena										
bua//nggi									x	
buik//sio						x				
bubui//kokondo *bubui//kokono*	x		x							
bulan//ledo	x	x								
buna//dula										x
buna//lusu					x					
buna//pena			x							
[-buna//-pule] *-buna//mpule*						x				
[bou//neka] *bou//ne'a*		x	x							
da//oe						x				
dae//namo	x									
dae//oe		x		x						
dae bafok//ledo sa'ak					x					

421

MASTER POETS, RITUAL MASTERS

Dyadic sets	1	2	3	4	5	6	7	8	9	10
dae bafok//lalai					x					
dae//lane					x					
dae-la'a//selu sue									x	
dae//nggoro										x
dae//tua									x	
[dadi//moli] dadi//mori	x		x						x	
dadi//tuda										x
dai//konda						x				
dai//noi							x			
dala//eno			x				x			
dale//lai	x									
dale//su'u					x					
dale//tei rala//tei		x	x		x	x				x
dalu//hida				x						
dasi//hala dasi//hara		x				x			x	x
data//hida		x				x				
[de'dea//kokola] de'dea//o'ola de'a-de'a//kola-kola de'a//kola	x		x		x	x				
dede'a//nafada	x									
delas//nitas			x							
deta//sama			x							x
deta//soi					x					
deti ledo//ndu bulan						x				
dilu//loe			x							
-dilu//-sesu							x			
dini(s)//oe						x				
dini(s)//uda						x				
[diu-dua//solo-lele] diu-dua//soro-lele		x								
do//beba						x				
do//fan				x	x					
do//hata		x								

APPENDIX

Dyadic sets	1	2	3	4	5	6	7	8	9	10
do-do//nda-nda										x
do//mbule						x				
do//tai		x								
do-na//seketu-na			x							
-dope//langu			x							
-doto//-se'e						x				
dua//telu lua//telu rua//telu	x	x				x	x			x
dula//lole								x		
[dulu//langa] dulu//laka dulu//langga	x		x		x		x			
[dulu//muli] dulu//muri	x								x	
e//opa		x								
-edo//-loko -edo//-roko						x		x		x
-edo//-eno										x
e'ekok//lali								x		
eo'o//seu								x		
ei//langga									x	
ei//lima							x			
eki//hika			x							
eko feo//lutu eko										x
eno//longe				x						
engga//latu					x					
fa//timu	x									
fa//uda	x									
-fade//-dea							x	x		
fae//foi				x						
fae//tipa			x							
fai//ledo fai//lelo		x	x		x	x	x	x		
[fali//-dua] -fali//-rua -fali//-lua	x		x							
-fali//-toa					x					
fali//tule			x	x						

MASTER POETS, RITUAL MASTERS

Dyadic sets	1	2	3	4	5	6	7	8	9	10
falo//sua				x						
falu//hitu									x	
falu//sio			x		x					
fara tanar//lulutu nasun						x				
fati//bou	x									
fati//hao					x	x				
fedu//tumbu						x				
[feo//loso] fefeo//roroso						x				
felo//masua	x									
fepa dea//kabak dok			x							
feto//ina	x	x	x	x	x	x	x	x		
fetu//hake	x	x								
fetu//hangge							x		x	
fina-koli//kaba sina									x	
fiu//te				x						
foa//lako				x						
foi//ladi							x			
foi-aon//lane-aon										x
fola//sei				x						
folo//hao		x								
fua//lutu									x	
fua dae//lutu batu									x	
fua poi//peda bafa	x									
fua//ndae					x					
fua//so'u								x		
fui//lasi				x						
[fui//paku] fui//pa'u	x	x								
ha//te				x						
haba//lilo				x						
hade//tua		x	x							
hae-lai//tene-tu			x							
[hai//hilu] hai//hiru	x									

APPENDIX

Dyadic sets	1	2	3	4	5	6	7	8	9	10
[ha'i//keko] ? ha'i//e'o							x			
ha'i//seu										x
hai//soi hahai//sosoi								x		
ha'i//tengga						x	x			
[hani//hulu] hani//huru		x								
hambau//tere-tasi	x									
hamu-le//tele-tasi			x							
hanu-le//tere-tasi										x
-hana//-tua							x			
-hapa//-sulu			x							
[hapu//pake] hambu//pake						x				
hea//seki	x									
-hena//-bani										x
hene//kae					x					
hene//ketu						x				
hene//kona					x					
hene//loe									x	
henu//lilo						x				
hele//hao				x						
[hele//ketu] here//etu		x								
huka//na-lo'o	x									
[huni//tule] hundi//tule									x	
[hani bafi//hulu manu] hani bafi//huru manu	x									
haradoi//kurudo					x					
haladoi//sisi							x		x	
hate//koni							x	x		
ha'u//uda						x				
hengge//ndae						x				
hengge//pa'a						x				
heu//mbeda								x		

MASTER POETS, RITUAL MASTERS

Dyadic sets	1	2	3	4	5	6	7	8	9	10
hi'i//latu				x						
hun//laon		x								
hu//oka			x							
hun//su'un						x				
hun//lesu							x			
huta//luli	x									
inde//kaba										x
idu//mata				x						
[ifa//ko'o] ifa//o'o		x								
i'ifa//mandak							x			
[iko//muli] iko//muri					x					
[iko//sula] iko//sura		x								
[ingu//leo] iku//leo		x	x	x						
[ingu//nggoro] inggu//nggoro									x	
ina//te'o		x	x							x
isi//nggi					x	x	x			x
isi tula//londa fepa	x									
kaba//tuli			x							
ka-boa//modo-peda [kae//hene] ae//hene	x									
kala//tepu (tepa)			x							
kali//ketu										x
kali//tofi									x	
[kapa//bibi] apa//bibi [kapa//bote] apa//bote		x								
[kapa//manu] kampa//manu				x						
[kapa don//fepa dean] aba don//fepa dean	x									
[kapas//tua] abas//tua	x									

APPENDIX

Dyadic sets	1	2	3	4	5	6	7	8	9	10
ke//mpesi				x						
ke//nggio				x						
[kea//bui ?] ea//bui	x									
-kea lutu batu//dede lasapo na'u									x	
[-kedu//-tani] -edu//-tani -kendu//-tani	x	x	x			x				
keko//lali e'o//lali					x	x	x			x
kelu-kea//tunu-hai				x						
[ketu//kolu] -etu//oru	x			x						
-ketu-meti//-tu-tongo				x						
-ketu//-toko							x			
[ki//kona] i//ona	x					x	x			
kiki tua//nesu ingu			x							
ko-nau//nilu-foi		x								
koa kako//dulu pila	x									
koa//nggia										x
koa ore//nggia mese										x
koa tua//ngia sina				x						
[koko//poe] koko//mpoe				x						
[koko-nau//poe-le] koko-nau//mpoe le				x						
kola//sau		x								
kola//soke			x							
kono//monu				x						
ko'o//ifa					x					
kou//noe			x							
kuma//ni	x									
la'a//ndoe									x	
labu//meko							x			
lada//lole						x		x		
lada mbeu//lole heu						x				

MASTER POETS, RITUAL MASTERS

Dyadic sets	1	2	3	4	5	6	7	8	9	10
ladi//tule						x				
lafa//pou						x				
lafe//rambi										x
[-lai//-tu'u] masa-rai//manga-tu'u						x				
lalo//nggongga									x	
[lali//pinda] rali//pinda	x									
lali//tu'u								x		
lalo//sapu		x							x	
-lama//-leu			x							
lama-nau//mengge-batu									x	
la'o//lope		x								
-laik//-ngetu (nese-laik//ngge-ngetu)									x	
lai//seko			x							
lai//sue	x	x		x					x	
-lake//-holu			x							
lane//to	a							x		
lane ai//to batu								x		
lane dae//tine to								x		
[langa//lima] langga//lima							x			
langga//nggoe					x					
lano//toko			x							
la'o//lope						x				
lapo//kono			x							
lasi-okan//tete don										x
lasi//nula					x					
lata-dale//setele			x							
le//lifu		x	x							
le//na'u					x					
[le//tasi] re//tasi										x
re retan//tasi sun										x
leak//luak					x					
le'a//nole									x	

APPENDIX

Dyadic sets	1	2	3	4	5	6	7	8	9	10
ledo//uda			x							
ledo-ha//uda-te			x							
lefa//kono			x							
lela//ndolu										x
lele//tepo				x						
-lena//-lesi							x			
[leno//sole] *lendu//sole*							x			
[leo//ingu] *leo//iku*	x									
lesu//o							x			
lesu ngi//tona kala				x						
lete//mo		x	x				x			
li//nafa		x	x							
-li//-mu							x			
lifu//meti	x									
lifu//na'u				x						
lifu//nusa	x									
limba//oli						x				
[-lini//-sufuk] *-rini//sufuk*						x				
liun//sain			x	x	x	x	x		x	x
-lo//-meli										x
lo//uma *lo a//uma*	x	x		x				x		
[loa//nalu] *loa//naru*		x	x			x	x			x
-loe//-pelu		x								
-lodo//-sopo									x	
lole//selu		x							x	
lole hala//selu dasi		x							x	
-lole//-tetu										x
lolo//tenu										x
-lo'o//-nggou						x				
losa//nendi										x

Dyadic sets	1	2	3	4	5	6	7	8	9	10
[losa//nduku] losa//ru'u losa//ndu'u		x								x
losa//ndule						x				
loti//pele	x									
lou//nggi							x			
[lu//pinu] lu//mpinu				x						
luli//sangu luli//sanggu ruli//sanggu			x	x		x	x	x	x	x
lui//pode			x							
[lui//sau] rui//sau		x	x							
lui//soke			x							
luku//sake			x							
lungu-lai//sema-kona				x						
mafo tua//sao ai									x	
mafo//sao									x	
mada//meti	x					x				
[malole//mandak] malole//mara malole//mana'a	x			x		x				
manukudu//tau-ana										x
masi//tua					x					
melu//lani [meru//rani]					x					
mepen//tean			x							
mete//mita						x				
mete//relu	x									
mete//suru						x				
meti//namo			x				x			
meti//tasi	x			x	x	x	x	x		x
modo//tua		x								
molek//sodak			x	x						
monu//tena			x							
molo//tabu			x				x			
mula//nitu									x	

APPENDIX

Dyadic sets	1	2	3	4	5	6	7	8	9	10
muti//nggeo							x			
[na//ndia] na//ria na//lia		x	x							
nabi//keke				x						
nalek//uak			x							
nalu//tua							x			
namo//oli	x									
namo//nembe						x				
namo//teno									x	
namo tua//teno dae									x	
nao//nggoe									x	
nata-tuak//timi-di'i			x							
[natu//lifu] natu//rifu	x				x	x				
-nda//-tetu					x	x				
[nda//toe] ra//toe		x								
nda//tonggo				x	x		x			
[ndadano//toto'o] rarano//toto'o	x	x								
[ndae//sua] rae//sua	x					x				
[ndai//seko] rai//se'o	x	x		x	x	x	x	x		
ndai//solo							x			
ndai//sudi						x				
-ndeni//-ta'a						x				
-nea//-sala	x									
nea//tama		x								
neda//ndele									x	
nembe//oli						x				
nembe hun//oli su'un					x					
-nene//-harakara [?]						x				
-nene//-nia nenene//ninia										x
nesu ingu//tua timu			x							
-neta//-tonggo			x							

MASTER POETS, RITUAL MASTERS

Dyadic sets	1	2	3	4	5	6	7	8	9	10
nggeli-tua//solo-langga										x
nggi//oka						x				
nggi-lesu//oka-o						x				
-ngelik//-tulek		x								
-noko//-onda	x									
noi//sanga			x							
nosi//titi					x					
[nula//lasi] nura//lasi	x									
nusa//lete	x									
omba hade//lane tiner				x						
oli//tasi					x					
olu-olu//selu lida									x	
osi//tini			x							
parida//koasa					x					
[pau//liti] mbau//riti						x				
pedan//hun						x				
[peda//ndae] mbeda//ndae					x					
[peda//tao] mbeda//tao						x				
[peda//tu'u] mbeda//tu'u						x				
peda//udok									x	
pela-oe//tasi-oe			x							
pele laka-namo//no do dae	x									
pepisin//tatain									x	
peu//to	x									
peu//lele		x								
peu tua//lele hade		x								
pena abas//beba tua	x									
[pila//nggeo] mbila//nggeo										x
polo//suma		x								
posi pedan//unuk hun					x					

APPENDIX

Dyadic sets	1	2	3	4	5	6	7	8	9	10
posi//unuk						x	x			
[poti//pa'a] mboti//pa'a						x				
[pua//no] mbua//no							x			
-pulu//-sengi			x							
rada//tia						x				
retan//sun										x
rene//tine	x									
[Safu//Ndao] Safu//Rao	x									
Safu//timu				x						
saka//tuka		x								
sala//singgo					x					
sala//tute		x								
-sau//-tusi							x			
sea//seki		x								
sele//tane						x	x			
sena//tia		x	x							
sesa//tati	x									
sida//susi				x						
solokaek//tasi-oe				x						
sonu//tipa			x							
suma//tek			x							
su'u//una							x			
suru//tai					x					
ta'ek//touk						x			x	x
ta'e tena//tou landus										x
[tafa//silo] tafa//siro						x	x			
tai//topa			x							
takadema//torano							x			
tama//tesa		x	x							
-tane//-teni			x							
-tatali//-sese'i							x			
tata//fule	x									

MASTER POETS, RITUAL MASTERS

Dyadic sets	1	2	3	4	5	6	7	8	9	10
[tati//siro] tati//siro					x					
tau do//futu aba								x		
tema//tetu		x		x					x	
tenda//seru					x					
tete//toli						x				
timu//sepe					x					
tipa//toko			x							
to batu//lane tiner					x					
-tu//-sele	x									
-tuda//-sasi				x						
tun//saon					x					

1 = Landu
2 = Ringgou
3 = Bilba
4 = Ba'a
5 = Thie I
6 = Thie II
7 = Dengka I
8 = Dengka II
9 = Dengka III
10 = Oenale

Bibliography

Dahood, M. 1975. 'Ugaritic–Hebrew Parallel Pairs' and 'Ugaritic–Hebrew Parallel Pairs Supplement.' In L. R. Fisher (ed.), *Ras Shamra Parallels: The Texts from Ugarit and the Hebrew Bible*, vol. II. Rome: Pontificium Institutum Biblicum, pp. 1–33, 34–9.

Dahood, M. 1981. 'Ugaritic–Hebrew Parallel Pairs' and 'Ugaritic–Hebrew Parallel Pairs Supplement.' In S. Rummel (ed.), *Ras Shamra Parallels: The Texts from Ugarit and the Hebrew Bible*, vol. III. Rome: Pontificium Institutum Biblicum, pp. 1–206.

Dahood, M. and Penar, T. 1970. 'The Grammar of the Psalter.' In *The Anchor Bible: Psalms III: 101–150*. Vol. 17a. New York: Doubleday, pp. 361–456.

Dahood, M. and Penar, T. 1972. 'Ugaritic–Hebrew Parallel Pairs.' In L. R. Fisher (ed.), *Ras Shamra Parallels: The Texts from Ugarit and the Hebrew Bible*, vol. I. Rome: Pontificium Institutum Biblicum, pp. 71–95.

Eaton, Margaret R. 1994. Word-Pairs & Continuity in Translation in the Ancient Near East. PhD thesis. Dunedin: University of Otago.

Edmonson, Munro S. 1971. *The Book of Counsel: The Popul Vuh of the Quiche Maya of Guatemala*. Publication 35. New Orleans: Middle American Research Institute, Tulane University.

Edmonson, Munro S. 1973. 'Semantic Universals and Particulars in Quiche.' In M. S. Edmondon (ed.), *Meaning in Mayan Languages: Ethnolinguistic Studies*. The Hague: Mouton, pp. 235–46.

Fox, James J. 1971. 'Semantic Parallelism in Rotinese Ritual Language.' *Bijdragen tot de Taal-, Land- en Volkenkunde* 127: 215–55. [Reprinted in Fox, James J. 2014. *Explorations in Semantic Parallelism*. Canberra: ANU Press, pp. 91–228.]

Fox, James J. 1973. 'On Bad Death and the Left Hand: A Study of Rotinese Symbolic Inversions.' In R. Needham (ed.), *Right and Left: Essays on Dual Symbolic Classification*. Chicago: University of Chicago Press, pp. 342–68.

Fox, James J. 1974. '"Our ancestors spoke in pairs": Rotinese Views of Language, Dialect and Code.' In R. Bauman and J. Sherzer (eds), *Explorations in the Ethnography of Speaking*. Cambridge: Cambridge University Press, pp. 65–85. [Reprinted in Fox, James J. 2014. *Explorations in Semantic Parallelism*. Canberra: ANU Press, pp. 129–148.]

Fox, James J. 1975. 'On Binary Categories and Primary Symbols: Some Rotinese Perspectives.' In R. Willis (ed.), *The Interpretation of Symbolism*. London: Dent, pp. 99–132. [Reprinted in Fox, James J. 2014. *Explorations in Semantic Parallelism*. Canberra: ANU Press, pp. 149–180.]

Fox, James J. 1977. *Harvest of the Palm: Ecological Change in Eastern Indonesia*. Cambridge, Mass.: Harvard University Press.

Fox, James J. 1979a. 'A Tale of Two States: Ecology and the Political Economy of Inequality on the Island of Roti.' In P. Burnham and R. F. Ellen (eds), *Social and Ecological Systems*. London: Academic Press, pp. 19–42.

Fox, J. J. 1979b. 'Standing in Time and Place: The Structure of Rotinese Historical Narratives.' In A. Reid and D. Marr (eds), *Perceptions of the Past in Southeast Asia*, no. 4. Kuala Lumpur: Heinemann Educational Books (Asia), pp. 10–25.

Fox, James J. 1980. 'Figure Shark and Pattern Crocodile: The Foundations of the Textile Traditions of Roti and Ndao.' In M. Gittinger (ed.), *Indonesian Textiles*. Washington, DC: The Textile Museum, pp. 39–55.

Fox, James J. 1982. 'The Rotinese *Chotbah* as a Linguistic Performance.' In A. Halim, L. Carrington and S. A. Wurm (eds), *Accent on Variety*. Canberra: Pacific Linguistics, pp. 311–18. [Reprinted in Fox, James J. 2014. *Explorations in Semantic Parallelism*. Canberra: ANU Press, pp. 355–364.]

Fox, James J. (ed.) 1988. *To Speak in Pairs: Essays on the Ritual Languages of Eastern Indonesia*. Cambridge: Cambridge University Press.

Fox, James J. 1989. 'To the Aroma of the Name: The Celebration of a Rotinese Ritual of Rock and Tree.' *Bijdragen tot de Taal-, Land- en Volkenkunde* 145: 520–38. [Reprinted in Fox, James J. 2014. *Explorations in Semantic Parallelism*. Canberra: ANU Press, pp. 295–313.]

Fox, James J. 1993. 'Memories of Ridgepoles and Crossbeams: The Categorical Foundations of a Rotinese Cultural Design.' In J. J. Fox (ed.), *Inside Austronesian Houses: Perspectives on Domestic Designs for Living*. Canberra: The Australian National University, pp. 140–79.

Fox, James J. 1997a. 'Genealogies of the Sun and Moon: Interpreting the Canon of Rotinese Ritual Chants.' In E. K. M. Masinambow (ed.), *Koentjaraningrat dan Antropologi di Indonesia*. Jakarta: Asosiasi Antropologi Indonesia bekerjasama dengan Yayasan Obor Indonesia, pp. 321–30. [Reprinted in Fox, James J. 2014. *Explorations in Semantic Parallelism*. Canberra: ANU Press, pp. 219–228.]

Fox, James J. 1997b. 'Genealogy and Topogeny: Toward an Ethnography of Rotenese Ritual Place Names.' In J. J. Fox (ed.), *The Poetic Power of Place: Comparative Perspectives on Austronesian Ideas of Locality*. Canberra: The Australian National University, pp. 91–102. [Reprinted in Fox, James J. 2014. *Explorations in Semantic Parallelism*. Canberra: ANU Press, pp. 265–276.]

Fox, James J. 2003. 'Admonitions of the Ancestors: Giving Voice to the Deceased in Rotinese Mortuary Rituals.' In P. J. M. Nas, G. Persoon and R. Jaffe (eds), *Framing Indonesian Realities: Essays in Symbolic Anthropology in Honour of Reimar Schefold*. Leiden: KITLV Press, pp. 15–26. [Reprinted in Fox, James J. 2014. *Explorations in Semantic Parallelism*. Canberra: ANU Press, pp. 283–294.]

Fox, J. J. 2005. 'Ritual Languages, Special Registers and Speech Decorum in Austronesian Languages.' In A. Adelaar and N. Himmelman (eds), *The Austronesian Languages of Asia and Madagascar*. London: Routledge Curzon Press, pp. 87–109.

Fox, James J. 2007. 'Traditional Justice and the "Court System" of the Island of Roti.' *The Asia Pacific Journal of Anthropology* 8(1): 59–74.

Fox, James J. 2008. 'Sun, Moon and the Tides: Cosmological Foundations for the Ideas of Order and Perfection among the Rotinese of Eastern Indonesia.' In C. Sather and T. Kaartinen (eds), *Beyond the Horizon: Essays on Myth, History, Travel and Society*. Helsinki: Studia Fennica, Anthropologica, pp. 145–54.

Fox, James J. 2014. *Explorations in Semantic Parallelism*. Canberra: ANU Press.

Fox, James J., with Asch, Timothy and Asch, Patsy. 1988. *Spear and Sword: A Payment of Bridewealth*. Film, 16mm colour. 25 minutes. Watertown, Mass.: Documentary Educational Resources.

Freedman, David N. 1972. 'Prolegomenon.' In G. B. Gray, *The Forms of Hebrew Poetry*. Reprint. New York: KTAV Publishing House, pp. viii–liii.

Garibay K., Angel María. 1971 [1953]. *Historia de la Literatura Nahuatl*. Mexico: Editorial Porrua.

Gevirtz, Stanley. 1973 [1963]. *Patterns in the Early Poetry of Israel, Studies in Ancient Oriental Civilization*. No. 32. 2nd edn. Chicago: Chicago University Press.

Gossen, Gary H. 1974. *Chamulas in the World of the Sun: Time and Space in a Maya Oral Tradition*. Cambridge, Mass.: Harvard University Press.

Gray, George B. 1972 [1915]. *The Forms of Hebrew Poetry*. Reprint. New York: KTAV Publishing House.

Jakobson, R. 1960. 'Concluding Statement: Linguistics and Poetics.' In T. A. Sebeok (ed.), *Style in Language*. Cambridge, Mass.: MIT Press, pp. 350–77.

Jakobson, R. 1966. 'Grammatical Parallelism and its Russian Facet.' *Language* 42: 398–429.

Jakobson, R. and Halle, M. 1956. *Fundamentals of Language*. 's-Gravenhage: Mouton.

Jonker, Johann C. G. 1908. *Rottineesch-Hollandsch Woordenboek*. Leiden: Brill.

Jonker, Johann C. G. 1913. 'Bijdragen tot de kennis der Rottineesche tongvallen.' *Bijdragen tot de Taal-, Land- en Volkenkunde van Nederlandsch-Indië* 68: 521–622.

Kern, H. 1889. 'Proeve eener Beknopte Spraakkunst van Het Rottineesch.' *Bijdragen tot de Taal-, Land- en Volkenkunde* 28: 633–48.

Koopmans, B. 1921. Memorie van overgave van de onderafdeeling Roti: Afdeeling Zuid Timor en Eilanden. Unpublished document, Ba'a. [Copies of this document are to be found in the Wason Collection of the Cornell University Library.]

Kugel, James L. 1981. *The Idea of Biblical Poetry: Parallelism and its History*. New York and London: Yale University Press.

León-Portilla, Miguel. 1969. *Pre-Columbian Literatures of Mexico*. Norman: University of Oklahoma Press.

León-Portilla, Miguel and Shorris, Earl. 2001. *In the Language of the Kings: An Anthology of Mesoamerican Literature—Pre-Columbian to the Present*. New York: W. W. Norton & Company.

Lord, Albert B. 1960. *The Singer of Tales*. New York: Atheneum.

Lowth, Robert. 1829 [1753]. *Lectures on the Sacred Poetry of the Hebrews*. Translation of *De Sacra Poesia Hebraeorum Praelectiones Academicae*. Boston.

Lowth, Robert. 1834 [1778]. *Isaiah*. Translation of *Isaiah X–XI*. Boston.

Newman, Louis I. 1918. *Parallelism in Amos*. Berkeley: University of California.

Newman, Louis I. and Popper, William. 1918–23. *Studies in Biblical Parallelism*. 3 parts. Berkeley: University of California Publications in Semitic Philology.

Ridder, R. de. 1989. *The Poetic Popul Vuh: An Anthropological Study*, Proefschrift, Leiden University, Leiden.

Tedlock, Dennis. 1987. 'Hearing a Voice in an Ancient Text: Quiché Maya Poetics in Performance.' In J. Serzer and A. C. Woodbury (eds), *Native American Discourse: Poetics and Rhetoric*. Cambridge: Cambridge University Press, pp. 140–75.

Tedlock, Dennis. 1996 [1985]. *Popul Vuh: The Mayan Book of the Dawn of Life*. Translation with commentary. Rev. edn. New York: Simon & Shuster.

Index

Adulanu, Stefanus ('Old
    Meno'/'Meno') 4, 29n.1, 31, 57,
    77–9, 163, 183, 243, 303–4
  as teacher xiii, 26, 146
  comparisons with 59, 62–5,
    68–76, 85–9, 101–8, 114,
    123–8, 150–7, 185, 192–5,
    256, 383, 387, 403, 407
  compositions 97, 112, 181
  imitation of 200
  recording of 29, 30, 77–8
  style of composition 30, 49, 52
  Suti Solo do Bina Bane version
    29–55, 198–9, 202, 206–8,
    321
  usage 104, 106–8, 151–2, 155–7,
    193
Akkadian 6, 8
Amalo, A. xiii, 349
Amalo, Ernst 3, 4
Amalo, Jaap 3, 4
Amalo, Stefanus xiii, 77
Apulugi, Zet 183–6, 191, 193–6,
    205, 207
Asch, Tim 91, 164
Atoni 308, 414
Austronesian 7

Biblical 6, 8–10, 11n.5, 14, 15, 233,
    325, 334
  see also Christian, Old Testament
bini 15, 22, 23, 24, 25, 91
  see also mortuary chants,
    origin chants

Biredoko, Frans 4, 29n.1, 111
Buehler, Alfred 317

Canaanite 6, 9, 10
canonical parallelism 15, 49n.4, 108,
    109, 414–15
  Biblical 8–9
  comparisons 5–6
  distribution of xi
  Jakobson perspective on 7–8
  Mayan 10–14
  rules of xi, 51
  strict 3, 5, 97
  tradition of 351, 362, 414
  see also parallelism
chants, *see* funeral—chants, mortuary
    chants, origin chants
Chinese 6, 8
Christian 317, 351
  canon 301, 417
  interpretations 328
  parallelism 24
  rituals 24, 233, 318, 418
  see also Biblical, Old Testament
Christianity 163, 197, 232–3, 303
  influence of 24, 417, 418
  references to 96, 300–1
concatenation 21n.13, 240, 387
Cuna 6

Dahood, Mitchell 9, 10, 11n.5
Dutch 3, 21n.14, 22n.15, 229, 231,
    232, 233, 234, 303, 346

441

recognition of Rote 18, 229, 230, 231
Dutch East India Company 18, 197, 229, 231, 232, 243

Edmonson, Munro S. 11, 12, 13, 14
Egyptian 6, 8
Europe 6

Finnish 6
Foeh, Hendrik 241, 274, 377, 378, 379, 383–7, 397, 400, 410–11
funeral
 ceremonies xiii, 22n.15, 182, 317, 418
 chants 15, 407, 418
 see also mortuary

Guatemala 11, 14n.6
Guru Pah, *see* Pah, N. D.

Haning, Paul 318, 331
Hebrew 5, 8–9, 10, 14
Hungarian 6
hus, see origin—ceremonies

Inca 6
India 6
Iu, Yulius xiv, 334

Jakobson, Roman 7–8
Jonker, Johann C. G. 234, 235, 236

Kiuk, Mias 4
Koopmans, B. 346

Lau, Frans 228, 241, 274, 351, 365–9, 374, 375, 396, 400, 408
Le Grande, G. J. L. 303
León-Portilla, Miguel 10, 11
Lesik, Simon 241, 351, 352, 365, 368
 recitations 353–64, 366, 383, 395–6

usage 387, 400, 409, 410
limbe/limba, see origin—ceremonies
Lönnroth, Elias 6
Lowth, Robert 5, 6, 7, 8

Mada, Alex 241, 243–5, 253, 255–7, 270, 364, 385, 390, 400, 402
Malay 232, 233, 303
Malaysia 78n.2
Malesi, Petrus ('Peu Malesi'/'Malesi') xiii, 78, 79, 183–4
 comparisons 85–9, 101–7
 recitations 91, 92–101, 108–10, 129, 200–2, 206–8
 usage 51n.6, 123, 125, 151, 153, 154, 156, 159–60, 192–3, 255, 349, 364, 385, 405
Manafe, D. P. 18n.10, 234, 235, 236
Manoeain, Laazar xiv, 77n.1, 241, 303–4
 recitations 304, 311, 392
 usage 312, 400, 407
Master Poets Project xiv, 147, 241, 275, 331, 333, 417
Medah, Kornalius 241, 275, 277
 recitations 276, 278, 300–1, 328, 391–2
 usage 296–8, 400, 404, 405, 406, 407
'Meno', *see* Adulanu, Stefanus
Mesoamerica 10, 11
Mexico 10, 11
Middle East 9
Mongolian 6
Mooy, Jonas 228, 241, 274, 318, 331, 335, 345
 recitations 332, 333–4, 345, 394
 usage 345, 347–8, 385, 387, 400, 409
mortuary
 bini 23, 24
 ceremonies 78, 79, 163, 183
 monuments 112
 see also funeral

mortuary chants xiii, 22n.15, 77, 78, 91–2, 300, 314, 417
  categories 24, 25
  composition 69, 113, 374, 406
  repertoire 401, 417, 418
  Suti Solo do Bina Bane as 40, 43, 91–2, 108, 182
  'widow and orphan' 24, 25, 78, 150

Náhuatl 6, 10, 11n.5
Ndun, Samuel ('Pak Sam') xiv, 241, 314, 315, 317, 318, 334, 344, 393, 400, 408

'Old Meno', *see* Adulanu, Stefanus
Old Testament 5, 9
  see also Biblical, Christian
origin
  bini 23, 24
  ceremonies (*hus, limbe* or *limba*) 23, 197, 232, 233, 255, 314, 327, 331, 334, 345–6, 348
origin chants 15, 36, 353, 362, 369, 379, 418
  composition of 30, 116, 182, 206–8, 212, 278, 304, 349, 384, 403
  repertoire 30, 43, 46, 78, 97, 181, 199, 300, 313, 318, 417
  Suti Solo do Bina Bane as 25, 30, 40, 43, 91, 92, 102, 108–10, 304, 314, 344–5, 383, 417
Ostyak 6

Pah, Ibu Guru Ena 318, 331
Pah, N. D. ('Guru Pah') xiii, xiv, 241, 314, 316, 317, 318, 344
  recitations 331–2, 334, 344, 393
  usage 318, 329, 349, 364, 400, 403, 405, 406, 408, 410
'Pak Pono', *see* Pono, Esau Markus
'Pak Sam', see Ndun, Samuel

parallelism 6, 8, 9, 89, 108, 240, 386, 389
  as oral composition 5–7
  Biblical 9n.2, 10, 334
  Christian 24
  compositions 7, 10, 11
  conditions of xi, 9, 10, 62
  definitions 5–6, 7
  literature 7, 8, 9, 14
  Rotenese 22, 143
  semantic 5, 12, 13, 14–17
  terms 6, 8, 9, 10, 11, 14
  traditions 5, 6, 7, 8, 11
  use of 5, 6, 7, 8
  see also canonical parallelism
Pellondou, Eli ('Seu Ba'i') xiii, 57, 58, 77, 78, 111, 113, 115, 147
  comparisons 68–76, 85–9, 101–7, 126, 138
  usage 114, 125, 151, 153–6, 158, 192–3, 207, 256
  recitations 59, 61–6, 123, 125, 199, 321, 199–200, 206, 208
Pellondou, Joel 146, 147
  comparisons 150
  recitations 147, 161, 204, 207
  usage 152, 154–5, 186, 192, 194, 209
Pellondou, Mikael xiv, 111, 129, 147
  analysis 138–43
  recitations 113, 115, 150, 202–4, 206, 208, 257
  usage 118, 122–7, 133n.1, 151–6, 160, 192, 194, 207–9, 255, 408
Pellu, Lintje xiv, 182, 228, 244, 260
'Peu Malesi', *see* Malesi, Petrus
Pono, Esau Markus ('Pak Pono') xiii, 163, 164, 165, 228, 260, 275, 333, 377
  analysis 176–7, 180–2, 192, 194
  recitations 204, 205, 207
  usage 208, 274, 362–3, 387, 403, 405, 408

Popul Vuh 8, 11, 12, 13, 14

Quechua 6

Ridder de, Robert 13
Ruy, Anderias (Ande) 228, 241, 259,
    261, 262, 275, 377
    analysis 260, 270–4
    recitations 257, 295, 390
    usage 296, 349, 364, 400, 404,
        406, 407

semantic parallelism, *see* parallelism—
    semantic
'Seu Ba'i', *see* Pellondou, Eli
South-East Asia xi, 6
Sumerian xi, 6, 8

Tedlock, Dennis 13, 14
Timor 7, 18, 230, 305, 308, 309,
    393, 398, 400, 414, 415
Timorese 235
Turkic 6

Ugarit 9, 10, 14

Vietnam 6, 7
Vogul 6

West Timor 229

Ximénez, Francisco 11

www.ingramcontent.com/pod-product-compliance
Lightning Source LLC
Chambersburg PA
CBHW040323300426
44112CB00021B/2855